Changing Lives

Women in Northern Ontario

edited by

Margaret Kechnie

and

Marge Reitsma-Street

Dundurn Press
Toronto & Oxford
1996

Copy editor: Wendy Thomas
Designer: Ron & Ron Design & Photography
Cover colourization: Ron & Ron Design & Photography
Printer: Webcom

The publisher wishes to acknowledge the generous assistance and ongoing support of **The Canada Council**, **The Book Publishing Industry Development Program** of the **Department of Canadian Heritage** and **The Ontario Arts Council**.
    Care has been taken to trace the ownership of copyright material used in the text (including the illustrations). The author and publisher welcome any information enabling them to rectify any reference or credit in subsequent editions.

J. Kirk Howard, Publisher

FEB 2 5 1997

Canadian Cataloguing in Publication Data

Kechnie, Margaret
        Changing lives : women in Northern Ontario

ISBN 1-55002-239-3

1. Women - Ontario, Northern - Social conditions.
I. Reitsma-Street, Marge.   II. Title.
HQ1459.O57K42 1996   305.4'09713'1   C96-932106-6

Dundurn Press	Dundurn Press	Dundurn Press
2181 Queen Street East	73 Lime Walk	250 Sonwil Drive
Suite 301	Headington, Oxford	Buffalo, NY
Toronto, Ontario	England	U.S.A. 14225
M4E 1E5	OX3 7AD	

for Jane Pitblado, with thanks

Contents

Acknowledgements

A s this project comes to an end we cannot help but reflect on the process we have gone through to bring this anthology to life. Recognition must go first to Anne-Marie Mawhiney, who as director of the Laurentian University Institute for Northern Ontario Research and Development (INORD) conceived the idea of a book about Northern Ontario women in 1994 and has been key to ensuring its publication.

The first step in the process was a symposium entitled "Changing Lives: Women and the Northern Ontario Experience," held May 19, 1995, at Laurentian University. This book is the result of that gathering. The help of Ashley Thomson (director of INORD for 1994–95) in organizing the symposium and carrying out the initial editing of the chapters is greatly appreciated. Joyce Garnett, director of the J.N. Desmarais Library of Laurentian University, also helped with the selection of papers and continues to be a supportive friend of the book.

The support we have received from the INORD office throughout the process and particularly from Jane Pitblado, INORD's projects coordinator/editor, cannot be overstated. The copy editing by Wendy Thomas and David Kechnie is appreciated. We are grateful for the grant that was received from the Social Sciences and Humanities Research Council to cover the expenses of the academic participants at the symposium and also some of the administration costs. Recognition must also go to the Miners' Mothers' Day collection of the Sudbury Women's Centre for the photographs of Sudbury women that are used in Chapter 10 and elsewhere in the book. We also thank the various other contributors of photographs in the book.

Finally, we deeply appreciate the thoughtful contributions of both the authors and the women, young and old, who participated in the research projects reported in the various chapters. The process of uncovering the unknown has at times been painful, at times joyful. It is our privilege to be part of the journey to make more visible the diverse lives of Northern Ontario women.

Margaret Kechnie and Marge Reitsma-Street
Sudbury, September 1996

INORD Books

Changing Lives: Women in Northern Ontario is the fifth in a series of publications sponsored by INORD and deriving from INORD conferences and symposiums. The previous books are *Hard Lessons: The Mine Mill Union in the Canadian Labour Movement* (1995) edited by Mercedes Steedman, Peter Suschnigg, and Dieter K. Buse; *Rebirth: Political, Economic, and Social Development in First Nations* (1993) edited by Anne-Marie Mawhiney; At the *End of the Shift: Mines and Single-Industry Towns in Northern Ontario* (1992) edited by Matt Bray and Ashley Thomson; and *Temagami: A Debate on Wilderness* (1990) edited by Matt Bray and Ashley Thomson. All of these books have addressed issues of particular relevance to Northern Ontario, and all have fostered healthy dialogue between academics from a variety of disciplines and interested members of the relevant communities (including women activists, labour leaders, mayors, Aboriginal leaders, and environmentalists). The efforts to produce these books, all published by Dundurn Press, have been liberally supported by both the Social Sciences and Humanities Research Council and the Ontario Heritage Foundation.

A Ukrainian woman catching her first fish in the northern bush, Brett Lake, 1934.

Introduction

The Bibliography of Northern Ontario/La Bibliographie du Nord de l'Ontario 1966-1991[1] reveals that comparatively few books or articles have been written about the lives of Northern Ontario women. The publications of the Northwestern Ontario Women's Decade Council constitute a notable exception. Working out of Thunder Bay, the council has made a major contribution to understanding the daily lives of women in Northern Ontario, particularly in describing the way women have responded to community needs by lobbying for childcare services and transition homes. Subsequent to the publication of the bibliography, the 1994 fall issue of Canadian Woman Studies features women of the far north.[2] As well, Joy Parr's recently published collection, Ontario Women 1945-1980, has several articles that include women's activities in Northern Ontario.[3]

Once the need for more information on the lives of women in Northern Ontario had been identified, the Institute of Northern Ontario Research and Development (INORD) at Laurentian University proposed that its fifth symposium be devoted to issues concerning women in Northern Ontario. Thus in the spring of 1995 a symposium was held at Laurentian University called "Changing Lives: Women and the Northern Ontario Experience." This book is the result of that symposium.

The theme of both the symposium and this anthology is that women are changed by life in the north, and in turn they have themselves changed the north. Change has been shaped by the diverse experiences of women – a reality that contemporary scholars and activists are seeking to understand.[4] Differences in race, ethnicity, class, sexuality, and age have shaped and transformed the experiences of northern women. Who are the women in Northern Ontario? What are their lives like? What impact did the north have in shaping their lives? What do these women share in common and how did they bring change to relationships, families, and the communities in which they lived? These are some of the questions pursued by the contributors to this volume. The various authors seek to understand how women cared for their families, earned money, and survived the pressures of life in the north; they also seek to understand how women, both young and old, influenced the development of the north.

The most profound changes for the people of Northern Ontario have been among the Aboriginal populations. Even though Native cultures vary greatly, concepts such as private property, economic inequality, and political subjugation inherent in European civilizations were not part of Native traditions. Eleanor Leacock has argued that Native women had a level of influence and autonomy within their society that is unknown in contemporary social structures.[5] The destruction of Aboriginal cultures and the ensuing breakdown in the relationships between Native women, men, and the land occurred as European laws and values displaced Aboriginal traditions. Women were devalued and their oppression soon mirrored that of European women.

European and other settlers to North America have generally viewed Northern Ontario as hostile, cold, and barren; it was seen as a place where men hunted and fished, and hardrock mining and lumbering dominated. Those who hold this limited view of Northern Ontario have seen only part of the picture. The chapter by Eileen Goltz, based on census data, shows that European men greatly outnumbered the women living in the north during the early years of

Marian Beauregard

British war bride, Doris Peterson, arrives at Wavel, Ontario, 1947.

immigration. The imbalance quickly changed as wives and daughters joined the men who had already moved to the north in response to the promise of well-paid jobs in the resource industries.

Throughout the book authors describe the experiences of the women who are representative of these cultures: Cree, Ojibwa, Finnish, Ukrainian, Spanish, and, more recently, women of African descent. While many women from other countries may have come reluctantly with either fathers or husbands, others came with anxious anticipation of what a fresh start could mean in a land of lakes, trees, and rocks. Aboriginal women had to adapt to the invasion of women and men from these various ethnic groups. The newcomers had to cope with the challenges of carving farms out of the bush or living in single-industry towns that offered them few opportunities for either paid work or leisure. While Aboriginal women lived through the period of the residential schools and forced assimilation, women of all backgrounds endured the booms and busts associated with the mining industry and the restructuring of jobs caused by the advent of computer technology. Many women met the changes by reviving the positive parts of their own individual, familial, spiritual, and cultural heritages and by passing them on to the next generation.

Over the years the women who moved to Northern Ontario from foreign countries, Quebec, and Southern Ontario did many kinds of jobs. They worked as nuns, nurses, teachers, domestic workers, and farm labourers. Karen Blackford tells the story, for example, of Elva Sullivan's teaching experiences during the 1930s. Varpu Lindström provides an interesting look at Finnish women working in northern lumber camps. While women normally worked at

New home near Matheson, 1947.

jobs seen as "women's work," some did work in areas that had usually been male-dominated. This non-traditional work is evident in the chapter on successful Northern Ontario business women by Blanco, LeBrasseur, and Nagarajan; but it is particularly marked in the chapter by Jennifer Keck and Mary Powell, who have studied women who worked in Inco's mining operations in Sudbury.

Regardless of the inroads some women have made in the north, household routines, social relations, and economic decisions have generally been shaped by the dominant masculine preoccupations with resource industries, private property, and European morality. These preoccupations meant women often faced daily stresses of low income and poverty, worry about accidents and inaccessible health services, long days working inside and outside the house with little help, and fear of partners on whom they depended for money and shelter. Nancy Forestell's chapter considers the daily stresses that the wives of gold miners in Timmins faced as they worried about mining accidents that might maim or kill a partner and the suffering and impoverishment that would follow such misfortune. Poverty among older francophone women is the theme of Marie-Luce Garceau's chapter; Carol Kauppi and Marge Reitsma-Street focus on poverty among females of all ages and cultures. The case histories of 18 northern women recounted by Marian Beauregard show how isolation can lead to abuse. These concerns are explored further in Carole Suschnigg's study of 177 women who also describe the lack of sensitivity to their health problems. Too often women must deal with stress individually, which may account, in part, for the higher levels of smoking and health problems among Northern Ontario women compared to those in Southern Ontario, as described by Roger Pitblado and Raymond Pong.

As many other chapters in this volume show, however, Northern Ontario women do not just endure and adapt. They also resist and attack the forces that hurt them and their communities.In fact, many of the contributors to this anthology describe how women have worked both individually and collectively to improve their lives and those of other women. The Women's Institutes in the early part of the century, the various Women's Centres established over the last two decades, and more contemporary efforts, such as the co-operative housing movement, le Collectif des femmes francophones, the Congress of Black Women of Canada, as well as the development of distance education programs, are but a few of the ways, described in various chapters in this book, that women use to alter their environment. Despite distance, cold winters, and pressures to stay at home, women, both young and old, have shown a determination to meet one another and work together for change.

Most women found that change starts small. They learned to listen to one another as they talked around kitchen tables. They broke the silence that shrouded subjects such as suffrage, wife abuse, health concerns, and the economic power that large corporations hold over family life. In the organizations that grew out of these gatherings, women tried new ways of decision making based on what is best for everyone. Change is facilitated when people help each other, as is most evident in the chapter by Kuyek and Broad on the development of women's consciousness. Small actions and a change in consciousness can lead to transformations in the way affordable housing is provided, as discussed in the chapter by Ginette Lafrenière and Barbara Millsap, or the way small businesses are financed as dealt with by Dawn Madahbee. To mitigate the systemic stresses of poverty, abuse, sickness, and racism that northern women deal with, the efforts of many women are needed. Sustaining collective efforts to change organizations and laws takes time, money, and courage in the face of intergenerational and intercultural tensions and setbacks.

This volume, *Changing Lives: Women in Northern Ontario,* will bridge the gap in our knowledge of women in Northern Ontario. The stories and voices of northern women, however, have not just been missing, waiting to be discovered. All too often the lives of women are made invisible. In the poem "Dead Letter," Valerie Senyk evokes the image of a young woman as "folded tight, tight,/square and symmetrical" like a dead letter without a name or destination. Thus, *Changing Lives: Women in Northern Ontario* does not just uncover missing stories, but it also describes the forces that push women into the corners. It speaks of the struggles women engage in as they attempt to emerge into full view.

Many of the authors who have contributed to this anthology look at why women's lives are so often gathered inward and made invisible to men, to other women, and to themselves. What are the forces that create invisibility? What coerces women to live their lives in corners, overworked and unnoticed, fearful of the men and organizations upon whom they are dependent for money and shelter? Why do women feel compelled to earn money and yet retain primary responsibility for housework and childcare, as argued in the chapter by Elaine Porter and Carol Kauppi? Why must some girls and women develop double identities, hiding their sexual orientation for fear of losing friends, family connections, jobs, and housing as revealed in the stories of some Northern Ontario lesbians, told by Pat Tobin and the anonymous co-author?

The invisibility of northern women is not primarily due to inherent lack of ability or poor motivation among women of all ages. Throughout the book we learn that public laws and organizational practices force women down and that private prejudices and stultifying beliefs hold women back. The law has also been used to oppress women. For example, Nancy Forestell writes about the "moral clauses" appended to the Workman's Compensation Act in 1925 that rescinded the miserly pensions of women who did not remain chaste after the death of a husband in a mining accident. In a similar vein, Dawn Madahbee speaks of the nearly 50 percent unemployment on Northern First Nations' reserves and the laws that make it difficult to loan money to individual Aboriginals to start businesses. Keck, Kennedy, and Steedman speak of the blindness that renders invisible the diverse complexity of women's lives. Ten years after organizing the "Every Miner Has a Mother" photo display, the authors explore the reasons for omitting the contributions of Aboriginal mothers.

Changing Lives: Women in Northern Ontario aims to make the lives and struggles of northern women more visible. All chapters have been written expressly for this anthology. A variety of people including artists, activists, and academics have used different methodologies to collect the data and to recall experiences and stories for this anthology. Theresa Solomon-Gravel writes lovingly as she documents her interview with her mother, Eva Solomon. In the historical chapters by Varpu Lindström, Linda Ambrose, and Nancy Forestell, the authors draw upon archival sources such as minute books, sessional reports, and letters. Various authors analyze quantitative data from large, random samples, while others draw a picture of everyday life from qualitative data using small samples, as in Susan Vanstone's portrait of young feminist activists.

The research process itself can be an important source of making the lives of women more visible, not just to the readers of this book, but also to those who participated in the research for each chapter. Consciousness-raising is one step in making small and larger changes, as women (and men) look more deeply into what they take for granted and try to understand their own lives. Marie-Luce Garceau, Johanne Pomerleau, and Kitty Minor comment in their chapters on the participatory action approach they used to establish the questions for their research as well as to analyze and interpret the results. In this respect, Carole Suschnigg's contribution is most explicit, as the 15 members of the Women's Health Research Steering Committee worked to established research priorities, organize focus groups, interpret data on the well-being of women, and explore alternative visions of health care.

A book of this length cannot capture all the types of diversity among women. The history of raising children is slipped into several chapters, but the work on creating quality, affordable childcare services is sadly missing. We regret too that the experiences of women living in urban settings, especially in northeastern Ontario, are more thoroughly represented than the lives of those from smaller towns or from northwestern Ontario. Some of the work of women in unions has been addressed in previous publications sponsored by INORD, notably the chapters "Women and New Issues in Labour Organizing" by Laurell Ritchie and "Women and the Changing Face of Labour in Northeastern Ontario" by Mary Powell and Jennifer Keck in *Hard Lessons: The Mine Mill Union in the Canadian Labour Movement*.[6] Women have spent most of their time both now and in the past doing work, usually unpaid. But they have had occasional moments of leisure.There is little in this book that visits these rare moments.

Although Northern Ontario women have not stood out in politics, whether at the local, provincial, or national levels, their contributions call for more attention. The Honourable Shelley Martel, member of the Ontario legislature since 1987 and former Minister of Northern Development and Mines, spoke at INORD's May 1995 symposium on Northern women as did Karen Shaw, Sudbury councillor since 1991. Shaw argued that without the involvement of more women at the council table, "the expenditure of municipal tax dollars will most likely continue to be focused on sewer, water, and road programs...[limiting] the opportunity of creating programs and services that enhance our quality of life."[7]

Since work on this book began, the Progressive Conservatives were voted into power in Ontario in June 1995. They have instituted swift legislative changes and radical funding cuts, while the Liberal federal government continues to erode the supportive entitlements of Canadians. The work worlds and daily stresses of North Ontario women (and men) are seriously affected by the deep cuts in welfare, daycare, and prevention programs for children and the elderly; by the rollbacks in employment and linguistic protection; by the freezing of support for affordable housing; and by the substantial transfer of fiscal responsibility for health, education, and social services from national to municipal governments. The profits from the bond market and the promised tax cuts to middle- and upper-income people living in Ontario will barely be noticed by women. They rarely earn enough money to buy stocks and bonds,

National Museum of Finland, Sakari Pälsi Collection (VKK 158:43)

Lumber camp cook taking a rare moment of rest, north of Thunder Bay, 1927.

nor are their incomes high enough to benefit from tax cuts. The movements for change included in this book will be challenged. The base budgets of Women's Centres, First Nations Friendship Centres, universities, and co-operative housing organizations are being cut or eliminated. The need for new sources of change, especially through political movements and with the help of younger and older women in all their diversities, is urgent.

Voices of Five Women

The organizers of "Changing Lives: Women and the Northern Ontario Experience," the symposium held at Laurentian University in May 1995 that gave life to this anthology, were somewhat apprehensive about the closing session. We feared that many of those who attended would drift away, particularly as the duties of the home called women and men to those important tasks. As Valerie Senyk, a faculty member of Laurentian's department of theatre arts, read her poems, we could not help but be moved. Many of us have heard the voices before; some of us are those voices. They are voices we cannot, should not forget. This is why we begin the book with these five poems.

Voices of Five Women

Valerie Senyk

Dead Letter   (Barbara's Voice)

As a girl I learned
to fold myself up like
a nice neat piece of paper –
no straggly corners
or bits sticking out.
That way, people would
always smile at me,
say how good and obedient I was.
"Barbara's an example," they'd say.

They never saw the inside –
dark words and storms raging,
inkblots, scratches…
That wouldn't do.
I stayed neatly folded
as the years passed,
doing everything people told me.
I could be counted on;
I never changed.

Finally,
I stuck my head out,
saw that there were other women
just like me, walking about
so neatly tucked away.
They all looked and
sounded the same: sad.
I thought about it,
but did nothing.

A man came along.
He was unlike the others
I had always disdained.
Suddenly, I remembered
that I had breasts,
and a place between my legs,
and a beating heart
just for such a man.
I had folded them all away.

The words inside me
started to shout,
but the sound was muffled.
I wanted him to notice me,
but there was nothing to notice.
I was folded tight, tight,
square and symmetrical.
I was like a dead letter:
no name, no destination, no delivery.

Making Pictures   (Jeanette's Voice)

Let me make you a picture....
...my childhood was spent in Batchawana.
It was my paradise...we were all
the same there...
we looked the same and dressed the same;
there was no competition.
I had many cousins to run with,
and our grandparents lived next door...
they denied being pure Indian so
we wouldn't be sent away to boarding schools.
The never-ending lake was always nearby,
always in the picture,
and we played among the tall timbers.
The timberwolves hovered so near
we mistook them for nice doggies...
I didn't know it then,
but we lived with nature.

My dad got work in the city so we moved –
that was a shock that lasted and lasted...
If anything was stolen,
We got blamed for it. If I went
to school with a rip in my dress,
children pointed and laughed; everyone competed.
We had to become something different
than we were, and we didn't belong.
Do you see this picture?
There was no nature around us –
no tranquil moments...
It was all buzz buzz, and hard edges...

It was like being off-balance on a tightrope;
I made a bad marriage very young:
beatings, drugs, alcohol...
but when I left it I didn't run for counselling,
I decided to try university instead.
I've taken Native Studies and other
courses I like, and I make pictures.
People like my pictures,
so I think I'll keep on making them.
I like colour, and I like to make
beautiful things...

Sure, I'm a grown woman now,
with almost-grown kids –
but I still see myself as that happy little girl,
no worries, surrounded by nature,
happy, so happy...
At least, that's what I like to see.

When Push Comes to Shove   (Marielle's Voice)

They say wide hips is good
in a woman...
well Jessie – she's my first –
was a hard labour.
I guess I sweated her out
for over twelve hours.
Joe, he was pacing
the hallway – he wasn't

havin' anything to do with
birth and pain.
I screamed, I know,
and he heard me, too –
They gave me two needles;
I was beyond carin'.
When I shoved that baby out
I felt I had run a marathon
and thank God it was over.

Three more babies came…
The work got a little easier
with each one – except maybe Justine.
She was breach, but
they managed to turn her around.
It was scary, but I was prayin';
Joe was drinkin' somewhere,
listenin' to his friends' jokes,
hiding his head like an ostrich…
It was all worth it, I guess…

But the hardest labour? –
that's the one where
I tried to get ME out,
get ME born…get me free!
That was a battle –
fighting my mother, my aunts,
my sisters…fighting ghosts.
And that town we lived in,
and Joe, and the kids –

and my own self in the mirror
saying, "What kind of nonsense
is this? Who do you think you are?
What makes you think you're so special?"
But when push comes to shove –
and believe me, in birth it always does –
you got to use those muscles
the good Lord gave you
and bear your own
fruition.

When Feathers Fly   (Gina's Voice)

The lake is a camera
it captures clouds trees rock sky birds moon
It has carried my wavering image
ever since I was a round-faced child
Now I am grown – when last I bent
over the surface of the water
the folds under my eyes
and the lines around my mouth
made me wonder who I was

I used to pretend I was a loon
their cries at dusk
unnerved me until they
became a lullaby I loved
I imagined my self far out
on the middle of the lake
surrounded by stillness
where no one could get me
 – crying out
having my say
but only in my imagination

Now I call goodbye to the lake
as I circle high above it
I finally told my friend Shirley:
Shirley, you got to help me
and she listened and said:
Telling is all it takes –

Then I told my man his temper
makes me sick. I told him:
no more pushing me and the children around

I told my old dad
that he should have gone to jail
for what he did to me with his filthy body

I told ma that she was dead
wrong to stay silent all those
faraway days ago

I told my kids, yes, yes
we are going and never looking back.

Man, when I did all that telling
the feathers flew – !
Now I am
now I am

Mining   (Joy's Voice)

They say this is a mining town, so
one day, in a rare fit of daring,
I planted dynamite
under my life; I'd decided
to go for the motherlode.

The explosion hurled the bits of me
up to the heavens
and my eyes separated,
their vision
freed from the vault of my brain,
and individual fingers groped
and stroked the unknown atmosphere,
disparate limbs danced
upon the hot current,
and my mouth gulped
to stay alive…

until I gently fell back to earth
in a new arrangement…
in pain but no loss;
I was whole

and I swing the lunchbox
that my dear one packs for me
each morning as I set out –
still a miner,
but in other people's lives,
helping them go deep,
explode if they have to –
transform the base metal into
something precious.

This path I know now...
stone and earth,
brain and heart and soul,
so I don't need to look down,
but forward...
and hear the birds' sweet calls
among the trees...

Yes, I went mining,
found gold,
and the gold is in me.

Part One

Understanding Diversity

Women are not a homogeneous group. However, as the various groups presented in this section demonstrate, the notion of family is central to the lives of women. Using the census as her lens, Eileen Goltz begins the discussion on the diverse nature of women in Northern Ontario. What is evident from her chapter is that in the early part of the century the north was a "man's" world. It was not until the middle of the century that there was a more equitable gender balance in the European population.

The census tells us little about the lives of First Nations women whose traditional religious practices were labelled "pagan" by racist census takers. Theresa Solomon-Gravel's interview with her mother, Eva Solomon, and Mary Ann Corbiere and Sheila Hardy's conversations with mothers and daughters in Wikwemikong attempt to correct this lack of knowledge. Their work shows how First Nations women were sustained in difficult situations by both traditional Native values and their Catholic faith. What is clear is that they saw the importance of passing on both traditions to their children.

The dual themes of preserving culture and strengthening family are evident again in the chapters by Helena Debevc-Moroz on Ukrainian women, Carol Stos on Hispanic women, and Dorothy Ellis on Black women. For these groups the importance of retaining language and taking pride in cultural practices is compelling as tensions arise between the older and younger generations.

Pat Tobin and the anonymous co-author deal with a different kind of diversity. Lesbians in Northern Ontario have been a particularly invisible group, and yet like other women, lesbians are also concerned with family. They strive to build bridges of understanding between themselves and their families, friends, and co-workers and to create a community in the north where they can both grieve their losses and celebrate their successes.

1

A Census of Northern Ontario Women

Eileen Goltz

The growing importance of women numerically, economically, and socially in Northern Ontario is reflected in their increasing visibility in the Canada Census Reports over the 130 years from 1861 to 1991. Women, who had been outnumbered by men in the 1861 Census, had gained numerical superiority by the 1991 Census. They were part of a population that, although it was predominantly of British descent, also had French-Canadian and Aboriginal elements and, as the period progressed, included people from Continental Europe, Asia, India, and Latin America. During the period under review, the women of Northern Ontario increasingly left the confines of home and family to engage in wage-paying occupations, some of which they eventually dominated. By 1991 women were prominent in several occupational spheres and were gaining acceptance in professions and occupations that had been traditional male preserves. As the period closed, Census Canada acknowledged that women were raising families on their own and recognized that family heads might be either male or female.

Northern Ontario is not a census geographic designation. It consists of districts, which are territorial divisions similar to the counties of Southern Ontario. For the purposes of this study, Northern Ontario is the total of the districts, including Muskoka and Parry Sound, that existed during a census period. Changes in the number and size of the districts over the 130 years of this study were of a bureaucratic nature, designed to facilitate enumeration.[1] The census, a snapshot in time, describes Northern Ontario as it was on Census Day. Fortunately for this study, enumerators divided total population figures into male and female sectors throughout the 130-year period. Such divisions, however, rarely extended to the areas of ethnicity, birthplace, and religion; age divisions and marital status were often divided by sex, while literacy and school attendance data were only sometimes divided by sex.

Nineteenth-Century Northern Ontario, 1861-1901

Official records relating to the presence of women in Northern Ontario are sparse prior to the first official counting undertaken by the Province of Canada in 1861. Aboriginal women had certainly lived in Northern Ontario from the earliest days, and English women lived on Hudson Bay in 1683.[2] The record is silent concerning the presence of French-Canadian women.

The population of nineteenth-century Northern Ontario was numerically dominated by males; women were decidedly in the minority. That factor, together with population ratios of the number of men to every 100 women and the number of married men to the number of married women, indicate the settled or unsettled nature of the area. As the ratio of men to women approaches 100:100, and the numbers of married men and women become more equal, settlement and stability are the norm. When men pursue employment and adventure, they frequently leave their wives and families elsewhere – in more comfortable, more appropriate, and perhaps safer surroundings – while they savour life in less settled, more exciting, frontier areas. This phenomenon occurred with the male population of Northern Ontario. Much of it was transient and not interested in settling permanently in Northern Ontario.

There were 175 males to every 100 females in Northern Ontario in 1861, and the ratio of married men to married women was 1,016 to 624. However, the imbalance existed almost solely in Nipissing District – one of the two districts making up Northern Ontario in 1861 – where industry was limited to logging and hunting, where there were 822 males to 100 females, and 1,400 married men to 137 married women. Obviously, the population of Nipissing was transient and the district was unsettled and unstable. The situation was different in Algoma, the other district, where there had long been settlement nodes, and where the population depended on a broader economic base comprising agriculture, fishing, hunting, mining, lumbering, and related industries. The ratio of 111 males to 100 females and 1,996 married men to 1,700 married women in Algoma approached a more equal division.

Table 1. Population of Northern Ontario By Sex, 1861-1901[3]

YEAR	TOTAL POPULATION	FEMALES	MALES	RATIO MALES/100 FEMALES
1861	7,010	2,547	4,463	175
1871	15,728	7,052	8,676	123
1881	47,524	21,595	25,929	120
1891	81,391	36,405	44,986	123
1901	134,075	57,367	76,708	133

As the nineteenth century progressed, the ratios evened out, and with each decade, the total population increased. In 1871, due to a tripling of the female population, the sex ratio became 123:100, and in 1881 the ratio was reduced to 120:100. By 1891, as the male workforce expanded, the ratio increased to 123:100. The same fluctuation appeared in the ratio of married men to married women, and by 1891 there were 3,000 more married men than married women living in Northern Ontario. Although relatively settled, Northern Ontario was evincing less stability as the twentieth century approached. By 1901, however, the ratios had changed dramatically. While both the male and female segments of the population had expanded, with 133 males to 100 females, there were fewer than 2,000 more married men than married women. The in-migration had been single males, aged 5 to 40, and married men accompanied by wives and families.

Table 2. Birthplaces of the People, 1861-1901[4]

BIRTHPLACE	1861	1871	1881	1891	1901
Canada	8,919	11,098	34,912	66,886	111,979
Ontario*	---	10,224	33,277	58,277	58,303
Quebec*	---	661	1,187	6,889	12,328
Aboriginals*	3,223	4,317	5,068	NA	9,084
Britain	909	3,431	9,963	10,521	11,453
China	---	---	---	10	25
France	---	28	62	84	160
Prussia, German States, Holland	10				
Germany (Poles)	---	139	479	654	884
Italy	---	1	1	174	1,826
Russia (Finns)	---	---	69	322	1,259
Scandinavia	---	15	370	326	961
U.S.A.	160	773	1,185	1,917	3,694

*Included in Canadian totals

Women in nineteenth-century Northern Ontario lived within a population that comprised Aboriginals and migrants from other parts of Canada, primarily Southern Ontario and, to a lesser degree, Quebec. The number of French Canadians in Northern Ontario increased from 1,291 in 1861 to 22,909 in 1901, while the Aboriginal population grew from 3,223 to 9,084 over the same period. The population, dominated by people of British background, included few immigrants from countries other than Britain or the United States, although towards the 1890s immigrants began to arrive from Finland, Germany, Italy, Poland, Russia, and Scandinavia.[5]

The prominent religions in Northern Ontario from 1861 to 1901 were the ones normally associated with an Ontario-based population – Roman Catholic, Church of England, Presbyterian, Methodist, and Baptist. The total number of adherents to the non-Roman Catholic faiths far exceeded the number that declared themselves to be Roman Catholic, although for most of the nineteenth century there were more Roman Catholics than any other one denomination. The Lutheran contingent, which had numbered only six in 1861, had swelled to over 3,000 by 1901, a reflection of Finnish immigration. The census enumerators designated those Aboriginals who chose not to ally themselves with main-line churches as "pagan."[6] Despite the population identifying itself with specific religions, there were no formal church buildings in Northern Ontario until after the 1871 Census had been taken.

Although relatively newly settled, Northern Ontario in 1861 had a population of 84 widows, most of whom lived in Algoma District. The corresponding number of widowers was only 51. Widows remained in Northern Ontario either as heads of families where there were young children or as matriarchs in adult families. The number of widows increased throughout the nineteenth century, both in actual numbers and relative to the size of the female population, until, by 1901, there were 2,174. By 1901, census enumerators had begun to record the number of divorced persons, and that year there were nine divorced women living in Northern Ontario.

As might be expected in a newly settled area, the population in 1871 was dominated by people who were young or of an age to be working, with the largest number of both sexes occurring in the 5-40 age group. There were some family groups, as evinced by the number of children under the age of five. As the number of married women increased throughout the nineteenth century, so the number of children under the age of five increased. With a growing population, there were additions to all age groups. Most striking is the large number over the age of 60 who remained in the area. For them Northern Ontario had become home.

Table 3. Ages in Northern Ontario, 1861-1901[7]

YEAR	SEX	UNDER 5	5-20	21-40	41-60	OVER 60
1861	Female	223	608	516	178	58
	Male	121	886	765	358	79
1871	Female	1,336	720	556	680	210
	Male	1,448	807	772	942	283
1881	Female	3,720	8,739	5,691	2,404	527
	Male	3,577	10,138	7,860	3,310	812
1981	Female	4,532	11,043	9,848	4,226	1,146
	Male	4,690	11,510	10,991	9,848	1,808
1901	Female	7,911	18,587	17,658	7,267	2,335
	Male	6,967	20,166	28,992	11,961	3,386

What did women do in Northern Ontario prior to Confederation? We can safely assume they undertook tasks normally assigned to women – all aspects of homemaking and child-rearing. According to the census enumerators, few engaged in employment outside the home, and the enumerators ascribed occupations to only 32 women in all of Northern Ontario. Among these were twenty-five servants, four teachers, one dressmaker, and one housekeeper (a type of servant). Their occupations fall into the modern categories of service and professions, with service including the servants and the dressmaker, and professions including the teachers. These categories formed the basis of the female workforce in Northern Ontario throughout the nineteenth century. Undoubtedly, in most communities there was an informal workforce, where women acted as midwives, nurses, dressmakers, or housekeepers for neighbours.

As the century progressed, more women worked outside the home, despite the larger numbers of children in the care-requiring ages. The scope of their endeavours did not broaden; they continued to work in the service and professional spheres, although there was more opportunity for them within each sphere. In the service sector, besides servants and dressmakers, there were milliners, laundresses, seamstresses, tailors, and weavers, and some women worked in bakeries, factories, and woollen mills. In 1891, 256 Northern Ontario women worked in industrial establishments. The professional sphere included teachers, nuns, midwives, and nurses, and by 1891, there were doctors, one of whom practised in the Town of Sudbury in Nipissing District, where she specialized in the diseases of women and children.[8]

Prior to 1871, a paucity of schoolteachers foiled most formal educational efforts. For example, in 1871, with 29 teachers in all of Northern Ontario, only 700 of the 1,700 girls aged six to sixteen attended school. Compulsory school attendance legislation[9] encouraged the building and staffing of schools, thereby improving literacy rates so that by 1891, four-fifths of the women living in Northern Ontario were able to read and write. School attendance, by then, was considered desirable, as evidenced by the presence in Algoma in 1891 of two boarding schools for "young ladies," having a total of 57 residents. By 1901, almost 9,500 girls over the age of five attended school in Northern Ontario; thus, half the girls in the 5-20 age grouping were at school. Such a large proportion of girls at school reflected two things. First, the success of the aforementioned legislation, which in 1871 gave every child aged 7 to 12 the right to attend school, and which in 1881 required that all chidren aged 7 to 13 attend school. Since the legislation targeted children of elementary school age, elementary schools were the norm. Second, despite the distances to be overcome in Northern Ontario, schools were easily accessible, suggesting a more urban than rural setting. Although, by 1901, the proportion of urban dwellers in Northern Ontario had greatly increased over that of the nineteenth century, secondary schooling had not yet become an important factor.[10]

In 1861, there were 677 families and 681 dwellings in Northern Ontario. Not surprisingly, in an area that was heavily forested, most dwellings were single-storey log structures, although frame and stone multi-storey houses were beginning to appear in the more settled parts of Algoma District. By the end of the nineteenth century, there were 25,285 families living in 25,696 houses, with the average house being a one-storey, wooden building with four rooms. A close second was a two-storey wooden building with four or more rooms. While stone and brick houses were being built, they were in the minority. Most women lived in four-roomed, single-storey frame or log houses.

Twentieth-Century Northern Ontario
– The First Half – 1911-1951

Northern Ontario women were aware their world was changing from one in which the mainline churches and Aboriginal faiths dominated to one in which churches catering to immigrants from Continental Europe flourished. While life for these women was similar to life for women elsewhere in the province during this period, women living in Northern Ontario also experienced the boom-and-bust existence typical of areas that depend on resource development industries. The first half of the twentieth century was a confused time for Northern Ontario. World War I began in 1914, and its finale in 1918 was followed by a deep recession that extended into the early 1920s and was accompanied by an exodus of workers. This was followed by an economic upsurge during the 1920s and a consequent influx of workers. The Great Depression of the 1930s saw many workers stranded as employment possibilities in Northern Ontario disappeared. During World War II, from 1939 to 1945, many men left for military duty. Women continued to be outnumbered by men, but the excess male population was no longer married men living apart from their wives and families; it was single men of marriageable age.

Table 4. Population of Northern Ontario by Sex, 1911-1951[11]

YEAR	TOTAL POPULATION	FEMALES	MALES	RATIO MALES/100 FEMALES
1911	262,539	104,412	158,127	152
1921	313,361	140,177	173,184	123
1931	408,993	180,064	228,929	157
1941	508,026	230,556	277,470	120
1951	588,478	273,845	314,633	101

The ratio of 152 males to 100 females for 1911 was a reflection of in-migration occurring in response to resource development expansion. There were at this time only 10,000 more married men than married women in Northern Ontario, but there were 40,000 more single men than single women in the population – a situation that may well have pleased women. Ten years later, in the midst of the recession, the excess number of single men was 28,000, while the number of married men was 7,000 more than the number of married women, an indication of out-migration. In 1931, the ratio of 157 males to 100 females reflected a movement into Northern Ontario of unemployed men from across Canada seeking non-existent employment. They added to the numbers drawn to the area during the 1920s and laid off as resource development declined. The next census – taken after the beginning of World War II, when Canada was sending troops abroad – indicated the male-female ratio in Northern Ontario had dropped again to 120:100. In 1951 the ratio reached an all-time low of 101:100.

Despite fluctuations in the ratio, Northern Ontario had become a settled, stable place. The number of married men relative to the number of married women had remained constant at 7,000 more for 1921 and 1931, had increased to 8,000 more in 1941, and had fallen to 6,000 more in 1951. Given the size of the population in Northern Ontario for any particular census year, these changes were minuscule and reflected local situations only.

Women in Northern Ontario during the first half of the twentieth century lived within a population that continued to be primarily Canadian-born and largely of British descent. Within the Canadian-born grouping, the French-Canadian population grew from 48,495 in 1911 to 63,182 in 1941, while the Aboriginal population grew from 11,972 in 1911 to 17,306 in 1941. There was a growing cosmopolitanism resulting from the increased numbers of immigrants coming from Continental Europe, including Finnish, Italian, Polish, Scandinavian, and Ukrainian peoples. The group born in China, although never large, almost doubled from 1911 to 1951.

The expansion of the numbers of adherents of the main religions was a reflection of an overall population expansion in Northern Ontario. The growth of the Lutheran membership from 3,000 in 1901 to 25,000 in 1951 reflected Finnish and German immigration. The appearance and subsequent growth of the Greek Orthodox and Ukrainian Catholic churches was due to the expansion of the Ukrainian community. After 1911 the term "pagan" ceased to be used in the census reports to designate Aboriginals whose religious beliefs did not fit census categories. The numbers espousing the Jewish faith had increased in 1901 and again in 1911. Thereafter, their numbers remained static.

The number of widows living in Northern Ontario increased from just fewer than 4,000 in 1911 to 14,000 in 1951. Widows remaining in the area also indicated settlement and stability. These women were able to stay, either as self-supporting people or as members of families or households. While there were not as many divorced women as there were divorced men living in Northern Ontario, this number increased steadily from 54 in 1911 to 190 in 1951.

Table 5. Birthplaces of the People, 1911-1951[12]

BIRTHPLACE	1911	*1921	1931	1941	1951
Canada	190,134	116,741	264,054	409,513	500,245
Ontario†	169,425	NA	232,214	347,350	411,356
Quebec†	23,321	NA	20,723	34,738	41,475
Aboriginals†	11,972	14,963	13,979	17,306	19,864
Britain	27,166	31,611	28,715	30,579	25,141
Foreign	---	40,593	---	---	---
Austria/ Hungary	‡16,816	---	1,367	3,958	---
China	391	---	688	687	---
Finland	6,293	---	12,602	21,159	---
Germany	§1,456	---	994	1,195	2,174
Italy	6,932	---	5,015	5,518	7,672
Poland‖	---	---	7,887	8,545	8,829
Russia	2,420	---	1,123	---	---
Scandinavian countries	4,143	---	4,520	4,623	4,170
Ukraine	---	---	1,139	---	---
U.S.A.	9,185	---	9,033	10,277	9,031
U.S.S.R.	---	---	---	3,119	889

* The Census Report for 1921 does not provide information on individual birthplaces
† Included in Canadian totals.
‡ The immigrants from Austria/Hungary prior to World War I were mostly Ukrainians.
§ These would have been mostly Poles.
Poland became an independent country after World War I.

Table 6. Ages in Northern Ontario, 1911-1951[13]

YEAR	SEX	UNDER 5	5-20	21-40	41-60	OVER 60
1931	Female	22,573	62,551	52,570	29,457	9,549
	Male	23,187	66,110	74,172	43,119	13,880
1941	Female	26,864	73,169	72,273	38,502	14,644
	Male	27,546	75,347	90,205	59,889	21,222

Ages by sex are not available for 1911, 1921, and 1951.

It is necessary to project age-sex data from 1901 through to 1931 and 1941. Similar data for 1911, 1921, and 1951 are not available. Although the population remained young and family-oriented, there was an increase in the population aged 60 and older. In 1901 there were fewer than one-half as many men and women in the 41-60 age group as there were in the 21-40 age group. In 1931 and 1941 this proportion increased to just over one-half. The same phenomenon occurred with those 60 years of age and over. In 1901 there were one-quarter as many men in that grouping as in the 41-60 age group. Women fared better in 1901, having one-third as many members in the over-60 age group as in the 41-60 age category. In 1931 and 1941 there were one-third as many men and women in the 60 plus age group as there were in the 41-60 category. Obviously, the population was evening out by age, and men and women were continuing to live in Northern Ontario into their declining years. Northern Ontario had ceased to be a sojourning place where people stayed to make their fortunes prior to returning "home" and had become home to the population.

Women became more prominent in, and an integral part of, the workforce in Northern Ontario during the first half of the twentieth century. Most continued to work in the service sector as waitresses, hairdressers, servants, saleswomen, boarding-house keepers, and in the laundry and drycleaning business. With the appearance of ready-made clothing, seamstresses, dressmakers, and milliners became obsolete. In the professional grouping, women were nurses, teachers, and librarians, while a few were doctors, dentists, accountants, social workers, and notaries. The new clerical sphere – which included bookkeepers, receptionists, stenographers, and other office workers – was dominated by women, as were the semi-clerical positions of telephone and telegraph operators. The printing and publishing business provided skilled employment for women as proofreaders, bookbinders, compositors, typesetters, and press operators. Women also worked as real estate dealers, some owned businesses, and some supervised employees – usually other women. The occupations women normally entered during this period were low-paying and lacked opportunities for advancement. Society continued to believe that women would marry and transfer their dependence to the spouse. During World War II women worked at non-traditional jobs, those occupations normally allocated to men. For example, the 1941 Census recorded women working in agriculture, other primary industries, manufacturing, and construction, although their numbers were eclipsed by the plethora of women working in the service and clerical sectors. By 1951 these opportunities for women had ceased to exist, and women returned to more traditional employment, leaving "men's work" to the returning war veterans.

School attendance during this period accelerated, as did literacy rates. By 1921 only 7,700 females aged 10 or older were unable to read and write. By 1941, 48,500 girls were attending school, out of a population of girls and women in the 5-20 age group numbering 73,000. Thus two-thirds of the females in the appropriate age group were at school. The third not attending school either had not begun or had finished. In 1919 the Ontario Legislature had extended mandatory school attendance to age 16,[14] and although permission could be obtained to keep children out of school, going to school was the norm by the 1950s.

The number of families living in Northern Ontario increased from 25,000 in 1901 to 143,000 in 1951. Over the same period, house-building had kept pace, and the number of dwellings available had increased from 26,000 in 1901 to 143,000 in 1951. Of the accommodation available in 1951, half was occupied by renters, and half by owners. The commonest types of accommodation were single-family dwellings, semi-detached houses, apartments, and row housing.

Twentieth-Century Northern Ontario – The Latter Half

The Northern Ontario of this period was very different from that of the earlier years. Postsecondary institutions had been established within Northern Ontario; women had embraced the contraceptive pill, thereby affecting population growth; the resource development industries had reduced their workforces; and the population of Northern Ontario was, for the first time, barely increasing. Yet some aspects of life in Northern Ontario remained the same. Most of the population was Ontario-born; the Roman Catholic Church had a larger following than any other; education continued to be desirable; and women continued to swell the ranks of the employed.

Table 7. Population of Northern Ontario by Sex, 1961-1991 [15]

YEAR	TOTAL POPULATION	FEMALES	MALES	RATIO MALES/100 FEMALES
1961	778,511	370,974	407,537	109
1971	836,675	406,390	430,285	105
1981	857,953	425,945	432,008	101
1991	870,460	437,180	433,280	99

The male population had increased during the 1950s, and by 1961 the ratio of males to females was 109:100. As the latter part of the twentieth century progressed, the ratio fell to 105:100 in 1971, 101:100 in 1981, and in 1991, with a ratio of 99:100, women had finally become the majority. The 1961 increase in the male population had resulted from expanding work opportunities, while reductions during the balance of the century reflected industry's efforts to reduce costs by eliminating highly paid workforces through reorganization and mechanization. This resulted in a movement out of the area of people – primarily men – seeking employment elsewhere. Many left Northern Ontario permanently. The total population of Northern Ontario increased by only 100,000 between 1961 and 1991. A more positive result of the industrial down-sizing was a decreased dependence on resource development industries in Northern Ontario and a move to diversify.

As in the earlier part of the twentieth century, the over-abundance of men comprised an influx of single men, rather than married men living apart from their wives and families. In 1961 there were 43,000 more single males than females, but there were only 4,000 more married men than married women in Northern Ontario. By the 1950s and 1960s married men, accompanied by their families, were moving into Northern Ontario to accept employment. By 1981 there were 31,000 more single males than single females, but only 115 more married men than married women.

Northern Ontario women during this period lived among an increasingly cosmopolitan population. While most of the population had been born in Ontario, the roots of these people were less frequently British. There were French Canadians, Italians, Americans, Germans, Poles, Ukrainians, and Aboriginals. The French-Canadian population, most of which was Ontario-born, increased only slightly during this period, from 204,035 in 1961 to 212,225 in 1991, a difference of only 8,190. The Aboriginal population increased by 4,673, from 27,062 in 1961 to 31,735 in 1971, the last year for which population statistics are available for this group. A sprinkling of visible minorities was also beginning to appear – from African countries, the Caribbean, Latin America, India, Pakistan, the Middle East, Vietnam, and Korea.

Table 8. Birthplaces of the People, 1961-1991[16]

BIRTHPLACE*	1961	1971
Canada	658,927	737,055
Ontario†	552,940	NA
Quebec†	48,811	NA
Aboriginals†	27,062	31,735
Britain	28,694	22,750
Africa	---	595
China	---	1,125
Germany	9,075	6,840
India and Pakistan	---	710
Italy	17,767	17,275
Poland	7,908	5,970
Scandinavian countries	3,784	---
U.S.A.	9,266	9,070
U.S.S.R.	7,667	5,870
West Indies and Latin America	---	1,210

* Birthplaces not available for 1981, 1991
† Included in Canadian totals

The growing cosmopolitanism of Northern Ontario was reflected in the religions represented in the communities. The Roman Catholic Church continued to grow and to attract more adherents than any single church in Northern Ontario, while the United Church was the largest of the non-confessional faiths. The Lutheran Church had increased its following from 25,000 in 1951 to 46,000 in 1961. Thereafter, the numbers of Lutherans declined slightly. The Greek Orthodox Church grew steadily and quickly during this period, while the Ukrainian Catholic Church grew for a period, then declined slightly, reflecting immigration changes and out-migration. Places of worship dedicated to the Islamic, Hindu, and Sikh faiths appeared towards the end of this period.

Although the number of widowers living in Northern Ontario remained relatively constant from 1941 to 1981 at between 7,000 and 8,000, the number of widows escalated from 12,000 in 1941 to 33,000 in 1981. Obviously widows did not re-marry, while widowers did.

Table 9. Ages in Northern Ontario, 1961-1991[17]

YEAR	SEX	UNDER 5	5-20	21-40	41-60	OVER 60
1961	Female	52,694	116,150	102,260	69,525	29,839
	Male	54,754	121,716	112,209	80,613	37,616
1971	Female	32,140	137,765	110,595	82,460	42,070
	Male	39,205	144,240	115,750	87,000	43,550
1981	Female	32,290	114,510	129,250	87,870	57,105
	Male	40,745	119,940	133,526	91,070	52,915
1991	Female	25,120	94,930	136,935	98,675	77,385
	Male	31,120	99,860	138,370	97,080	65,460

Beginning in 1971 and continuing through to 1991, there were fewer children in the under-5 age category for both boys and girls. These reductions were reflected in the smaller number of people, both male and female, in the 5-20 age categories for 1981 and 1991. After 1961 the use of oral contraceptives became common, and women using this method were better able to regulate the number and timing of their pregnancies. People had begun seriously to limit the size of their families. Although there were fewer people in the 0-20 age categories, such was not the case at the other end of the scale. More people were between the ages of 21 and over-60 each decade.

Although family sizes had decreased, the number of families living in Northern Ontario continued to increase during the latter half of the twentieth century. Throughout the history of Northern Ontario, there had been either slightly more or slightly fewer dwellings than there had been families, and it was obvious that some families must have shared dwellings. After 1951 the situation changed, and during the latter half of the twentieth century there were many more dwellings available in Northern Ontario than there were families living in the area. In 1961 the difference was not significant, but by 1991 there were 77,000 more houses than there were families. Although from the earliest years of settlement some women had had to assume responsibility as "head of the family," Census Canada did not recognize such situations until 1971, when it designated women as family heads; in 1981 it noted that there were single-parent families without indicating the sex of the head. In 1971, 13,685 families were headed by women, and in 1981, there were 24,580 single-parent families.

Women had long complained that they did not earn as much for their work as men did. This situation changed during the latter part of the twentieth century with the movement of some women into high-paying non-traditional employment and with pay equity legislation. Women, nevertheless, continued to dominate the service and clerical sectors and certain aspects of the professional sphere. There were many women teachers, social workers, librarians, and nurses, and while there were more women dentists, physicians, lawyers, and accountants than there had been previously, these professions continued to be dominated by men.

The 1961 Census recognized women in managerial positions, but their numbers were only 20 percent of the numbers of males occupying similar positions. Women had made advances in the manufacturing and recreational fields, and they had invaded many of the non-traditional work areas. This was different from the 1940s, when women were permitted to do "men's jobs" while men served in the armed forces. Women now operated transportation equipment, worked on construction and in the primary industries of logging, mining, and farming, and were paid the appropriate salaries. These occupations were perceived by women to be careers; they were not replacing men who would one day return. Many more women were engaged in employment outside the home, some because they wished to pursue careers, others because they were single parents supporting children, others because their financial contribution was needed within the family, and others who believed that women should be able to support themselves.

School attendance rates continued to be high, and the advent of postsecondary educational facilities in Northern Ontario presented opportunities hitherto unavailable locally. Prior to the 1960s, people seeking postsecondary education had had to travel to Southern Ontario or elsewhere. During the 1960s universities and community colleges were established at several points in Northern Ontario, and the presence of these institutions attracted students from places other than Northern Ontario. They came from Southern Ontario, from other parts of Canada, and from off-shore, and they shared their experiences with students from Northern Ontario. Moreover, many faculty members teaching in these institutions were from elsewhere, and they brought with them customs and experiences to share in the new environment. Northerners had long complained that young people did not return to the north after attending college or university. With postsecondary education available in the north, more young people tended to remain in the area. In addition, the presence of postsecondary educational facilities allowed adults, long out of school, to resume formal learning without leaving their own communities.

Conclusion

Census reports inform us that from 1861 to 1991 women in Northern Ontario were part of a population that was primarily Ontario-born and that supported the traditional churches found in most Ontario towns. In 1861 most of the population had moved to Northern Ontario from other places in the province and most claimed British descent. By the late twentieth century, however, although most of the population had been born in Northern Ontario, many claimed Continental European ancestry, and many supported churches that had not been present in 1861. Where visible minorities had been few in 1861, their numbers had notably increased by the 1990s.

According to those same census reports, women in Northern Ontario from 1861 until the late twentieth century had been outnumbered by men, and during that period their presence in the workforce had expanded. The entry of women into the employment market had been almost as slow as their numerical growth vis-à-vis men. Until the 1960s they had worked primarily in the service and clerical sectors of the economy and in some aspects of the professional sector. During the 1960s women began to pursue professional careers other than nursing and teaching and to enter non-traditional types of employment. With the ability to limit family size and to schedule pregnancies, women had the security to undertake professional careers and to invade employment spheres previously closed to them. The early insistence of the Ontario government that all children attend school and the later establishment of institutions of higher learning in Northern Ontario allowed women to obtain the education and training necessary for career advancement.

2

Nokomis and the Changing Times in Her Life: Interview with a Woman Elder

Theresa Solomon-Gravel

E va Alma (Pelletier) Solomon came into this world on July 15, 1913. At the time of her birth she was named *Nimkiikwense*, a name that, in accordance with one Ojibwa naming tradition, reflects something of significance that was occurring within the natural world at the time of her arrival.[1] Anyone who knows her well and also knows something of Ojibwa traditions might well see the connection between her name and her life as she has lived it. For, according to Ojibwa traditional teachings, the "Thunder People" are teachers whose work it is to restore the balance in the world around us.

Eva and her husband of 57 years, Art Solomon, are respected Elders within the Anishinabe community. Through their commitment to each other, to family, and to community, they serve as role models, not only to their own children but to many others as well. Eva's love of family comes out of her experience as a sibling in a very large family, and it is evident in the dedication she has shown in her commitment as mother to her own ten children. There are many others as well – among them three foster children who came into her family in the 1960s – who, if asked, would attest to the fact that Eva has willingly opened both her heart and her home to them and who can always be assured that there is a place for them in both.

Eva is a very faith-full person whose strength comes from both her traditional spirituality as well as her Roman Catholic religion. She is among Canada's many Native people who have lived the experience of life on the reserve. Her earliest years were spent on the Spanish River (Sagamok) and Wikwemikong Indian reserves, on the north shore of Lake Huron and on Manitoulin Island, respectively. She lived and received all her formal education at the residential school in Spanish near where she grew up. For some of her life she has lived in very isolated communities; at other times she lived in the city. Eva is no stranger to poverty and hard times, but through it all, she has managed to maintain an attitude of optimism that has enabled her to be forever hopeful and forward-looking. This positive attitude is what enables her to face head-on the present challenge of ill health that her husband now experiences, as well as her own recent experience with a stroke.

With humour and an infectious smile, Eva has managed to affect the lives of all who have come in contact with her. She does this in the quiet and gentle manner that is her way. She epitomizes the Ojibwa traditional teaching that our responsibility as human beings is to live the four gifts that the Creator endowed us with at the time of Creation: kindness, sharing, honesty, and strength. Today, Eva is *Nokomis* (grandmother) to 26 children, and *Gchi-Nokomis* (great-grandmother) to five, with another on the way at the time of this writing.

Theresa Solomon-Gravel and her mother, Eva Solomon

Thank you for accepting to be interviewed for this project, Mom. What I would like to talk about today are the changes in your life and some of the things that you have experienced that you would like to share with us. I wonder, perhaps, if we can start with you sharing a little bit of your own childhood and upbringing and what it was like where you came from.

It wasn't very exciting. I grew up on a farm on the Spanish River Reserve, which is now Sagamok. Our farm was situated on the widest part of the river, about ten miles from the community of Sagamok itself. To go to the nearest village, Walford, we first had to cross the river, then walk three miles into the village. Sometimes we took a short cut through the bush and over a mountain to get there, because along the highway it was three and a half miles. If we wanted to go to the community of Spanish, we had to go five miles, so we often walked along the railroad track. Our closest neighbours were about a mile or two away, so we didn't get to see others very much. Once in a while we went to visit though, or they came to visit us and, of course, I had nine brothers and eight sisters at home.

You were born right there at that farm too, weren't you? Were all your brothers and sisters born there as well?

Yes, I was born at home, and so were all those younger than me. As far as I know, all the older children were born in Wikwemikong on Manitoulin Island.

You will be turning 82 years old this year. I remember a very interesting story that you used to tell us when we were young, about the day you were born. Would you like to share that with us now?

Well, I was born on July 15, 1913. They say there was a great big thunderstorm the day I was coming into this world. My mother always had the same woman for her midwife, a Native woman who lived about a mile and a half from our place. She gave me my name as soon as I was born.

That's your traditional or "spiritual" name, as it is called in our culture?

Yes, she called me *Nimkiikwense*. In English, it translates to "Thunder girl."

It is my understanding that one of the Ojibwa traditions surrounding naming is that a person may be given a name that refers to something of significance that is occurring in the natural world at the time of their birth. It is obvious that she named you according to that tradition. I find it interesting that you started out in life with a different name than you have now, but that seems to be the pattern throughout your life too, I've noticed. I guess that is what happens to all women who become mothers and grandmothers. Tell me a little bit about your father. I understand that he was a musician.

My father was a musician, he was a carpenter, a shoemaker, and he was a harness maker. He did all of those things. He came from Wikwemikong. His name was Onizime Pelletier, but everyone called him Tawanaa or Dan.

And your mother, where was she from?

My mother came from Harbour Springs, Michigan. Her name was Cecilia Miller. I don't know very much about her family though.

Did your dad basically just farm in order to raise your family, or did he work somewhere else as well?

No, he just farmed. In the wintertime he and the boys did lumbering. He had the contract to supply wood for St. Joseph's Convent, the Indian residential school in Spanish where I went to school. There were two schools there. The girls' school was called the "Convent" and the boys' school was called the "College." They were across the road from each other.

How old were you when you left home to go to residential school?

I was eight years old when I left home to go to the convent, and I stayed there for six years. The farm was only about five miles from the convent. But since we lived by the river, we had no way of going back and forth to school every day, so we stayed right there. My parents were pretty well educated themselves and they felt it was important for us to get an education and that was the closest school to us.

What was a typical day like in school?

The day began at 6:30 in the morning. Mass was at 7, breakfast started at 7:30, and we had to be finished and ready to begin work at 8. We had to do everything. We had to clean up the kitchen, do the dishes, prepare the dining room for the next meal, and clean the halls and the bathrooms. Some girls worked in the laundry, others worked in the garden or in the barn looking after the cows and chickens. Those who worked in the barn had to go back out at 4 p.m. and take care of the animals again (milk the cows and everything). We rotated jobs every month and the "senior" girls, as they were called – the older ones – supervised ten-girl work parties of "junior" girls. All the work had to be completed by 8:45 a.m. because classes started at 9. There were about 100 to 120 girls at the convent at any given time, so there were lots of hands to do the work.

What time did you get out of school?

Classes were over at 4 o'clock. Then we would all return to the playroom. That's where we always had to assemble whenever anything was finished. Whatever we did always started and ended in that room. When classes were over, we would all get in line to receive our "after school lunch." Everybody got a slice of bread; just dry bread, no butter, nothing else. Then, at 5 o'clock the older girls had to go to sewing class. Lots of girls liked sewing. We had a good sewing teacher, who was very nice to us. Supper was at 6 o'clock. We always knew what we were going to have for our next meal too, because they always served the same combinations of food on the same day each week.

With over a hundred girls in the school, how did you remember everybody's name?

We didn't. We used to call each other by our number; my number was nine. Everything we owned had a number on it and we just used that number to remember each person. It was easier because a lot of them had the same first names. I remember when we went to Expo 67 in Montreal, I got a chance to visit with some of the women who came from Caughnawaga (now Kahnawake), who had been in residential school with me. When I looked them up I knew their names, but I remembered each of them by their number and they remembered me by mine. The same thing happened to me one time when I met a friend at a conference in Spokane, Washington. I remembered a lot of the girls that way. We didn't have to do it like that, we just did.

How many of your sisters and brothers were in school at the same time as you?

Oh, Johnny was there for a little while, and Albert (Pius), and Eugene. They were at the boys' college when I was in the convent. Irene was in school with me for a short while, maybe a couple of years or so, then I left.

How often did you get to visit or spend time with your brothers?

Well, we used to go to chapel in the boys' college every morning. Sometimes we would see them on the boys' side of the room. But we only got to visit with them about one hour per month. It wasn't really much of a visit though; they would bring us together in the same class-room and we would sit in the desks. We used to see them across the road when we went outside to play, but they never allowed the boys and girls to play together.

Did you get home very often to see your parents?

No. I used to see my dad sometimes when he would make the weekly wood delivery to the convent. And we were luckier than most of the children there because my parents used to come to church in the chapel at the boys' college, so we would see them then. In the spring and early summer they would sometimes bring a picnic lunch with them when they came to church. On some occasions when they did that, we would all go down to the river and have lunch with them for an hour or so. In the wintertime my brothers used to sneak home to see my parents. They would skate down the river to visit with them, when they were supposed to be outside playing.

Did you ever go home for Christmas and holidays like Thanksgiving or Easter?

No, we just stayed there. We always spent Christmas at the convent, but when school was out for the summer, of course, we would go home. But some children never got to go home.

In recent years, we have heard that many children who attended residential schools had really terrible experiences while they were there. What kind of experience was it for you, personally?

For my part, I didn't mind it. I didn't have any really "bad" experiences while I was there. Some of them didn't like the place, that's true, but, "Where do you go in this world where everything goes good for you?"

One thing often mentioned when people talk about their experiences in those schools is the fact that the children were punished for speaking their own language. I can recall you mentioning that you also experienced that. That must have been very hard.

That's right. When I was in the convent, we were not allowed to speak our language. If we got caught speaking our own language, we got a penalty for it. Sometimes that penalty was not too severe; perhaps it would be that we were not allowed to play with the rest of the kids. We were made to sit down somewhere or maybe read or do whatever, but we couldn't play. As a result, many of the girls forgot their language while they were there. Some of them were at the convent for many, many years, you know.

You did have one sad thing happen to you while you were in the convent, even though it didn't have to do with the school itself. You lost your mother while you were away at school, didn't you?

Yes, I did. I was about 11 years old when she died.

Losing your mother at such a young age must have been pretty traumatic for you. How did you handle that? Did it make you feel like you grew up all of a sudden?

I don't know, it was hard. But no, I never got the feeling that I grew up all of a sudden; possibly because my older sister Lena sort of stepped into the role of mother until my dad remarried some years later. Lena was about 20 years old when our mother died. And then there was my father's sister Annie who used to come over very often; plus, my grandmother was there all the time.

Your grandmother lived with you?

Yes, my grandmother Madeline, my mother's mother, always lived with us, from the time my parents got married. Oh, she would go back to Harbour Springs in the summertime because she worked for tourists in Manistique, but she would always return to our farm in the fall. She died about two years after my father remarried.

Some of the children were still pretty young when your mother died. Did your father remarry right away?

No, not right away. About three years after my mother died, he went away to work in Flin Flon in northern Manitoba for about a year. We moved to Cutler while he was away. When he returned, we moved to Wikwemikong, where he ran a store for one of his cousins. My grandmother moved to Wiki with us as well.[2] It was there that Dad married Jane Zack; then we all moved back to the farm on the Spanish River again. I stayed with them on the farm for about a year, then I left to go to Toronto.

How old were you when you moved to Toronto, and what ever made you go there?

I guess I was about 16. My sister Lena was already working there for a couple who were both dentists. They were looking for someone to help her with taking care of the children, so she asked me if I wanted to come. I spent several years working for different families while I was there. I did mostly housecleaning and taking care of children. While I worked for the Allen family, I went to Robertson's hairdressing school. When I finished school, I got a job in a hairdressing shop.

What kind of wages did you make taking care of children, in the early 1930s?

I worked for the big sum of five dollars a month! It wasn't much better at the beauty shop. Shortly after that I came back up north. When I first returned home I worked for a French family in Blind River. They had ten children and only the two older ones spoke English. I was with them for quite a while. I didn't learn to speak French, but I was able to understand it.

Do you remember very much of the traditional ceremonies at that time when you were growing up on the Spanish River reserve and in Wikwemikong and those different places?

Not really, they weren't really happening "in full" at that time. We were under the Jesuits. They were pretty strict, you know, so nobody practised their own traditions – at least not openly. If they did, it was on their own, because at that time the missionaries didn't believe that our traditions and spiritual ways were as good as theirs. But I remember when we were in Killarney, your Grandma Jane and others from Wiki used to come over and they would dance and do a pow-wow because people wanted to see the dancing traditions. But they didn't do anything like the sweet-grass ceremony and all the other ceremonies that people do today.

I remember you telling us stories about your childhood and some of the traditional things you saw your dad doing.

Well, he never really explained much to us about the meaning behind those things that he did. We just saw him doing things like burning cedar as an offering, the way we use tobacco now. He always used cedar. Also, around the first of November, All Saints' Day, he always burned a plate-ful of food as an offering for those who were gone. There was a grave-yard not far from our place too, and I remember in the fall the people from the reserve would come there. They would bring offerings of food and they put it on the graves of their family members or friends. And my grandmother used to put tobacco down whenever she went out in the bush to collect medicine. She made a lot of medicines. We didn't understand then why she put the tobacco down, she never told us; but we did see those kinds of traditional things being done.

At different times when we were growing up, I can recall seeing you burn small amounts of cedar boughs on the top of our wood stove at home as well.

Yes. Cedar was more our medicine than sweetgrass. We used a lot of sweetgrass but we didn't use it for prayer then the way we used the cedar. The sweetgrass was used for making articles like placemats and baskets and so on.

Did you do a lot of traditional basketry and things like that when you were young?

No, not on the farm. There was never enough time for that – too much work on the farm! My grandmother did though. She would go and collect bark and do a little bit once in a while, maybe make birchbark place-mats with sweetgrass trim. She taught me how to make sweetgrass mats and things. We had lots of sweetgrass on the farm. Sometimes we did make birchbark cassots for collecting maple sap when we worked in our sugar bush.[3] We used to do that if we didn't have enough cans. The boys would gather the birchbark for us and they would also collect cedar bark that was stripped and made into a string-like material that we would use to tie the cassots with. After my dad remarried, my step-mother taught me how to make porcupine quill baskets, but I didn't do much of that.

After your mother died and your father remarried, what were some of the biggest changes you had to adjust to?

Well, for one thing, when my dad married Jane, she was much younger than he was; in fact, she was younger than my brother Gustin and she had two children of her own. Bringing two families together was a big adjustment, for them as well as for us, but we got along not too badly with them. And then, of course, my dad and Jane had children of their own.

How did you end up in Killarney?

Well, your uncle Johnny got married in 1935 and I went to Killarney for his wedding. I wasn't planning to stay, but then I met your father. I worked there for a couple of years. Then your dad and I went back to Blind River. He went to work with my brothers on my dad's farm where I grew up. They did some lumbering there at that time. Then on April 27, 1938, we got married – in the chapel at the boys' college. We lived in Spanish and your dad worked on the highway all that summer. They were building Highway 17 then, the Trans-Canada.

And then you started your family in 1939?

Yes, Donnie was born on February 15, 1939. We did a lot of moving around for the first few years after we got married. Donnie was born in Sudbury. Then we moved back to Killarney for a couple of years. For a while after that, we lived in Blind River and then we came back to Sudbury for a time.

So there was a lot of travelling from one community to the next. Was that a time when jobs were really hard to find?

Yes, times were hard then and you went wherever the work was. It was also during this time that your dad started to become very ill. In 1944, he was diagnosed with Bright's disease, a kidney disorder. We were living in Sudbury and he was working at Frood then. The doctor told him that if he wanted to keep on living that he'd better get out of the city. So, we moved back to Killarney at that point.

Was that when he was told that he only had from two to five years to live?

Yes! We just didn't know what was going to happen in the next five years. He gradually got his health and his strength back though. But you know, because he wasn't sick in bed and was able to walk around, some people thought that he was just not a worker, that he didn't want to work.

Kidney disorders are like that, you just don't appear to be sick. Art's aunt Nancy was about the only one who really knew how serious his condition was. That was really one of the hardest times in my life. And you know, there was no such thing as welfare in those days. There was no help like there is today. Those were very, very hard times – for me anyway!

So how did you manage to feed all of us and keep us dressed and everything?

Well, we did the best we could. We always had a big garden. I did a lot of canning of fruits and vegetables and I also made pickles. There were some people in the community who were very good to us. One of Art's aunts always sent us food and clothing. I would take those old clothes and make them over into clothes for you kids. Sometimes I didn't know where I was going to get even the essentials like flour to use for the house, but Father McHue and several other people were very good to us. Sometimes they would send over staples like flour and sugar and tea, that kind of stuff. I remember one year we planted our garden really late. Everybody said we were crazy to plant then, because all their gardens were already up; it was July by then. But we said, "Well, if it comes up, it comes up; if it doesn't, well, we'll have to take the consequences." We were lucky though, we had a good year. Our garden grew fast because the ground was already warm when we planted, so it wasn't hard for it to start to grow.

There was a real sense of community in this little place then, people really helped each other out?

Yes, always; they still do.

What are some of your best memories from those times, even though they were hard?

Oh, it wasn't all bad; we had some good times. We used to go out picnicking every Sunday. We would take our supper out in the boat with us and go across the bay or up the channel. Your dad built water skis and Donnie and Raymond would go water-skiing with their friends. They had some good times.

How did people get back and forth from Sudbury to Killarney in those days? There was no road into the town at that time.

We had to go by way of Little Current. In the summer we would go by boat to Little Current, and in the wintertime we would go across the ice. Sometimes there were two or three teams of horses that used to go to Little Current every week in the winter. Some would go to pick up the mail, some to pick up supplies. Once we arrived in Little Current, we would take the train or drive to Sudbury.

The next thing I would like to ask you about, Mom, is your experiences with living with the effects of assimilation and imposed acculturation. I can remember you talking about the fact that many Native people, even in a small isolated community like Killarney in the 1940s, seemed to be turning away from their culture at that time. Today people know that this was largely due to the cumulative effects of the experiences of residential schools, the loss of language, and the outlawing of traditional spiritual practices that were part and parcel of the Canadian government's assimilation policies directed towards Native people. What I would like to know is, how did that affect you personally? How did you feel when you saw others around you denying their heritage; and more importantly, how did you manage to keep such a strong sense of your own identity and culture?

I think those changes were happening there long before I ever went to Killarney. But, yes, there really was a strong belief at the time that Native people should become like "everybody else." It was occurring all across Canada. I don't think I realized then what the full impact of it really was; so, at the time, I don't know that I was aware of how it affected me personally. I did see what was happening but I felt that if others chose to deny their heritage it was not up to me to criticize them. They had a right to choose who they wanted to be. As far as keeping my own sense of cultural identity, I know that it was the strong influence of my parents and grandparents that helped me to know who I was. My grandmother who lived with us never spoke to us in English, she always spoke Ojibwe. And my father's mother always spoke Ojibwe as well; I believe that is what helped me to hold on to my culture, the fact that I could speak my own language.

The last time you moved from Killarney was in the early spring of 1958. What kind of experience was that for you, moving with ten children, and having to bring them across the ice to Little Current in order to get to Sudbury?

It was kind of scary because it was in March – and in March, you know, the ice is not always at its best. Anyway, we left as early as we could in the morning and we got to Sudbury that night. We drove in a car, but there was also a truck that brought all of our things over for us at the same time.

That particular move to Sudbury was the beginning of some really new experiences for you and your family, wasn't it? There was a big change in the family dynamics at this time, as a result of Dad becoming more politically active and having to be away from home more than he had been in the past. Also, shortly after the move, some of the older children started to leave home and I'm sure you had some adjustments to make in this regard as well. Was there ever a time when you experienced what is called the "empty nest" syndrome?

Yes, that time came when everyone was gone from home. I always knew that at some point in your lives, you would be leaving to follow the path you were choosing in life. I enjoyed having all of you home, but I also saw this as a time when I could begin to take some time for myself. So, I welcomed this opportunity to travel with your dad and to experience the kinds of things that his work was bringing to him. He was really at the forefront of the Native cultural rebirth and re-awareness that was happening at that time.

Yes, the 1960s was a time of great social change. I would venture to say that this was probably the decade of the greatest change within this century. Among other things, it was an era that witnessed a rebirth of Native people's identity. How did it make you feel when Dad started getting involved with all of the organizations that he did at that time – the Nickel Belt Indian Club, the Indian and Eskimo Association, the American Indian Movement (AIM), and all of the others? Did you ever think of where these organizations were going?

Well, when we moved back to Sudbury we got involved in the Nickel Belt Indian Club and that's when he began to change. I didn't mind because I always had a very strong cultural identity myself. I wasn't sure where these organizations were headed, but I thought it was good. I thought I would just wait and see.

I remember that there was some pretty harsh criticism of what these organizations were trying to do at that time. Some people said that they were trying to go back to the way things were in the past.

A lot of people did think we were turning backwards. They used to think we were crazy to turn back because we could never live the way our people had lived years ago. But that wasn't really the meaning of it. Those people just interpreted it that way. There were some, it's true, who did want to go back to the old ways of living – even some people locally – but I didn't see how we could do that and survive in this day and age.

How did you feel about the revival of Native spiritual traditions, like the use of sweetgrass and cedar and those things?

I felt all right about the spiritual part of it. The only difference between what I saw at home and what was happening with the revival of traditions was that we used to use more cedar when I was young. Cedar is what we considered as our sacred medicine in this area.

How did you feel about the people learning how to do traditional beadwork again, and things like traditional dances coming back at that time?

Well, I liked it. I was glad to see that people were finding their own roots again and beginning to follow them.

I remember lots of people coming to our home on Maley Drive when I was growing up. No matter what time of year it was, there was always someone coming there to see you and Dad. What I remember most was the hospitality that you showed them. It didn't matter how many people arrived at one time, you always managed to feed them and offer them a blanket and a place to sleep, if they needed it. Do you remember how many people came through your doors in the 1960s, when people were coming back to their roots?

Oh dear, I couldn't remember that! There were so many of them: some young, some Elders, some middle-aged. There were lots of people who came there. I'd imagine that within a couple of years, there might have been a few hundred or so who passed through the house. Some of them stayed over, others just wanted advice from your dad, or to talk to him; then they would keep on going. Sometimes the only bed there was for them was on the floor. We didn't have much, but we shared what we could with them.

Are there any experiences that you had during this time that were really "special," that you would like to share with us?

Well, I really enjoyed it when we travelled with Ernie Benedict and a group of young people from Akwasasne in what was called the "Iroquois Travelling College." We also went on a trip with a second group that was part of that travelling college, called the "White Roots of Peace," and we travelled all across Canada and into the States. For most of one winter we travelled in the southwest and went from college to college and university to university giving talks. That's where your dad got started with all his talks, with that group.

I remember hearing you tell an interesting story about what happened the year that a delegation of North American Native people went to make a presentation before the United Nations in Geneva.

Oh yes, we went to Switzerland in 1977. There were hundreds of us who went, and when we went to the Palace of Nations to make our presentation, we walked. There was an old man from the States who said a prayer in his own language and from where he said the prayer, the people began to march towards the palace. They marched with drums drumming and people in traditional dress and by the time we got to the main hall where the meeting was going to take place, you could look in any window in that palace and there were faces looking out at you. The people said they had never before seen anything so beautiful.

Not all the gatherings you came upon in your travels were always peaceful, were they? I'm thinking of, for example, the situation at Anishinabe Park in Kenora in the late 1970s, where some people appeared to be very militant. Were there ever times when you feared that the outcome of certain events could be really dangerous?

Yes, there were times when I was concerned, and there were some gatherings that tended to be more militant than others, but I didn't agree with their militancy.

During the 1970s Dad began to work extensively with Native people inside the prisons, and I remember that you accompanied him on several occasions. Were you ever afraid when you went into those situations?

Yes, I was afraid for him, because I was concerned that he could be in danger from anyone, either guards or prisoners, who might take offence at the things that he was saying.

There were other changes at that time too that Native society as a whole was undergoing. Some of it involved people gathering together and sharing the history of Native people as they knew it, especially the Elders. What were some of the most profound things that you learned from attending Elders' conferences and similar gatherings?

For one thing, like the ceremonies, it had been against the law for Indians to congregate in large groups when I was growing up, so we never experienced that then. But when we went to Elders' gatherings in the 1970s and '80s, a lot of the Elders talked about what they remembered of how things were in the past. Some of them told us that at one time the women were the ones who ran the communities and that the men listened to them. But, I guess eventually there came a point where the men became more important than the women. But today women are beginning to take their place again in Native society. At least I think they are. Many people look towards them as leaders now.

What would you like people to remember about you?

I'd like them to remember something good about me, such as my friendship towards them. I'd like them to remember the good things I did for them and how I appreciated their goodness.

We have talked about a lot of changes that you have experienced throughout your lifetime. As you think back on your life, what would you say, from your perspective, were the most profound or the most significant changes that you experienced?

Oh, I would have to say that was when I got married and settled down. Then looking after our first son and watching him grow. Later on, of course, having the other children added more responsibility. Taking care of children can be rather demanding at times because each child needs special care. It was also a big adjustment for me when your dad started travelling and doing the work he did, especially in the prisons. I enjoyed the opportunity to travel with him when I could. And today, of course, we have the reality of your father's ill health to deal with. I know that being on dialysis is very strenuous for him, and then there is my getting over the stroke that I had two years ago. But I'm really grateful to all of you children for helping us out now.

Do you have some really fond memories from different stages in your life that you would like to share with us?

Well, when I was very young, about five or six years old, I can remember looking forward with great anticipation to my grandmother returning from her summer work in Manistique, Michigan. She would always bring gifts for each one of us. I remember her bringing home fabric for all of the girls. My mother would make dresses for us with it; she was a good seamstress. She never used a pattern to make our clothes; we would look at the pictures of clothes in the catalogue and she would make us things that looked just like them, including coats and everything.

In the wintertime my brothers would take us for a horse and cutter ride on Sunday afternoons. I also remember when my cousin Basil would come over to go skating with my brothers on the river. He would always take me for a ride on the sleigh as he skated down the river.

Some of my best memories though, are of watching my children growing up and remembering the good times we had when we went out together; like those summer blueberry-picking expeditions or going across the channel for a picnic. I also remember how much everyone enjoyed our winter outings when we would take our supper and go out and make a big bonfire and go sliding or snowshoeing for the day. These are good memories for me and it's always nice to hear you kids speak of them today.

If you could leave a message to your grandchildren and others, what would you tell them?

I would tell them to honour their parents, to be good to them and to all the elderly people. I would tell them to remember all the goodness that has been given to them. Always remember all the good things and the good times they have experienced.

And what about the not-so-good things?

Well, there are times when things don't go right. It could be sadness, violence, uncharitableness; and these are not nice things to think about, that's true. If you find yourself in a situation where "bad" things keep happening over and over again, you should seek help. There is always somewhere that you can get help. I don't think that anyone likes to think about the not-so-good things. I don't, anyway. They're gone and they're not going to come back, and the sooner you let them go, the better off you are. If you don't learn to let them go, you will never be at peace. That's the way I feel. I don't like to hang onto something that's made me feel sad, or angry, or hurt me, in other words. It's gone and it won't ever come back so just let it go and learn to forgive, and to love others.

What do you think the future holds for the children of today?

I have no idea. I don't even know what the future holds for me. I just have to take it as it comes. I certainly hope that there's a good future for our children. I also know, though, that it doesn't look good at times. But never give up hope! Never, ever give up hope! No matter how bad things are, they'll never get so bad that they won't get better ... at some point – they'll get better.

3

Women of Quiet Strength: Nishnaabe-kwek Mothers and Daughters

Mary Ann Corbiere and Sheila Hardy

The task of recounting the values and experiences of Native women posed a challenge to us. A traditional academic format did not seem like an appropriate way to present the voices of Native women. We interviewed eight Native women – four daughters who work in postsecondary educational settings, and their mothers – and present the stories of these women in the context into which they were born. The interviews were semi-structured conversations, lasting from 60 to 90 minutes and moving through several questions on early childhood, significant events and influences, goals, values, responsibilities, and roles. We were interested in comparing the answers of the two generations. "Roles" is a static English word; our word is *enaagzheng*, better translated as "one's task or job." Our word for "responsibilities" is *enendaagzing wii-zhichgeng*, translated as "what one is obliged to do."

The women who shared their stories for this chapter are Ojibwe/Odawa or *Nishnaabe-kwek*, from Manitoulin Island and the North Shore of Lake Huron. The names Odawa or Ottawa, Ojibwa or Ojibwe need some explanation. The first two refer to people of the same culture. The same is true of Ojibwa and Ojibwe. The two groups, Odawa/Ottawa and Ojibwa/Ojibwe, speak essentially the same language. Despite this, their cultures were different historically, with the *Odawaak* practising agriculture and the *Ojibwek* living a life based more exclusively on hunting and trapping. In their language, both the *Odawaak* and the *Ojibwek* generally say they are *Nishnaabek* and those who speak the language say *"Ndoo-nishnaabem,"* meaning "I speak Indian." With the extensive intermarriage that has occurred between the two groups and with a closely related third group, the Potawatomi (or *Boodewaadmiiyig*), individuals are hard-pressed to identify themselves as being of one particular "tribe." Regardless of the mixed ancestry, however, all identify themselves as *Nishnaabek*, and the women as *Nishnaabe-kwek*. We do not claim that the picture of Native women provided here is definitive; what we hope to provide is a richer understanding of the multi-dimensional character of a particular group of Native women and their experiences. Hopefully, the images presented will eliminate some of the stereotypes about the "traditional Native woman."

The Manitoulin And North Shore Context

The culture into which these women were born had, by 1900, been affected and dramatically altered by the work of missionaries and by other European influences. Morrison writes:

> [By] 1843, there were some twelve hundred Indian people settled on the "Odawa Minising" [and of] these, more than half were already Catholic, another two hundred Anglican or Methodist .... [Furthermore, it] was their Christianity which most distinguished the Manitoulin Islanders from their compatriots at Walpole Island.[1]

The Jesuit objective of persuading the Native people of Wikwemikong (known familiarly as "Wiki") to take up farming so as to ensure that the children would go to school and the people generally would attend church had evidently been achieved by the 1850s. Morrison notes that besides learning to farm, the "Ottawa and Ojibwa males also learned to be blacksmiths, carpenters, and boatbuilders and their wives were competent seamstresses and domestics."[2] Morrison questions, however, the extent to which Natives assuming European work habits was due to Jesuits teaching or to the fact that the way of life promoted by the Jesuits was not entirely new to the Natives. He argues that "the great majority of the inhabitants of Wiki ... had already been living in semi-sedentary villages for hundreds of years. Unlike the Ojibwa, [the Natives at Wikwemikong] practised extensive corn agriculture and did not spend the entire winter out on the trapline."[3]

Whatever the reason for the mission's success, the descriptions of life in the 1930s provided by the women give a clear sketch of a farming and trades-based subsistence on Manitoulin Island in the early part of the twentieth century. Morrison also suggests that the Indian women of Wikwemikong were spinning wool and producing cloth as early as 1854. One of the mothers recalled a household where there was a *biimtegan* (a spinning wheel) and outlined what was involved in *biimtegeng* (spinning wool). This woman grew up on a small farm and in turn married a farmer. Another described rather nostalgically the fall fairs that used to be held when she was a young woman. She remembers the teams of horses, the cattle, and the diverse produce that the farmers would proudly show off.

This is not to suggest that the people of Wikwemikong necessarily embraced the new way of life or the religion the Jesuits offered. Morrison notes that the "Indian people continued to ... adhere obstinately to certain traditional beliefs."[4] Devens demonstrates that in Sault Ste. Marie and Upper Michigan, it was the women who most resisted the missionaries' proselytizing and typically "converted" only due to coercion from the husbands.[5] Her book, unfortunately, does not examine the reactions of the women of Wikwemikong to Jesuit preaching. Whatever the degree of reluctance or enthusiasm to adopt the new religion, however, it is clear from the interviews and other anecdotal evidence that by the 1920s and 1930s, most in Wikwemikong – including the women – were practising Catholicism.

The Mothers' Stories

When asked about their early education, what women most frequently remembered is learning reading and writing and *kachiim* at the girls' school then in existence in Wikwemikong. (*Kachiim* is the Ojibwecized version of "catechism," as used by one of the women interviewed.) This education was "furthered" at the residential school in Spanish, Ontario, which came into existence in 1913 as a major Native education centre. It was there that young Native women and men were taught domestic work, farming, trades skills, and, of course, *kachiim*.[6] Few Natives bypassed this formative experience. Most Native children acquired the ways and mores taught by the Jesuits and the Sisters who worked at the school in Wikwemikong.

Regardless of the extent to which Christian observance appears to have taken hold in Native communities, underneath the veneer of Christian ways lies a solid core of Native values. The mothers do not give conscious thought to which of their values or ways come from their Native background and which come from the newer Christian teachings. The fact that the traditions they often describe and practise are Christian ways does not mean that they have rejected Native values. When the women were asked which values they see as most important, they stressed respect and honesty. One stated that "one must respect others despite what they may do" and "be honest with everyone." Another woman has described the lessons of humility that she learned from her mother-in-law, a devout Catholic who died in 1963 at the age of 87. She remembers the mother-in-law saying of a woman who would make a big show of going to church, *"Niimshkagen da-nmihewin"* ("She wears her faith like a showy headdress"). Respect, honesty, and humility may be highly valued in Christian culture, but they are also among the values described in the Teachings of the Seven Grandfathers: wisdom, love, respect, bravery, honesty, humility, and truth.[7] Thus there is evidence of a synthesis of the two sets of values. If the mothers' perception of "traditional values" does not pose a contradiction in their minds, this seems to be the reason. This is also why the mothers' sense of identity as *Nishnaabe-kwek* is firmly intact, why the fact that they follow a Christian faith with greater or lesser degrees of devotion does not cause them to feel any less *Nishnaabe*.

When the mothers interviewed compared the roles of women today with the roles of women when they were young, they indicated that the most noticeable contrast is the variety of educational and employment opportunities available for women today as opposed to the limited opportunities available to them in their day. Education was mainly controlled by the church and stressed limited roles for women. The predominantly farming, logging, and trades economy that provided their families' livelihood held few opportunities for women. The mothers recalled that in their early life the natural course for a woman was to get married, have a family, perhaps co-manage a small farm with her husband, and periodically supplement the family income by working as a domestic in a home of non-natives on the island or the mainland.

The mothers also remember that the standard of living for Native people was exceedingly low by today's criteria. They recall that those who were "well-off" had a few head of cattle, chickens, and a thriving garden plot. Some families who were "really poor" had mothers who were working off-reserve and were able to come home only once every few weeks. The children were raised primarily by aunts, grandparents, or great-aunts.

Many of the mothers who talked about *Gii-gchi-gdimaagak* ("when there was great poverty" – one woman's term for the Great Depression) managed to find something humorous to lighten their anecdotes, or to chuckle in amazement over how they managed to survive. They laughed not to deny the poverty of the times, but to deal with the reality of their lives. Not all, of course, could so easily discuss the hard times.

The coping mechanisms these women used when recalling the past demonstrate their resiliency. As one mother said, "Times were tough, we had our ups and downs ... but I prefer to remember the good times." Two other mothers stated that they did not like to talk about the hard times, and they didn't. Other women talked about the "good old days," while at the same time frankly acknowledging the dreadful uncertainty of wondering where the next meal was going to come from. They also recalled the gratitude they felt when they found a job cooking or doing laundry and other housekeeping chores in some "well-off" non-native household. As one has said:

> Everything is so expensive now. I remember when a pound of butter cost ten cents. Now, imagine! Having to pay over two dollars nowadays for the same amount of butter! Mind you, we weren't paid as much as youse are these days. When I worked, I would get paid $5 for the month. Imagine that – $5! But that could buy an awful lot back then.

She remembered, laughing at the memory, her young daughter saying to a visiting friend, "We're rich now." The daughter had been proudly setting the table for supper using her mother's new plates. Decorated with fading pink roses and bordered in worn gold trim, the dishes had been picked up by an aunt at a rummage sale in Sault Ste. Marie. Acquiring household items in such a fashion, of course, was not seen as demeaning in the culture of this reserve. That was life. One treasured the beautiful and practical things that might be discovered in a box from a rummage sale and was neither bothered that the things were cast-offs nor ashamed that this was all one could afford.

The mothers did not look back on those times with either regret or bitterness. There is no evidence of any poignant sense of loss over the fact that they cannot describe traditional Native rites. They may regret – especially given the new interest in Native culture – that they did not record the old songs and stories that they had heard from their mothers, aunts, or grandmothers. As one often says when asked to tell a particularly entertaining story again, "I wish I had thought to write down the stories my mother-in-law told before she died," or "There's another good story she used to tell, but I just can't remember how it all goes."

What the mothers see as distressing are the loss of their language by the youth of today and the apparent loss of respect for the values that guided them as they were growing up. The loss of sharing with one another is a value that the mothers feel is particularly disappearing: feeding a visitor however little food one might have in the cellar, helping each other out without consideration for how much one might be paid, keeping one's door always open to someone who might be in need, and working for one's own sustenance. The mothers recognize the difficult economic realities of today. Still, they are dismayed that "young people don't do odd jobs in the community when there's lots of people and elders, too, who could use help with housework, garden work, and other things. Everybody expects to be paid so much. Even if they get paid a few dollars for the odd jobs here and there, that's better than nothing. And it is certainly more than we made when we worked in the old days."

While not all of the mothers interviewed talked about marriage, some indicated their disapproval with the light attitude of many young couples towards their marriage vows, and the perceived unwillingness to work to provide for themselves and their families. Some of the mothers who discussed marriage shake their heads in disapproval over the separations that seem to follow weddings so frequently these days. They are also appalled at the apparent lack of foresight on the part of couples when neither partner has either a job or the prospects of one and yet they undertake marriage and the responsibilities that go with raising children.

Although some of the mothers with whom we talked did indicate disapproval of separation, other evidence reveals that separation and divorce are accepted by the mothers interviewed if the reason for the separation is abuse. One of the mothers had actually travelled to a city several hundred miles away to retrieve her abused daughter and her children. Furthermore, this was at the encouragement of her *dindaawaa* (the mother of her son-in-law), who had told her of the abuse she had seen her son inflict on her daughter-in-law: "You should go and get your daughter and bring her home." In cases where divorce or an annulment has been obtained, however, the mothers have not accepted as willingly their daughters' plans to marry another man in the church if the "ex-husband" is still alive, since the previous husband is still technically the husband in the mothers' eyes. When such a marriage does take place, the daughter's new partner is accepted as her new mate, but not as her husband.

The mothers do not see marriage as an imperative for every woman. When asked about her thoughts on the role of women, one mother suggested that there's no reason why a woman has to marry. "Look at [so-and-so]. She's living perfectly well. She works, is able to buy nice clothes for herself, and built her own house. Same with [so-and-so]. Since she left her husband, she's perfectly happy, she got her own house, and she's working." The woman went on to say that if a woman did not have children she could still be fulfilled. Another mother wondered why her daughter, who has been through three relationships, wanted to marry her fourth partner. "She's working, there's no reason for her to marry him." She recalls the widow who "made the mistake" of marrying a widower and alienating her children as a result. She herself is a widow and reflected on her reasons for not remarrying. Her main consideration, she explained, was the well-being and happiness of her children. Besides, once the mother being interviewed realized how self-reliant she could be, she came to prize her independence.

Related to the notions about marriage held by the women interviewed is the importance they attach to their children's independent decision making. Mothers said time and again that their children need to learn on their own. They believe that they must make their own decisions, whether right or wrong. "It's their life, they need to be the ones to decide. I can only encourage and support," said one mother. Despite the fact that their daughters sought advice from them concerning careers, marriage, and children, the mothers contended that noninterference was a form of learning about life. All but one of those we have talked to indicated that they do not directly advise their daughters on how they should live. One gave indirect guidance through gentle parables illustrating how another person dealt with a similar problem to the one faced by the daughter. The parable showed the ramifications of the actions that had been taken. The mothers would tell their daughters that today's young people are so much more educated and in a better position to know what is the best thing to do.

While two of the mothers indicated great pride when their daughters had children and eventually married their common-law mates of several years, they never exerted any pressure on them either to have children or to marry. While the mothers feel that children need to learn on their own, they are adamant about one thing: the importance of education. "You can't survive without that these days. See the world. Don't tie yourself down when you are too young." The consistent message from the mothers to their daughters is to be self-sufficient, not to be overly dependent on anyone else for one's sustenance and survival. Notwithstanding this, when the daughters did marry, and particularly when they were married in the church, there was much happiness on the part of the mothers. This serves as another example of the dual value system at work. There is no perceived need to get married especially at a young age, and no undue pressure to do so even if one has had children. However when one does decide to marry, a church wedding is seen as important. Neither a wedding before a justice of the peace nor a traditional Native ceremony is recognized by the communities as official and legitimate.

In fact, the mothers interviewed do not seem to know what the traditional Native way of getting married is. They have only heard of the Native ways that are being brought from other parts of the country. To the mothers a traditional marriage is a Christian wedding ceremony. It was not just that the mothers preferred the traditional church wedding ceremony: they considered the members of the community who had been married in a newly revived Native way as not being married at all. On this key rite of passage, in the view of the mothers, the newer Christian mores clearly prevail over the traditional Native ones.

The acceptance of a Christian standard for a valid marriage does not mean that the vows "until death do us part" must be followed absolutely. As illustrated earlier, abusive marriages cannot be condoned, demonstrating that concerns for the well-being of children supersede Christian dogma. The acceptance of children born outside of Christian wedlock serves as another indication of this flexibility. While there are no statistics to show how many Native women have borne children without being married and raised them alone, as compared to non-Native women, it does seem that keeping all babies has been more common in Native communities than in Canadian society generally. For example, it is well known in Native communities which children were born before their mothers married and were raised by step-fathers. While some may have been stigmatized by their status, many were not.

A story told by of one of the women illustrates the willingness to accept all babies. She recalled the day that the woman she understood was her grandmother told her matter-of-factly that the man who had raised her was not her biological father. The woman remembers nothing in the way her step-father and his mother had treated her that suggested she was anything other than their blood relation. She remembered how she did the gardening chores with her "grandmother," and how her grandmother prayed and recited the rosary with her on their noon break under the shade of a tree. "Never forget to pray," her grandmother would tell her. When the woman herself became pregnant at 17, she had planned not to tell her parents. Rather she would have the baby at an unwed mothers' facility on the North Shore and give it up for adoption. When her "father" heard of her plans, he said that under no circumstances would he let her do that. He said: "We'll go and get that baby and raise it ourselves if she's going to give it up." The girl changed her mind and kept her son, and the grandmother treated the "illegitimate" son of the "illegitimate" granddaughter as her own flesh-and-blood great-grandchild. Although there is a somewhat derogatory Ojibwe term for "illegitimate" offspring – *gimniijaagan* – one rarely hears it. One's parentage is noted so that one knows all one's relations.

Examples of parental responses much like this abound in Native communities. There are many instances of a younger "sibling" in a family actually being an older sister's child. Seldom is the unwed woman forced to "succumb to the shame" inflicted by the Christian mores and made to go into hiding to await the birth of her child and return home childless. That course of action was seen in the community's eyes as committing a wrong even greater than the "sin" of premarital sex. While the Christian ideal of the virgin bride has been accepted, the human desires that mark young adulthood were also understood and accepted. Men and women marry with full knowledge and acceptance of any children that either partner might have from previous relationships.

However, a woman who does not have her baby baptized as early as possible is seen by the Native Catholic mothers as committing a grave omission. Baptism is still generally considered mandatory by the mothers we interviewed. A traditional Native naming ceremony is seen as not fulfilling the parents' obligations; a traditional church baptism should be performed. "Otherwise," as one woman said, "what if the baby should die without having been baptized?" Naming ceremonies, however, did have a place up until perhaps the 1940s, but they do not seem to have been considered obligatory. One mother described the naming ceremony as taking place on *Gimaa-giizhgag* ("when it's king's day" – the term by which the Feast of the Epiphany was called in Wikwemikong). These are among the times that the mothers describe as the "good old days." On this holy day each year, a feast was held at someone's house. Everyone in the community was welcome and each household attending brought something to eat. The hostess would be responsible for preparing a large batch of *skaanensan* ("little scones"), and of hiding in one *skaanens* a coin – perhaps a dime or a quarter. Each guest would take a *skaanens* and whoever found the hidden coin would host the following year's celebration. This celebration seems to have been seen more as a social occasion than a sacred function. These days, naming ceremonies are being revived in certain communities.

Underneath the adherence to Christian values is the persistent Native view that one's responsibility resides first and foremost with the children one brings into this world. These responsibilities include the children's physical and spiritual care, which accounts for the importance placed on the rites of baptism and matrimony. One mother quietly expressed concern for her daughter's spiritual health, saying, "You shouldn't neglect to pray and to teach your children how to pray as well." This is as close to interfering with her daughter's child-rearing as she will get. Another noted disapprovingly the practice of "dropping off the kids at the daycare every day, where they always get sick because they have illnesses passed on to them from all the other kids there." Yet, they will not tell their daughters, "You should stay home with your kids." They recognize the economic necessities that require – and have always required – Native women to work outside the home.

The residential school in Spanish was a significant factor that shaped the lives of the mothers we interviewed. Some entered the residential school at

seven or eight years of age; others at 12 or 13. Being separated from grandmothers, mothers, aunts, and other kin posed hardships. However, many see
the experience as having a positive side. For example, the teaching they
received is considered by most to have been good. One woman who did not
attend the residential school – because "my parents wanted to keep me with
them, I suppose, to continue helping them on the farm" – expressed a certain
sense of frustration that she did not get an education like some of the other
children did.

At Spanish, the mothers also first realized the negative consequences of
being "different." Being *Nishnaabe* was a difference that to this point had not
created any particular problems for them. Priests in Wikwemikong had
learned the Ojibwe language and used it with the people. At Spanish, the
mothers were punished for speaking their mother tongue. When they left
Spanish to go to work, they recognized for the first time the racism that existed
in Canadian society. One of the mothers said that she "never let it bother me. I
let [non-natives] have their own opinion." Another recalls that the racism she
felt when she went to work changed her: "I lost my self-confidence.... I wasn't
in their [non-natives'] league."

However bleak the "Spanish experience" was, it gave the mothers the
skills to function in the world in which they had to live. They forged ahead as
best they could to try to make a better life for themselves and their children.
What else could they do?

That they did not escape these experiences unscarred is not to be disputed.
For some of the mothers interviewed, the hardships while in the residential
schools are something they prefer not to talk about. Others who are able to talk
freely of their early life show evidence of lasting hurt as well. The scars
nonetheless are visible. One woman claims that even within her family, she
can't cry when someone dies. Some of the women have never been able to say
to their daughters "I love you." Expressions of love come through letters or in
words of encouragement to their daughters such as, "Keep your chin up" or
"You can do it," which are said when the daughters are discouraged and question their ability to succeed.

Despite the humiliation inflicted by residential school staff, the mothers
demonstrate their resilience and their quiet, unassuming determination that
their daughters will survive and be equipped to secure a far better life for
themselves than they had. Without being conscious of it, the mothers rely on
the value of bravery, a traditional Native teaching.[8] Some express it in terms of
faith. In one mother's words of encouragement, *"Yaa debenjget"* ("There is
one who owns [takes care] of all things"). When asked to identify the factors
that helped them to survive, a typical response was a look of wonder that one
could ask and expect an answer to such a question. To them, one simply did
what one had to do and just dealt with challenges as they arose. One did not
have a clinic in the community to go to, or a bank from which to borrow

money, so one simply obtained whatever help was available from fellow Nishnaabek or the church, and coped.

Without the help of either modern psychoanalysis or the traditional methods that shamans and other healers would have had in pre-conversion times, these mothers have survived and transcended their humble, and often humiliating, early years. Forging ahead despite feeling they were not in the same league as others shows the strength of character that can belie the seemingly shy exterior of some of the mothers. Building a solid and good path from two very different value systems, Native and Christian, demonstrates a resourcefulness and a flexibility acquired despite, in their words, a "limited education."

The Daughters' Stories

Daughters become strikingly like their mothers as they mature into adult women. Technology, medical advances, and access to education affect the lives of everyone. Their impact on Native people is even more significant. Historically, Native people have been marginalized from society and thus have not been able to access as readily the advances that have benefited other groups. In recent years, however, educational policy has changed so that both access and retention of Native people in the schools has improved. While struggling within this environment of change, the daughters interviewed, like their mothers, have faced significant hardships in their lives. Many are the same hardships as their mothers faced – poverty and racism. Some of the difficulties differ from those of their mothers – separation, divorce, and striving to complete an education in a non-Native milieu.

Certainly for these daughters – who are now between the ages of 35 and 55 – mothers, grandmothers, and aunts were the women who had a significant impact in their lives. That solid core of traditional Native values mentioned earlier in the chapter seems to be what ensures continuity from one generation to the next. As values are transmitted, so are ways of knowing and ways of doing. This is particularly satisfying to those working to retain Native tradition, culture, and language. The interviews with the daughters show that they have retained much of what their mothers, grandmothers, and aunts have taught them. Our role as women is to "teach them [our children] our values: that life is precious … to have balance in one's life … and that we all have responsibilities." Those core values that they were taught by their mothers, grandmothers, and aunts – "respect and honesty" and "caring and sharing" – are the values that guide to this day the daughters interviewed. As one of the daughters said, "I guess I was really taught to share whatever I had and they [mother and aunt] taught me I could do whatever I wanted … and that I should be proud of who I am [a *Nishnaabe-kwe*]." What is different is that the daughters tend to identify more explicitly these values as Native.

Both mothers and daughters interviewed envisaged women's responsibilities as first to their children, if they had them. "My mother taught me to care for my children first and to love them." The daughters see the role of women as "keeping the family strong, spending time with children, supporting, teaching, and nurturing them." However, mothers and daughters did acknowledge the need for the women of today's generation to work outside the home for economic reasons, but both stressed the importance of the mother's presence in the early life of a child. The daughters were quick to point out that "housekeeping" is not solely their responsibility but rather a job that is shared equally between partners. This is not to suggest that the role of men is less valuable than that of women, but for these Native women, nurturing and teaching children in the early years of life is clearly a woman's responsibility. One daughter stated that men and women are "equal, yet different, with no one job being more important." Yet, as Wynne Hanson states,

> The aspirations of Indian women are to combine the best of two worlds, to survive and to keep their families intact. To achieve these goals many Indian women must enter the world of the employed and this creates conflict by dividing loyalties between family and career. Because Indian culture is usually emphasized in the instruction of the children, the responsibility for teaching cultural traditions usually falls on the Indian women.[9]

What each of these daughters had to say about hardships was that they were able to get through them with the help of family, friends, and for some, the Creator. They attribute who they are today – hardworking, determined, and educated – to a combination of their upbringing, which instilled in them pride and a set of core values, life's lessons in dealing with hardships, and the sheer determination to succeed, which was passed down from a mother, grandmother, or a special aunt. Even with the added responsibility of working in Native postsecondary education, on or off the reserve, these daughters are expected to "help out" with many of the same responsibilities as their mothers had. For instance, they describe their mothers as people who "held the family together, making sure our needs were always met." For the majority of the daughters, life continues to be centred on the family and on working to make it better for their children and their people.

Being self-sufficient was an ideal that these daughters took to heart. Statements such as "Going on welfare just wasn't an option" and "I didn't want to be on welfare, mother's allowance until 65" express their values in clear, unequivocal terms. It has become evident that the mothers' determination to make things better for the next generation has been passed on to their daughters. All knew that obtaining an education would be key to their survival. As stated by one daughter and echoed by others: "Education was always encouraged."

The daughters felt family, friends, and community encouraged further education. But after graduating and returning to serve one's community on reserve or off, they had a sense that one's Native "identity" is being tested. Many people, both Native and non-native, seem to assume that education makes one "less Native." This struggle is something the mothers did not have to face. They were accepted for who they were. Despite these pressures, all the daughters have developed a strong sense of Native identity and pride in who they are and where they come from.

It is interesting that for both mothers and daughters, the significant person who influenced their life was a female, most often the mother or grandmother and frequently a special aunt. All reiterate that these were their first teachers. The mothers interviewed spoke of their mother, grandmother, and aunts as the people who held the family together by being "loving and caring" to all people, not just to blood relatives – "An extra potato in the pot didn't matter." Daughters echo the same people as being influential.

While the roles and responsibilities of women in society have undergone redefinition in many instances, those of the Native women interviewed for this chapter remain constant. Values of family strength, responsibility towards children, and preciousness of life are part of the core traditional Native values that have been retained.

In conclusion, the intent of this chapter was to add to the reader's understanding of Native women from one particular culture and to begin identifying what has helped or enabled these women to survive in a rapidly changing world. What emerge as key factors to their survival are the flexibility and adaptability of these women. The mothers we interviewed were able to blend two contrasting value systems, European and Native, drawing upon each as appropriate for a given circumstance. The daughters are similarly adept at reconciling different value systems. They have maintained a strong sense of their own identity and values while functioning successfully in work environments that operate on a value system and structures that are foreign to the Native traditions. Such is the consistency of their identity and sense of place in this world that all the women say they are not Catholic, not traditional, but simply Native women – *Nishnaabe-kwek.*

4

Ukrainian Women in the Sudbury Region

Helena Debevc-Moroz

Учітеся, брати мої,

Думайте, читайте.

І чужому научайтесь,

Свого не цурайтесь.

Taras Shevchenko

In an 1845 poem entitled "To the Dead, to the Living, and to Those Yet Unborn, My Countrymen All, Who Live in Ukraine and Outside Ukraine, My Friendly Epistle," Taras Shevchenko, the greatest Ukrainian national poet, exhorted his countrymen to "study, my brothers, think and read, learn the ways of other peoples, but do not shun your own traditions" (writer's translation). Brief as it is, the above fragment of the poem expresses certain values: notably those of education and learning the traditions of other peoples while preserving the traditions of one's own people.

Taras Shevchenko is venerated by virtually all Ukrainians, regardless of their political or religious persuasion. Monuments to Shevchenko have been erected not only in all the major Ukrainian cities, but also by Ukrainian immigrants, in such unlikely places as Washington, D.C., Buenos Aires, Argentina, and, most recently, in St. Petersburg, Russia. In Canada, Shevchenko monuments can be found from Oakville to Winnipeg and beyond. The above passage is widely known among Ukrainians, and for many Ukrainian immigrants it has represented a guiding light for their lives in diaspora, particularly since it was in part directed to Ukrainians living outside of Ukraine: while one must learn to adapt to the life in a new country, one must not spurn one's own traditions.

The present study is concerned with the degree to which these traditions have been preserved in Sudbury and, more particularly, with the particular role of women in the attempts to preserve these traditions.[1]

The Ukrainian community in the Sudbury region is very diverse. Although Ukrainians speak the same language, they come from various regions of Ukraine and different religious backgrounds. In general, Eastern

Ukrainians are Orthodox, whereas Western Ukrainians are Catholics of the Eastern rite. This reality is reflected in the fact that in most Ukrainian communities, including Sudbury, there are both Orthodox and Ukrainian Catholic churches. A small minority among Ukrainians belong to Protestant denominations. Some Ukrainians have left the traditional Ukrainian churches and have joined non-religious organizations, like the Labour Temples, which more accurately reflect their aspirations. However, whatever their religious or political background, the respondents in the study viewed their Ukrainian heritage with great pride. Descendants of several waves of immigration still live and work in the community and remain active in their respective Ukrainian organizations (Ukrainian National Federation, Association of United Ukrainians, Ukrainian Senior Centre, for example). The influx of the postwar refugees resulted in a substantial population increase in the Sudbury region from 2,260 in 1941 to 5,625 in 1971.[2] Different waves of immigration settled in the region when local industry needed a labour force and thus their personal history, as well as the history of the community they belonged to, became inexorably linked with the history of the region. Numerous Ukrainian organizations existed and still exist, representing the different needs and different political philosophies of the diverse Ukrainian community.

It is a historically well-documented fact that confrontations existed between the various political factions in the Ukrainian community between World Wars I and II as well as in the postWorld War II years.[3] New immigrants formed organizations that reflected their own views and aspirations, and the conflicts within the Ukrainian community continued. To speak of a cohesive Ukrainian community is not really possible. Any portrayal of the Ukrainian women in the Sudbury region must reflect the reality of different communities within the Ukrainian community here. Every effort has been made in the selected sample of interviews to reach as many women as possible belonging to different organizations within the Ukrainian community. Although this study does not claim to be indicative of the point of view of the entire Ukrainian community, it is based on a sample believed to be fairly representative of that community.

The Research Process

Eight existing Ukrainian organizations in the Sudbury region – covering the entire political, cultural, and religious spectrum – were contacted by letter.[4] The purpose of the study was outlined and the assistance of the organization was requested in publicizing the study among its women members. In addition, the heads of the organizations were also requested to suggest the names of women of Ukrainian origin who would be willing to participate in the study. The letters were followed by phone calls and subsequent interviews of volunteer subjects, who read and signed a consent form. Some Ukrainian women were also approached through personal contacts within the Ukrainian community. Twenty-six women were interviewed, primarily in English but also in Ukrainian, in interviews lasting from two to five hours. Questions were asked on family history, education, immigration, and heritage issues. All the women who volunteered for this study were eager to tell their story. Most of them were not born in Northern Ontario, but they helped build a vibrant modern community here. They spoke with pride of their identity and their attempts to preserve their Ukrainian heritage. This is their story.

Identity and Heritage

The subjects of this study were women of Ukrainian descent of various generations. When it became apparent that differences in the perception of the issues discussed were clearly drawn along generational lines and also reflected the difference in the pattern of immigration to Northern Ontario, the subjects were divided into five groups. When the women were asked to identify themselves by nationality, it became clear that there is a generational divide in women's perception of themselves. Although they identified themselves differently, none of the women felt that she had a problem with either her identity or her loyalty to Canada. Collectively they constitute a group that considers itself very comfortable as part of Canada's mainstream society.

Group I: Women of Ukrainian descent in their sixties and seventies, born in Canada to Ukrainian immigrants who came to Canada in the early twentieth century. The overwhelming majority identified themselves as Canadians of Ukrainian descent or Canadian Ukrainians.

Group II: Ukrainian women who emigrated from Europe as young adults following World War II, often labelled the "Displaced Persons." All these women identified themselves as Ukrainian.

Group III: Canadian Ukrainian women in their forties, born to Ukrainian parents, at least one of whom was also born in Canada. They referred to themselves as Canadian Ukrainians or Canadians of Ukrainian background.

Group IV: Women in their late thirties and mid-forties, the majority of whom were born in Europe and came to Canada as small children. They are the daughters of the "Displaced Persons" generation. The majority chose the Ukrainian Canadian designation.

Group V: Ukrainian women in their thirties and forties who recently immigrated to Canada. These recent immigrants identified themselves as simply Ukrainian.

The women of the older generation (Group I) had vivid recollections of their parents' lives as well as of their own childhood. Their stories are of survival, of their fight for social justice, of hard work, of building a community and practising their Ukrainian traditions, and they reflect pride and joy at being able to worship freely in the churches they helped build.

The younger generation (Groups III and IV) first followed in their parents' footsteps, but the world they grew up in differed from that of their parents. They had new struggles and aspirations and their experience was perceived in the Canadian context.

Ukrainian Women and the Northern Experience

As with other aspects, the impact of the north on Ukrainian women and how they shaped the north can be clearly drawn along generational lines. The answers ranged from the older generation's comments about "pure survival" in a mining town, to the recent immigrants' finding that the north meets most of their expectations.

For the older women (Group I) who came to Northern Ontario as children with their immigrant parents or as young adults from the prairies, the north looked like a dark, barren, dreary place. It did provide an opportunity for steady work. Most women said they adjusted quickly and felt northerners were friendly, but what was most reassuring was that they found fellow Ukrainians in their communities. "There were lots of Ukrainian restaurants and hotels" and although the town was "just a mining town," it had "more modern facilities" than a little hamlet in the prairies. The north they helped build was a place for people with a pioneering spirit: their occupations ranged from running a supply store in the virgin bush in Swayze in the mid-1930s, to working in the boarding-houses catering to the miners, to the building of Ukrainian halls that reflected every political persuasion. All women stressed how hard those times were, but they felt a tremendous sense of pride not only in helping create the northern community as it is today but also in preserving their traditions in doing so. "Our first thought was of survival," and it was "work that made all the difference."

For some young women, coming to Sudbury from the west was an "adventure." The north was "just as cold as the West," so they knew they could manage, and although the landscape was quite different from the western landscape, these women were fascinated by "all the water and all the lakes." Some women in this group who came as young children "fell in love with blueberry-picking." The words of one woman echo the feelings of many other women about Northern Ontario: "I got to love the complexity and diversity of the north," where "people are willing to help and to share."

Work brought the Group II women and their young families to the north. These women felt that the existing Ukrainian community did not reflect their political aspirations, so they helped build their own organization. They used the organizations as cultural centres for children and adults, perpetuating Ukrainian traditions and their language. The north became their home; they feel that they have roots in the north and none of them has any desire to leave the north.

Some of the women in Group III felt that the northern experience has had a profound influence on their lives. Besides work and family that tie them to the north, their political activism has shaped their lives and given them direction. They see their contribution to the community at large by making the north a better place to live for those who need support. Others see work, family, and the quality of life in the north as the most important reason for staying here.

Very few women in Group IV grew up in the north. The vast majority came because of their partners' opportunities for work here. They perceive life in the north as peaceful and safe for their children. Easy access to nature and the numerous recreational facilities have certainly made many of them converts to the northern way of life. Many came from big cities and they appreciate the friendly, unhurried pace of life here. However, many find the north culturally and socially too quiet. They find the Ukrainian community not active enough, not providing enough stimulation for them and their children. Had they lived in larger centres where the Ukrainian community is more numerous, they would not have any difficulty in finding appropriate programs for their children. In Northern Ontario, they felt they had to be the pioneers and organize cultural programs, language classes, and Shevchenko concerts themselves for their children since the Ukrainian community did not provide the services for their children that they deemed essential. Their pioneering work was challenging and time-consuming, but they do not regret the effort. Their overwhelming concern is that they do not see another generation continuing the work that they started.

The recent immigrants' experience (Group V) in the north has been very positive in spite of the initial "fear of so many rocks." The north provided them with steady work. Northerners were helpful and friendly, accepting of their "foreign accent" – of which they are still somewhat self-conscious. But it is the presence of a Ukrainian community that they found in the north that affected positively their quality of life and made the necessary adjustment to the community at large much easier.

Preservation of Ukrainian Traditions

Ukrainians in Northern Ontario are like Ukrainians everywhere in Canada: they have preserved the colourful and festive traditions that are unique to their culture. Many of these traditions have pre-Christian origins: the colourful Ukrainian Easter eggs, *pysanky,* for example, symbolize rebirth in spring. The *hopak,* the spirited Ukrainian dance, has become an instantly recognizable part of the Northern Ontario culture, and the beautiful choir music accompanied by *banduras* (a Ukrainian string instrument) or mandolins has become a tradition that the Ukrainians in Northern Ontario have come to share with others. The traditions of song and dance serve to unify the

Ukrainians in Northern Ontario, and local groups – for example, the Veselka dancers and the Dnipro choir – have achieved international reputations. Ukrainian embroidery is found in practically every Ukrainian home in Northern Ontario. Residents of Northern Ontario look forward every year to some festival where they might experience first-hand the vibrant culture of their Ukrainian neighbours.

Then there are the Ukrainian gastronomic delights. Is there a northerner who has not tasted *borsch* (beet soup), *holubtsi* (cabbage rolls), *varenyky* or *pyrohy* (filled dumplings)? These foods have become part of the northern menu.

private collection

Ukrainian singers and dancers, Sudbury, 1980.

These are some of the visible symbols of Ukrainian culture in Northern Ontario. Ukrainians themselves share many more, and the majority of Ukrainian women interviewed listed the same traditions.

The traditions most often cited by the women are connected with Ukrainian Christmas and Easter. The Ukrainians in Northern Ontario follow the Julian calendar and their Christmas festivities fall on January 6 (Christmas Eve) and January 7 (Christmas Day) of every year. Ukrainian Easter festivities coincide with the Gregorian calendar approximately every four years. The traditional ritualistic foods feature prominently in the preservation of tradition. From the 12 meatless dishes on Christmas Eve – some like *kutya* originating in pagan times – to the colourful Easter baskets full of traditional foods blessed in church before Easter, to decorating the *pysanky*, these traditions are still thriving.

Other ritual holidays, such as *Zeleni Sviata* (Whitsunday) commemorating the dead, are sacred in many families. *Malanka*, or the Ukrainian New

Year on January 13, is rich in tradition and ritual. Song, dance, and occasionally fortune-telling make up this delightful holiday, still practised by many Ukrainian seniors in the north. A Ukrainian wedding would not be a wedding without a *korovai,* a traditional braided bread decorated with symbolic dough ornaments and periwinkle flowers.

Preservation of Ukrainian Language

The most controversial issue in the preservation of Ukrainian heritage was the issue of language and its role in the preservation of the Ukrainian culture and traditions. The answers about this important and sensitive issue were divided along generational lines and are recorded by groups.

Ukrainian is written in the Cyrillic alphabet (see an example at the beginning of this chapter), which immediately distinguishes it from English or French, which use the Latin alphabet. When the relationship between language and culture was discussed, there was a marked discrepancy between what the women believed, what they practised, and the current linguistic reality in the Ukrainian community in Sudbury.

In Group I, almost all the women listed Ukrainian and English as the languages that they spoke. Knowing Ukrainian constituted for them part of their identity: it provided them with roots. In their early youth it also provided them with the window on the world that was shut off by Canadian society. Some had either a passive or an active knowledge of another Slavic language, and some had a fairly good command of French. When asked to assess their level of proficiency in Ukrainian, most women said that they received no formal education in Ukrainian; they spoke Ukrainian at home with their parents who had emigrated from Europe and spoke no English. Some of the women in their seventies grew up in the west and came to Northern Ontario as young adults. They recalled how school authorities forbade them to speak Ukrainian among themselves.[5] Some younger women as well recalled being discouraged by local teachers from speaking Ukrainian to their parents. Multiculturalism certainly did not exist as a policy then! The parents, however, made every effort to send the children to Ukrainian language classes in different Ukrainian halls and churches. With their own children, they tried to speak Ukrainian when the children were small but most of them admitted that the dominant language in their own households was English.

They cited several reasons for this. Some decided that, being Canadian-born themselves, they would not press the use of Ukrainian at home. Others said that their Ukrainian was not good enough to sustain them past their children's grade school. Then there were those who married outside the Ukrainian community, making the preservation of the Ukrainian language even more difficult.

Still, almost all the women interviewed sent their children to Ukrainian language classes organized by various Ukrainian organizations or the

Ukrainian churches. When the Sudbury Board of Education started offering the heritage language programs, the women encouraged their children to take Ukrainian. Few of the adult children of these women speak Ukrainian. And the children's knowledge of the Ukrainian language is limited to a few phrases and words that deal with Ukrainian traditions and Ukrainian food.

Women in this age group were almost evenly split when asked what they considered more important, language or tradition. Some regretted losing the Ukrainian language, feeling that they owed it to their heritage to preserve it. At the same time they felt that linguistic compromise was inevitable.

The Group II women were young adults when they immigrated after the war, and speaking Ukrainian at home was for them quite natural. Preserving their native tongue was a question of honour and a positive step in a multicultural world. They had a very strong sense of national identity and saw no reason to speak English to their children. They believed that the Canadian schools would take care of their children's English. Some of them learned English along with their young children, and they refused to speak to their children in "broken English." They also refused to be intimidated by the local English education establishment, which chided them for encouraging their children to speak Ukrainian at home. Some of them learned English well and went on to further their education. For these women, preserving Ukrainian culture and traditions without the language is inconceivable.

A very revealing attitude towards language and culture came from Group III, Ukrainian women whose parents were born in Northern Ontario. Some of these women spoke only English, others spoke English and some Ukrainian. They came from different backgrounds and therefore wanted to preserve different aspects of the rich Ukrainian culture. For some, it was the Ukrainian music and dance that constituted the magical force of the Ukrainian culture in Northern Ontario. For others it was the richness of the Ukrainian religious tradition with its music, its *pysanky* – the very distinctive tradition of decorating the Ukrainian Easter eggs that has become a visible symbol of the Ukrainian presence not only in Northern Ontario but in the entire country. What is very surprising is that the women in this group also felt that culture and tradition could not survive without language. When confronted with the apparent contradiction between this and the practice of the Ukrainian traditions without the active use of Ukrainian, they admitted that the coexistence between language and culture is an ideal that is absent from their lives. Some women felt that as long as the language is tied to a tradition that is perceived as relevant, it is worth preserving. Others considered language part of their heritage and felt that their experiences in visiting Ukraine would not have had the same depth and dimension without the language.

Practically all of the women in Group IV, educated children of the postwar immigrants, speak Ukrainian to varying degrees of proficiency and all of them still speak Ukrainian to their parents. Their "Ukrainian immersion" was intensive: several hours of Ukrainian language and culture a week, Ukrainian extracurricular activities, Ukrainian summer camps, and an ongoing observance of Ukrainian language and traditions at home. Many of their parents were professionals belonging to the educated élite, and they insisted that their daughters actively participate in all aspects of Ukrainian life in the diaspora.

A very small minority still speak Ukrainian to their children. One-third speak some Ukrainian to their children, and one-third speak no Ukrainian to their children. The abandoning of Ukrainian is sometimes due to intermarriage and sometimes because of the tremendous effort and dedication that such linguistic demands would entail. Although the majority of women married sons of "Displaced Persons," this did not automatically guarantee the preservation of the Ukrainian language. Most of the women in this group abandoned their Ukrainian language when the children reached school age. Ukrainian was further eroded when the children entered high school. Few women make the effort to upgrade their own Ukrainian skills by reading relevant Ukrainian literature to be able to discuss contemporary issues with their children in Ukrainian, issues such as science projects, sports, and extracurricular activities. When asked which was more important to them – the preservation of language or of culture – two-thirds said that both were important, while the rest were divided between language and tradition.

This particular group is very sensitive about the language issue and is either regretful or defensive about losing or not practising the language. While *baba* (Ukrainian for "grandmother") was alive, the language was easier to maintain, but sometimes even the presence of a Ukrainian *baba* is not enough to preserve the language. The effort to communicate in Ukrainian is just too overwhelming for most grandchildren.

Very emotional responses regarding language came from the daughters of the "Displaced Persons." References to Ukrainian language being part of "one's soul," constituting one's "essence," or being "woven into one's being" were quite frequent. Many women in this group felt that, by preserving the Ukrainian language, they were paying homage to their parents and their struggle in the new land.

There were also some dissenting voices in this group. They expressed the feeling that language can become "exclusive," especially for their non-Ukrainian partners, whether within the family, or in church, or in keeping the traditions that are inexorably tied to language. They felt that a compromise on the language issue was very difficult.

The recent immigrants of Group V are delighted that they can speak Ukrainian freely in Canada. For them, preserving the Ukrainian language gave them a sense of identity, roots, and a feeling of pride. The political conditions in the countries where they lived in Europe usually made them confine their use of Ukrainian to their homes. At school and at work, they spoke a different

language. While they find the Ukrainian community in Northern Ontario welcoming, they fear that their children will quickly become linguistically assim-
ilated and they feel rather powerless to do anything about it.

Perception of Multiculturalism by Ukrainian Women in the North

One of the many stipulations of the Canadian Multiculturalism Act of the
Government of Canada is to "recognize and promote the understanding that
multiculturalism and racial diversity of Canadian society and acknowledge the
freedom of all members of Canadian society to preserve, enhance and share
their cultural heritage." Two of the specific mandates of the multiculturalism
policy are to "encourage the preservation, enhancement, sharing and evolving
expression of the multicultural heritage of Canada" and to "facilitate the
acquisition, retention and use of all languages that contribute to the multicultural heritage of Canada."[6]

Although most of the women interviewed were aware of the existence of
the multiculturalism policy in Canada, they were not familiar with the scope of
its mandate beyond its promotion in this country. Some were aware of calls for
review of the government's policy on multiculturalism, particularly because of
government subsidization of a variety of multicultural programs.[7]

The perception of multiculturalism by the Ukrainian women in Northern
Ontario was generally very positive. Their responses, however, again reflected
the generational gap between the women.

The most important aspect of multiculturalism for the Group I women
was to provide official government recognition and acknowledgement of, and
respect for, diversity. The women felt strongly that the contribution of
Ukrainian settlers in Northern Ontario and the rest of Canada should be recognized in textbooks used in educational institutions. "We are a people too....
We have a past and a history ... and people should know about it."

No amount of government recognition or subsidy, according to the women
of Group II, will help preserve the Ukrainian culture in Northern Ontario unless
the organizations rethink their orientation and become self-sufficient organisms
that create jobs to keep the new immigrants in the community.

The women of Group III felt that whereas the multiculturalism policy
gives some direction, it is up to the Ukrainian groups themselves to define
their priorities.

Sharing the Ukrainian culture and learning from other cultures is the leit-
motif of Group IV.

Often unable to practise their language or culture openly because of political circumstances before their emigration, the women in Group V welcomed
the *right* of keeping their own language and traditions in the new land. They
found invaluable the help they received through the multicultural association
in the north.

The Future of Ukrainian Culture and Language in Northern Ontario

The women of all the groups wanted the survival of some parts of the Ukrainian culture, but many saw assimilation as a threat. Although most women were cautiously optimistic about the survival of Ukrainian heritage in the north, their concerns could be traced along generational lines.

The women of Group I have seen the northern community change from a strictly mining town to a flourishing community. On the whole these women are rather optimistic about the survival of Ukrainian heritage in the north, provided some significant changes take place. Their concerns ranged from fragmentation within the Ukrainian community to lack of commitment of younger generations in volunteering in their respective organizations. They felt that the older generation was often too critical of the younger generation and did not give it enough credit or opportunity to institute any changes. The organizations that this group of women helped build served a real need in the Ukrainian community in the past. They provided a social and cultural haven. Some organizations were a hubbub of political activity. Today some of the ideologies they embraced seem outdated and no longer relevant. This is a time of transition, and the important question is whether the younger generation will want to promote the organizations that it no longer perceives as relevant. The younger generation sees no need for a communal family to meet its social, political, or cultural needs. The women in this group were unsure what form Ukrainian heritage in the north will take in the future. Some cautiously mentioned music and dance, but most would not venture any predictions about the future.

The Group II women hoped very much that the Ukrainian heritage in the north would survive. They, too, felt that the current status of the existing organizations in the community had to be reviewed. Some major restructuring was in order, they felt. The volunteers who built the vibrant Ukrainian community were getting tired. Intermarriage of their children, in their opinion, will also change the nature of the Ukrainian heritage. As to what form the Ukrainian heritage would take in the future, the answers varied between active co-operation with Ukraine to keeping the community at large vibrant enough to prevent the exodus of their educated children from the north.

If the various Ukrainian groups joined their efforts, the women in Group III felt some cultural aspects of the Ukrainian heritage (music and dance) would survive. This might be possible with the younger generation, who might not carry the political baggage of the past. The cultural aspects of the tradition would survive only if they are perceived to be relevant to the way we live in the 1990s.

Although Group IV women said an overwhelming yes when asked if the Ukrainian heritage in the north will survive, their answers often seemed to contradict the reality of the situation around them. Young people come to fewer and fewer events sponsored within the Ukrainian community. In inter-marriage the women often adopt their husbands' traditions because there is no language barrier. Members of this generation are service- and career-ori-ented and this does not leave much time for the volunteer work that sus-tained the Ukrainian community in the past. They seem to depend for the heritage's survival on a number of committed individuals who keep the tra-

Ukrainian Seniors Centre, archives

Traditional Easter Bread workshop, Sudbury, 1994.

ditions and culture alive. They seem to be reconciled to the fact that some traditions will die or become modified once *baba* dies. Members of this group acknowledged the lack of commitment of their generation to both the Ukrainian community and the Ukrainian heritage, and some expressed deep concern regarding the end result of this benign neglect. They acknowledged that the language is dying in Northern Ontario and that the majority of Ukrainian Canadians found the effort of keeping it alive with their children on a daily basis too much of an effort. Furthermore, they recognized that the language they use is a Canadianized version of Ukrainian and a far cry from the Ukrainian spoken in Ukraine. Most members of this group commented on the possible impact of the influx of new immigrants on the revitalization of the Ukrainian heritage. They had great reservations regarding the new immigrants' interest and commitment to the restructuring of old Ukrainian organizations.

What will survive are the nonverbal elements of the cultural legacy – Ukrainian folk music and dance and Easter egg decorating. In one woman's words, "Some traditions are too nice to let go."

The new immigrant women (Group V) felt very divided in their views. Some saw the solution in promoting guest artists from Ukraine. They felt such contacts would give Ukrainian traditions in the north a fresh meaning. Others felt that eventual total assimilation was inevitable.

Conclusion

Ukrainian women of different generations and different waves of immigration share their pride and deep emotional bond for their heritage. They perceive it as something worth preserving because it enriched and sustained their own lives, yet they face the future challenges with uncertainty. Most women view their Ukrainian heritage as a visible and integral part of Northern Ontario culture. They are beginning to examine the values that sustained the previous generations to see if they can sustain them in today's environment. They are trying to find ways to make the preservation of language and traditions relevant in today's world. They are examining the global economy to see if they can make the language issue more relevant, thus giving their children "an edge" in the competitive world. They are conscious that being sensitized to different cultures is an asset. In the consumer society of the 1990s they realize that they cannot take their heritage for granted. If it is to survive, they must be willing to find new ways of promoting it and making it relevant in the future.

5

Traditions / Transitions / Translation: Hispanic Women in a Northern Community

Carol Alexis Stos

When I began the research for this article on how Spanish-speaking women immigrants are responding to the challenges of living in Northern Ontario communities, I anticipated responses from both Spanish and Latin American women and consequently chose to use the adjective "Hispanic" in the broadest sense of the word, meaning "Spanish-speaking." Although all the participants are from Latin America (Mexico, Central and South America, and the Caribbean), I have chosen to continue using "Hispanic" or *hispanohablante* ("Spanish-speaker") in order to be as inclusive as possible.[1]

Forty letters in Spanish explaining the nature of this study were sent to women on a general mailing list used to inform the Hispanic community about cultural events in northeastern Ontario. Two women personally distributed an additional 20 letters. Information was gathered through taped conversation sessions, loosely based on a general questionnaire that dealt with emigration information (when, with whom, why), first impressions and experiences (personal and professional), difficulties and challenges (linguistic, personal, familial, professional), and responses and reactions to living in a northern community. There were 12 respondents in all. It was fewer than had been anticipated, but understandable in light of comments such as "I have answered too many questions about where I come from."

Because both the mail-out and the replies were from available Hispanic women, and because the number of respondents was small, I have made no attempt to categorize the responses statistically according to country of origin, age, marital or socio-economic status, etc., although the majority of the women who replied were either married or widowed, with children, the remainder being young (18 to 25), childless, single women. For purposes of anonymity, no particular locations in Northern Ontario are identified nor are any of the participants assigned pseudonyms; furthermore, no specific countries are mentioned.

Taking into consideration the limitations imposed by a small subject response, is this study representative? It is, as a general appreciation of the changes Spanish-speaking women face, endure, and overcome in living in northern communities. The individuals in this study tell their own stories about their own experiences in Canada. They reflect upon their struggles, put them into the context of their present-day situations, and measure their successes and disappointments accordingly. And in the telling, even as each one is establishing her own identity in a new land, she also shares in the common experience of Hispanic women changing their lives in Northern Ontario. I spoke with women between the ages of 18 and about 45; who have been living in Northern Ontario, some for only 3 or 4 years, others for up to 25 years; who had studied English in Latin America or spoke not a word of English when they arrived; who fled their country for political reasons or came to Canada because of a love of challenge and adventure or love of a new husband; who had to leave their extended family behind but who have nurtured and encouraged their nuclear family here; and whose lives in Northern Ontario have been radically different from what they would have known in Latin America. I am enormously grateful to those who voluntarily participated in this study and who so willingly and generously shared the stories of their experiences in coming to Canada and learning to live in Northern Ontario.

When most Hispanic women first come to Canada, they have either very little general knowledge about this country – certainly nothing specific about Northern Ontario – or, perhaps, a rather romanticized image of a vast land of great forests, many lakes, and sparkling snows. Those who arrived in the late spring, summer, or early fall say that they found the climate different but not unpleasant, the general look of the land strange but not forbidding. Arriving in winter was another story altogether: not one was prepared for the experience, either physically or emotionally.

Coming from a tropical or at least a very temperate climate, these women had no warm clothing, certainly nothing remotely suitable for a Northern Ontario winter and often no opportunity to acquire any. One young woman explained that, despite the concern of her new Canadian husband, she had no choice but to arrive wearing a light sweater and sandals in February. Worse still was the first breath of frigid winter air: "No one warned me that my nose would freeze immediately, my throat would become numb, and that I would feel my lungs stop because the air was so unbearably icy." For many the cold was not just a shock but an intensely painful and even frightening physical experience: "The cold is excruciating. It is a sharp pain in my head."

This unfamiliarity with winter weather can make the most recent immigrants reluctant to venture out of doors and some become housebound, isolated, and depressed (particularly if unemployed) during the winter months. Adjusting to the extremes of northern temperatures requires acclimatization in the most elemental sense of the word for the *hispanohablante*. One woman, however, learned to delight in the variety of the changing seasons. She now is enchanted by a pristine fall of new soft snow and more practically remarked,

"I put on another sweater, a warmer coat, and heavier boots." After several years here, another woman is proud of the fact that she can go outside in the winter without a hat: "That is something truly Canadian!" Reflecting on these kinds of experiences and putting them within the context of her own life, yet a third woman simply stated: "After revolution and civil war in my country, getting used to winter isn't insurmountable."

Of all the experiences they share, difficulty with English is the most common: learning it, speaking it, and understanding it. Sometimes these women have studied English in their country of origin for several years, but usually without much opportunity to truly practise it. They discover, upon their arrival in Canada, that the colloquial version is not what they had learned, and that varied accents make the spoken language sound different and more difficult to understand.

Their linguistic experiences here range from being the only Spanish-speaking family in a small community (managing entirely on their own until the fortuitous acquaintance of some missionaries with knowledge of rudimentary Spanish), to having lived for several months with new Canadian parents-in-law before overhearing someone speak Spanish in a store. This latter experience caused such an overwhelming reaction of joy and recognition for that particular woman, that when she tried to introduce herself, ironically, in the excitement of the moment her mother tongue deserted her and she blurted out the few words of greeting she had learned in English. In a more extreme instance, another woman lived in a somewhat larger centre for a year without speaking any English whatsoever. Family circumstances obliged her to remain in her home, isolated from any community contacts, either with other hispanohablantes or the community at large. When she was finally able to attend English as a Second Language classes, it was a wonderful revelation to realize that she was not alone; many others from different origins shared a similar situation.

But English continues to be a problem. No matter the length of time spent studying and speaking it, whether in Latin America or in Ontario, most are either still struggling with the language to some degree or conscious of speaking with an accent and, perhaps, not perfectly. The children, however, speak both Spanish and English fluently, whether they are born here or in Latin America. As well, they generally are enrolled in either Core French or French Immersion courses. At home, especially if the husband also speaks Spanish, that is the only language spoken to the children and so consistently that one young mother was surprised and amused when her little boy said: *"No me hables en inglés, Mami. ¡No te entiendo!"* ("Don't speak to me in English, Mommy. I don't understand you!") Her English is perfectly intelligible; he simply could not reconcile the idea of his mother speaking to him in English when Spanish is their exclusive means of communication.

With little or no knowledge of either English or French, everything is a challenge; all the mundane tasks that make up daily routine are fraught with confusion, indecision, uncertainty, frustration, and even minor disaster. One woman stated earnestly, "Most of the things I know, I have learned very painfully." Grocery shopping, for example, is at first done by pictograph, but what is actually in the container doesn't always look like what is on the label. They find it strange that so many items are pre-wrapped and packaged, particularly fresh fruit and vegetables. There are some amusing surprises, like discovering the difference between sweet milk and buttermilk, but more disconcerting is the realization that the results of one's own cooking are not the same here. Often in Northern Ontario supermarkets, it is impossible to find familiar ingredients and sometimes, as one woman explained, "Even though I prepare a traditional dish, it really doesn't quite taste the way I remember. Perhaps I should not be surprised. After all, I am in Canada now, and these are Canadian vegetables, so of course they have a different flavour."

It isn't always easy to be philosophical about how strange it all is here. "I lost it all, everything familiar. Everything changed: the culture, the food, the language. And my family was far away. The difference was like night and day." Initially, this woman was quite fearful of not doing what is proper or right in this new country of hers because everything is truly different: housing, the daily schedule, hours of business, the law, the political system, credit, banking, and other financial matters, social customs, social occasions, the celebration of holidays. Often acculturation finds its beginning through cultural misunderstanding.

Many women commented on the difference in attitude they perceive between Canadians and their fellow *hispanohablantes*. In general, they think that people in Latin America are happier and more relaxed, although the lower and middle classes have much less money and fewer material goods. Among friends and relatives, relationships are somehow more open and less formal. One woman who has lived in Northern Ontario for many years laughed about how, during her first year here, her impromptu, unannounced, and lingering visits to her new Canadian friends must have discomfited them. She was equally taken aback by invitations extended here that often indicate both an arrival and a departure time. Learning to develop friendships in Northern Ontario can be unexpectedly uncomfortable. Another woman discovered that although *una fiesta* translates as "a party," there is almost literally a world of difference in the cultural interpretation of this event. The Hispanic version includes much music, dancing and singing, lots of good food, drink, and conversation, and a combination of old and young – little children, adolescents, parents and grandparents – all enjoying themselves and each other into the early hours. By contrast, a "Canadian" party can seem rather exclusive, subdued – and short. This same woman, however, happily remarked that her Canadian friends do enjoy themselves at a real *fiesta* and everyone likes to learn to *salsa*.

Even for those who come from large and cosmopolitan cities in Latin America, life in general here seems *muy agitada,* very nervous and hectic; so much is complicated and people seem to be pressured to do so many things at once and quickly. As one woman pensively observed, "Here all we seem to do is work to pay our debts, insurance, our bills," while in Latin America it seems easier to relax, to spend more time with family and friends, to talk more to each other, to somehow have a fuller life. But she immediately qualified her words as only a nostalgic reminiscence and not a complaint about Northern Ontario. She, like the other women in this study, is very resilient and sees that she must make the most of her time for study and employment, taking advantage of the opportunities despite the demands of juggling home and family in a new culture and environment.

Partly because of language difficulties, partly because of the need to gain Canadian equivalency for their skills, training, and education, and often because of a young family, it is never easy to find a job. Nevertheless, every woman interviewed for this study has made every effort to continue with her education, accessing all that is available to her through government-sponsored courses, community college up-grading, and night-school courses.

Often, because of personal circumstances (a combination of a lack of spousal support, finances, language difficulties, no knowledge of the system, young children at home), some of these women never manage to regain the possibilities for advancement or professional self-development that were left behind in order to come to Northern Ontario. Their first employment in Northern Ontario is often at the lowest entry-level category of domestics, clerks, and child-minders. These are women with specialized skills, diplomas, degrees, and experience in careers ranging from executive secretary to primary school teacher to social worker and early-childhood educator, among others. Although all the participants interviewed have progressed to better-paying, supervisory positions or self-employment, none, as yet, has achieved the equivalent of her profession in Latin America. The one participant in the study who has occasionally managed some work in her field, but only on contract or part-time, is frustrated by her inability to gain economic stability and security and misses the personal satisfaction she would realize from fully utilizing her education, training, and experience: "The biggest challenge for me living in this community is to find full-time employment. I have so much to offer!" The most poignant comment, however, comes from a woman who has been promoted several times at her place of work, in a field totally unrelated to her previous expertise. In stressing that she is neither discontent nor unhappy with her life as it is now, she still had to say, "I could have been something more than what I became. It was very, very hard."

What is the single most important thing that would make life here in Northern Ontario easier or less complicated for these women? One woman speaks for all, declaring, "If only I could have family nearby, or win the lottery so that they could come to Canada often, to visit!" More than anything else, the lack of daily contact with one's family – the lack of emotional and moral support – is the most difficult part of living in this country, or anywhere else for that matter. The extended family is an integral part of life in Latin America; nothing can substitute for the lack: *"La familia es la familia"* ("Family is family").

Missing one's family is a common immigrant experience, but for the *hispanohablante* in a northern community, the cultural and linguistic isolation, coupled with the absence of an extended family is, perhaps, more profound because so often there is no Hispanic community or organization to turn to for assistance, companionship, and support. Even in those centres with other families from Latin America, it isn't always easy to become part of a group because of the national and cultural differences among *hispanohablantes*. "There are 23 Spanish-speaking countries in Latin America and each has an extremely complex history, as well as its own political, social, and economic reality. In many cases regional differences are so marked in dialect and customs that one would hardly believe the people belonged to the same country."[2] Compounding the problem, as one woman declared, is the fact that "so many Canadians seem not to know much about Latin America. It seems to me sometimes that they are unaware of what our way of life is like, and they are unconcerned about what we have gone through. They just do not realize how diverse and different Latin American peoples and cultures are." This perception of a general ignorance about Latin America in Canada contributes to a feeling of isolation, further intensified in northern communities, which, in turn, are themselves somewhat isolated.

It is possible to identify different stages in the long-distance family dynamic. One relatively recent immigrant explained that, because she is so intensely involved in adjusting to her new life here, even though she misses her family very much, she feels that their relationship has not changed. For her, for now, frequent correspondence and phone calls seem to be enough. Another woman, who left Latin America over 20 years ago, has found that letters and long-distance calls, no matter how constant, cannot replace the intimacy of almost daily contact, nor can they truly substitute for the mutual moral, emotional, and physical support that so characterizes the family in Latin America. The sense of participating in the lives of her extended family becomes ever more tenuous over the miles, as the years multiply.

> The distance means that I am no longer a member of the group. When you live in another country you become the one from outside. You come for a few days and then you go. Although you want to be, you are not truly a part of the family. It is different. They do not forget you but you cannot share your daily concerns. I do call when there are problems but not often just to chat. Sometimes I think that I share more of my troubles than my joys with them.

Nevertheless, the important traditional role of family continues to be reinforced at home in Northern Ontario. In general, it is felt that *hispanohablantes* are more strict than most Canadian parents, and their children concur. Children are taught to be respectful of their elders, to value time spent together as a family, to put the needs of the family first. It is very important that children be true to family values and principles, develop a strong sense of morals and decency, and always strive to further their education. As mothers, these women strengthen family bonds and continue traditions in the same way that their mothers and other female relatives did and do in Latin America.

Those who have daughters enjoy and encourage a close relationship with them, much as their own mothers and grandmothers did. If the children are adolescents, most think they may have a more open relationship with them here in Northern Ontario. One woman specifically mentioned that she speaks much more freely about sexual matters, spousal abuse, and family violence simply because these are issues more openly discussed in Canadian society, and her children – her daughters – must be educated and made aware for their own protection. However, another woman also speculated that if her relationship with her daughters is different from that of hers with her mother, it is more of a generational difference, "it is because of who we are, rather than where we are or the culture that surrounds us."

Would they go back to live in Latin America if they could? Answers to this question depend on many variables. Those who have come to Canada fairly recently as political refugees and whose country of origin is still just beginning to recover from the ravages of war do not want to return. The political situation is still unstable, their sons would be drafted at age 18 for obligatory military service, and there is much more theft, crime, and violence in the streets because so many people have been dispossessed and are now unemployed. Canada is safe, and they can visualize their family's future, especially that of the children, a future they are not willing to jeopardize.

Those who have been in Canada for more than 10 or 15 years now have roots here, too. Their children or grandchildren are Canadian-born; they are in school or living and working happily in Northern Ontario or another province; they have settled into a home, a job, a comfortable pattern, and a familiar daily routine; the family has become a part of the fabric of their community. Several have been able to go back to Latin America for a visit, but it can be unexpectedly difficult: "I have changed and my country has changed, but in my mind and in my memory I expect things to be as they were when I left. Now I am surprised and made to feel uncomfortable in a place where I expect to feel automatically at home. It is very strange." One woman remarked that she found she speaks Spanish differently now; after so many years in Northern Ontario she is unaware of new vocabulary, the current slang, and even changes in patterns of speech in her country of origin.[3] Another felt that friends and neighbours of the family may treat her differently too, feeling suspicious of how she and her attitudes may have changed and become Canadianized. It can be a bittersweet experience to return to the country of her birth. Coming back to Northern Ontario is often much easier.

There are still other factors that alter the northern experiences of Spanish-speaking women immigrants. Those married to a non-Hispanic (a Canadian or Euro-Canadian) may have had a somewhat easier introduction to Northern Ontario, given that they returned with their husband to a country where he knew the language, the customs, and the rules. It was no less stressful, however, since, as one woman observed, she still suffered a tremendous culture shock and often had to contend simultaneously with adjusting to married life in a foreign land and living with her new in-laws, no matter how welcoming they may have been. Another explained that her sense of isolation was heightened because neither she nor her husband spoke each other's language very well, and she, like others married to a Canadian with his own ethnic heritage, had to deal with his traditions and community while attempting to adjust to the broader context of Canadian culture and society.

With only one exception, none of the participants in this study ever felt that they had been discriminated against because they were Hispanic, although a number of them spoke about friends or relatives who had experienced derogatory remarks because of their appearance or language. Most commented that people sometimes perceived them as being rather unintelligent but that was, they felt, a reaction to their difficulties in speaking and understanding English. Once their language skills were adequate and they were more familiar with the way of life here, they no longer noticed that response. However, it was disquieting and disheartening for those whose husbands had strong ties to another culture to discover that they were not as readily welcomed into that particular community.

Young women, between the ages of 18 and 25, who arrived in Canada as adolescents or pre-adolescents with their parents and who have spent most of their formative teen years in Northern Ontario, have a very different set of experiences as Hispanics growing up "Canadian." They also have gone through a process of acculturation, but theirs has been a constant and daily series of adjustments and re-adjustments, a balancing act between their behaviour at home and within the Hispanic community, and at school and within the larger community.

Parental and cultural expectations follow Hispanic custom and tradition; daughters are supposed to be their mother's helpers, to take on their share of domestic duties, to be obedient and always behave circumspectly, to be a credit to the family. Many times, because they learn English much more rapidly than their parents, they also assume, at a very young age, the responsibilities of translator and interpreter for everything from a shopping excursion to visits to the doctor. While they come to terms – not without some chafing – with these familial obligations and restrictions, and their parents' over-protectiveness, often it is frustrating to try to explain their situation to non-Hispanic friends at school who have much more freedom. It is difficult, as well, to try to integrate into a network of friendships at school because they are never permitted to go to or to have a sleep-over, to go to a public playground after school "with the gang," to go to the movies with a mixed group of friends. Consequently, the best and most enduring friendships and relationships develop among other Hispanic girls and young women. "It's just easier. She knows what it's like without me having to explain. She understands why I have to put the family first a lot of times; why my Mom is going to worry if I'm out past 10 or 11 o'clock at night; why my brother, who's younger than me, has so much more freedom." Ironically, one young woman discovered that while she may not seem sufficiently Canadianized to her non-Hispanic acquaintances, to a young woman her age who recently arrived from Latin America she is not Hispanic enough; what she thought was the beginning of a really good friendship was abruptly terminated when she was told that she just didn't behave in an acceptable (Hispanic) manner and there could be no real exchange of confidence in their relationship.[4]

Difficulty in making friends is not exclusively an adolescent problem; mature Hispanic women may have many Canadian friends of varied backgrounds, but their best friend, with whom they have the most intimate and trusting relationship, is usually another *hispanohablante* in the community or a girlhood companion who may live thousands of miles away. It is as if there is a certain essence of their identity that cannot be easily understood by those of another culture. There is a sense of being different, separate, of not truly belonging, which stands in the way of forming really close relationships with other women who are non-Hispanic.

The experiences of professional women, with postgraduate degrees, and highly skilled entrepreneurs coming from Latin America are mitigated by a number of factors. In many instances, they already speak English (and a third language) very fluently; they have lived, studied, and worked in large cosmopolitan centres in Latin America. Although not all have travelled abroad, in general they have a more global awareness of different cultures and customs, which makes their transition to a Canadian society somewhat smoother. Although they also still must make many daily adjustments, sometimes the greater change for them comes with moving from a Latin American metropolis to a much smaller Northern Ontario community, where they face a double culture shock. Not only must they adapt to a multicultural Canadian society, they must also adapt to small-town life. Women accustomed to the variety of films, theatre, art galleries, museums, concerts, lectures, and other such activities available in large metropolitan centres experience an additional sense of cultural isolation in Northern Ontario. This experience is carried over in their contacts with their Canadian colleagues, whom they find extremely well trained but not as "educated" (in the sense of having a wide range of cultural interests and knowledge) as their professional counterparts in Latin America. It is difficult to make friends and develop personal relationships when it seems that the only common ground or interests are work-related.

They are isolated, as well, in the workplace. Professional women, particularly if their expertise is in a traditionally male-dominated field, find that they face a certain amount of discrimination, not because they are Hispanic, but simply because they are female. If female entrepreneurs have difficulty in financing their independent ventures, it is not because of their country of origin but because of their gender. Although some of these experiences date back more than 15 or 20 years, the same kind of situation is still painfully true for their daughters who are pursuing postgraduate studies in non-traditional careers for women. One woman, however, is optimistic, since she feels that at last "the doors are open. They had to be forced open, but at least they now are open for my daughters." It is ironic that through these gender-based discriminatory experiences the Hispanic professional woman is very much a part of the broader context of Canadian society.

Despite the difficulties faced by all those who immigrate to a new country, not one of the participants in this study regrets her decision to come to Canada nor to stay in Northern Ontario. For each one, positive aspects can be measured by the political and social stability here, as well as by the opportunities for education and employment. *"El Canadá es un país muy seguro"* ("Canada is a very safe country"). Children have a better chance at a brighter and more secure future here, and that is of the utmost importance to the family. For some women, living in another culture has given them the opportunity to reflect on their own, to see it from another perspective: "I have come to appreciate and admire my culture more, even though I recognize all the advantages in this culture and how much easier my life is here. I see what is valuable in both countries and I am grateful for everything I have from each of them." Other women have come to recognize a truly personal change as a result of adapting to life in Northern Ontario: "I am a better human being for coming to Canada. I have more tolerance, more acceptance of others, more respect for people doing their jobs well, no matter what that job is; I can more readily accept people for what they are."

The traditions that are apparent in the homes and families of these hispanohablantes in Northern Ontario are sometimes as tangible as the food on the table, the ornaments and decorations on the walls, and the music on the tape-deck. More often, and perhaps more significantly, the traditions that endure are the language, the importance of familial relationships, the emphasis on education, and the resiliency necessary to adapt to changing conditions and circumstances. All the participants in this study have struggled, to a greater or lesser extent, to make the necessary transition to living in a multicultural northern environment, and translating their experiences from one country and its culture into another has meant profound changes in every aspect of their lives. The results can be rather ambiguous. Several women spoke about a part of their heart that will always belong to their country of origin, but they prefer living in Canada. One Spanish-speaking Canadian citizen explained that "when I travel abroad, I am proud to be Canadian and I miss Northern Ontario; but, in Latin America, I'm *latina* and don't think about this country." Young women who have spent their adolescence in Canada remain engaged in a more constant and complex process of transition. Acculturation has been perhaps much easier for them in many ways, but they, more than their mothers, are still caught between the influences of two cultures, both of which are unequally their own.

The women who participated in this study have all adapted, to the best of their own abilities, to the circumstances that both welcome and challenge them in Northern Ontario. As immigrants and *hispanohablantes,* their shared experiences offer a general reflection of how women's lives can change in northern communities. But each one also is defining her own identity within a Canadian context. "We are not all the same. I feel that my voice is different." Each voice adds to the chorus but it is as individuals that they continue making community, and we are richer for their experiences.

6

The Experiences of Black Women Across Northern Ontario

Dorothy L. Ellis

The population of Black women in Northern Ontario is growing. Most of the women who live in the north emigrated from Haiti, Trinidad/Tobago, Guyana, various parts of Africa, Jamaica, some Spanish-speaking countries, and the U.S. Virgin Islands. There is also a small concentration of Black women in the north from Nova Scotia. The largest number of Black women in the north reside in the Sudbury area, but many live in places such as North Bay, Elliot Lake, Kirkland Lake, Timmins, and Kapuskasing. Across Northern Ontario, in general, the numbers of Black women are small and decrease as you move farther north.

Black women came to Northern Ontario for several reasons, the majority because their husbands emigrated here to work in the mines. There was a need for medical doctors across the north, and some women moved here with their husbands who were doctors. There were those who came as doctors themselves. In the sixties, a shortage of teachers brought some Black women from the West Indies to work as teachers, still others came as domestics.

In my discussions with Black women in Northern Ontario, they talked about the quality of their lives when they first came to the north. Life was not easy for these women. In attempting to make a life for themselves and their families, they faced numerous problems in a region where the majority of the population is white. While the obstacles were often enormous, Black women in Northern Ontario communities faced the challenges with courage and determination. This paper discusses both the problems they had to confront and the strategies they use to overcome discrimination.

Comfortable housing was hard to find, due either to the low vacancy rate or to the reluctance of property owners to rent to Black families. As the communities began to accept their presence, many of these women and their families built or purchased their own homes.

Shift work is common in Northern Ontario and presented a challenge to the newcomer. As several of the husbands were involved in shift work, the mothers often had the sole responsibility for running the home and raising the children.

Most of the Black women who immigrated to Northern Ontario had little or no formal education and found it difficult to access the educational systems. They talked about the uncomfortable feelings they experienced when they visited schools to meet with teachers about their children. They mentioned the lack of visible minorities in the school systems. As a result, many of them stayed away from parent-teacher meetings and avoided both upgrading and postsecondary education even when it was available.

The majority of Black women are members of large extended families. Living in Northern Ontario punctured the fabric of the extended family. A large number of Black youths raised in Northern Ontario leave the north when they finish their education in order to obtain employment in one of Ontario's larger urban centres. A number of these young people are still under-employed outside of the north. For Black women, this exodus of their children changed the structure of the extended family as they had known it.

There are few Black women working in education and other government ministries compared to the number of Black women working in the private sector. A very small number of Black women sit on boards of non-profit or voluntary organizations, and virtually no Black women are in any of the full-time paid positions of any of these organizations. As a result, there is a great deal of untapped expertise and under-utilized talent among the population of Black women in Northern Ontario.

Many Black women came to Canada with credentials from their countries that were not recognized here. Therefore, there was a need to be educated as to what services were available in their communities and how to access them. A number of these women were under-employed or unemployed. Agencies such as Career Preparation for Immigrants (CAPRI) and the multicultural centres provided training and retraining for them. Their involvement with organizations helped them become more involved in their communities, and in many cases these organizations also served as support systems for them and their families.

Black women developed ways to overcome isolation, make a contribution to their community, and bring about social change. Black families developed communities of their own, and in the process they developed sound relationships in their districts. They held various gatherings, like barbecues, domino games, and parties, at which they would eat, drink, dance, play music from various countries, and share stories about their places of origin. Small clubs started to crop up in communities across Northern Ontario. Unfortunately many of these clubs were domino clubs and did not include Black women.

Black women, though small in number, continue to make contributions in communities across Northern Ontario. Many are involved in sharing cultural activities with other ethnic groups and take part in sensitization seminars and workshops regarding the needs of visible minority women in their communities. They have become involved with organizations such as multicultural centres, visible minority networks, race relations committees, Women Across Cultures, the Congress of Black Women of Canada, and agencies like CAPRI. The fact that there are few Black women in the towns and cities means that they often feel alone, and their sense of isolation frequently brings them into these organizations. Where English is not their first language, this feeling of isolation can be compounded.

Twelve years ago, the Congress of Black Women of Canada was formed in Regina. At present, this national organization has chapters in almost every province in Canada. Its purpose is to lobby for support on issues that are critical to the well-being of Black women and their families and to serve as a support system for them. The northeastern Ontario chapter of the congress is based in Sudbury and acts as a liaison with Black women across northeastern Ontario by holding meetings and seminars in various centres. At this time, northwestern Ontario does not have a chapter of the congress, but efforts are being made to encourage the development of one.

The recent federal budget cuts will have an adverse effect on the lives of Black women in Northern Ontario; most of the cuts were to training programs that helped improve the quality of women's lives. Reduced funding will also affect programs that encouraged communication through conferences, seminars, and workshops on issues that affected the lives of Black women and their families.

Black women across Northern Ontario have made and continue to make progress towards full integration into northern communities through continuing education and community activity. There is, however, a need for the inclusion of these women in full-time paid positions, on boards, in the educational system, and in both the public and private sectors in the north.

7

Invisible Lives, Visible Strength: Stories of Northern Ontario Lesbians

Pat Tobin and Anonymous

There will be those who will read the authors' names and be perplexed. Some will think it strange that an author would use the pseudonym "anonymous" in a country where freedom of speech is taken for granted. But many who read this inscription will understand immediately why the author had to hide her identity. Most of the women who spoke to us of their experiences as lesbians in Northern Ontario certainly felt the same way. While each spoke passionately about the need to have "lesbian stories told, retold, and remembered,"[1] they also spoke about the frustration of not being able to identify themselves publicly as lesbian.

We do not presume to speak for all lesbians living in the north. Rather, we present a collection of stories told through interviews and discussions with lesbians living in Northern Ontario.[2] The women interviewed welcomed us into their lives. We talked, listened, wept, laughed, and expressed our anger at the discrimination against lesbians. We spoke of the relationships, intimacy, and support we find in the lesbian community. We reminded each other of how far we have come, and how far we have yet to go. These are the quintessential paradoxes of daily lesbian life and the predominant themes in each story told and now retold.

Through the retelling, we hope to achieve three goals: to document and preserve these stories; to give back to lesbians living in Northern Ontario some of what we have been given – support, hope, and the energy to continue to work for change; and to offer the reader an opportunity to hear the stories of women who might otherwise have remained invisible.

The invisibility of lesbians means much more than not knowing our names. It also means not knowing about our relationships, our families, our friends, our leisure activities, our lives. This invisibility is commonly referred to as "being in the closet." Metaphorically speaking, the closet is "an emotional hiding place where one does not have to disclose one's [sexual] identity."[3] The closet is not a structure we willingly enter. We are forced into closets by virtue of a difference. We are kept in closets by society's reaction to that difference. Becki Ross notes that "approximately nine-tenths of the 'lesbian population' live in fear of disclosure and the attendant loss of family, friends, jobs, and the custody of children."[4] Discrimination knows no boundaries; it is a universal socio-political problem. Fear can fill our lives. One of the women we spoke to expressed it this way:

> I encounter fear-filled people every day. Fear of difference, fear of the unknown. People think they know me. I fear telling them much about myself. Fearful that I will lose my job, my home, whatever respect and trust I have worked so hard to earn in many relationships. I choose carefully who to tell: some of my family, but not all; some of my friends, but not all; some of my colleagues, but not all. I must choose wisely and dangerously who to tell. Some choices are beyond my control ... the possibility of broken confidence, being outed at any time, laws that continue to discriminate against myself and my partner ... my family as I choose to define that.

Lesbians in Northern Ontario identified several elements that they believe are particular to northern living. The size of cities and towns in the north, for example, makes maintaining anonymity much more difficult. The lack of visible lesbian-positive services in northern cities and towns often has an impact on both networking and outreach. The distance from urban centres with a variety of cultural events, recreational activities, and professional services limits accessibility. So why do we stay in the north? As one woman said:

> Because I love Northern Ontario. I like what it has to offer. What makes it difficult for me is also what makes it inviting. I don't like the impersonal nature of big cities, the fast pace, the miles of concrete and pavement. I like the warmth of the people, the sense of community and the rhythm of life in Northern Ontario. I like being surrounded by lakes and bush. My life is here, my roots are here.... Northern Ontario is home, I don't want to live anywhere else.

For most of the lesbians we spoke to, leaving the north is unthinkable. It is not the solution. The women are convinced that living in Northern Ontario is not the problem. The real problem is the pervasiveness of heterosexism and homophobia.

Heterosexism defines heterosexuality as the norm and demands conformity in all social structures and relationships. From a social and legislative perspective, sexuality, intimate relations, and the institution of "family" are synonymous with heterosexuality.[5] Two-parent (father and mother) families are considered the fundamental social unit of society, the model to which people are expected to conform. It is the model upon which social and legislative systems have been designed and constructed. The expectation of heterosexuality is an essential element in all aspects of the socialization process.

As children progress through stages of human development, the social lessons they learn about intimate relationships prepare them for participation in heterosexual social relationships and structures. Successful transitions from one stage to another are marked with ritual and celebration. The first co-ed party, the first date, going steady, the engagement, the wedding, and the birth of children are significant milestones celebrated by family and friends. The importance or celebration of heterosexual relationships is not what lesbians dispute; rather what we take exception to is the social script that makes heterosexuality compulsory.[6]

Inextricably linked to heterosexism is homophobia, which can be defined as "an individual reaction to gay, lesbian, and bisexual people – a reaction of hatred, fear, or discomfort – acted out through discrimination and violence."[7] Heterosexism and homophobia are the cornerstones of lesbian oppression and construct the closets that render lesbians invisible.

Homophobia, therefore, reinforces the status quo. "To be a lesbian is to be perceived as someone who has stepped out of line."[8] As lesbians we challenge the dominant cultural assumptions of sexuality, intimate relationships, and family. To speak of our differences, and to live our differences, has been and continues to be a profoundly difficult experience. One woman told of her experience in coming out:

> I never actually had the opportunity to "come out" to my parents. In the late 70s they managed to figure out that I was a lesbian, although I don't recall them ever actually saying the word. What I do remember was their reaction. My parents had me admitted to a psychiatric ward of a local hospital. There I spent ten days alone, frightened, confused, and struggling to make sense of what was happening.

In another interview, a woman told us:

> Shortly after my sixteenth birthday, my relationship with a young woman was discovered. The decision was made by my parents to have me admitted to a mental health facility. It still amazes me today when I think back that the question of my sexual orientation was never discussed. I attended the out-patient clinic three times a week to speak to a counsellor. I quickly learned that the lies were more acceptable than the truth. I continued with my relationship and told everyone else what they wanted to hear.

Granted, these events occurred some 20 years ago. Since then, homosexuality as a "psychiatric disorder" has been removed from the American Psychiatric Association's Diagnostic and Statistical Manual (DSM) and is no longer a basis for institutionalization.[9] However, it remains highly probable that a lesbian will encounter professionals who exhibit a strong heterosexist bias in their practice,[10] and there remain many parents who still experience discomfort and anxiety with their daughter's sexual orientation.[11]

Disclosing one's sexual orientation is a topic frequently discussed in the lesbian community. Since most people (parents included) assume heterosexuality, lesbians most often either pretend they are heterosexual or come out. Coming out is described as "a process involving innumerable decisions regarding whom to 'tell,' when, and how much to do so."[12] The decision to come out is never an easy one, but deciding to come out to parents is perhaps the most difficult coming-out decision to make. The possibility of losing affection, acceptance, and family ties is the risk lesbians take when coming out to parents. One of the authors reflected on her experience as follows:

> The costs of identifying as a lesbian I measure in losses ... lost relationships with parents, siblings, and relatives. Although I continue to live my life with integrity, these losses have produced a wound that never really heals. At every holiday, every birthday, and every milestone, I am painfully reminded of the absence of these significant people in my life.

Not all parents react in the same way, but we have yet to hear a coming-out story where parents are without some reservations. Here is another story from a woman we interviewed:

> Seven years ago when I decided to come out to my parents, I wrote them a letter because I was too afraid to tell them in person. The world around me has never affirmed my sexual orientation, and I was only too familiar with the experiences of other lesbians who had come out to their parents. I was afraid that they would reject me and ultimately abandon me. My parents were devastated. As they struggled to understand and accept me for who I was, they were alone in their confusion and fear. In their small Northern Ontario community of 1,500 people, there were no support systems, nor were there any support systems in the neighbouring city of 50,000 people.

In this situation the process of re-establishing a positive relationship took approximately five years. This might not have been the case if information and support had been readily available. In small northern towns and cities there are few strangers, and one is more likely to be acquainted with the librarians or receptionists in places where a lesbian would go for information. The fear of discovery, or more specifically the fear of negative reactions when sexual orientation is discovered, poses a considerable barrier for individuals and families needing information regarding sexual orientation.

The lack of visible lesbian-positive services in cities and towns in the north also makes information and support much more difficult to access. If this family had been living in Toronto, or even in a more rural community in the surrounding area, they would have had access to several resources.[13] For instance, there is an organization called Parents and Friends of Lesbians and Gays (P-FLAG).[14] This group was established for people struggling to accept the sexual orientation of their children or significant others. It provides both information and a forum for support. They are located only in large urban centres such as Toronto and Ottawa. As yet there are no P-FLAG groups in Northern Ontario, which illustrates the regional dimension of the lesbian experience.

The struggle to accept sexual orientation is often made all the more difficult when religious beliefs are considered. As one woman told us:

> When I came out to my parents they were shattered. Their religious teachings defined lesbians as immoral and against the laws of the church. This was further complicated by the fact that my parents held positions of responsibility within the church.... Their community of support were fellow parishioners who also believed homosexuality was a sin.

Religious institutions have traditionally played a significant role in constructing the closet for lesbians.[15] The social system defined heterosexuality as the norm and the medical system reinforced the definition with the label of "abnormal" for homosexuality. The church, however, applied the full weight of moral authority and defined homosexuality as "evil" and a "sin" against God and nature.

Today, most organized religion continues to oppose any legal or social recognition of same-sex individuals and couples. In May 1994, Bill 167 – legislation that would have sanctioned equality for same-sex couples – was introduced by Marion Boyd, Ontario's attorney general at the time. During the debates at Queen's Park on the bill, there was tremendous opposition from organized religion. In calling on the members of the legislature to vote against the bill, the Catholic Women's League claimed that Catholic doctrine taught that homosexual alliances cannot be considered conjugal relationships.[16] Members and adherents of Kingsway Baptist Church in Etobicoke protested against Bill 167, claiming that the proposals it put forward – including legal rights for so-called same-sex couples and marriages and their right to adopt children – were contrary to the revealed laws of God as set forth in Holy Scripture. They argued further that the bill would denigrate lawful marriage bonds and result in the "increased breakdown of the family, to immorality in society, and to the further physical and spiritual harm to the lives of individuals and of our society as a whole."[17]

According to Barbara Donaldson, executive assistant to the Honourable Marion Boyd, literally hundreds and hundreds of letters outlining religious opposition to equality rights for lesbians and gays were received by members of parliament.[18] Religious doctrine is persistent in its teaching of heterosexuality as the only sacred expression of intimacy, and the heterosexual couple and their children as the only sacred expression of family. The struggle to reconcile religious beliefs with sexual orientation is not restricted to parents of lesbians; lesbians themselves can also be caught up in it. As one interviewee said:

> My coming out coincided with my decision to enter seminary training for ordained ministry.... I found myself struggling with some profound questions. Would God or the church accept me as a lesbian, when I wasn't sure I could accept myself? I felt like a wanderer in a foreign land ... a feeling that was to return throughout my six years as a parish minister in Northern Ontario. The lessons I learned in seminary and parish ministry about survival were: do not tell, lie when asked, offer no information, don't ever be vulnerable, and never let your guard down.

These are painful lessons to learn. The methods by which lesbians are taught these lessons are not exclusive to the enduring social mores and religious doctrines. Often they are reinforced by the actions and reactions of people who have internalized negative beliefs about lesbians. A lesbian couple recounted the story of their relationship being discovered and made public in a small northern town:

> We endured obscene phone calls and on many occasions we were awakened during the night by the pelting of rotten fruit and eggs on our home. During the day the whispers, furtive glances, open stares, and stony silences turned our daily routines into trials of inner fortitude and perseverance. Concerned about our welfare, and the welfare of our children, we moved.

This family relocated to a new community in the north and they are carefully rebuilding their lives. They go to great lengths to conceal their lesbianism from all but a select group of trusted friends. Not all lesbians encounter this level of overt hostility, but we are all aware that the potential exists. As another lesbian couple explained:

> Our daughter is going on 11. We have often wondered when the day would come when she would have to ward off some form of homophobia. It is frustrating. Small northern town. Small minds. The day has come, almost six years after our family was formed. Six years of sweat, tears, and happiness. Six years of hoping she would not come home crying or injured because she has two mommies. Although no

violence has thankfully come her way yet, the neighbourhood kids are talking. We have to "de-dyke" the house every time she has a friend come over. Then there is the fear, our fear, that she will reject us as her peers begin to reject her. She lied to a friend about us just the other day. Her pain was not in the lie, but in her perceived betrayal of us.

In varying degrees, all lesbians have experiences of being denied the freedom to live visible lives. The factors determining the consequence of visibility are as enigmatic as human nature itself and as complex as societal institutions. Being out often hinges on the personal views of our families, friends, neighbours, and co-workers. Even when social support is available, anxiety can be present. In the experience of one of the authors:

> Most people who know me would identify me as a lesbian. My family, my friends, my colleagues, and my political community all know me as a lesbian and accept me for who I am. My family and friends continue to love me, my workplace welcomes diversity, and my political community joins with me in the struggle for equality. Even with this security and support, I question the wisdom of my decision to put my name in print. I have forfeited the possibility of public anonymity, and I have no way of knowing what the consequences will be. Will there be a price to pay and how much will it cost? Should I ever need to seek employment again in Northern Ontario, will this affect my employability? As a therapist in private practice, will I find professionals who will hesitate to make referrals? As a training consultant, will I lose contracts?
>
> When I told my sister about this article she reacted with, "You're coming out in public? Are you ready for that?" I thought I was ready, but the writing of this article has renewed my fears of the unknown.

For most lesbians, the freedom to be out depends not only on the responses of people around us, but also on the arbitrary policies of workplaces and the social, legal, and medical institutions with which we interact. Lesbians find it difficult, for example, to adopt children. We also encounter problems in health care: if one partner becomes ill, the other can be excluded from the decision-making process. We worry that our job applications may be rejected if it is known we are lesbian, even when we are well qualified for the positions. As one lesbian stated: "Rejection has been an all too familiar consequence of identifying as a lesbian."

The enactment of legislation that would guarantee our civil rights would not necessarily temper individual homophobia; however, it would be a significant step in dismantling systemic discrimination and would reduce the consequences of living visible lives. Lesbians in the north are acutely aware of the political resistance to recognition of our rights and our protection when those rights are violated. While the federal Bill C-41 – an Act to Amend the Criminal Code – will offer a degree of protection for lesbians and gays in hate-motivated crimes, it was not lost on our community that delays in passing this bill were due to the inclusion of sexual orientation.

The provincial Bill 167 was intended to provide some equality and protection in the workplace and in family law. On 9 June 1994, the bill was defeated. As the final vote was announced, we felt as though we had just been physically assaulted. In the words of one author:

> My partner and I and every other lesbian in this province had just been told we were not legitimate people, that we didn't deserve the same rights and privileges as everyone else. And then we watched the police, wearing latex gloves and carrying billy clubs, remove people from the spectators' gallery. We were horrified and outraged. Throughout the evening we spent a great deal of time on the telephone talking to other lesbians in our community and in other communities in Northern Ontario. The conversations were filled with anger, pain, and grief, and by the end of the evening we were exhausted from crying.

In retrospect, lesbians did not expect that Bill 167 would be the solution to all our problems. We were well aware of the backlash it had generated. Bill 167 did, however, seem like the first of many steps towards equality and the possibility of living a more visible life. The defeat of the bill produced an overwhelming sense of loss. We were again reminded of our tenuous status.

Many of the lesbians we spoke to in Northern Ontario talked of being forced to maintain a double identity – a public and a private one. Absent from the public realm is any discussion about who we really are privately. As one woman said, "People need to understand that we are just like anyone else. Being lesbian doesn't make you different on the inside." We share the same human needs, hopes, and dreams. We survive the same daily struggles of life; we want what all people want: happiness, health, prosperity, and security. Yet we are forced time and time again to hide who we are.

The effort that goes into hiding our relationships is considerable. The necessity for invisibility has an enormous effect on the subtleties of lesbian lives. As lesbians we are constantly forced to modify or censor any language or behaviour that might suggest we do not conform to the heterosexual roles expected by this society. If you are heterosexual, try to imagine the following. You are deeply in love with someone. The world around you does not accept this relationship. When you are alone with each other, you speak and behave in ways that demonstrate your love for each other. You hold hands, you use terms of endearment, you exchange glances that say "I love you." But you don't live in a vacuum. You have to interact with the world. When you enter into a social situation, you must become hyper-vigilant about any language or behaviour that would expose your relationship. As one lesbian said:

> I find myself constantly on guard, monitoring my language, both verbal and body. I am careful not to use phrases that might suggest a "couple" relationship. I avoid the use of "our" when describing ownership of any belongings. The apartment is "mine," not "ours." I avoid the use of "we" when describing events. "I" went south for my holidays, not "we" went south. Many times it is not simply a matter of changing pronouns. It is a complete denial of part of my life. Living a double life becomes a way of being. I carry with me the fear of being discovered every day, but every time I deny my relationship I am filled with pain and anger.

Questions such as "Are you dating?" "Do you have a boyfriend?" or "Don't you want to get married?" are often asked as a matter of course in social conversations. The questions are innocuous in and of themselves but they are laden with the assumption of heterosexuality and create painful dilemmas for lesbians. On some days the effort and emotion required to hide are simply too demanding. One woman explained it in this way: "I can't even begin to count the number of times I have left a room or a group when the conversation has turned to relationships. Sometimes it is just easier to avoid the topic than to be put in a position where I have to lie."

Without experiential knowledge, it may be impossible to comprehend fully the intellectual and emotional calisthenics involved in this camouflage. Nonetheless, it is important to make deliberate and consistent attempts to take our reality into account. One woman commented that "people need to understand the nature of our oppression and the consequences we suffer on a daily basis. They must not minimize, however unintentionally, the seriousness of our oppression and the destructive power of homophobia."

The lesbians we spoke to talked about the consequences of forced invisibility. They often referred to the emotional toll exacted. As individuals, couples, and families, we pay a tremendous price. One woman described her situation as follows:

> Living in the closet affects my personhood, it affects how I feel about myself. What living and working in the closet has created is a situation where I have had to seal off emotions and major parts of who I am. I feel like I have lost the language of my emotions. After years of living this way, I have forgotten how to feel. The struggle then for me is to reconnect with my feelings and learn how to express them.

Despite the suffering caused by systemic discrimination and the unrelenting opposition to our rights, to our relationships, to our families, and to our lives, lesbians have always built community and chosen to celebrate. Reflecting on her lesbian experience, a woman said, "I drink in the small joys and intimacy of a lesbian community that quietly celebrates our daily joys and sorrows."

In the absence of social recognition or observances of rites of passage, lesbians are creating and observing our own milestones. Special occasions such as commitment ceremonies, house-warmings, anniversary parties, and so on are celebrated. We also commemorate sorrowful passages such as separations and the loss of those we love. One woman reported, "My circle of friends has grown to about 30 womyn. We celebrate with each other the joys and sorrows of our lives. We have goddess ceremonies, full moon rituals. We meet for birthdays, keep each other informed on political issues, and congratulate each other on accomplishments."

On a day-to-day basis, our relationships and our community provide a buffer from the antagonistic world around us. As one woman put it:

> My relationship with my partner is my source of sanity in this crazy world of double identity. Within this relationship I love, I am loved, and most importantly, I self-love. In much the same way, it is my friendships with other lesbians that nurture and strengthen who I am. It is within the community of lesbians that I find support, solidarity, and the freedom to be me.

Although the lesbian community provides an invaluable infrastructure for social and emotional support, the necessity of anonymity can make the community difficult to locate. This was especially true several years ago. Prior to the early eighties there were virtually no visible organizations for lesbians. The experience of one of the authors is indicative:

> When I was in the process of coming out in Sudbury in 1981 I had no way of making contact with the lesbian community.... There were no organizations, there were no support groups, there were no organized social events, there wasn't even a nightclub I could go to. I knew there were lesbians living here, but the community was so closeted it took months before I was able to make contact.

To be a lesbian in the north has been, and still is for many, an isolating experience; however, we are seeing changes. Today there are lesbian/gay organizations, support groups, information phone lines, social events, and meeting places in many communities.[19] We have lobbied for, and have achieved in some instances, recognition for ourselves and our families. There are now workplaces, organizations, and institutions in the north that recognize lesbians, their relationships, and their families.

It is with determination and pride that we northern lesbians have told our stories. Why? Quite simply, because whether one lives in Northern Ontario or anywhere else, "there should never be a price to be paid for loving another human being."

We agree, but there will be some who will continue to believe that heterosexuality is the norm and that nothing should change. Others, having known all along that discrimination must end, will be reaffirmed in their commitment to equality for all women. We end with the words of one Northern Ontario lesbian, who speaks of both the ongoing discrimination and courageous fight for change:

> How and where does one begin to talk about the reality of one's life? ... The language, the box of labels I have been handed and that I and others pin on me, speaks volumes. They are also limited attempts to define who I am, and how I choose to live my life: lesbian, feminist, Caucasian, Christian, clergy, lover, partner, mother, sister, oppressed, privileged, blessed.
>
> My life thus defined is an unbelievable number of contradictions. I have gone past the oxymoron stage to the insane. I love the woman who gives my life joy and meaning, my life-time companion, my lover, my partner, without whom I would be bereft. My faith in a loving compassionate creator of all goodness and beauty beckons me to live in such a way as to embody goodness and wholeness for myself, and to enable goodness and wholeness for others.
>
> In the midst of all that continues to make my life painful and fearful, I choose to live boldly and well. I choose – with as much cunning, wisdom, and passion that the creator gives me – not to be victimized by the hate, fear, and ignorance of many. I also choose to live and work in whatever small way I can to make the changes needed for the transformation that will put an end to the contradictions in my life. I choose to live times of celebration and recreation with my lesbian sisters, and times to cry with them when this world is cruel to us.

Part Two

The Worlds of Work

Work, either paid or unpaid, is central to the lives of most women regardless of time or place. Varpu Lindström's contribution to this section looks at Finnish immigrant women who took jobs as either domestics or cooks in northern lumber camps. Both married and single women found the isolation of camp life tough, even though for single women the pay provided a level of independence. As Karen Blackford discovered when interviewing Elva Sullivan, isolation could also be a problem for young, unmarried teachers in the north. School boards operated with limited financial resources, and teachers such as Sullivan learned creative ways to get around the problem.

Work traditionally done by women such as Sullivan is often ignored or taken for granted. Jennifer Keck, Susan Kennedy, and Mercedes Steedman were interested in reclaiming the invisible work of women when they began the Miners' Mothers' Day project in 1983. When they revisited the project ten years later, they were struck by the way they had themselves contributed to the invisibility: the collection of pictures focused only on white women, and excluded the work of Aboriginal women. The visibility of women's work outside the home began to change in the 1970s. Access to mining jobs at Inco changed during this period as demands for women's equality began to make a difference. Jennifer Keck and Mary Powell have studied the employment records of 72 of the women hired between 1974 and 1976 and who later quit or were laid off.

Whether women worked in lumber camps, taught school, or worked in mines, most faced a "double day" of paid and unpaid work. Elaine Porter and Carol Kauppi's chapter argues that although one-third of the women in their study contributed more than 50 percent of the family income, they continued to be responsible for the bulk of household work. The tension over understanding who has the power to decide what work is important emerges in Karen Dubinsky's reflections on the stories she heard from her Ukrainian grandmother. Dubinsky uses these stories as a methodological approach to interpreting oral history.

The need to work long hours to achieve success comes out in the interviews done by Blanco, LeBrasseur, and Nagarajan on successful women entrepreneurs. The 22 women interviewed talked about the long hours and the challenge of working in a "man's world," but they also reported pride in their achievement. Dawn Madahbee's interview with Marge Reitsma-Street echoes this theme. The First Nations Community Economic Corporation is an example of the way in which Aboriginal people are taking control of their lives by reviving traditional values, dealing with social issues, and developing a local economy.

Anna Johnson Peterson, prospector around Matheson, 1930s.

8

Finnish Women's Experience in Northern Ontario Lumber Camps, 1920–1939

Varpu Lindström

"It was the money all right, that's what drove me to the bush; eventually I even learned to like it there."[1]

Untamed Canadian wilderness held a special attraction for Finns, who were among the first pioneers, trappers, and homesteaders in Northern Ontario communities. Here they found sought-after work in the emerging resource industries and in building the railroads. By the 1920s the lumber industry had become the most important source of livelihood for Finnish men, who began to dominate large sectors of Ontario's pulpwood camps. Many of these lumber workers were newly arrived immigrants. Between 1921 and 1930, more than 37,000 Finns arrived in Canada. Since the very beginning of Finnish immigration to Canada in the late nineteenth century, Ontario has been the favoured destination. In 1931, two-thirds of all Finnish immigrants lived in that province. The majority of the new settlers were men, but by 1931, 11,000 Finnish females (43 percent) had also made Ontario their home.[2]

Finns did not have strong family-chain migration in the fashion of many southern and eastern Europeans and, hence, could rarely rely on financial or housing support from their families. The Finnish "chain" consisted of friends, acquaintances, and, to some extent, siblings. Unlike women of most other nationalities, Finnish immigrant women were universally literate and most of them arrived as single women. As a significant consequence, single women were not restricted by their husband's choices. Many Finnish women, therefore, had considerable independence to choose where they would live and work.[3] Although women were more likely than men to settle in large urban areas of Montreal, Toronto, and Vancouver, the majority still chose to settle in the smaller Finnish communities, especially in Northern Ontario.

The decisions Finnish women made and the experiences they had in Northern Ontario were clearly influenced by their gender, culture, and class. As was the case with all women seeking employment during the 1920s, and especially during the Depression, their options for work were limited. Because they were immigrants, their opportunities were further curtailed by prejudice and by their inability to speak English or French. They were, however, also subject to their own cultural conditioning and value systems. Furthermore, as members of the working class, most did not have financial resources to acquire professional skills necessary to seek out better-paid occupations. It is within this multi-layered reality that Finnish women tried to carve their place in Canada. Some decided that the best employment opportunities for them were to be found in the lumber camps.

This chapter will examine the working and living conditions of Finnish women – both single and married – in the Northern Ontario lumber camps by giving voice to the women through extensive use of interviews and letters. It will analyze the economic, social, and political consequences of camp living and will argue that, for some Finnish women, work and life in the lumber camps was a positive experience that offered an opportunity for relatively independent work, self-respect, and some savings, within a protected, ethnically exclusive, and culturally sanctioned environment.

Canadian scholars have found it puzzling to explain how Finnish women gained access to the camp cookhouses "at a time when so few other women entered the traditionally male domain."[4] A closer analysis of their community organization, economic needs, and cultural values will provide some answers. This chapter will also attempt to determine the extent to which the presence of Finnish women in the lumber camps had any lasting impact on aspects of the Northern Ontario lumber industry.

Employment Opportunities

Finnish immigrant women, like Finnish immigrant men, came to Canada primarily for economic reasons. They were, therefore, not only interested in survival but hoped also to save some money. Since Finnish women had little family support, the meagre factory wages were simply not enough to pay rent and to support themselves in an urban setting. Hence, they looked for other opportunities more suitable to their specific needs.

By the 1920s, the Finnish communities were well equipped to distribute information about vacancies via employment agencies, newspapers, and, of course, word of mouth. The most common occupation for a Finnish immigrant woman was to be a live-in domestic, but women also worked in a variety of service industries with live-in options such as Finnish-run rooming and boarding houses. These traditionally female occupations had many advantages for the newly arrived immigrant: instant housing, boarding, and an opportunity to learn about the Canadian way of life. Finnish women usually started out as domestics and slowly graduated to "more independent" work. Perhaps the most lucrative legal option, which also provided room and board, was to work in the lumber camps. The only other highly paid options for unskilled immigrant women in Northern Ontario were bootlegging and prostitution.

Although most Finnish women worked first as domestics, some chose to go directly to a lumber camp. One such woman was Martta Laitinen, who described herself as a stubborn, independent, and hardworking woman. She had arrived alone in Sioux Lookout in December 1923. Her husband had left a few months earlier from Finland for Canada, but Martta had no idea where he was. Upon arrival Martta's first priority was to get a job and her second priority was to find her husband. She describes her employment choices: "There were two jobs available, one was to be a dishwasher in a *poikatalo* (men's boarding-house) and the other was to be a dishwasher in a lumber camp." Martta chose the lumber camp. She was not afraid of the dense forest nor the cold climate, both of which were familiar to her from Finland, and she certainly trusted that she could "handle the men." [5]

Martta heard about the jobs by word of mouth, but most would read about them in the Finnish newspapers. The advertisements were designed to attract experienced and hard-working women. Women could be married or single but preferably without children. They had to be willing to work long hours and to sign a long-term commitment to work in a lumber camp. If no work seemed to be available, women would also place their own advertisements. The most opportune time to look for lumber camp work was in August and early September. In August 1923, for example, Vapaus, a socialist Finnish Canadian newspaper, ran the following advertisement: "A married woman with years of experience wants to come and work at a lumber camp. A small camp is preferable. My primary objective is cleanliness. Notice! I will not bring children with me."[6]

With the exception of a few Depression years, the demand for Finnish women in the Northern Ontario lumber camps seemed to be greater than the supply. During the 1920s most cultural groups would restrict women's movements. Chaperons were required for single women, and family honour demanded that women not be left alone with men who were strangers. Thus, for women in many southern and east European cultures, work in the lumber camps was simply not an option. For more established Canadian women, work in an isolated camp with "foreigners" was not deemed to be respectable. Finnish women had no such cultural or community-imposed restrictions. They were expected to work hard and to be in charge of their own reputation. Most Finnish women, however, also preferred to stay in the cities and resource towns to enjoy the lively social activities and modern amenities. Work in the lumber camps was not for everyone. It required physical strength, good health, and self-confidence. Women who chose the lumber camp alternative had to believe that the high wages were worth the many personal sacrifices.

Living and Working Conditions
Martta Laitinen was satisfied with her working conditions. She did not expect much and she knew in advance that the work would be physically demanding

and the living conditions crude and primitive. She liked the men who worked
at the camp:

> There were 25 men working at the lumber camp. It was a small
> lumber camp run by a Finnish man and his wife and they needed a
> dishwasher … and they wanted a three-month contract for January,
> February, and March. So I agreed. I was a tiskari [dishwasher] and I
> had to work long days. I started in the morning already at four
> o'clock and worked till night as they had no other helper. I had to
> clean the men's camp, the one where they lived, that I cleaned and I
> had to help the Mrs., she was the cook, and I had to do the dishes and
> all that other kind of work. The men there were really good, they
> came at night when I was doing the dishes and they would dry the
> dishes for me, they would carry wood for me into the kitchen, and the
> men helped in this way.[7]

The dishwasher worked hard but not as hard as the cooks. Impi Kanerva
recalls:

> You had to work hard but at least there was some time off. It was
> really hard to bring in the supplies for food. We bought nothing ready
> made. The cook had the worst job. Often the cook had to put the
> alarm on in the middle of the night to make the dough to be ready to
> bake bread in the morning. We dishwashers could sleep the night
> although it still made for a long day. The men were called to breakfast
> at 6 o'clock. The food was good, you see it was a Finnish camp. We
> made mountains of cookies.[8]

In the larger camps, the cooks had several people assisting them. After
years of working in the bush, Nelma Sillanpää's mother became the head cook
of a large lumber camp.

> She had to do all the cooking and baking for the camp. She also
> had a girl to wait on tables and to assist her whenever needed. They
> had a pump for water over one of the sinks for drinking, washing, and
> cooking purposes. A chore boy did the dishes, cut the meat, peeled
> vegetables, and brought in the wood.[9]

Men could put up with cold bunkhouses, pine branches as mattresses,
lice, and crowded conditions, but if the food was bad or the cook inadequate
the men would either quit or organize a strike. One Finnish bush worker,
Reino Keto, remembers a rebellion in his camp because of poor food: "We put
on pressure and finally we got so organized that we said if the cook doesn't

leave, the men will. We got a new cook."[10] Another man recalls the very primitive living conditions but then adds, "The cooks were Finnish women and they made sure, taking into consideration the circumstances, that the food was pretty good."

Finnish women soon earned a reputation as good cooks and the demand for their services increased with each positive experience. One reason Finnish

Finnish-Canadian women worked as cooks and dishwashers in the remote and isolated lumber camps. North of Thunder Bay, 1927.

cooks were in demand and their food appealed to the Finnish men is that they cooked familiar ethnic foods. Beans and bacon, the standard fare in many lumber camps, was foreign to the Finnish taste. For a newly arrived immigrant the food seemed plentiful – eggs served from large wash basins. William Eklund couldn't believe his ears when he asked how many eggs he could have and the reply was, "Take as many as you want!"[11] After a few years in Canada, Finnish lumber workers learned to demand plenty of meat and potatoes, a variety of soups, such as fish, meat, and pea soup, porridge, pancakes, eggs, and rye bread. In addition, Finns were "addicted to coffee," which was served with pulla and cookies.

The women, too, enjoyed the plentiful food in Canadian camps. They even complained about gaining weight. One woman wrote home to Finland, "I am fat as a pig – couldn't get 12 to a dozen – I don't understand why the devil one has to gain so much weight when one first comes to this country."[12] One female camp clerk described the food at a large lumber camp behind Night Hawk Lake:

The food was wonderful – many kinds of everything. Breakfast
at 6 o'clock; most men would make their own lunches, everything
was ready for them. Then they'd go into the bush. Those working
near the camp would come in for coffee about 10. There was all kinds
of goodies, cakes and stuff. There was always quite a few at lunch.
All afternoon there was coffee, then supper, and evening coffee. It
was really something![13]

Not surprisingly, some woods managers who ranked Finns among the
best bush workers in Northern Ontario also complained that "Finns used too
much butter and sugar, and cost 15 percent more to feed than French
Canadians."[14]

*Finnish lumber camps offered bathing facilities. Anna Kauppi heating the
sauna, north of Sault Ste. Marie, c1930.*

In addition to their ability to cook a variety of tasty dishes in primitive
conditions and in large quantities, the Finnish camp women were also
praised for their cleanliness. They boasted of having spotlessly clean
kitchens, which of course also added to their already heavy workload. One
non-Finnish lumber worker explained, "But not a man could stand half up
to the Finnish women. God, they even used to scrub the benches that guys
sat on."[15] In addition, they tried to take care of their personal appearance.
Many camp photographs depict clean, starched, lace-lined aprons and hair
done up and covered by nets or white head gear. Although most camps did
not have electricity and water had to be carried from nearby streams or

wells, Finnish dishwashers were expected to use boiling hot water and to rinse their dishes carefully.

While the conditions in the camps were rough, Finnish women found at least one redeeming factor in the Finnish camps – the sauna. According to Ian Radforth, the leading Canadian scholar on Northern Ontario bush workers, Finnish camps were unique in that they offered bathing facilities, and Finnish bush workers gained a reputation for their cleanliness.[16] Linne Korri explains, "Finns always built a sauna, the men built it even in non-Finn camps. We [women] heated it up twice a week."[17] An additional benefit of the saunas was that they provided convenient and warm laundry facilities. "The women washed clothes at the sauna too. A large barrel, which the men filled up, provided the water for laundering."[18] In fact, the availability of a sauna became a standard requirement for Finnish women and many Finnish men who worked in the bush.[19] Yrjö Kyllönen, who worked in the lumber camps near Kirkland Lake, makes this point clearly: "I went to another camp but there was no sauna or washing facilities so I left!"[20]

Others recalled the democracy and camaraderie in the bunkhouse kitchens. "The kitchen was built so that there would be always room for everyone to eat at once, bosses and men alike, all ate the same food at the same time, sitting around large tables."[21] At night, however, the women were separated from the men. In some camps they slept by the kitchen at one end of the bunkhouse, but at other camps they had their own log building or one that they shared with "the boss."[22] During the afternoon women would sometimes have an hour or two to rest. If they worked in the camps with other women, this was time used for socializing, having a cup of coffee, writing letters, or even going tobogganning. Women found comfort in one another's company, especially since they shared the same language and culture. Relatively speaking, then, the women – dishwashers, cooks, and cookees (cooks' helpers) – enjoyed better living conditions and more privacy than the men. But their working hours were longer. The cooks never had a day off. Rain or shine, the hungry workers had to eat several meals every day of the year.

Economic Opportunities

The hard work and long hours of the lumber camp women were compensated by good wages. Martta Laitinen, for example, was very pleased with her wages as a dishwasher in the winter of 1924. Fifty-five years later she still recalled with pride the size of her paycheque after three months in the lumber camp: "I received a good salary, I got $45 a month and free room and board. So I had over $100 when I left the camp to meet my husband in Vancouver."[23] Similarly Impi Kanerva chose the lumber camp because of its high wages: "I got $80 a month wages as compared to $30 a month in the city as a maid, and that included food and board."

After some experience as dishwashers and cook's helpers, the women graduated to become bakers and cooks and the wages improved significantly. Mary Erickson recalls that before she was married (in the late 1920s or early 1930s) she worked in a lumber camp as a dishwasher and got $35 a month. She adds, "Then I was a cook so I got $75, even $100 [a month]."[24] This possibility for upward mobility and for exceptionally good wages brought women back to the camps year after year despite the heavy work regimen. The larger the camp, the better the wages. Perhaps these perceived economic opportunities are best expressed by Aino Norkooli, a young, single woman who wrote to her sister in Finland from a lumber camp north of Thunder Bay in 1925:

> There are 20 men here and I am here to cook for them.... I have one boy as my helper.... I get $60 a month wages which is a good salary but I sure have to work hard for it.... In the morning I must get up about 5 o'clock and then I run non-stop till 9 o'clock. All the time I have to work and try to bake as much as I can manage.... I am trying to learn to become a cook because there is always work for them and good salary. I know even now around here in the camps women get sometimes over $100 a month when they cook for 50 men and that is an excellent salary. And one day I will get it too and then I will come to Finland because I have decided that when I get $300, then I will come to Finland. Maybe I will have it by next spring.[25]

Many factors contributed to the extraordinarily high wages paid to the Finnish lumber camp women. The laws of supply and demand were in women's favour and they had earned a good reputation as clean, capable, and hard-working women. This, however, does not suffice to explain their exceptionally good pay; female cooks could, in fact, earn two or even three times more than the male bush workers. According to statistics compiled by Ian Radforth, cooks during the 1920s earned between $90 and $125 a month and room and board. Such a salary was unheard of for unskilled immigrant women who sought work in the service industries in the urban areas.

Although cooking is traditional female work, cooks in the lumber camps had been exclusively men. When Finnish women began to work as cooks in Northern Ontario camps, they did so on the terms established earlier by male cooks. The common pattern in many occupations women entered between the wars was that wages would decline along with the feminization of the work force. This did not happen in the lumber camps because, throughout the 1920s and 1930s, men continued to dominate in the camps' cookhouses. As long as the women remained in the minority, they were not threatening the position of male cooks. If the Finnish women could work as hard as the men and cook comparable or better meals than the men, their jobs and wages also continued to be set according to the male wage scales.

During the Depression the wages declined, but relatively speaking still offered economic opportunities not attainable in the cities. Aino Norkooli, who was earning $60 in 1925 and expecting to increase her wages to $100 in a few years, wrote home in 1936 that she was working as the only woman in a lumber camp with 25 men and earning $45 a month.[26] According to Radforth, the camp cook's wages were at their lowest in 1932 at $60 a month.[27] Despite the decline in wages, opportunities for women to work in the lumber camps continued to provide interesting, and relatively well-paid, alternative employment to those willing to put up with the long days, gruelling schedules, primitive living conditions, and isolation.

Women with Families

Sometimes married couples would work in the same camp, the women as dishwashers and cooks and the men as bush workers.[28] This was easier for women who did not have children. Couples often took out contracts and worked in mini camps. In this case they sometimes lived in tents or hastily

MHSO, MSR 6891 Part I No. 8

Finnish families in the Northern Ontario bush, north of Thunder Bay, 1905.

built small homes. When on contract there was no time to waste. Artturi Saari's letter describes this well:

> Now we have our own camp. We have six men altogether and one man's Mrs is our cook. We built this camp in the bush, one end of the bunkhouse is for the cook and the other end is for the men. And then we also built a sauna (in one day) and now we are building a stable on Sundays so that we don't waste any working days.[29]

Women would also help in the logging, and some wives followed the men into the bush. One woman explained, "It is so good that I enjoy working outdoors. I much rather pull stumps than do the dishes."[30] In her recent autobiography Nelma Sillanpää describes how many Finnish families lived in the bush cutting pulpwood and adds, "sometimes the women helped, working side by side with their husbands."[31] There is also at least one instance where a woman, Ida Konnila, became a lumber camp operator near Sprucedale and advertised that she was hiring 20 men. She promised them $2 a cord and guaranteed "satisfaction as far as food is concerned."[32]

Camp life posed greater difficulty for women with children. Sometimes mothers would leave their children behind with relatives or with paid babysitters, especially if a child was very young. Boarding, however, was expensive. Aino Norkooli, who left her 11-month-old son in the city, wrote to her mother that the childcare cost $20 while her wages were $45.[33]

Some children grew up in the camps in rather carefree conditions. Their mothers were busy working and the lumber workers didn't have much time for them either. Older children often found the experience a lonely one. One woman recalls: "I had no one with whom to play. So, I always had a pack of cards in my pocket, hoping that someone would play cards with me."[34] Usually there were no schools within travelling distance, so children were sent to board in the cities, where they spent months separated from their parents. Or, like Nelma Sillanpää, they could study independently: "As was the case with most of the children there, I had been enrolled in a correspondence school, I had my lessons to do every day."[35]

Some Finnish families became lumber camp operators. Depending on the size of the operation, the wives either worked as cooks or, if they had the necessary language skills, they could work as clerks in the company store and as bookkeepers for their husbands. The lumber camp clerks were also highly paid, especially in larger camps. Alva Korri remembers when she was a clerk in a camp office after she married: "There was lots of paper work. And you had to sell clothes and things: it's like a little store.... I made all of $75 a month. I was offered $65 but I said, 'No I want $75.' And I got it! Ha Ha. We didn't pay for food. I worked for many years. Two years at one camp, three years at another."[36]

Similarly, Irene Hormavirta spent years as a clerk at Algoma Central Mile 155 camp owned by her and her husband. This large lumber camp was a long-term operation and the Hormavirtas built a beautiful log house on the site.[37] Most married women, however, lived in very modest log cabins. Nelma Sillanpää describes her parents' cabin in the woods: "It was a tiny, but warm and cosy cabin. Dad always joked that it was so small that we had to go outside to turn around."[38] During the off-season (summer) the families would return to their small homesteads or to their homes in the cities, but some stayed behind and utilized the empty lumber camps, thus living with their families in remote, isolated cabins all year around. Nelma Sillanpää recalls:

> In June, we travelled by train to another camp still within the beautiful Algoma District. We disembarked near a pile of logs that was marked with a pole showing a mileage number on it. There were many abandoned lumber camps in the area, and anyone could live in them free of charge during the summer months. We were two families.... We took the cook camp because it was smaller than the other. The other family took the men's bunkhouse. The camps were beside a small stream that flowed down the hill to a lake. Across the stream was a sauna.[39]

Thus, lumber camps also offered opportunities for married women. Many Finnish families spent years in the wilderness, sometimes raising their children in the Northern Ontario bush. Ian Radforth cites the case of Nelma Sillanpää's sister-in-law, Elsa Sillanpää, who began working at the age of 15 as a cookee in a lumber camp. The following year she worked in a small camp where she learned to cook. For the next few years she cooked in ever larger camps, increasing her wages accordingly. She then married a bush worker and brought her young children to the camp. When her children grew to school age, she either sent them to town or cooked in a boarding house of a sawmill town. Thus, what often began as seasonal, short-term contract work could stretch into a long, lucrative career and a distinct way of life.

Social Conditions

Isolation, which often lasted for months, was one of the hardships of lumber camp life. Some Finnish women adjusted to the isolation well, even professed to like it, while others couldn't stand it for long. Unlike in domestic service where Finnish women frequently changed employers, the women who hired themselves out to the camps were expected to sign contracts for the whole season. Many stayed for seven to eight months of the year, while some jobs were year-round. One woman from South Porcupine recalled that the longest stretch she stayed at a camp was nine months, "then I had to see a dentist and I spent a day in town and was back again in the bush.... But I didn't mind it at all. You just work and the time passes."[40]

Once again, the great incentive that kept women in isolated camps was money. Hilja Rantala explained in a letter: "I have been already in the bush for four months and things are not easy for me now, but what can I do when I want money so that I could shake off that old country poverty." She added that her bush camp at the time was 198 miles north of the closest major city, Sault Ste Marie.[41] While the isolation improved the women's economic opportunities and their abilities to save, it could have many psychological and social drawbacks. Minni Lahtinen wrote from Hearst:

I am one of those children of great misfortune. I buried myself
into the dense forest and was quite afraid of people when I came to
populated areas. Then I just worked in the lumber camps and I was
there many years with hard work and long hours, so I really didn't
feel like letting anyone know about me. I had my daughter and son
there with me.[42]

Nelma Sillanpää's mother, after a particularly rough season in the woods,
"vowed that she would never again go to a logging camp. It was too tough and
lonely for a woman." Yet, that summer she was once again cooking for 75 men
in a summer lumber camp.[43]

Another cause for concern for the women in the camps was an almost
total lack of health care. It could take days to reach the nearest doctor or hospital. Accidents and deaths were quite frequent, and some Finnish women ended
their immigration journey in a grave by some remote lumber camp. A particularly sad tale involves a single mother who died in a camp after a short illness.
We know about her from the story of her son, Eino Kuusela. This young
orphan, who had lived all his life in the lumber camp, was assigned to a
Canadian farmer who abused the boy, which led him to escape. He lived alone
"like a fox in a hole" in the midst of winter for 76 days before he was appre-
hended. He had not had any formal education, but he surely had learned the
survival techniques required of people living in the wilderness.[44] Sometimes
the Canadian press would report lumber camp accidents, such as the story of
the scalding of Mrs. H. Saari, a camp cook who was badly burned while lifting
a pot of boiling grease off the stove.[45] Mothers with young children were particularly worried about the long distances to doctors and hospitals. It was not
uncommon to read about sad accidents to children in the camps.[46] For example, Vapaus reported in February 1928: "Eight-month-old little girl burned to
death at a lumber camp while her mother was fetching water."[47]

On the positive side, camp life could offer some social advantages, especially for single women, who worked in the male environments. Nowhere
were the odds tipped so heavily in women's favour as in the lumber camps.
The codes of behaviour were strict: "One did not touch the lumber camp
women!" One bush worker remarked that there were "never any shenanigans"
and noted that "the girls were treated with respect because they demanded
it."[48] Or, as one woman over a hundred years old explained, "No, the men
wouldn't touch me. No fooling around in the camps. You couldn't annoy the
cook. If the cook left, the camp might have to close." And then she added,
"Oh, but how many times I wished that they had!"[49]

With such close proximity, some romances were inevitable as women
socialized with men in the camps. Although many complained of being
exhausted at night and falling asleep at 9 o'clock during the week, the women
would partake in men's social activities on Saturday night and holidays. This

included long, political debates, reading, letter-writing, storytelling, singing. Some would play cards, and, according to one woman, "there was always someone playing the accordion, a Finn worker with his own accordion. He played real nice old Finnish songs."[50]

Alcohol was disallowed at most lumber camps and, overall, the men stayed sober. Occasionally some alcohol was smuggled into the camps, and in remote small bush camps where families worked independently on contract it was not uncommon to find moonshine operations.[51] If fights broke out and rowdiness occurred in the Finnish camps, it was more likely caused by political disagreements than alcohol. "At the camps our entertainment was to argue over politics. If there were Finns, there were Reds and Whites."[52] Unlike in the cities, where the arrival of the lumberjacks after long periods in the bush sometimes erupted in uncontrolled partying, drinking, gambling, and visits to brothels, in the camps the men, by and large, behaved "politely and courteously" towards the women.

Some women were quite calculating about their opportunities. Hilja Rantala wrote from Algoma Central Railway Mile 198 in 1929: "Yes, there would be [suitors] for me too as I am here in the forest cooking for nine men and soon more are coming." But she adds that she has decided to stay single.[53] The fact that women had plenty to choose from was not, by any means, a guarantee of marital bliss, as one woman noted: "There were 60 men to choose from and I chose such a wretched drunk who spent all his money on cards. I had to go back to work to the camps to earn food and clothing for my small children."[54] While lumber camp life could be lonely and isolated, far away from health care, it could also offer women a distinct social advantage.

Political Activism

During the 1920s and 1930s the organized, social, cultural, and political activity in Northern Ontario's Finnish communities was dominated by the Finnish-Canadian left. Many lumber workers had arrived in Canada after Finland's bitter Civil War of 1918, where the "white army" was victorious. Some had endured persecution and prison camps, or seen their families and loved ones shot. There were martyrs on both sides of this fratricidal war and the scars were deep. It was not an easy task to try to achieve united political action in Canada among people who were so deeply divided. Yet in the lumber camps the Finns distinguished themselves as union organizers. Radforth points out:

> Although the Finnish immigrants dominated the work force in the pulpwood camps near Lakehead, up the Algoma Central Railway, and along the Canadian Northern Railway west of Sudbury, their participation in early unionization drives was far higher than their numbers in the industry as a whole. Their activism grew out of the radical, Finnish-immigrant culture that thrived so vigorously in the north.[55]

There were many kinds of Finnish radicals – "wobblies," socialists, communists, and social democrats – but during strikes they managed to pull together to form "united front strike committees."[56]

Finnish men were most active in the Lumber Workers Industrial Union of Canada (LWIUC); in fact, they were its founders, organizers, and main supporters. The task of organizing was not easy, but conditions and wages in the camps were so poor and labour practices frequently so dishonest that the men were driven to strike. Northern Ontario was also the scene of many labour battles and bitter strikes between the Finnish-run unions and bush workers and their sometimes Finnish owners. The most celebrated martyrs of the Finnish Canadian left are John Voutilainen and Viljo Rosvall, two lumber camp organizers who were allegedly murdered by Finnish anti-union men. According to Radforth, the first of the significant strikes in the Ontario lumber industry occurred in September 1926, and for the next decade "there was at least one major strike involving several hundred Ontario lumber workers nearly every year."[57]

Women working in the camps were, of course, affected. During the strike they lost their wages, but often their work continued as they tried to provide soup kitchens to the men manning the picket lines. It seems that many of the women working in the camps were fully supportive of the strikes although aware of and annoyed by the gender inequity within the union movement. Gertie Gronroos, who went to work in a lumber camp kitchen in 1937, remembers with some bitterness that women were not allowed in "those unions," yet women in the kitchen had to go out on strike, without any strike pay, although their conditions didn't improve. "The men got better wages, not us!" She also recalls the hardships caused by the strikes: "Today we don't know what a strike is, you go hungry before you know what a strike is. If the small farmers in the area hadn't brought in supplies, the men would have starved."[58]

Despite the inherent sexism, Finnish women seemed ready to support strikes. *Metsätyöläinen* – a newspaper for Finnish lumbermen – described an attempt to organize a particularly strong anti-union camp north of Port Arthur in 1932. According to the newspaper, the ten-man-strong organizing group had to return to the city without success except for the women. "The cook with her helpers promised to leave."[59]

When union organizers were successful in emptying out the camps, they sometimes made allowances for married couples. Minutes describing a lumber workers' meeting in October 1934 at Algoma Central Railway Mile 122 state: "It was decided that men with families can stay until they can get all of their belongings by the railroad tracks and can in the meanwhile be on picket duty."[60] One reason this was possible was that the women could feed the striking men.

During the strikes most women would return to the Northern Ontario cities and towns where they would become involved in strike support activities and in fund-raising for the strikers: "Before I got married I worked in lumber camps [near Wolf Siding].... My husband belonged to the LWIUC, always we took part in supportive strikes. We had social events at the hall to collect money and equipment for the strikers."[61]

Finnish women's organizations challenged their counterparts to provide funding in an organized fashion. For example, in 1934 the Sudbury Finnish Women's Labour League (WLL) decided to donate $5 to the striking Algoma lumber workers and challenged others to follow suit. "Women of the working class, hurry and fill your obligation [literally, debt of honour]. The lumber workers strike of Algoma must succeed by our united efforts!"[62] Within a few days the Sault Ste. Marie Finnish Women's Labour League decided to follow the example and donate their $5 to the strike fund, and then to publish this decision in a Finnish newspaper and to urge all WLL branches to do the same. "If you have no money, that's no excuse, you must think how to make some." As an example, they cited the efforts of the WLL in Sault Ste. Marie where they had planned to organize an entertainment evening and to give women's handicrafts as door prizes.[63]

Although most of the lumber camp women seem to have shared the men's radicalism and supported their unionizing drives, some did not. In the intolerant political climate, these "white" women could be chased out of the unionized camps. Many camps had their own "committees of investigation," where men would determine whether the newly arrived immigrants were supporters of the working class. One class-conscious Finnish woman complained that women sometimes got away with their conservative political opinions in lumber camps if they were good cooks. She was pleased to report, however, that just recently they had fired an experienced camp cook "because she had cooked for the white army in Finland."[64]

Organizing, striking, and fund-raising helped to consolidate the women's class consciousness, but at the same time these activities also revealed the sexism inherent in the labour movement and in the Finnish radical organizations.

Conclusion

Of the limited options available to working-class immigrant women in Northern Ontario, the lumber camps made sense on many levels: they offered food, housing, a culturally familiar environment, and an opportunity to earn unusually high wages. Because this traditional female work was done mainly by men in most lumber camps, women were able to argue for equal wages. Unlike wages in most other occupations that women entered after World War I, the lumber camp wages remained high and at par with male wages. Lumber camp women, especially if they were cooks and had no family obligations, could indeed achieve their economic goals and save money.

Lumber camp life, however, was clearly not for all women. Only independent, strong, and healthy women survived in the camps. They had to be familiar with cold winters and dense forests and be able to put up with months of isolation. They had to be able to make their own decisions and be free of culturally imposed restrictions on women's mobility. For such women the camps offered a unique lifestyle, where women enjoyed considerable respect, some social advantages, and, at times, found themselves in positions of power. Camps could simply not function without the cooks. The work was clearly demanding, even gruelling, at times dangerous, and isolation could take its toll. The negative aspects of camp life, however, could be partially alleviated because the Finnish women worked almost exclusively within the cultural safety of Finnish lumber camps and in many camps enjoyed the camaraderie of other Finnish women and men.

Within these camps the Finnish women raised the standards of food and cleanliness and had an overall civilizing impact on camp life. As a result, many men, as they moved from camp to camp, began to expect and demand similar standards in non-Finnish camps. It is no surprise then, that in addition to wages, unions began to pay increasing attention to living conditions. Women also made a significant contribution by supporting the many lumber workers' strikes, some of which were successful. Thus, it can be argued that the presence of the Finnish women in the camps had an impact on the living and working conditions of the camps that reached far beyond the particular camps where they happened to work.

Finally, as the first women in the bush camps, Finns pioneered the way for other women who wished to work in Northern Ontario lumber camps. After World War II, when camp life gradually became modernized and conditions improved, women from many cultural groups sought work in the camps. By then, the presence of women in the camps was no longer a novelty but often an expectation. The path for the lumber camp jobs had been cleared and the standard set by Finnish immigrant women.

9

Elva Sullivan, a Teacher in Northern Ontario, 1931–1939

Karen Blackford

When interviewed about her life in Biscotasing, Elizabeth Griffin was emphatic about the role one of her teachers played in shaping her life: "She taught us school work and how to live right."[1] This chapter is based on the teaching career of Elva Sullivan, who taught in outpost schools in Northern Ontario from 1931 to 1939.

After completing Grade 13 in her hometown of Arthur, Elva Sullivan entered Normal School, graduating a year later with a first-class certificate. Since there were few employment opportunities in Southern Ontario during the Depression, Sullivan looked to the north where school boards were having difficulty recruiting teachers. Unlike many young teachers who feared the loneliness of the north and were discouraged by tales about the Communists and Russians who populated northern communities, Sullivan gamely wrote to a northern school inspector whom she had known when she was a student in Southern Ontario. She was grateful when he offered her a teaching contract at the Dryden and Falconbridge School located just outside of Wahnapitae (20 kilometres east of Sudbury). As road conditions were poor, Sullivan recalls having to ride on horseback to the school. "It was one of those western ponies and every time you went to get on the saddle, it would turn around and bite you." Getting to school turned out to be one of Sullivan's lesser problems. There was little protection against improper advances made by students to young inexperienced teachers such as Sullivan. For example, on one occasion, "a young guy came back and propositioned me. I thought fast. He could've handled me I'm sure because back then I was a skinny little thing. We got no help with that kind of thing."

When she arrived at Wahnapitae, Sullivan was unaware that a situation for which she was totally unprepared was about to erupt. Shortly after her arrival, she discovered that her appointment had been made over the objections of many school board members. They opposed the fact that she spoke only English while most of the people in the village were French-speaking. The newly appointed teacher had replaced a popular francophone woman whose qualifications had been questioned by the same inspector who had hired Sullivan.

Initially, some of those who opposed the appointment used verbal threats to scare Sullivan into leaving the community. In one instance, "they tried getting rid of me there by saying that the Wahnapitae River is pretty deep." Shortly after that, the son of her strongest opponent attempted to shoot her. "When I got to school, all the children were standing outside and some of them were white as snow. 'He didn't get you?' they asked. I didn't know what to

Elva Sullivan

Almost the whole village of Wahnapitae, c1930.

say. I took it to be an accidental shot. One of them blurted out what had happened, that he went out to shoot me 'cause he wanted to get rid of me."

As a result of the stress of the situation, Sullivan broke out in hives. The hives were then used by those who wanted to get rid of her to further discourage her. "They said I had smallpox and brought a policeman and a doctor. The doctor started to laugh. He said, 'Well she sure hasn't got smallpox.'"

These discouraging events ensured that Sullivan would not renew her teaching contract at the end of that year. However, a combination of factors, including her determination to teach, the scarcity of other job openings, and the cost of a return trip south, kept her in the north. In fact, Sullivan did not move far to find a teaching position. She was hired to replace a teacher temporarily on leave at Coniston, another small town near Sudbury.

While any type of contract was welcomed, Sullivan was determined to obtain a full-time position. Therefore, when it was evident that the teacher she was replacing was going to return to work, she wrote to Toronto to find out if there were any jobs in Ontario. "They wrote back and said if I joined the Federation of Women Teachers' Association of Ontario [FWTAO] they would help me get a job." As a recent graduate of a Normal School, Miss Sullivan was understandably proud of her newly acquired professional status. She had been reluctant to join the teachers' federation, which was considered to be radical at the time.[2] The $2 membership fee for FWTAO was voluntary, and up until this time she had avoided joining the organization. It was now time to join.

Elva Sullivan

Elva Sullivan on "Tom Brown," 1930. The log school was about three to five miles from Wahnapitae depending which way you went.

In 1934 with the help of the FWTAO, Sullivan accepted a teaching position at the Loughrin School near Markstay, a small community 50 kilometres east of Sudbury. This was a "Back to the Land" school and part of a government settlement program. This program was a joint venture between the federal Ministry of Labour, the provincial Ministry of Lands and Forests, and northern municipalities that chose to participate in the project.[3] Under the Ontario Relief Land Settlement Act of 1933, Canadian families on welfare were relocated to areas in Northern Ontario. These families were expected to grow their own food and harvest timber for fuel. Those chosen to participate in the program had to be in good health and to have some farming experience. The intent was to have heads of households travel north and choose a lot from the Crown land available. They built a house with tools and materials supplied by the government and then sent for their families. It was the children of these families who attended the school in which Elva Sullivan was placed. According to her account:

These people came from the city on account of the Depression. They lived in Sudbury and found it cost too much. So they moved out to Markstay. The government gave them the land as long as they improved it. They had to live on it so many months per year or they couldn't have it. It was government land they were living on. They were given underwear, jeans, dresses, shoes. They got a certain amount for food every three months, I think. They were to produce their own food. They were only allowed to charge me $12 a month for board. At that rate, it wouldn't even feed a person.

The large number of families who returned to urban life suggests that many were poorly prepared for rural life in the north. Inadequate knowledge of the northern wilderness and attempts to clear land in the fall rather than the spring contributed to the difficulties they encountered. Many of those who participated in the project expected that the monthly welfare stipend they received in the city would continue when they reached the north. Instead, they were allocated only $10 a month regardless of family size.

Her sense of affiliation with people in this community was increased because she boarded with some of them and came to know their situations. She observed the humiliation, fear, and moral regulation they experienced by continuous inspections from relief workers. She was aware from a comparison with her own annual salary of $600 just how limited the family's monthly $10 stipend was and knew how much they relied on her contribution for room and board.

While the government paid to relocate teachers to these schools, isolation and difficulties with transportation still presented hardships for teachers. "I had to walk in snowshoes about two and a half miles through the bush to the school in Markstay." Regardless of the difficulties, Sullivan was encouraged by the positive relationship she developed with her students, their parents, and the community. In contrast to the hostility she encountered at Wahnapitae, she felt welcome at Markstay: "They liked me, they wanted me to visit."

In dealing with the hardships of northern isolation, Sullivan had support for her teaching from a number of sources. Charitable agencies in the Markstay area such as the Independent Order of the Daughters of the Empire (IODE) provided supplies for both the schools and the families associated with the Back to the Land program. "The group of IODE women in Sudbury used to send a great big box full of gifts to all the Back to the Land schools at Christmas. There'd even be a gift for the teacher. They would also send a big box of used books." Support also came from the northern branch of the FWTAO located in Sudbury:

When I was in Markstay I came up to the teachers' convention in Sudbury. I had to ride on one of these wagons with a spring seat on it.

I got the worst cold. You didn't have conveniences like cars to go places, especially in the Depression. They got me to make a big speech about Back to the Land schools. They had a couple of other teachers make a little speech on that too. I could remember the convention being held in St. Andrew's Church.

A 1933 Sudbury Star report of this FWTAO meeting reveals how Sullivan used her platform as speaker at that meeting to advocate for families on welfare.[4] "Life is not easy for the settlers," she declared, "how would you like to have only $10 to clothe a family for five months?"

This combination of support from students' parents, charitable organizations, and the FWTAO gave this young teacher the confidence to persist throughout her contract and to be innovative in meeting her students' learning needs. Sullivan recalls that there were times when "we didn't even have notebooks." She recalls further:

We went out and got bark off birch trees and used it to write down what we wanted. I didn't have to worry about having something for a science lesson. Two lads brought in a porcupine one day. They had long sticks and they guided this porcupine along until they got to school. So we had a lesson on porcupines.

It was not unusual to have children in the classroom who had little previous opportunity for school attendance. "In Markstay I got children in that school that were 12 years old who had never been to school." To meet the needs of these children, Sullivan often adapted her pace of teaching even though the curriculum was supposed to be standard across the province. In fact, the goal of one inspector was to have every student read the same page of the same book on the same day of the week.[5]

Down at Markstay, there were two girls anxious to learn. At the end of the first year they had finished Grade 4 and were in Grade 5. The next year I gave them two more grades. Later they wrote their government exams for Grade 8 and they passed.

In Markstay, Sullivan taught children from families who spoke French, Russian, or other languages at home. To do this she adapted the materials readily available to her: "I cut pictures of a man and a woman, a girl and a boy, out of the catalogues. Then I'd put their names on them and put them up on the wall. They seemed to learn English fast."

She also responded to the wishes of the parents of her students and changed the traditional curriculum so that children learned things that were relevant to the everyday lives of the settlers' children:

Parents wanted the children to learn how to send money orders to Eaton's and Simpson's and how to write both a business letter and a friendly letter. They didn't give two hoots whether their children learned science or social studies as long as they learned how to use money. They figured if they could do those things, they would manage.

Through her experience at a Back to the Land school, Elva Sullivan came to realize that in addition to the standard methods encouraged by her teacher's training, innovation was valuable in assessing the needs of students and in developing creative ways in which to teach. "Maybe I didn't do things conventionally, but they worked and that's what counts," she commented.

Sullivan came to see parent-teacher relations as important for an understanding of children's learning needs, and the young teacher developed a rapport with both her students and their parents. "Down in Markstay it was great! In fact, there were people who didn't have children who invited me, including an 'old maid.' They were like that."

Sullivan eventually brought her growing confidence to a teaching position in Biscotasing. From 1936 to 1939 Sullivan taught in this lumbering, trapping, and railroad community 150 kilometres northwest of Sudbury. "Bisco," as it was known by residents, was on the main CPR line and could be accessed only by rail or canoe in 1936.

Even though women teachers made sufficient wages to live independently, the social expectation that they would be models of decorum dictated that they board with families in the district. The homes offered to Sullivan sometimes left a lot to be desired: "I could tell you some things about the boarding-houses. How would you like to sleep with a cat at the foot of your bed that you had coaxed into staying with you because you were scared of the rats under your bed?" In Biscotasing, she initially boarded with an elderly couple. The meals were good and the house was spotless, but "the damned bed bugs" were a major concern. Sullivan also found living in a boarding-house confining. Often she was not welcome in the kitchen, and some places did not allow her to have friends visit. In one place she was afraid to use her radio because "the landlady's husband was kind of grouchy." However Sullivan recalls with pleasure her last home in Biscotasing, where her landlady was the local midwife. She "let me cook some meals myself and we both enjoyed the radio programs, especially the hockey games!" As well as finding a comfortable boarding-house in Biscotasing, Sullivan discovered the community offered a social life. There was a town hall and dances were common. This was quite a change from some of the other Northern Ontario towns where Sullivan had taught.

As was the case elsewhere, the Biscotasing board was unable to finance either textbooks or teaching materials for students. Again she improvised:

You were required to teach geography and pretty near all the other things that were on the curriculum. But you didn't do them the way you would if you were in Southern Ontario. There was that little boy who couldn't read or write. Although printing wasn't permitted, I taught him to print his name. The inspector couldn't believe it. He asked me how I had gotten him to print his name.

Elva Sullivan

Pupils at Biscotasing from primer to Grade 8, from both rooms, c1936. Grey Owl (Archie Belaney) is at the back. Elva Sullivan is at far right in second row.

Sullivan's unconventional approach was rewarded. "When the inspector went back to Toronto, I got two huge boxes of paper, crayons, pictures to colour, sewing cards, something to make little vases. We got all kinds of stuff." Sullivan employed other unusual teaching methods. At Bisco, for example, she had students participate in community events. Sullivan also prided herself on a liberal approach to religious affiliation and was determined to ensure that both her Protestant and Catholic students felt comfortable. Students sang at both Catholic and Protestant funerals and weddings.

Sullivan's idea of who she was appears to have changed during her stay in Northern Ontario. This can be seen in her personal relations and activities, as well as in her teaching philosophy and methods. When she first arrived in Wahnapitae, she presented herself with the most proper decorum possible. Her dress was modest and she did not encourage close personal relations with people in the community. This professional distance from the community dissolved in Markstay, where she increasingly felt part of the neighbourhood and identified with the Back to the Land families. By the time she arrived in

Biscotasing, she attended dances and purchased a radio. Both of these activities on the part of a proper schoolteacher and single woman might have been looked upon with raised eyebrows by some circles in Southern Ontario at that time. The personal growth Sullivan experienced during those years becomes most apparent if we consider her new-found interest and participation in athletics. In Arthur her mother did not allow her to skate, but by the time she was living in Biscotasing she was playing on a women's hockey team!

While these signs of transformation were evident in Sullivan's personal life, changes had also occurred in her educational practices. She arrived in the north proud of her First Class Certificate and determined to uphold the Normal School philosophy that she had been taught to sustain. No doubt, she saw that part of her role in the north was to uphold the authority of the Ministry of Education and was to represent her superintendent's wishes in Wahnapitae. Instead, over time, she became an advocate for northern children and their parents. With their needs in mind she became flexible in her approach to teaching. She adapted curriculum and modified teaching materials in order to meet the needs of the students, their parents, and the community.

As a teacher in the 1930s, Sullivan conformed in many ways to the social expectations of women teachers of her generation. Yet through her own determination and grit, she showed her students in Northern Ontario that while education was important for passing government exams, it was equally important for managing everyday life. She demonstrated for teachers that travelling alone to remote communities and taking on a profession was possible for women. Today's students and teachers are beneficiaries of the contributions of teachers such as Elva Sullivan.

10

"Every Miner Had a Mother"[1]

Jennifer Keck, Susan Kennedy, and Mercedes Steedman

Throughout history women have taken on the difficult task of looking after the physical and emotional needs of their husbands and children. In the paid workforce we have continued to support the largest
needs of the community, again largely as caregivers and service
workers. As mothers and housewives we labour alone, and as workers in the community our work is underpaid and undervalued. This,
despite the fact that our work has and continues to play a major role
in building and maintaining a labour force.[2]

In the spring of 1983, the Sudbury Women's Centre sponsored a Mother's
Day tea and photographic exhibit entitled "Every Miner Had a Mother."
Both events were part of the Women's Centre's contribution to the City of
Sudbury's centennial celebrations in 1983. The theme "Every Miner Had a
Mother" was in reaction to the city's centennial logo, which featured two male
miners, one of the past and one of the contemporary period. While the logo
went a long way towards acknowledging the role that male industrial sector
workers had played in building the community, it rendered invisible the contribution of women. As Women's Centre activists, we set out to reclaim women's
past. We sponsored a number of centennial events that would make visible the
role that women played in building the community.

Two of the authors, Jennifer Keck and Susan Kennedy, were directly
involved with the organization of the Women's Centre's project in 1983.[3]
Mercedes Steedman and Jennifer Keck rejuvenated the photographic exhibit
for the INORD symposium, "Changing Lives: Women and the Northern
Ontario Experience," in the spring of 1995. Both events focused on the need to
reclaim women's history in Northern Ontario. It also showed the importance
of building links between the political projects of academics and the work of
activists in the women's community.

Although Sudbury began as a small stop on the Canadian Pacific Railway,
it was destined to become one of Canada's largest mining centres. In 1886, the
Canadian Copper Company set up its headquarters in the Sudbury Basin, and
from then on Sudbury expanded as a company town. For over 70 years the
economy was dominated by two major multinational corporations:

Falconbridge and Inco and their predecessor companies. One hundred years after the community was founded, its character had changed: it had become a service centre, with a regional population of around 100,000.[4] Despite considerable economic diversification, the city was still perceived to be a single-industry "town," and mining and the mining unions continued to influence many of its cultural and social activities.[5]

Even though Sudbury has a history of labour activism that dates back to the early twentieth century, industrial unionism established itself in the Sudbury community only in the closing years of World War II. Following the war, the community experienced several bitter strikes. The late 1950s and early 1960s saw fierce inter-union rivalry between the Canadian Union of Mine, Mill and Smelter Workers and the United Steelworkers of America. These events continue to shape the cultural and political landscape of the community.

Yet all of these events are remembered as men's struggles. Men's life stories mark the historical record of the community and women's lives remain invisible. There are notable exceptions, to which a film documenting participation of wives during a 1978 strike at Inco can attest, but on the whole there have been few attempts to discuss the role of women in building the Sudbury community.[6]

Sudbury Women's Centre and the Centennial Project

In the fall of 1982 representatives from the City of Sudbury announced plans to celebrate the city's centennial the following year. With representatives from the municipality and the local historical society, the Centennial Foundation unveiled the city's official centennial logo – two male miners, one past and one present – with considerable fanfare. A representative from the foundation described the symbolism in the logo as recognition of the "price and dedication of the people who had built the community."[7]

The reaction from the local women's community was swift. Sudbury, like many other northern communities, had had an active women's movement since the early 1970s. After the logo was announced, members of the Women's Centre steering committee wrote a letter of protest to the Centennial Foundation. The centre objected to portraying only men in the logo. The women who had contributed to the building of Sudbury were totally absent. The Women's Centre received a polite reply suggesting that our organization might sponsor a centennial event during the year (the Centennial Foundation had already extended an invitation to groups from the community to sponsor events commemorating the centennial).

The logo – and the Centennial Foundation's response to our concerns – presented a particular dilemma for members of the centre. On the one hand, the logo acknowledged the role that working-class miners had played in building the community. It was difficult to argue against the central role that mining and resource extraction had played in the local economy. It was also difficult to imagine that after investing money in the design of a logo and a promotional campaign, the Foundation would likely change its plans to accommodate our concerns. On the other hand, the logo ignored our history and the part our mothers and grandmothers had played in building the community.

Sophie Sawchuk outside her boarding-house on Frood Road, Sudbury, 1932.

It was unclear what course of action would be most effective. A public protest would gain "publicity for a day" but be lost on the general public. We also risked alienating the mine workers who were honoured in the logo.There was need for a political project that would confront the symbolism in the centennial logo, but one that would at the same time bring the majority of the community "along with us." We decided that with a little creativity and a sense of humour, we could come up with an idea that would highlight the role women played, while gently poking fun at the Foundation's oversight.

Amid gales of laughter at our first organizing meeting, we decided that the city fathers needed to be reminded that "every miner had a mother." We claimed Mother's Day as the logical date for our event. What started out as a spoof on City Hall began to take shape as the evening progressed. We wanted to highlight the historical contribution of women's work and to attract as many people as possible to the event. The decision was made to sponsor a tea in the tradition of our mothers and grandmothers. It would have all the makings of a traditional tea, complete with pink and green triangle sandwiches, but our tea would make a political statement – that "every miner had a mother."

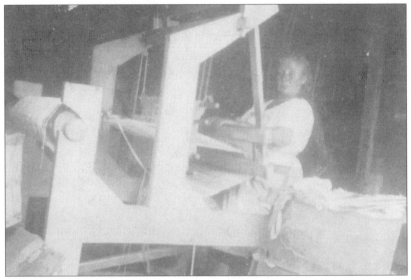

Lempi Kauppi emigrated from Finland in the 1920s. She wove mats to augment family income. The picture documents the type of women's work that is often absent from official collections.

Our proposal to the Centennial Foundation included three related projects: a logo, a mural, and a photo exhibit.

The logo was designed by local artist Brenda Fuhrman and featured two women – an older woman with flowers on her hat and a younger one with a miner's hard hat. The latter image reflected the move of women into production jobs at Inco's Sudbury operations in the early 1970s.[8] This logo was featured on a range of items, including buttons, sun visors, and T-shirts, that the centre sold during the year.

Fuhrman also undertook to paint a mural featuring women that would be donated to the City of Sudbury to form part of a series of similar artwork that was featured on the local Canadian National Railway fence in the downtown area. All the pictures in the existing collection featured prominent "great (white) men" in the city's history. Our mural featured three women and a child, including an older and a younger Euro-Canadian woman and an Aboriginal woman. The third project involved a photographic exhibit that would be featured at the Mother's Day tea. Using the theme "Every Miner Had a Mother," we planned to gather photographs from both official and more informal sources to prove that women had been there too.

The Centennial Foundation was cautious about supporting the proposal, but in the end funding was granted. No doubt its reservation stemmed from the fact that by 1983 the Sudbury Women's Centre had a reputation for inviting controversy. However, the project clearly promised to highlight the contribution of women to the community, making it impossible to reject the proposal.

"Every Miner Had a Mother" logo.

The Photographic Exhibit

With Fuhrman in control of both the design of the logo and the painting of the mural, other women turned their attention to the photographic exhibit. It would prove to be the most ambitious part of the project. Three women worked on the exhibit: Maureen Hyman, who was at home with a young child, and Susan Kennedy and Jennifer Keck, who were working at the time as federal civil servants. All three of us were white, anglophone, and in our late twenties and mid-thirties. Each had been involved with the women's movement in Sudbury and other cities over the previous decade; only Keck had been raised in Sudbury. Ties to the anglophone and francophone communities through family, work, and the women's movement united all the women at the Women's Centre, but few First Nations women were involved in the Women's

Centre at that time. The resulting project reflected our concerns and historical memory.

We wanted images that portrayed women's work and community contributions both inside and outside of the home, but these aspects of community-building were not to be found in traditional community historical records, which meant that the usual sources for visual history were of little use. We were interested in the work that women did raising families, keeping house, farming, and a host of other activities related to volunteer work in hospitals, schools, unions, and other community organizations. As we turned to obvious sources – the local library, university archives, and prominent community organizations – our enthusiasm waned. There were only a limited number of photographs featuring women's work.

Miners' Mothers' Day collection

It is often difficult to find pictures of the work women do in community halls and church basements. This photograph and the facing one appeared in The Sudbury Star, *c1950.*

When we turned to local employers of women, we had more success. Local stores and the hospital proved to be important sources of pictures of women's work in traditional occupational sectors in the postwar period. The local newspaper photographic archives proved to be a worthwhile resource, as women's volunteer work was often recorded in the newspaper. Yet we still had few photographs featuring the social history of the community and the more informal aspects of women's work.

We put an immediate call out to all members of the Women's Centre. We called our friends, relatives, neighbours, and co-workers to search for pictures of women's work in their family picture collections. We placed a public announcement in one of the local newspapers. We were careful to define women's work as work that included work in the home, the community, and the workplace. We had some difficulty explaining to people that we were not just interested in old pictures of women working at wage employment. We wanted to draw out other aspects of women's work – as mothers, wives, sisters, and community members.

Miners' Mothers' Day collection

The results of these efforts were overwhelming. Contacts with our own informal networks provided us with a wealth of pictures: over a period of two weeks with many 18-hour days, we collected more than 120 pictures of women from the French, English, Finnish, and Ukrainian communities. We also collected several written and taped interviews on women's lives in northeastern Ontario, giving us the beginnings of a chronological history of women. Each interview seemed to raise new issues and questions, many of which remained unanswered by the end of the project. What began as a spoof on City Hall became a politicizing experience as we gathered photographs, heard stories, and began to unravel aspects of the "herstories" of women in the community.

We discovered, for example, that the process of collecting pictures also meant unearthing the stories of the women and families depicted in them. One of our co-workers in the federal government brought in the picture of her grandmother, Azilda Belanger, the matriarch of a large Franco-Ontarian family and the namesake of Azilda, a large Franco-Ontarian community on the outskirts of Sudbury. An older woman residing at a local nursing home responded to our advertisement in the newspaper and provided a picture of women picking potatoes on a farm just west of the city in the 1930s. She described an average working day that began at 6 a.m. and extended to the late evening when she put the last of her children to bed and finished the day's mending.

Working for Lafrance Furs, Sudbury, c1950.

Miners' Mothers' Day collection

Despite having formal education as teachers and nurses, several women told us stories of having to quit teaching or nursing in the 1950s when they married or were expecting a child. Many of these women turned to volunteer work at the local hospitals or with the Red Cross. One Women's Centre member contributed a picture of her mother with a small child in her arms. She then told us how her mother had delivered babies for women at home. When the local maternity ward did not have available beds or when the distance to the hospital was too far to travel over dirt roads or when the cost was prohibitive, home births were necessary. Another colleague contributed a picture of her mother when she worked as a nurse with the Victorian Order of Nurses (VON). On the back of the photograph is a short note describing a visit to a family during a snowstorm. She explained how the weather had forced her to stay overnight with this family. Each picture had a story to tell.

Sudbury women's experiences during World War II featured prominently in our collection. At the local newspaper archives, we uncovered a number of pictures of women selling war bonds and volunteering for the Red Cross. In family albums, we discovered pictures of women who joined the war effort as members of the armed forces or workers at war industry plants.

Azilda Belanger and her family were among the first families to settle in the outlying farming communities surrounding Sudbury.

Several themes began to emerge from the photographs. There were pictures of early pioneering women, women working during the war years, women participating in traditional occupations, and women labour activists in the postwar period. Women's contribution to the community was extensive, and we now had the visual evidence to prove it.

The 1950s are often seen as a period of women's retreat into the home, but we found that women were actively involved in labour struggles in their community. Images of women's labour activism highlighted the role that women played in building the Mine, Mill and Smelters' Workers union. Their roles as workers during the war years and as members of the Ladies' Auxiliary during the 1950s and 1960s told a different story. The image of Sudbury as a "male" union town was clearly not an accurate picture of the community. Women's union activism stretched beyond the mining unions into the service and public sectors. There were pictures of women involved in the first restaurant strike in the 1950s, there were pictures of public sector strikes in the late '70s and early '80s, and there were pictures of women members of the United Steelworkers of America Local 6500. Some photos also depicted the work of women involved with "Wives Supporting the Strike" during the 1978 strike against Inco.

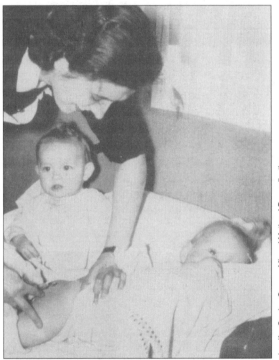

VON nurse Betty Sharpe administering penicillin, Sudbury, January 1947.

As we gathered more pictures and stories, it became clear that our photographic exhibit was really only the beginning of our struggle to make women's work in the community visible. We were now more conscious of our own ignorance. Why did we not know this part of our own history? The project made us sensitive to the patriarchal nature of historical memory, a political issue made more acute in a resource sector community. Why was it so difficult to find sources that would help us piece this project together? Why did official collections not include aspects of women's work? Even more compelling, why were the women we contacted so willing to lend their stories to help us build this project?

This last question was answered, in part, by the large numbers of women who came to the Miners' Mothers' Day tea and the popular press coverage the event received. Over 450 women (and men) attended the event in May. Most of these women had never attended a Women's Centre – or feminist – event before. Some came because photographs of their family or neighbours were included in the exhibit. Others offered their own stories and promised photographs if we wanted to continue to research and expand our collection.

Women from the Sudbury region joined the armed forces during World War II. Jacqueline Fournier (Keck) and friend were members of the Royal Canadian Navy.

The tea was a tremendous success. The mayor and a provincial member of parliament unveiled the mural and it was donated to the city. The chair of the Centennial Foundation attended the event and proudly sported a button with the Women's Centre's alternative logo beside the "official" centennial symbol. The picture collection and the logo became a focal point for the Women's Centre's contribution to the centennial year celebration. We decided to keep the photograph exhibit together for the rest of the year. Throughout the centennial year celebrations, the photographic exhibit was displayed prominently at various events and in the foyer of City Hall. Our logo created quite a sensation. The centre was bombarded with requests for buttons with the alternative logo. One elementary schoolteacher came to the centre (for the first time) the week after the tea with a request for 25 buttons to sell at her school.

The Miners' Mothers' Day exhibit marked a critical turning point for many of us who were active with the Women's Centre. The project was an important first step in our efforts to regain our past. The photographic exhibit was a tribute to our mothers and grandmothers and to the other settler women who had helped to build Sudbury and other communities in Northern Ontario. The project provided many of us, as young feminists, the opportunity to hear the life stories of another generation of women. It taught us about the importance of unravelling this part of the city's past.

Noella Cayen (now Blackwell) and Ethel Pitman (now MacLean) left Creighton in 1943 to work at a factory in Ajax, Ontario, that made anti-aircraft artillery. They are shown outside the residence where they stayed in Ajax.

The project also taught us that there was more than one way to fight City Hall. The Miners' Mothers' Day event was effective in its efforts to attract a wider audience, in part because it allowed us to tap that secret anger that many women feel about the way their work has been underpaid and undervalued. Using humour also allowed us the opportunity to bring members of the Centennial Foundation and other event organizers "along with us." The project captured the imagination of local journalists and editorial writers by providing an alternative symbol that used humour to make a political statement. Women had played a role in building the community and we had the pictures to prove it! In the end, we were able to show people why we were upset and what we wanted to change – but with creativity and humour we were virtually unassailable.

Mike Solski Collection, Sudbury Public Library

Local 902, General Workers Union strike at Radio Lunch 1950.

Ten Years Later

Jennifer Keck and Mercedes Steedman pulled the photos out again ten years later for a slide presentation at the 1995 INORD symposium on women in the north and for this book. As academics, we usually work with official public records that often fail to represent the struggles of working-class peoples to build more humane and democratic communities. We also fail to recognize the pervasiveness of racism in the way we define our history. In 1995 these issues are now on our minds. We noted that First Nations peoples were absent from the slide presentation. But rather than trying at the last minute to add images of First Nations women, we wanted to raise an issue that has always been a sub-text to the Miners' Mothers' Day historical research project – these slides come out of our own racism.

The history of female white settler society was too frequently intended to be a representation of all women. Historian David Roediger, in his study of working-class white male culture, makes the point that the whiteness of history begins its misrepresentation in the selection of questions to ask, stories to tell, and images to project. Race is imbedded even in these beginning stages of research.[9] As white women, we look to the known, our families' stories and photos, and fail to address the question of how whiteness becomes meaningful to us. As we became aware of our own complicity in this process, we became more conscious of the images of women that the slide show portrayed. The development of settler society in the Sudbury Basin is one part of a larger story of this area, a brief history in a long panorama of settlement.

We found one image of a family from Manitoulin Island in the Sudbury Public Library collection. It gave no names for the faces that stared into the camera. The same portrait style was used for family photos in the settler soci-

Cartoon in the Sudbury Star, *4 May 1983.*

ety, but if the image had been of white people, it would have included the names of the family. (Actually, it would likely have identified them as Mr. John Smith and wife.)

As white women, we are aware of the consequences of being treated as other, of our stories and historical experiences being set aside and marginalized, of women being unnamed. The Miners' Mothers' project was an attempt to challenge that construction of women's identity, yet because we were less sensitive to the place of racism in the construction of settler women's gendered identity, we too ignored First Nations women's contribution to the construction of the Sudbury community. We need to take feminist author bell hook's warning seriously: "To ignore white ethnicity is to redouble its hegemony by naturalizing it."[10] If we were to remain silent on this issue, we would be in danger of falling into just that trap.

When we presented our slide show in May 1995, we needed to articulate our bias. This collection was an attempt to make visible the experience of

Euro-Canadian women and was not intended as a history of all women in Northern Ontario. In our struggle to reclaim our past, we cannot ignore the fact that Aboriginal women have a much longer history and claim to this region than we do. We need to build on our sense of outrage at the invisibility of our past and build alliances with Aboriginal women who are struggling to reclaim their voices and make the history of First Nations people visible.

During the 1978 strike at Inco women organized Wives Supporting the Strike. This picture shows women preparing a bean supper for striking families.

The Miners' Mothers' Day project also points to the need for greater collaboration between activists in the community and women working in academe. The act of taking control of historical memory and consciousness is part of a struggle to socialize and recover our history. Inevitably, it becomes a political act. It is instructive, for example, that this project did not originate in academe but rather from the feminist activists in the community. While there has been further scholarship on the history of Sudbury and Northern Ontario in the period since the photograph collection was first put together, there is still more work to be done.[11] We need to challenge the political exclusion of these official community histories that focus on the role of resource extraction and industrial-sector workers without taking into consideration the role that women played in the development of towns and communities.

Finally, this project offers important insights on the politics of "doing history" and the importance of acknowledging that fact in the work we do as academics and political activists. In order to confront the ideological hegemony in bourgeois history, we need to challenge the "objective" assertions of mainstream academic work and learn to use the stories and experiences of working people, who built their communities. To do so involves an analysis of class, gender, and race – and a willingness to bridge the distance between activism and scholarship that often characterizes work in universities. Uncovering our past can and should be a politicizing experience, but we need to be willing to address the anger women feel about the hidden aspects of their history and make it part of our larger social and political project.

Manitoulin Island, c1910.

11

Working at Inco: Women in a Downsizing Male Industry

Jennifer Keck and Mary Powell

This chapter provides an overview of women in mining at Inco operations in Sudbury and a profile of women hired in Inco production and maintenance jobs during the mid-1970s. Inco became one of the first mining companies in Canada to hire women for hourly rated jobs; between 1974 and 1976, the company hired 100 women for production and maintenance work. In this chapter, we provide a brief history of women in mining that sets the context for the 1974 hiring and, based on data gathered primarily from employment records at the Inco Archives, we focus on one group of the women hired from 1974 to 1976: *those who exited.* This work is part of a larger project that began as a result of a request by the Women's Committee of Local 6500 to explore women's experiences in production and maintenance jobs at Inco in conjunction with the twentieth anniversary of their hiring.[1]

We argue that women took jobs at Inco because they could earn substantially more than at the jobs they left and that their earning power was important because a majority of them were unattached women, supporting themselves and in some cases supporting children. Despite a conventional view that women lack the staying power for such jobs, women were more likely to stay on the job or to leave involuntarily (layoff, death, disability) than they were to quit. Evidence from the employment records of those who exited indicates that, in addition to seniority, factors affecting worker mobility may help explain variations in the length of time on the job. In general, women who were young and had finished high school tended to work for about two years and then quit; in contrast, women who were older and had not finished high school worked more than six years on average and more of them were laid off than quit. We must emphasize, however, that this sketch is drawn from those who exited. Some of these conclusions may not apply to the women who are still employed at Inco, but that is a subject for future research.

Women's Work: The Sudbury Labour Force
Our research on women in production and maintenance jobs at Inco focuses on women who are not typical of the female labour force in Sudbury. Mining has

historically been a male-dominated industry, with women comprising less than 1 percent of the Inco hourly workforce. The prohibition against women in mining was not simply a matter of traditional hiring practices; women were by law prevented from working in mines and mining production. The legislation was temporarily suspended to allow female employment during World War II and was changed permanently in the 1970s as part of the broader pattern of changes in the status of women. Inco's decision to hire women in 1974 opened up relatively high-paying, unionized jobs for women workers in an industry that had been historically closed to women. Access to these jobs had particular significance in a local economy that was dominated by a single industry – mining – and in a labour market that was shaped by the hiring practices of two large multinational mining corporations.

Over the period from 1941 to 1991, Sudbury exhibited the same trend of steep increases in female participation that occurred in Canada as a whole. But Sudbury lagged behind Canada by some 3 to 4 percent in the first four censuses examined here. The main reason is that the dominance of the mining industry affected men and women differently – that is, the lower proportion of women in the labour force in Sudbury compared to Canada is related to fewer employment prospects for women in Sudbury's mining-based economy, and the percentage of men in the population (and thus the labour force) is higher in Sudbury than in Canada, because men were attracted to the area by employment prospects in the mining industry.

Table 1. Women in the Labour Force, Sudbury and Canada, 1941-1991

	1941	1951	1961	1971	1981	1991
Sudbury: Women in Labour Force	1,997	3,082	7,289	11,960	17,890	22,130
Sudbury: Women as % of Labour Force	15.6	17.9	24.5	30.6	41.1	46.7
Canada: Women as % of Labour Force	18.5	22.0	27.3	34.3	40.4	44.9

However, by 1981, the percentage of women in the Sudbury labour force was ahead of the figure for Canada (41.4 percent compared to 40.4 percent), and by 1991 the labour force in Sudbury was 46.7 percent female, compared to the Canadian workforce that was 44.9 percent female.[2] These differences are accounted for by changes in the Sudbury economy in the direction of fewer jobs for men and more jobs for women. In particular, the largely male workforce at Inco and Falconbridge, the region's largest employers, began to shrink. In Sudbury, as in Canada as a whole, mining is an industry in absolute employment decline, a process that began in Sudbury in 1972, was clearly a long-term trend by 1977, and was evident nationally by the mid-1980s. Employment growth in the region in the 1980s came primarily from the public sector, which hired more women than men for its clerical and service jobs. The 1974–76 entry of women into the Inco hourly rated workforce was thus not only an historic shift in a significant industry but also a profound departure for Sudbury's female workers, who had for many years been severely limited in the jobs they could get, in the wages they could earn, and in the job security and employee benefits available to them.

Women in Production and Maintenance Jobs at Inco

In the history of Inco, Sudbury's largest employer, women entered production and maintenance jobs in three distinct periods: during World War II, when women were hired because of a shortage of male labour; during the mid-1970s, once the legislative prohibition against women in mining was ended; and during the early 1990s, when office and technical workers were offered production and maintenance jobs as an alternative to layoff. In the first two periods, women were actually hired from outside the company for production and maintenance work; in the third, however, women who moved to production and maintenance jobs were already employed at Inco but their original white-collar jobs had disappeared in company restructuring.

In the early years of Inco, women were not employed in production because Ontario mining legislation had since 1890 prohibited the employment of women in mines. The original legislation[3] provided for a complete prohibition but amendments in 1912 and 1930 allowed women in mining only if they were working in a "technical, clerical or domestic capacity." Excluding women from mining was of little consequence to the industry during the first part of the twentieth century, because there was no shortage of male workers.

But the situation changed dramatically early in World War II, when the supply of male labour dropped and demand for nickel increased because of its importance in military and industrial uses. Not only was nickel an essential war material, but the Sudbury region had a virtual monopoly on nickel production: "about 90 percent of the world's nickel originated in district mines, mostly Inco's."[4] Average Canadian production of nickel between 1940 and 1944 was more than 274 million pounds, almost 20 percent above the prewar peak. To achieve this level of production, Inco needed workers, and this led to federal government action to override the provincial legislation barring women from mining production. Using its powers under the War Measures Act, the Dominion Cabinet issued an order-in-council on 13 August 1942 allowing Inco to employ women in its surface operations in Sudbury.[5]

Within two weeks, 17 women from Sudbury and Copper Cliff had been hired to work in the Copper Cliff smelter, the first women in Ontario to work in mining production.[6] According to the regulations established for female workers, they were restricted to surface operations, had to be at least 18 years of age, and were to work not more than 48 hours a week, with "a qualified matron or attendant" on duty during the night shift and during "all shifts with more than 12 women workers." Their pay was "to be fixed in accordance with rulings of the National War Labour Board which [had] recently advocated the principle of equal pay for equal work."[7]

Over the course of the war, Inco hired over 1,400 women in production and maintenance jobs.[8] These women, comprising just under 15 percent of the average wartime hourly workforce, started out as sweepers or general labourers, but

Women workers at Inco's Garson Mine, 1943. Back row from left: Fern Dwenell, Ellen Portelly, unknown, Isobel Hofbauer, Ruth McGee, unknown, Cora Hyde, Florence Daust. In front from left, Ruby Carr, unknown, Bea Cull, unknown.

they went on to do a variety of surface jobs, including "soldering cables on batteries, operating ore distributors, repairing cell flotation equipment, piloting ore trains, operating heavy moulding machines, and working on lathes."[9] They earned about 60 cents an hour, considered a good wage for women in the 1940s. For most of this time, the workforce was not unionized but in February 1944, following a certification vote the previous December, Local 598 of Mine Mill (the International Union of Mine, Mill and Smelter Workers) became the bargaining unit for Inco workers. Women workers joined the union – indeed, some had helped organize it.[10] The first contract did not increase wages, which were frozen by wartime regulations, but the union made "major gains ... in terms of working conditions and union recognition."[11]

Although the women worked well at their jobs, it was generally understood that employing women was strictly a response to the wartime labour shortage and that they would have to leave Inco and "return to their natural jobs"[12] when the war ended and male workers returned home. In November 1945, the Cabinet rescinded its order-in-council, arguing that "the supply of male labour now becoming available renders the continued use of women ... unnecessary."[13] By 31 December 1945, only 62 women were still working in production and maintenance jobs, and they were soon laid off.[14]

The end of war saw the end of women's employment in production and maintenance and a return to lower, peacetime levels of nickel production.[15] To the extent that women could work in the mining industry, they were still limited to working in a "technical, clerical or domestic capacity." A further legislative amendment in 1948 added "or such other capacity that requires the exercise of normal feminine skill or dexterity but does not involve strenuous physical effort."[16] The wartime experience was not soon repeated.

In general, from 1941 to 1971, the trend of production and employment at Inco was upward. In the first part of the period, the expansion was war-related. Once World War II was over, Inco shared in the postwar expansion of the civilian economy and also increased production to keep up with military demand, particularly from the United States' involvement in the Korean War and later the Vietnam War. Employment rose and fell, but there was a long-term increase from an average of 11,500 workers during the 1940s (mostly men, but about 15 percent women during 1942 to 1945) to about 13,000 in the 1950s and about 15,000 in the 1960s.

Although this was a period of increase in employment, it was also a period of rapid capitalization: "in the period 1948–73, the dollar value of Canadian mineral productions grew almost eightfold, while the number of persons employed increased only 25 percent."[17] By the 1970s, capitalization continued to increase, but employment did not. The historic peak for the Inco workforce – 18,966 hourly workers – was reached in 1971. In the mid-1970s, levels of employment rose and fell, but by 1977, mining in Sudbury entered a period of absolute employment decline. By 1994, the number of hourly rated workers had dropped by 75 percent to 4,780.[18]

The decline in employment at Inco is marked by several sharp drops, indicating significant layoffs and, more recently, early retirement offers (see Figure 1). When the company wanted to step up production, it recalled laid-off workers and, occasionally, when the number recalled was not enough, Inco hired new groups of workers, as in 1974 and 1975.

It was during this period – a temporary expansion in the long-term trend of employment decline – that the first women to work in production and maintenance jobs since World War II were hired.[19] A number of factors helped set the stage for this decision, including the general pattern of social change affecting the role of women, the dramatic increase in female labour force participation, and a vigorous women's movement with its demands for an end to discrimination against women and for policies of affirmative action. Public policy reflected and influenced these changes, including the appointment of the federal Royal Commission on the Status of Women, which recommended extensive changes to legislation and policy in its 1970 report. In the case of mining, a provincially regulated industry, the 1970 change to the Ontario Mining Act[20] eliminated the prohibition against women in surface jobs, but the prohibition against underground work remained on the statute books until 1978.[21]

During 1974, there was a labour shortage in mining generally,[22] but no such shortage existed in Sudbury. In a front-page article in the Sudbury Star in

Figure 1. Decline in Employment at Inco for Hourly Rated Workers, 1970-1994

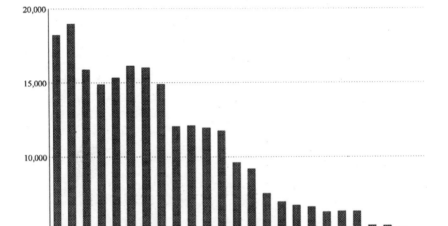

January 1974, Inco public affairs director Don Hoskins, replying to a question about women in production jobs, was quoted as saying that the company did not have women in such jobs "simply because no women have applied."[23] Several months later, Inco issued a press release indicating its willingness to hire women in production and maintenance, and the story was given considerable attention in the local print and broadcast media. Response to the news "was immediate [and] overwhelming," and Sudbury women began to apply for hourly rated jobs.[24] Beginning at the end of May 1974, with three women recruited for the newly opened nickel refinery, a total of 57 women were hired in 1974. In its operational report for 1974, Inco gave indications that it intended to continue hiring women; in the mining and smelting division "new facilities ... [were] being planned" to accommodate an increase in the number of women workers.[25] By October 1976, 100 women had been hired to work in a number of surface operations. As with women during World War II, they started as general labourers, usually in jobs involving routine maintenance – shovelling, hosing down dirty areas, unloading supplies, and sweeping. Unlike women during the war, they did not work in groups. On the contrary, it was the experience of most women that they worked only with men; even if two or more women were assigned to the same plant, they usually did not work together because of different work areas and different shifts. Women worked at eight surface sites: the nickel and copper refineries, the Copper Cliff and Levack mills, the Copper Cliff smelter, the Copper Cliff reverbs, the Frood-Stobie rockhouse, and the matte process plant.

Inco Triangle, August 1974, from the article "Ladies, First Ladies"

Like most hourly rated workers, women began as general labourers. Melody Midena (née Maki), Laurene Wiens, and Rachel Barriault were among the first women hired at Inco in May 1974.

But the general trend of employment was downward, with major layoffs in 1978 and in 1982, the year in which Inco reported its first loss in 50 years. With the 1982 layoffs, the number of hourly rated workers fell below 10,000 for the first time since the 1930s. The decline in employment has continued since the mid-1980s, with attrition and early retirement replacing layoffs as the vehicles of workforce reduction. Many of the women hired in the 1974–76 period were among those who left. Inco hired new workers occasionally during this period, but only eight of the new employees were women. However, for the first time and after some resistance, Inco did allow women to work underground. The legislative restriction against such work had been lifted in 1978, but women at Inco were limited to surface jobs until September 1992, when a woman who had made repeated efforts to move to an underground job was finally assigned to one. Eighteen women entered production and maintenance jobs in 1993–94, as a result of restructuring in the Inco technical and clerical sector.[26]

By 1994, there were 14,186 fewer workers in hourly rated jobs at Inco than there had been in 1971. Of the 4,780 who were employed, 46 (about 1 percent) were women and only 20 were 20-year veterans.

Profile of Women at Inco: The Employment Record Data

It is clear that the women hired in production and maintenance jobs between 1974 and 1976 were exceptions: by virtue of their jobs, they were an exception to the low-paid clerical and sales workers who made up the majority of the female labour force in Sudbury, and by virtue of their gender, they were an exception to the overwhelmingly male workforce at Inco. But who were these women? Were they so very different from the female labour force[27] and the Inco workforce? Why did they go to work at Inco? Were they conscious feminists working to break down gender barriers in the workplace, or were they motivated by the high wages and security that an Inco job offered?

At this stage we have only indirect evidence about the women's motivations and very little about their political views. The 20 women hired between 1974 and 1976 who are still working at Inco today are being interviewed individually as part of the larger research project, as are the 26 other women who have joined them since. All are being asked why they took the jobs, how they see themselves, and how they would characterize their work experience. But the 20-year veterans are very much the minority among the group of women hired in the 1974–76 period. Four times as many – 80 women – no longer work at Inco. It is these women who are the focus of this chapter. Our analysis is largely based on data drawn from the employment records of 72 of them.[28] First, we describe the group in terms of age, education, former occupation, marital status, and language. Second, we turn to work-related issues: length of time worked, layoff, and type of exit.

Age. Conventional wisdom suggests that it is young, single women, often taking their first job, who hire on for what used to be called non-traditional work. However, evidence from the 72 women who exited is that these women ranged in age from 18 to 46 at the time they were hired, with an average age of 28.

Education. Of the exit group, 13 had a grade school education and 37 had some high school (Grade 9, 10, or 11). A further 15 had completed high school (Grade 12 or 13), and 5 had some postsecondary education.

These data illustrate the rising educational requirements in Canadian industry (and perhaps also the general tendency of females not to leave school as early as some males). Between 1951 and 1971, the percentage of men in mining with less than a Grade 9 education dropped from 65 percent to 39 percent; there was a similar drop, from 54 percent to 33 percent for men in mining-related manufacturing.[29] In contrast, only 19 percent of the women in the

Inco Triangle, December 1976, from the article "Lunchpail Ladies ... here to stay!"

Debbie McLaughlin, process labourer, measures the level of feed in a surge bin at the Fluid Bed Roasters Building, Copper Cliff Smelter, Inco.

exit group had less than Grade 9. A total of 72 percent of women in the exit group had some (or had completed) high school, compared to 50 percent of men in mining in 1971 and 56 percent of men in mining-related manufacturing. About 11 percent of men in mining in 1971 had more than high school education, compared to 7 percent of the women hired in the mid-1970s. Apart from the small postsecondary group, the women hired in the mid-1970s were better educated than the average male workers. However, the data are not strictly comparable, because the data for men include all male workers, not only those newly hired.

Former occupation. All but one of the exiting women had worked at other jobs before joining Inco, but their previous jobs were not always typical of the Sudbury female labour force. One in five had worked in male-dominated occupations (n=14) before being hired at Inco; these included labourers, loggers, and factory assembly line workers. For the remaining women with previous job experience (n=55), the single most common occupation (n=14) was waitress in a restaurant or bar. (Normally this is considered as a service occupation, but it is presented separately here because of its size.) It has been suggested that working as a bar waitress was good preparation for working in a male-dominated workplace like Inco, because the women were accustomed to dealing with men, had worked with "all kinds," and had already developed coping skills that would enable them to deal with on-the-job problems.[30] Three other occupational groups were represented: sales (n=16), clerical (n=13), and other service (n=12).

There is little doubt that better pay was one of the factors attracting women to production and maintenance jobs at Inco. Table 2 provides comparative average wage data for the jobs these women left when they were hired at Inco. For those who worked in female-dominated occupations, average wages ranged from $2.25 to $2.50 per hour. Women who worked in male-dominated occupations received somewhat higher wages, $2.50 to $3.50 per hour. However, all stood to gain by going to work for Inco and becoming members of Local 6500 of the Steelworkers, covered by a collective agreement in which the lowest rate, for process labourers, was $3.99 an hour.

Table 2. Average Wage Comparison, October 1974

Female-Dominated Occupations		Male-Dominated Occupations		Principal Inco Occupations	
Occupation	Hourly Rate	Occupation	Hourly Rate	Occupation	Hourly Rate
Secretary	$2.50	Construction Labourer	$3.50	Process Labourer	$3.99
Waitress	$2.25	Sawmill Worker	$2.75	Mining Labourer	$4.16
Sales Clerk	$2.39	Truck Driver	$2.50	Miner	$4.74

Source: Wage Rate Survey, 10 October 1974, Regional Municipality of Sudbury, Community Profile, 1975, 11-17

Marital status. We have suggested that women went to work at Inco because of the wages they could earn. The importance of their earning power is underscored by the fact that almost 60 percent of the women (n=43) supported themselves on their own, either as single women (n=23) or separated, divorced, or widowed (n=20).[31] The remainder were married or lived with a partner (n=29).

It is more difficult to give an accurate picture of the number of women who had children. Records indicate that some unattached women named children as beneficiaries, which provides a minimum estimate. Others, who were married or had partners, may have had children but they were not necessarily mentioned on their records. In any case, employment records indicate that 24 of the 72 women had children and of these, one had five children and at least three others each had four children.

Language. In terms of language, the women were typical of the Sudbury community. All of them spoke English, which was the language of work at Inco; there was little explicit recognition of other languages, even though a third of the Sudbury population speaks French as its first language and there are large Finnish, Italian, and Ukrainian communities. The employment records do not always make reference to language; however, in more than a third (n=26) it was noted that the employee spoke French, and for a few (n=3), it was noted that the employee spoke Finnish. No further data are available on the ethnic or racial composition of the group, though given the population of Sudbury it would not be surprising to find that some women had Aboriginal heritage.

Work-Related Issues

We have indirect evidence, based on wage surveys, that women entered the Inco workforce because they could earn better wages. In addition to the question of entry, however, we are interested in their on-the-job experience. From employment records, we examine three issues: how long women worked, the incidence of layoff, and the type of exit. We begin with a comparison of those who are still employed with those who have exited (see Table 3). The average length of time worked for those who exited (n=78) is 4.35 years compared to an average of 19.16 years for those still employed (n=20).[32] This contrast is only to be expected because, by definition, those who exited did not work as long as those who stayed. It is worth noting that the figure for those who have exited is made up of two distinct parts: those who quit (n=38) after having worked an average of 1.69 years, and those who exited involuntarily (n=33), who worked 6.17 years on average.[33]

Table 3. Employment Status and Type of Exit

VARIABLE	VALUE	LENGTH OF TIME WORKED (yrs)	N	Total N
Employment Status	Still Employed	19.16	20	98 (2)*
	Exited	4.35	78	
	Quit	1.69	38	71 (7)*
	Involuntary	6.17	33	

* Number of missing cases in brackets.

Average length of time worked varies with variations in education, former occupation, age, marital status, and language, though not all the variations are sizeable. Education appears to be of considerable importance (see Table 4).

Among those who exited, there is an inverse relationship between education and length of work, with those with the least education staying the longest (average=5.68 years) and those with some postsecondary education the shortest (average=1.91 years). This inverse relationship holds true even if we examine those who quit separately from those who exited involuntarily. For both subgroups, those with the least education stayed the longest.

Table 4. Comparative Average Length of Time Worked

VARIABLE	VALUE	AVERAGE LENGTH OF TIME WORKED (yrs)	N	Total N
Education	Primary	5.68	13	70
	Grade 9, 10, 11	4.99	37	
	Grade 12, 13	2.37	15	
	Postsecondary	1.91	5	
Age	under 21	3.20	15	72
	21 to 29	4.13	27	
	30 to 39	4.89	21	
	40 to 49	5.64	9	

Average length of time worked also varies with age. In general, the older the woman was at the time of hiring, the longer she was likely to work. This generalization applies to the exiting women as a whole and to the main subgroups (those who quit and those who exited involuntarily). There may be some element of maturation involved; that is, older workers, with more experience of working and of life itself, may be less restless and more motivated to stay with a good paying, unionized job or, to put it less positively, they may be more fearful of insecurity and less confident about finding another job. But the age effect may be less the influence of age per se than of age-related elements such as education.

Although our findings are preliminary, it is likely that factors affecting worker mobility are important for understanding variations in the average length of time worked. Age and education may influence length of work because of their contribution to mobility (or lack of it). When we examined these variables in combination, the two largest groups that emerged are in a sense the poles of the mobility argument. One group is young (between 18 and 24) and had finished high school or had some postsecondary education. These women (n=14) worked an average of 2.04 years, and 11 of them quit. Their youth and education gave them greater mobility, and they took advantage of it to leave their jobs at Inco. The second group is the opposite: they were older, with an average age of 36, and had less education (the two best educated in the group had Grade 11, and eight had Grade 9 or less). These women (n=14) worked an average of 6.73 years, and more of them were laid off than quit. For them, education and age combined to restrict their mobility. They had good paying jobs at Inco and they tended to stay with them. Some of this group did quit (n=5) and it would be worth exploring the extent to which age-related or service-related health factors were responsible.

Two major layoffs occurred during the period under consideration, one in 1978 and another in 1982. In 1978, workers were laid off as of 13 February. At this time, one-third (n=23) of the 69 women still employed out of the original 100 were among the workers laid off, while the other two-thirds had enough seniority to avoid the layoff. Of the 23, 7 did not return from layoff, while the remaining 16 were recalled during the summer of 1979.

The second layoff was in 1982. Most Inco workers were off the job from 31 May 1982 until 4 April 1983, first for a month-long strike, then an eight-month shutdown, and finally the layoff. Twenty-one women were laid off in this group, including 8 who had escaped the 1978 layoff and 13 who were being laid off for the second time. By the time recall rights for this group expired in December 1986, only 2 of the 21 had been recalled. Ultimately, lay-off was the end of employment in production and maintenance jobs for 26 of the 31 women who experienced layoff.

The group of women we are discussing is defined by one particular characteristic: exit. Eighty of the original 100 women hired have exited, with quitting the most common type of exit (n=38). Although the quit rate is lower now, as jobs have become scarcer and more insecure, turnover in production and maintenance jobs has traditionally been high in the mining industry. Wallace Clement, referring to a study done by the Mining Association of Canada, notes that the turnover among unskilled labour in Canadian mining in 1973 was 127.8 percent and among skilled miners it was 49.8 percent.[34] Among the women at Inco who quit, company records note "reason for leaving" in 18 cases: five left town, five quit for health reasons, three returned to school, three went to other jobs, and two did not return to work after their maternity leave.

Involuntary exit, the alternative to quitting, accounts for 33 exits. Layoff (n=26) is the most important component, followed by death or disability (n=6).This latter group includes the only woman killed on the job. One woman was fired, and she is also included in the involuntary exits. As might be expected, women who exited involuntarily worked longer (average = 6.17 years) than those who quit (average = 1.69).

To review the employment status of the original 100 women hired, 20 are still employed, 38 quit, 33 are involuntary exits, and the remaining 9 are exits of unknown type. It will be useful to compare these data with turnover data for the general Inco workforce to see if the pattern for men is similar. In view of the high turnover cited by Clement, and given that 53 percent of the women hired either are still on the job or left involuntarily, it is possible that these women have a lower turnover rate than their male co-workers.

Summary Comments

Our research focusing on women in production and maintenance jobs at Inco underscores perhaps the most fundamental of all points about gender discrimination in the workplace: it is gender itself that is used to keep women out of jobs. While there are disagreements about the true extent of gender discrimination underlying "traditional hiring practices," there can be no doubt in the case of women and mining. Women were excluded from the mining industry as a matter of law beginning in 1890, a prohibition that remained in place for surface jobs until 1970 and for underground jobs until 1978. Federal order lifted this prohibition during World War II: 1,400 women were hired between 1942 and 1945 for production and maintenance jobs. When the legislation was finally changed, Inco took the historic step of hiring women in production and maintenance jobs. Mining is an important industry in some regions of Canada, and the entry of women has contributed to breaking down gender barriers in the workplace.

This chapter profiles 72 working women hired between 1974 and 1990 in blue-collar jobs at Inco who had all left by 1994. In going to work in production and maintenance, they were leaving the minimum-wage, non-unionized jobs available to women and moving into the well-paid jobs that had in the past been available only to men. Although there is still much to be learned about the women themselves (as opposed to what the employment records can tell us) and about their experience, the data we have here suggest important lines of inquiry. In particular, although there may have been other motives as well, the chance to earn high wages was an important factor in women's entry into Inco production and maintenance jobs, especially for the majority of women who were on their own. We have suggested that factors related to women's mobility – in particular, education and age – may be important for understanding length of time worked. In further research, consideration should be given to characteristics of the worksite (particularly workplace culture and relations of authority) and to women's physical and psychological resilience in an often-harsh physical environment and a male-dominated workforce. Also, despite a popular view that women "can't hack it doing men's work," the opposite conclusion – that women have a lower turnover rate than men – is worth exploring, based on the evidence here.

Since the 1970s, mining in Sudbury has been an industry in absolute as well as relative employment decline. This decline makes it more difficult for women to enter the industry, especially if there is no policy of employment renewal of a rapidly aging workforce. To the extent that there are more women now than a decade ago, most of the increase is due to the restructuring of the workplace, which involved the transfer of women from office and technical jobs that were being eliminated to production and maintenance work. For the future, the hiring policies that Inco pursues in renewing its workforce will be critical in determining whether women will ever obtain an equitable share of employment in mining. This is especially so given the absence of any government commitment to supporting full employment and, in Ontario, the current climate of official hostility to employment equity.

12

Women's Work Is (Almost) Never Done … (By Anyone Else)

Elaine Porter and Carol Kauppi

Families in Northern Ontario and throughout Canada are increasingly dependent on the incomes of both husbands and wives. Most of these families were dual-income, or the wife was the sole income earner.[1] According to Statistics Canada data, 64 percent of all married women in 1992 were in the labour force compared with 49 percent in 1981. The only published report to date of the workforce participation of Northern Ontario women shows a comparable number were employed: 60 percent of English-speaking wives and 56 percent of those who spoke French were in the labour force in 1991.[2]

Given that wives have added to their work day by assuming work roles outside the family, equity principles would dictate that husbands in dual-income families become more involved in household labour. By 1981, in fact, about three-quarters of all Canadians agreed that husbands should share in housework.[3]

The reality, however, is much different. Even by 1992, Statistics Canada survey data showed the sharing to be modest at best. Wives who had at least one child under five years of age and who were in the paid labour force spent 2.4 hours per day in domestic work and 2.1 hours in primary childcare, while their husbands spent 1.4 and .8 hours, respectively, in these activities. This discrepancy occurred despite the fact that working wives with children under five have reduced their absolute number of hours spent in domestic labour. Wives who were not in the labour force put in an average of 3.9 hours of domestic labour per day.[4] It seems that wives have assumed more of the breadwinning function in the last 30 years than husbands have reciprocated in housework.

This state of affairs, while regrettable, is not surprising. Although critical to family survival, women's domestic labour has always been undervalued, as have the kinds of jobs that women have assumed in the labour force. Baker and Lero have reported that, on average, Canadian working women earn only 64 percent of the salaries of their male counterparts and even women who work full-time and full-year still make only 72 percent of the earnings of men.[5]

This chapter reports on the household labour of a diverse group of 514 wives who were employed full-time in the labour force in Northern Ontario and 204 who were employed part-time. We examined the effects of factors that have been found in other studies to increase husbands' participation in housework. These factors can be divided into those that have do with women's ideas about women's and men's roles and those grounded in the economic resources that wives bring to the struggle to equalize household responsibilities.

Benedicta Belanger Bryce cooking, Pine Street, Sudbury, c1944.

It is only since the 1970s and the path-breaking work of Ann Oakley that housework has even been defined as work and that there has been any serious academic effort to study it.[6] Domestic labour includes both the work involved in childcare and the routine household chores that women have usually done: meal preparation and clean-up, laundry, vacuuming, and grocery shopping. It also includes the less frequent, typically husband-dominated tasks of yard work, gardening, and minor car repairs. Paying bills is a task that is included in this study as an area that has not been clearly identified as belonging tradition-ally in either the wife's or the husband's domain.

The Sample and Data

The information analyzed in this study came from questionnaires answered by women and their male partners who were living in a marital or common-law relationship at the time of the study. Only women and men who were employed were eligible to participate. The data were collected by students enrolled in a university-level correspondence course in the Sociology of the Family at Laurentian University in 1992 or 1993. Each student collected data from four couples known to them. The students informed potential respondents of the purpose and voluntary nature of the study and provided a separate, self-administered questionnaire to each spouse.

The husband and wife were instructed to complete the questionnaires individually and then to seal them in envelopes that were provided to ensure confidentiality. The completed questionnaires were returned to the researchers at the university. A screening question, which asked whether the individual had answered the questionnaire previously, ensured that we did not receive duplicates.

Seven hundred and eighteen Northern Ontario women and their partners participated. The majority of the women (80 percent) were living in the four major cities in Northeastern Ontario (that is, Sudbury, 42 percent; Sault Ste. Marie, 11 percent; North Bay, 11 percent; and Timmins, 16 percent). The other participants were scattered in smaller communities primarily in Northeastern Ontario, such as Chapleau, Elliot Lake, Wikwemikong, Sturgeon Falls, Kirkland Lake, Sundridge, Kapuskasing, and Wawa. The population size of these communities ranged from 100 to 156,000. Only a small minority of the study participants (10 percent) lived in rural areas with 1,000 or fewer residents.

In terms of ethnicity, a majority of the women reported that they were of British origin or simply described themselves as English Canadians (53 percent). Just over one-quarter of the women were French Canadians (26 percent) and a smaller proportion reported an ethnic origin from a European country other than the United Kingdom or France (18 percent). Only 3 percent of the sample indicated that they were members of a visible minority group, such as Native Canadians, Chinese, or Caribbeans.

The age range of the participants was 21 to 76, with the average age being 42. Nearly all the women (96 percent) had one or more children, but some of these children were no longer living with their parents. The ages of their children ranged between one month and 42 years, with 17 percent having preschool children, 41 percent having primary school-aged children and 36 percent having adolescent children. An additional 7 percent of these women had adult children. Approximately one-half of the women reported that they required some form of daycare (either formal or informal) for their children.

Because educational attainment is linked to labour force participation, those women who volunteered to complete the questionnaires tended to be more highly educated than is true for the Northern Ontario population as a whole. Sixty-five percent of the sample had gone beyond high school compared with only 44 percent of women in Ontario as a whole. In addition, the study participants were much more likely to have university degrees (26 percent) than were Ontario residents as a whole (13 percent) or Northern Ontario residents (e.g., 9 percent in Sudbury).[7]

Laurie McGauley and Miners' Mothers' Day collection

Young northern children, 1920s or 1930s.

Extent of Sharing of Domestic Labour

The 718 women who were studied were asked about the extent to which they participated in 12 domestic tasks according to the following categories: (1) wife always; (2) wife mostly; (3) husband and wife; (4) husband mostly; (5) husband always. Husbands also responded to the same questions. Husbands' and wives' responses were grouped together and were compared so that we could see to what extent wives' estimates of their participation in domestic labour is verified by their husbands. We have combined categories 1 and 2 in Table 1 so that the comparisons are in terms of the percentage of husbands and wives who reported that the task was performed always or mostly by wives.

As Table 1 shows, both wives' and husbands' responses indicate that wives who participated in the labour force still did the lionesses' share of traditional female household tasks. Wives were much more likely than their husbands to cook the meals and do the laundry. Sixty-six percent of wives reported that they did the cooking and 80 percent did the laundry largely unaided. Although husbands tended to see wives as slightly less involved in performing these tasks than their wives reported, the husbands' responses generally confirmed the pattern of involvement that the wives reported. In those tasks in which the wives' participation was lower, the predominant pattern was shared work rather than one in which husbands were exclusive task performers. The only area of housework in which both husbands' and wives' responses showed that there was a rough equality was in the task of grocery shopping.

Table 1. Percentage of Husbands and Wives Reporting that Wives Exclusively or Predominantly Perform Domestic Labour

There was virtual consensus between husbands' and wives' responses that wives did not do many of the minor car repairs or much of the yard work.

Household Tasks	Husbands' Reports %	Wives' Reports %
Cooking Meals	61	66
After-meal Clean-up	44	55
Grocery Shopping	53	56
Laundry	74	79
Vacuuming	52	61
Daily Care of Children	44	48
Taking Children to Medical/Dental Appointments	56	62
Chauffeuring Children	19	27
Paying Bills	37	44
Minor Car Repairs	3	3
Gardening	27	32
Yard Work (mowing, shovelling)	4	6
Number of Participants	718	718

These tasks still tended to be in the husband's domain. The types of household tasks that husbands have performed traditionally such as car repair and yard work are less routinized and thus less frequent, as well as more discretionary than wives' tasks such as daily meal preparation and cleaning.

In the area of childcare it appears that, while most wives still did more of the work, there was more sharing here than in housework chores done by wives. Other studies show a similar tendency for husbands to move into the area of childcare.[8] Husbands in Northern Ontario appear to specialize in chauffeuring children, in that both husbands and wives report that about 80 percent of husbands performed this task. About 60 percent of wives routinely took their children to medical and dental appointments. Husbands and wives reported almost splitting the daily caretaking of children, although we would need to know more about the types of tasks each does in order to assess how equally the workload in this area was shared.

Responses on the performance of the other areas of housework that were included (that is, gardening and paying bills) indicated that these are tasks for which there was no clear pattern of performance by either wives or husbands. Both of these tasks were more likely to be shared. Only 32 percent of wives reported that they did the gardening largely by themselves. Nearly half of the wives took the lead in paying bills.

Comparisons Between Wives Working Part-Time and Full-Time

The next set of analyses compares the levels of housework between wives who were self-defined as working full-time and part-time.[9] The proportions of our sample of northern women who were employed full- and part-time were very similar to the patterns for Canadian women as a whole. The majority of the northern women in the sample were employed full-time (72 percent), while just over one-quarter were employed part-time (28 percent). Statistics Canada has reported that 26 percent of Canadian women worked part-time in 1993.[10]

Working part-time represents both an accommodation that women make for family roles and a result of labour market demand. Of Canadian women married and with children under age 16, 29 percent reported that they worked part-time for reasons of family responsibility, 44 percent because part-time work was their preference. Twenty-five percent could not find full-time work and the remaining 2 percent gave a variety of other reasons such as an illness or disability.[11]

As Table 2 shows, we found that across all but two domestic tasks, a larger proportion of wives who worked part-time did more of the housework than those who worked full-time. One exception is doing laundry; no matter what the women's work level, in most families the wife did almost all of it. About the same proportion of wives employed full-time and part-time, about 45 percent, had responsibility for paying bills.

The heavier workload at home of wives employed part-time compared with those who worked full-time in the labour force is not unexpected; differences were also reported in other studies.[12] As a strategy for adjusting to the dual pulls of job and family, part-time paid labour appears to leave wives with a considerable burden of household labour.

Table 2. Percentages of Women Working Full-Time and Part-Time Who Performed Domestic Labour Largely by Themselves

Household Tasks	Full-time %	Part-time %	SIGNIFICANT DIFFERENCES[a]
Cooking Meals	58	83	YES
After-meal Clean-up	53	63	YES
Grocery Shopping	53	67	YES
Laundry	77	83	NO
Vacuuming	57	70	YES
Daily Care of Children	41	59	YES
Taking Children to Medical/Dental Appointments	55	75	YES
Chauffeuring Children	25	31	NO
Paying Bills	45	44	NO
Minor Car Repairs	4	3	NO
Gardening	31	38	YES
Yard Work (mowing, shovelling)	5	7	NO
Number of Participants	473	194	667

[a] Following the conventional practice, we reported as significant any relationship that attained a .05 level of significance or beyond. This means that there is only a 5 percent probability that this difference could occur by chance.

Differences Among Full-time Working Wives

As a group, wives employed full-time still performed a disproportionate share of the household work compared with their husbands. However, the lower percentages of wives working full-time compared with those working part-time who had nearly exclusive involvement in household tasks suggests that there is considerable variation among them in how much housework they do by themselves. To investigate the sources of this variability, we examine four variables that have been found in other studies to reduce the proportion of housework wives perform relative to husbands.[13]

Table 3 shows how the full-time working wives are distributed across the characteristics of age, age of children, percentage contribution of family income, and beliefs about who has the obligation to support the family economically. The greatest percentage of full-time working women (55 percent) were of the baby boom generation, those born between the end of World War II and 1967. This is the period in which married women began to enter the labour force in significant numbers compared to those born prior to 1945.[14] The group born after 1968 has experienced the highest labour force participation rates while they had pre-school children, and those born before 1945, the least. Overall, only 17 percent of all respondents had pre-school children.

As would be expected, the women who were employed on a full-time basis contributed a larger proportion of the total family income than those working part-time. One-third of these full-time employed women provided 41 to 50 percent of the family income (compared with 13 percent of those employed part-time), and a further 29 percent provided more than half of the family income (compared with 10 percent of the part-time workers). This is somewhat higher than the the 16 percent of Canadian women who contributed to this level of family income.[15]

Table 3. Selected Characteristics of Wives Working Full-Time

CHARACTERISTICS			
Year of Birth	Before 1945	1945-1967	After 1967
	14%	55%	31%
Age of Children	Pre-school	School-age/Adult	
	17%	83%	
Percentage Contribution to Family Income	Under 50%	Over 50%	
	71%	29%	
Obligation to Support Family Economically	Husband's	Shared/Wife's	
	21%	79%	

Finally, Table 3 shows that 79 percent of women who were employed full-time rejected the idea that husbands had the sole obligation to support the family economically; in contrast, 21 percent continued to believe that husbands should have exclusive responsibility for family income.

Sources of Variation in Domestic Work by Full-Time Working Wives

The profile of full-time employed wives describes a group of women largely in their thirties and forties, with older children, making less than half of the family income, but the majority believing that they and their husbands shared an obligation to contribute to the economic situation of the family. The next and final question we address is how much of a difference these characteristics make in the amount of housework these full-time working wives perform.

Table 4 presents the results of a series of analyses of these four characteristics on the household and childcare tasks that have been in wives' traditional domain. Only relationships that are statistically significant are reported, that is, those group differences that could not have occurred by chance.

The one characteristic most consistently related to domestic work was the belief about the breadwinner role. Although most full-time employed wives rejected the breadwinner ideology (that is, the view that men are responsibile for earning income in the family), those who did endorse it were significantly more likely to do housework and childcare tasks unaided. The percentage of family income contributed by the wife was less effective in increasing husbands' share of housework across the range of tasks studied. Nevertheless, those wives employed full-time who contributed 50 percent or more of family income did do proportionately less cooking of meals and daily childcare. These are both onerous and time-consuming tasks.

Table 4. Effect of Selected Characteristics on Percentage of Domestic Labour[a] Performed by Women Working Full-Time

TASKS	% OF FAMILY INCOME		YEAR OF BIRTH			INCOME OBLIGATION		PRE-SCHOOL CHILDREN	
	<50	>50	Before 1945	1945-1967	After 1967	Husband	Shared/ Wife	Yes	No
Cooking Meals	63	44	74	59	49	75	53	46	60
After-meal Clean-up	--	--	--	--	--	67	43	42	56
Laundry	--	--	88	79	69	80	73	63	80
Vacuuming	--	--	68	60	48	71	53	46	60
Childcare	--	--	60	42	31	57	37	29	44
Appointments	--	--	--	--	--	67	52	--	--
Chauffeuring	--	--	27	25	25	--	--	--	--

[a] The percentages reflect the proportion of women predominantly or exclusively performing the tasks.

Both wives' ages and whether they had pre-school children were other areas of significant differences in the level of domestic work performed by wives employed full-time. A higher percentage of wives who were born prior to 1945 did more of the tasks unaided than women in the other two age groups, with husbands helping to take children to appointments and to clean up after meals. This was a linear relationship, meaning that the level of domestic work decreased progressively with ages of the women.

The involvement of husbands of full-time working wives in daily childcare, cooking, and after-meal clean-up was higher among those who had pre-school children. Husbands in families with pre-school children shared more in the overall workload of families, except that a higher percentage of wives retained their involvement in laundry relative to other tasks. The overall burden of work in a family with pre-school children increases so that both husbands and wives in these families may be putting more hours into domestic labour compared to those with school-age and older children. Our cross-sectional data cannot confirm whether the higher levels of participation in housework by the husbands of women with pre-school children will be sustained once the children are school-aged. However, the one interpretation of our data is that a more equitable division of labour could be emerging among families in the post-baby boom generation.

Since a woman's age and having pre-school children are interrelated, both these variables were operating together to affect the level of domestic work performed. In other words, the fact that those who were younger were less likely to have exclusive performance of housework and childcare could have been a consequence of a workload that was increased more by having pre-school children than by the age of the woman. However, since those women born between 1945 and 1967 had also reduced their level of exclusive participation in tasks relative to those in the group born before 1945, it seems likely that age contributes its own effect.

What stands out as a very important factor in amount of housework performed – bridging both part-time and full-time workers – is the extent to which the breadwinner ideology is endorsed. For full-time employed women, those who did not view husbands as having an obligation to be the prime income-earners in the family substantially reduced their exclusive involvement in after-meal clean-up and childcare (below the 50 percent level). That is, when wives believed in the importance of sharing responsibility for bringing in income, wives also appear to have expected more sharing of housework with husbands.

Part-time employed wives were much more likely than those employed full-time to endorse a breadwinner ideology: 55 percent of those employed part-time endorsed it versus only 21 percent of those employed full-time. We would need to know more about their other beliefs about women's roles. Pupo found that part-time working women were not necessarily traditional in orientation towards women's employment. They thought that working was appropriate for mothers.[16] Our study findings, however, indicate that married women in Northern Ontario who work need to believe in the importance of their economic contribution as well, whether they work full- or part-time.

We need to interpret the findings on ideology in conjunction with those on the income contribution of the wife. The percentage of income that wives contributed to the family economy turned out to be relatively ineffective in reducing the domestic workload of full-time employed women. The stronger findings on the beliefs about the importance of a woman's income indicate that it is not income alone that is important but how that income is viewed. If wives do not believe that their income makes a difference to the economic situation of their family, they may be less likely to exert pressure on their husbands to alter the division of labour on the household tasks that have been women's work.

We checked to see whether those who were younger and with pre-school children also had the most egalitarian beliefs about the importance of their income contributions. We found that they did not. This means that wives' ideas about the breadwinner role have effects on their involvement in housework and childcare that are separate from the effects of being younger and having pre-school children. Our results showed, then, that the wife's burden of housework was decreased and the husband's contribution increased by three factors: the woman being younger, having pre-school children, or earning 50 percent or more of the family income.

The importance of beliefs is underlined by one follow-up analysis we performed. We looked at the proportion of women performing the cooking, the one task in which both income contribution and ideology reduced the amount of housework exclusively performed by full-time working wives. We found that full-time working wives who contributed more than 50 percent of family income reduced their exclusive involvement in cooking a great deal more if they believed that they and their husbands shared the responsibility for the financial support of the family. Wives whose income was significant but who endorsed the breadwinner ideology had husbands who were less involved in housework in the area of cooking.

Summary

Northern Ontario women who join the paid labour force, working either full- or part-time, take on a double day of work inside and outside the household. We found, as did Pupo (1989), that attempts to accommodate family needs and work by taking only part-time employment simply add a substantial burden of work for women. Although we did not measure the number of hours that these women worked at their jobs, we should note that they could have worked a total of 35 hours and still have qualified as part-time work. Pupo (1989) found that the typical pattern of part-time employment for women is from 8 to 35 hours per week, with an average of 21 hours.[17]

The domestic workload of full-time employed women was high, given that they work 40 hours a week or more and 60 percent of them were employed in managerial or professional occupations. Almost one-third of women contributed to more than 50 percent of the family income. However, income contribution alone was not a strong factor in reducing wives' housework or increasing their partners' help. What reduced wives' workloads – regardless of a woman's age, whether she had pre-school children, or worked full-time or part-time – was their belief that they were making an important contribution to family income.

Our findings, along with those of Ferree,[18] suggest that wives need to see themselves as co-providers of family income in order to have their husbands participate in housework. Northern Ontario women have taken on the responsibility of contributing to household income; now they need to help themselves and each other to believe that they are entitled to have their husbands do their fair share of domestic labour.

13

Successful Women Entrepreneurs in Northeastern Ontario[1]

Huguette Blanco, Rolland LeBrasseur, and K.V. Nagarajan

When you look at the number of successful business women in this community, you do have an incredible level of talent and expertise here. (D.S.)

After interviewing 22 successful women entrepreneurs in northeastern Ontario, we agree with this belief. This chapter is the story of their lives, exciting lives but also very demanding ones. First, two women speak of their experiences and share their thoughts of what it means to run a successful business. We then present the methodology for this study, describe our sample, and report and discuss our findings. We conclude with the advice that these successful women want to give to those who are or may be thinking of starting a business and with some recommendations.

Self-portrait: Elva Evans, Owner of Airport Hotel Inc. in Timmins

The entrepreneurial bug. I have just floated into most of the businesses that I have had. I got into some of them not knowing what I was doing. Usually I talk to an accountant, a bank manager, and a lawyer. And I listen to people who have been in business before. I don't always take their advice but I listen to them and I read up on things, and then I evaluate it. I have lots of good friends, but about three years after my husband died I suddenly realized that I had a brain. So I started thinking things out on my own and using my own judgement, and it worked very well for me.

My first actual business was a beauty salon. At that time I also got into the cosmetics business: Merle Norman cosmetics. And then myself and two of my girlfriends started a business called Office Overflow. Later, with one of the girls who worked with me in the beauty salon, I bought the building.

While I was in my hairdresser and cosmetics business, I started this small hotel (ten employees) in August 1989. It all started by a visit to book a dinner for my investment group. I remembered hearing about this small place in

South Porcupine. When I got there I realized that the owners were getting old and tired and sick, and only the bar downstairs was operating. I was so disappointed because the building and grounds are very beautiful. I walked away thinking, "This place needs me." I phoned a realtor whom I knew because I heard that it was for sale.

Starting up. Destiny had a great hand in it, but you also have to help it along. I got all the financial reports, which didn't look good, but I am old and wise enough to see the potential. I knew that I was a woman coming into a man's business. There were a lot of old Ukrainian, Finn, and Russian people, and I realized that I had to come in and see what they want and I can't impose my ideas on them.

I asked the advice of a good family friend in the hotel business for many years, and another friend in the hotel business as well. I sold my home and cottage and that was my down payment on the hotel. The banks would not lend me money because it is on a flood plain, so I talked the owners into holding the mortgage. The bank did give me a bridge loan. There were other problems too: getting through some old wiring, remodelling the 30-year-old kitchen, and getting by the city by-laws.

Running the business. On average I work 15 to 16 hours a day, seven days a week. The cash flow from the business keeps the business going. I have passed the five-year mark for my mortgage. My goal now is to keep the building and grounds maintained and keep everything on an even keel so that I can pay my bills. I would like to expand the building but I probably won't because it will cost so much money.

I have five full-time and five part-time employees. Five are permanent positions including the chef, housekeeper, and bartender. With such a small business, everyone does everything. I tell them so when I hire them. I try to set an example myself; I will do everything except for cooking. I don't have staff meetings very often because they are on different shifts and have different problems. I try to discuss things with them on a one-to-one basis.

Networking. I belong to WIN, the Women's International Network, the Chamber of Commerce, the Hotel and Motel Association, and James Bay Frontiers. I belong to an investment group of 15 members. I feel good knowing these people and it is good to get away from my business and air my problems and listen to theirs. If I am a bit down, they perk me up. WIN has great business discussions and we always have a speaker and we have discussions about our businesses. And there's one couple who have been very supportive.

Getting satisfaction from a bit of everything in the north. My banker thinks that I put too much money back into the business. Most people think that it is awesome. I am pretty pleased with myself and have an idea to expand it, but not at this time. I am getting a bit of everything. I like the fact that it is keeping me busy and healthy. It gives me people to associate with and it gives me a sense of being proud.

I love the north and have been here since I was four years old. It has its challenges, like small numbers of people, and you have to cater to them. I think that Northern Ontario has caring, pioneering people. You have to be able to cope with these kinds of people.

Self-portrait: Marie Bouffard of Thermo Matrix Inc., Elliot Lake

Creating opportunities. My primary business right now is a manufacturing facility (19 employees) dealing with heating, ventilation, and air-conditioning, set up in October 1994. This is my third venture. The first one was a contracting service company in office services/management. It started in March 1987 and closed this year [1995] because of time constraints and market changes. The second venture, which is still functioning, started in March 1991: a sales, service, and contracting company in the heating, ventilation, air-conditioning, and commercial refrigeration industry.

We spent in excess of $100,000 to get a business proposal together. I went to my team of lawyers, an independent financial consultant, my chartered accountant, and my industry network. I hired a professional marketing company and two private sector manufacturing consultants. With personal money as well as reserves in the two other companies, we purchased a building and bought the inventory. I used the existing staff from my other two companies. I brought my marketing skills to the business and was trying to do two hours' worth of work in one hour. I was determined (and still am) to triple the size of the business.

My grandparents are entrepreneurs, and I have picked up courses here and there. But my biggest educator has been the written word (magazines and credible textbooks). I took one year of accounting at college after Grade 13 and a variety of industry-related certificates.

I used to work for the municipal government. I thought that starting my own business would give me more time to raise my family (I now work 60 hours a week).

Running the business – 50/50 with people. We have 19 employees including my son: 17 full-time and 2 part-time. All of them are permanent. Hiring is done according to skill: set criteria, interview, test, and then a trial period. We use the job description as a working tool for dividing the work. I'm result-oriented but I'm very much aware that the key to my success is my people.

Planning involves full financial projection for 30 days as well as day-to-day planning. The entire team is involved. I do the marketing. My working partner is in charge of the technology. The administrative officer handles resources planning, and our buyer helps the accounting clerk with cash-flow projections.

Finances are an on-going problem because the cash situation changes daily. You look at priorities. You use thoughtful decision making before spending funds and you make adjustments immediately when expected cash receivables don't come through for whatever reason.

I discuss my plans with a variety of individuals: primarily my working partner, secondly my spouse, and then various contemporaries. I have struck a business/friendship relationship with an entrepreneur in Kingston, Ontario. I turn to my spouse and my family for moral support.

Performance. At this stage of development, I judge my business performance by progress. My impression is that others do the same: my employers, the bankers, and other financiers. I am "about to be" financially successful but not there yet. Personally I think I'm very successful: job and personal satisfaction, feel good about myself, more independent, more money, and more prestige and status.

Double duty for a woman. I would advise a woman starting a business to square her shoulders and toughen up. Doing double duty is a heavy workload, and it is still a man's world out there. In Northern Ontario, the benefits outweigh the negatives. With two children (8 and 12 years of age), I manage by fire-fighting. It helps to have experience at it because it's a difficult part. I adjust my schedule according to the changing needs of my children.

The stories of Elva Evans and Marie Bouffard testify to the energy, drive, and business sense that women bring to their own businesses. Having introduced these two women as individual entrepreneurs, we now proceed to describe the study and present our findings.

Methodology

This chapter is based on 22 case studies of successful women entrepreneurs. We selected them by asking local Chambers of Commerce or women's business organizations to provide the names of successful women entrepreneurs in their area. A woman was judged successful if she was doing well in her business, if she had made or was making a significant contribution to her community, and if she had shown distinction in some manner. The sample of 22 women includes 13 recipients of a business award. The sample is diverse in that it includes different types of business and locations throughout northeastern Ontario. All the women contacted agreed to participate in the study.

A case study approach was adopted to avoid what Stevenson calls the "male bias" in the entrepreneurship literature, and to follow the advice of Stevenson and Campbell to avoid the use of highly structured surveys that oversimplify the dynamic nature of entrepreneurship.[2] The case study approach allows women to define entrepreneurship in terms of their own experiences.

Data were collected through open-ended telephone interviews of 45 minutes to one hour in length using a questionnaire constructed from the general framework developed by Brush (1992) in which the women's views are central. Women were asked to provide information about their organization, the process of managing their business, and demographic and personal data.

Characteristics of Women Entrepreneurs

Demography. Demographic characteristics vary widely. Ages range from 33 to 71 years, with a mean age of 47 years and a median of 43 years. Most (68 percent) are either married or living in common-law relationships, and 73 percent have at least one child. Like women in other studies (Hisrich and Brush 1983, Honig-Haftel and Martin 1986; Neider 1987), the women in this study are highly educated with most (82 percent) having either a college or university education.[3]

Type of business. Consistent with samples of women entrepreneurs from other studies, most of the women in this study own service businesses (82 percent), including retail stores (41 percent); hotel, restaurant, or tourist facilities (18 percent); and professional, health, or financial services (23 percent). Four women chose to run manufacturing businesses in such fields as ventilation equipment, filtration products for the mining industry, or food products. They chose their business field either because they recognized a need or an opportunity (64 percent) or because they were already working in that area (36 percent).

Entrepreneurial characteristics. Half of the women have been in their current business for less than ten years, and for 68 percent this current venture is their first business venture. Several women (27 percent) own at least two businesses. For the majority of the women (55 percent), entrepreneurial blood runs in the family, having at least another immediate family member who is or was an entrepreneur.

Prior to starting their current venture, 32 percent of the women had been self-employed and 45 percent had worked for someone other than themselves. Two women had been homemakers, two had been students, and one a politician.

Start-up Phase

Motives for start-up. The reasons given for starting their business were again diverse. Only one woman identified wanting to have more time with her family as a prime motive, and only one said that she wanted to make more money; for 27 percent, frustration in their previous job was the main motivation. Many (36 percent) had entrepreneurial motivations such as seeing an opportunity, realizing an ambition, or wanting control over their lives. Others (27 percent) saw starting a business as a way to adapt to the lack of job opportunity in the north. They explained:

> I never went into business to make money. I only wanted to make a living. I wanted to create (M.F.).
>
> I never went into business to become a millionaire. It would be nice if it happened, but that was never my goal. This was an opportunity to

do something entirely different, where I could bring my skills and grow something and achieve that kind of satisfaction (D.S.).

These reasons are typical of what has been reported in the literature. In addition to traditional motives such as desire for independence, desire to put a skill to use, economic necessity, and desire to be one's own boss,[4] workplace discrimination, such as job segregation and wage inequality, and the lack of mobility in the labour force that women face also tend to draw them into starting their own businesses. Therefore a combination of job frustration (push factor) and identification of a business opportunity (pull factor) leads them to start their own businesses.[5]

Skills and weaknesses. Looking back, these women are quite confident about the skills they brought to their business. Forty-one percent estimate that they had business-related skills, and 36 percent mentioned job-specific skills such as sewing or horticulture. The other skills mentioned are common sense and formal education. Consistent with the findings of other studies, people-related skills were identified much more often than financial skills.[6]

Half of them do not think that they had any weaknesses when they started. Most (64 percent) sought help before starting, turning mainly to professionals or friends in business for advice. Although half of them said that they did some research before starting, only 18 percent reported having done a formal study. As one woman stated, "If I had to start up a business like they say to do today, I would never have done it" (M.F.).

Resources. The women in this study relied principally on personal sources of funds to start their business. Forty-five percent also looked to the banks for some of their financial needs, while only 14 percent applied for federal government funding. This confirms the findings of Brophy, Hisrich, and Brush that women tend to rely on personal resources to start their business.[7]

Problems. Half the women faced business-related problems at first, including financing, dealing with suppliers, finding customers, or staffing. Twenty-seven percent had problems of a personal nature, such as not having sufficient time, making decisions, or combining family and business responsibilities. Regulations in general interfered in four cases.

Daily Life

Schedule. The entrepreneurial life is not one of leisure. These women work long hours: 59 percent report working over 50 hours per week on average in their business, and in addition, many are actively involved with business organizations such as the Chamber of Commerce of their community and other not-for-profit organizations. It is not surprising that many comment that there are not enough hours in a day. Working such long hours cuts into the time available with their family, and many feel guilty. One woman reported, "I must admit that I feel often, not as much now as in the beginning, like I was leaving the family out of it because we were overworked for a few years.... So I have a feeling of guilt" (H.V.). But having their own business gives them the flexibility to deal with family problems such as a sick child or other emergencies.

Management style. Most of these women realize that they have to manage both the tasks to be done and their employees, and most say that they have adopted a team approach and involve their employees in the decision-making process. Only two (10 percent) seem to be highly directive and make all the decisions. This contradicts previous findings that suggest that women entrepreneurs have a hard time letting go of the decision-making process.[8]

Planning. When asked about their business planning practices, most of them mentioned that they do plan, and planning is most often related to sales and customer services; financial planning, cost projection, and cash-flow forecast were only occasionally mentioned. Planning is most often done by the woman herself, sometimes with the help of her business partner or the employees, informally, and for one month. Only three women (14 percent) plan for a year and one for a year and a half.

According to the literature, planning is of utmost importance for the small enterprise because it forces the small business owner to assess his/her strengths and weaknesses, map out resource requirements, and consequently get involved in strategic thinking.[9] The majority of the women in our sample, however, are typical of small business owners who lack the time for detailed business planning and instead have a bias for action.[10]

Networking. About two-thirds of the women responded that they have established a personal network to help in their business. Most women (80 percent) belong to a business or professional organization such as the Chamber of Commerce or a women's business group, and many are or have been directors of these organizations. Referring to the usefulness of these networks, one woman said, "Public relations is one thing that is probably very vital in our business; and then the contacts; and that is one of the things that, I think, has helped us in our business" (L.C.).

Participants in the networks include business partners and employees, professionals such as accountants, lawyers and bank managers, husbands and other family members, friends, and members of professional associations. As expected, business partners are most important for discussing plans for running the business, but their role decreases when it comes to advice or moral support. Accountants and friends in business are most important for advice, and husband and other family members for moral support. Many of these women see their husbands as advisors and morale boosters but tend not to discuss their business plans with them.

Life in the North

"We love the north. We would not want to live anywhere else. We enjoy the people of the north" (G.C., native of the north). "I like the north. I am a big city person, but basically I like Elliot Lake" (L.B., a 14-year resident of the north). Most (77 percent) percent of the women interviewed for this study have lived their whole life in the north and they love it. The women who were not born in the north have lived here for at least eight years, are well established, and also love the lifestyle in the north. Only 18 percent of the women report some drawbacks such as: "The winter could be shorter" or "C'est un peu loin des centres." This high level of satisfaction with their life in the north does not mean that they did not face difficulties as businesswomen working in the north. The main challenges mentioned revolve around the large distances to markets or to suppliers and the high cost of transportation. Many in the retail sector note that they have to keep higher levels of inventory than they would in the south, thus increasing their costs. Others note the small size of the markets, the high dependence on the resource sector, and the lack of awareness by southern legislators of the needs of the north.

They have found ways to deal with these challenges. For example, L.B., a manufacturer of filtration products, has turned to phone or direct-mail marketing to cut costs; or L.K., a distributor of medical supplies, "looks for the best buys and works with suppliers who have the best shipping policies." Several find that a focus on people is the answer: "In Northern Ontario we do business on a more personal level, so you have to build your network" (D. S.). Others, especially in the hospitality industry, are very sensitive to their customers' needs and taste changes.

A few report that their northern location gives them an advantage. Marie Bouffard thinks that she is perceived by her national customers as being "more capable and better organized, a cut above the rest" because she is successful in the north. For another, "operating in the north gives us some advantage when it comes to getting and holding on to good staff" (G.C.). None of these women would think of moving to a southern location.

Measures of Success

How do women assess the success of their business? Although a study of women entrepreneurs in Great Britain found that "making money" was on the top of the list,[11] most studies report that women entrepreneurs tend to give more importance to non-economic dimensions of their business performance. In a sample of 58 business women in three eastern metropolitan areas in the United States, Cuba et al. found that only 9 percent of the sample chose profit as a prime reason for having the business.[12] Self-satisfaction and the desire for freedom and independence were higher on the list of business performance measures.

These women entrepreneurs differentiate between business success and personal success. They measure the success of their business in several ways. Although ten women (45 percent) mentioned a financial measure of success, the majority had other measures, such as satisfying their clients or maintaining their current operations. Many had multiple non-financial criteria. When asked what they personally were getting out of their business, only three women (14 percent) talked about money and wealth. As the quotes below indicate, the majority are not in business for the money but rather for job or self-satisfaction.

What am I personally getting out of the business? No idea. I have a riot! I love it (L.C.).
Success is to be happy and like what I am doing (L.T.).
We are not wealthy, wealthy in terms of dollars, but that is not a main concern of ours. We have time together, which is a major plus (G.C.).

Seventy-five percent of the 20 respondents to this question are at least satisfied with their financial performance, and 85 percent are personally satisfied with what they are doing; but there is no correlation between level of success in the business and level of personal success. For some, the long hours and hard work take their toll. Only one woman reports that although she is financially successful she is not personally satisfied. In her own words:

I would like to be more successful.... I feel that I have succeeded in what I have attempted to do in my business. I do not feel that I have succeeded in my personal and emotional end, because too much has been put into this business and I feel that I have shortchanged other areas, family for example (S.T.).

Although they are generally satisfied with the overall performance, 68 percent would like to expand, but they see several obstacles in their way. Their two most important worries: money, mentioned by 32 percent; and lack of time or energy, also mentioned by one-third. Many women saw more than one obstacle.

Comparing Large and Small Communities

Are there significant differences between the experiences of women operating in the larger communities (North Bay, Sault Ste. Marie, and Sudbury, with populations of 60,000 or more) and those of women operating in the smaller communities (Elliot Lake, Haileybury, Kapuskasing, Hearst, Kirkland Lake, and Timmins, with populations of less than 60,000)?

Women in business in the larger centres tend to have more formal education, particularly non-business education. They are more likely to have other entrepreneurs in their family and usually are associated with others in their business venture. Women operating in the smaller centres work longer hours (more than 50 hours per week usually), are more keen to expand their business, and are less formal in their planning. Managing the dual requirements of focusing on the business and focusing on the employees, more women from the larger centres believe that they achieve a balance between the two, rather than emphasize one or the other.

Advice of Women for Women

The participants were asked to give advice to a woman starting her own business in the north. Beyond the general business concerns, they emphasized four specific themes: workload and commitment, doubt of their abilities as businesswomen, difficulties of working in "a man's world," and the value of networks. The dominant theme was the heavy workload which included commitment to the business, and the need to adapt to the situation. In the women's own words:

> There are a lot of hours, a lot of sacrifices.... You are not physically and emotionally prepared (S. T.).
>
> I think you need commitment. You have to be prepared to spend a lot of time at it and you have to be open-minded (J. N.).
>
> Make sure that you like what you're doing, and be prepared to do a lot of work (L. K.).

The second theme centred on the perceptions of insecurity and doubt that women and others have of women in business. Overcoming these challenges adds to the load, but a determined woman can succeed. Here are some quotes: "Never be apologetic. Never let the fact that you are a woman get in the way" (L.B.); and "If you have the guts to do it, if you have a good feeling, go for it. I think it's a beautiful adventure going into business" (H.V.).

Doing business in a man's world frequently was mentioned as a difficulty in setting up the business. It would seem that once the woman entrepreneur passes this initial period, the business community recognizes her success, and relations become normalized. In a similar vein, the publicizing of successful women entrepreneurs helps to lower the barriers.

> Go for it.... At times it is a man's world out there. A woman probably has to prove herself a little bit more (R.G.).
>
> Trying to convince your banker ... and being a female starting out ... establishing a line of credit (L.C.).
>
> Bankers and other professional people whom I had to deal with often didn't take women in business seriously.... I think that the publicity that women business owners have been getting has changed this perception (D.S.).

Finally, the women interviewed pointed to the importance of networks of all kinds in supporting the entrepreneur and the difficulty some women have in finding a women's network:

Make sure that you have the support of your family and make friends with the bank manager. Always be totally honest with people. Work hard (E.B.).

Get the advice of a good lawyer and a good accountant. Talk to as many people as you can....You have to build your network (D.S.).

Get a good network of other women who are in business. They're hard to find (M.M.).

Conclusions and Recommendations

The 22 women entrepreneurs included in this study are success stories in the north. They demonstrate, according to their communities, the high levels of business success that women can attain regardless of how one defines success. We can draw a number of conclusions based on their experiences:

1. These successful women entrepreneurs are happy in their northern communities. They enjoy what they are doing and feel good about themselves.

2. They expend tremendous levels of energy in their businesses and are motivated by both finances and other incentives such as independence and challenge, and measure their success accordingly.

3. Many of them have faced financing difficulties when launching their business; many continue to give financial planning a low priority.

4. These entrepreneurs have extensive personal and professional networks but do not always have access to other women entrepreneurs, especially in the smaller communities.

5. Although the world of business is still a man's world, women can break its barriers and, once in it, they operate very successfully and attain positions of leadership in professional organizations.

Based on our study, we believe that the following policy recommendations would help those governmental and private organizations wishing to promote and support women in business:

1. Stories of successful women entrepreneurs should be publicized widely to demonstrate the variety of businesses tackled by women and the rewarding experiences of the entrepreneurs. Target groups should include both current and potential women entrepreneurs as well as male audiences. In particular, a concerted effort by government and private organizations to educate children in elementary and secondary schools about the possibilities, the challenges, and the rewards of business ownership may pay great future dividends.

2. An awareness campaign of the importance of financial planning should target current and future women entrepreneurs, and be linked to training opportunities.

3. The creation of women entrepreneurship clubs should be encouraged, especially in the smaller communities. One possible avenue would be to create chapters of larger organizations such as the Women's International Network (WIN) and the Association des femmes d'affaires francophones (AFAF).

4. Given the current low level of understanding that we have of the life and times of women entrepreneurs in peripheral regions like northeastern Ontario, we recommend that researchers delve into these topics. Our sample of 22 women gave us some insights into the entrepreneurial lives of women and provided some interesting preliminary findings. We need to validate these findings by using a larger sample size and by extending the research to other peripheral regions.

14

First Nations Community Economic Corporation

Dawn Madahbee with Marge Reitsma-Street

Marge: *How are Aboriginal women involved in developing the economies of First Nations communities?*
     Dawn: Aboriginal women have a strong partnership role in developing all aspects of First Nations communities, particularly in addressing socio-economic issues. The women in our communities have focused their efforts over the past two decades on reviving our traditional values while dealing with the many social matters such as child welfare, physical abuse, alcohol and drug abuse prevention, suicide prevention, health, and general community healing. A natural progression in strengthening the health of our community is the development of our local economies. Of course, a strong economy means employment, which in turn enables families to meet their own basic needs allowing them to lead happier, healthier lives.
     Therefore, as the social programs have become more developed through the efforts of women, many Aboriginal women are now focusing their efforts towards creating the needed employment. They are actively involved in starting up new businesses, strengthening existing businesses, heading community development corporations, business consulting, working as job developers, and in many cases, taking on the formal position of community leader.
     A partnership approach between women and men is crucial to community development, particularly when our communities have limited human resources. Within many of the smaller First Nations, it takes everyone in the whole community to become mobilized on the journey towards a basic standard of self-sufficiency.

What are some of the difficulties faced by First Nations people in developing their local economies?
     There are many obstacles, though not insurmountable, that must be dealt with by our people to build our local economies. Envision yourself living in a community where half of the families do not have a wage-earner; where the job prospects are basically limited to the few positions in the local government (Band) office or in housing construction; where almost

three-quarters of the families live below the poverty line; where only 30 people out of every 100 within the working-age population have graduated from high school and half of all the people have difficulty reading or understanding the English language; where the houses are in poor condition and there are no sidewalks or paved streets; where one-quarter to nearly one-half of the houses don't have running water; where you are unable to obtain a bank loan or mortgage for your home or your small business idea or, in some cases, for basic furnishings; where the only services you might have are a convenience store or gas station; and where many of your friends, family members, and neighbours suffer from low self-esteem and serious social problems.

Also imagine that you are restricted by many real or perceived brick walls from seeking outside employment to provide for your family. There are restrictions on where you can hunt or fish, as traditional family hunting and fishing areas are no longer available. When you travel to a nearby community for employment, you know the likelihood of finding a job is extremely slim when you see few, if any, faces from your community actually employed in these outside communities.

What is the story of Waubetek?

In the early 1980s, the federal government set up the Community Futures Program, which involved empowering local people to address job needs in regions across the country that were experiencing high unemployment. Our region, which is in the Manitoulin Island District of Northern Ontario, was one of the regions facing an unemployment rate of 25 percent. Through the Community Futures Program, local boards were allowed to establish Business Development Corporations that could be capitalized with an investment fund to lend to local entrepreneurs to start new businesses to create employment. Over 200 of these corporations were established nationally.

During the first five years that the Community Futures Program was established in our region, only two or three loans were made to Aboriginal people. The population of our region is 12,000, of which 45 percent consists of the Aboriginal people from eight First Nations communities. We had only one representative on the Board of Directors, even though we represented nearly half of the area's population and the First Nations unemployment rate was over 50 percent. Part of the problem in attempting to meet the needs of Aboriginal entrepreneurs was that collateral could not be secured for a loan on property situated on an Indian Reserve (First Nations territory). The problem is a jurisdictional issue as, in accordance with the Indian Act, all property on a reserve is held in common by all members of that community. Banks are reluctant to lend on-reserve as they cannot take on-reserve property as security on the loan.

With the lack of progress in addressing the needs of First Nations communities, our leadership came together to support the establishment of a separate Community Futures organization, which would work towards addressing the unique and different needs of the First Nations. One consideration or advantage to having a separate, Aboriginal-exclusive organization was that Aboriginals can take on-reserve property as collateral or loan security from each other, as property on reserve is held in common by the community. Therefore, an Aboriginal organization could, in effect, hold security for loans on the reserve. The First Nations leadership provided their support and co-operation to this new Aboriginal-exclusive organization by allowing Waubetek to take security on-reserve for the conduct of business and lending to Aboriginal business people. The federal government saw the validity of this proposal, and in August 1989 approved the establishment of the Waubetek Business Development Corporation. Waubetek is now one of four Aboriginal-exclusive corporations in Ontario among the 54 federally funded ones operating in the province. "Waubetek," by the way, means "the future" or "what is coming" in the Ojibwe language.

The establishment of Waubetek represented hope for our people, as now we had a significant say in the development of our communities as well as the financial means to assist our Aboriginal entrepreneurs in working towards achieving their dreams. We believe we are now on the road to creating healthier, prosperous communities.

What was it like in the beginning?

Scary. Here we were, approved to deliver this program where we could actually establish a bank for our people, and no one among us had any banking or lending experience. It was an awesome responsibility, but we had an excellent group of people from each of the seven (now eight) First Nations reserves to work at putting it all together. One of the areas about which everyone was most adamant was that our board of directors and staff be comprised of people from our own communities – Aboriginal people.

During this initial phase, the community representatives hired me to do the legwork in establishing the organization. It was something that I was very interested in as I believed strongly in the concept. I had had experience in setting up programs and services for First Nations in the past through consulting work with the First Nations. As for my academic background, I have a Bachelor of Arts degree in Political Science and Law – which is a far cry from banking, but it seems to work. My husband and I also ran a small business in our community, which also helped me in understanding the needs of our business people.

I believe strongly that when a group of people put their heads together to try to come up with ideas and solutions with everyone having equal say and input, the result is the best possible ideas and solutions. This is why Waubetek was established on fairly solid ground. When the group received the federal government approval, we held a planning workshop and underwent a visioning exercise. All of the seven founding members (three women and four men) joined me in envisioning what our communities would look like five years down the road, then ten years, through the efforts of Waubetek. Our minds, I believe, merged and we saw the same things: people working, happy children and youth with a future, better homes, basic services provided by our own people in our own communities, prosperous business people serving as role models, the establishment of businesses that respected the natural environment, and the revival of our traditional values and culture.

What are the services? What does Waubetek do?

In setting the direction of the organization, a five-year economic development strategy was prepared that highlighted the priorities and issues that needed to be addressed to develop our communities. Each year, the Waubetek board and staff meet with the community leaders and band economic development officers to revisit this plan and update it. So basically, Waubetek tries to co-ordinate the economic efforts of the First Nations on a regional basis.

We had to be creative in looking at ways to meet our community needs. Specifically, needs were identified in upgrading the skills of our people, in obtaining financing and business support for our entrepreneurs, and in building the needed infrastructure for our communities.

In response to the need for upgraded skills, Waubetek founded a training institute which provided accredited training in affiliation with a local college. For the business people, a loan fund was set up with business advisory services made available. Waubetek has also instituted a separate business consulting service that provides planning, bookkeeping, and advisory services. We have also given advisory assistance to band economic development officers in their efforts to improve community infrastructure and services.

While all of these services have been initiated through Waubetek with the full involvement of the communities, it is the business services that are most prominent and that have the greatest impact. Since May 1990 Waubetek has made 180 loans totalling nearly $4 million to Aboriginal businesses. With the loan fund, Waubetek has leveraged an additional $5 million for our clients and, as a result, they have created 360 jobs. The loan repayment has been excellent, with less than $10,000 having been written off to date. Waubetek has one of the best loan portfolios of all the Business Development Corporations in Ontario. There were many people who thought we would fall flat on our faces, that our loan repayment would be virtually impossible. However, we took up the challenge and our people have proven that given the opportunity they are excellent credit risks.

The Aboriginal business people deserve all the recognition for this organization's success to date. I believe that the business people recognize that Waubetek is their organization and that we have the potential to build something here for our future generations. We have to make it work.

Waubetek currently has a staff of five women and one man, all Aboriginal people from the area. Our staff work directly with the clients and prepare the business analyses for the board. While our business development officers do have accounting backgrounds, we have all had to learn our basic financing skills on the job. We have a strong team who work hard to see that the business people succeed. Since we are all from the local communities, we practically live side by side with our clients, which is a strong incentive to make sure we are doing our jobs effectively.

How are loan decisions made?

Waubetek has a nine-member board of directors made up of First Nation community representatives who have backgrounds in business, management, or finance. The board reviews all loan applications and makes loan decisions on a consensus basis. We have always had a strong board that has the interests of the clients in mind during each review, and there have been times when the board has increased the loan contribution to help the client obtain newer or more advanced equipment than was originally requested.

When we first began lending, the average loan size was around $8,000. We are now averaging $40,000 per loan. Our loan limit is $75,000.

It should be noted that we do not provide loans to directors or staff or to their families. This policy assures the community that we are not involved in delivering this service out of self-interest. We also maintain a strict code of confidentiality in order to maintain the trust of our clients.

Can you give some examples of new businesses that the loans have helped to start?

Waubetek has assisted in starting up a variety of businesses: restaurants, building contractors, masonry businesses, building supplies, silkscreening shops, gas bars, car washes, trucking and heavy equipment businesses, forestry operations, auto-mechanic garages, auto towing and wrecking services, golf course driving ranges, janitorial services, hair salons, campgrounds, gift shops, speech pathology services, fish cage operations, and so on. We are even involved in the establishment of a crematorium. We are fairly flexible in the type of business that we will finance, as long as the business is viable, significant employment is created, and the business is environmentally sensitive. The majority of businesses are family-run and usually have fewer than ten employees.

There are very few manufacturing companies at the present time. The lack of manufacturing or light industrial businesses is probably due to the fact that these types of business require a lot of capital for start-up. Waubetek can only lend so much money, and the clients are usually very hard-pressed to raise their needed equity for the business, so most clients start out very small with the full intention of expanding as the cash flow permits. Where manufacturing businesses have been established, it is usually a community-owned enterprise, such as the local log-building enterprise or the dock manufacturing company.

When I think back to some of the first businesses that we financed, one business in particular comes to mind, and I think it is typical of our clients. We were approached by a young mother who wanted to start a food-catering business. She had the needed cooking skills and a good reputation in the community for her food services. Unfortunately, she was unemployed, had no vehicle of her own, and didn't have a chef's or formal cooking certificate. Also, her first language is Ojibwe, which made it extremely difficult for her to communicate with the bank or any other funder. Because she was very determined, we assisted her with the development of a plan. She began taking chef's training courses towards her certificate, and then she started knocking on doors looking for catering contracts. Every time we gave her a task to do, she did it right away. When her homework and planning was completed, we provided the financing to help her purchase a catering truck, heating trays, and kitchen equipment. This young woman now employs eight people in her business.

Please elaborate on loans to women.

About one-third of our loans are to women. We find that where there are family-run businesses, women have a predominant role in the day-to-day management of the business. Also many of the women are interested in upgrading their business and management skills; they constitute the majority of participants in any training sessions.

What do you like about the work?

The type of work that we do is very positive, as we are able to help people realize their dreams and their potential. We get a lot of personal satisfaction out of seeing the Aboriginal business people, our people, succeed. We know that when the businesses succeed, more of those jobs we need are created. So together with the businesses, we are basically chipping away at that 50-percent unemployment rate. We can see the results of our efforts instantly and watch the confidence of our people grow.

In the tradition of our people, we like to take time to honour the achievements of those who have contributed to our communities. Waubetek hosts an annual business awards dinner where we recognize the accomplishments of the business people and hold them up as role models for our communities. This dinner is usually a much-anticipated event that we have a lot of fun arranging.

Personally, I enjoy the work, as it seems to be contributing to the larger picture of community healing. I want to see our communities develop in accordance with our traditional values so that we have better places and improved conditions for our children and the future generations yet unborn.

One of my greatest pleasures is working alongside my colleagues at Waubetek. We work well together as a team – everyone has strengths and weaknesses that they bring to the job. I think we complement each other as a team, and when there are issues to deal with, we generally put our minds together to seek resolution or to find a creative way to help a client. We are constantly looking for ways to improve the services, processes, or ourselves in meeting the needs of the client and the community. Most of us did not receive the formal training required for the work we do, but there is a strong sense of commitment and encouragement from amongst ourselves that seems to help each person realize his or her potential. It is not uncommon to see staff working in the office on weekends or until 10 in the evening. Everyone works until the job is done. We like to recognize the support of our families for allowing us to work the somewhat crazy hours by having gatherings at Christmas and each summer.

I believe that there is a strong sense that what we do today will affect our children tomorrow. That seems to be what drives most of us.

What lessons do you think are most important for First Nations women working towards economic development?

Some of the lessons we can learn and have learned are that our people have the capabilities to do anything we set our minds to; that it is impor- tant for us to trust ourselves; and that we must make sure that the deci- sions we make today will guarantee better, healthier lives for our great- great-grandchildren and all future generations.

We have already seen first-hand the small successes and achieve- ments made by our people when we work together. As a people, we have survived against many odds. I think that we might have been close to being on an "endangered species list," but I believe that society in general has come to recognize and appreciate the contributions that Aboriginal people have to offer in protecting the earth, working for the good of the community as a whole, and providing rich cultural values that can guide people in walking the good road.

15

"Who Do You Think Did the Cooking?" Baba in the Classroom

Karen Dubinsky

Baba herself would be surprised by this title, for she spent very little time in a classroom of any description. The only daughter of peasants who died when she was a child, Baba, like many girls of many families in many countries, was pulled from the world of ideas to the world of caretaking, and spent her childhood and early adulthood in Ukraine caring for her younger brothers. Yet when I was a student and now that I am a teacher of women's history, Baba has accompanied me in the classroom – metaphorically – numerous times. She is great company there, and more recently, she has found a sizeable and diverse community of other "babas" in my classroom to spend time with.

And here I am dragging Baba along to school again, for I want to talk about her here in order to explore individual life stories and oral history as pedagogical tools in teaching women's history. This project is in part autobiographical: I shall consider the life story of my own grandmother, a Ukrainian immigrant to Northern Ontario, and how she contributed to my own development as a women's historian. I will also discuss oral history "life story" projects I have used for several years in women's history university classes. Finally, I would also like to put both themes – individual life stories, and oral history as significant teaching tools for women's history – in the context of recent scholarly debates about the strengths and weaknesses of personal narratives, memory, and oral history.

I first brought Baba to school some years ago, when Professor Marilyn Barber, with whom I was taking an undergraduate Canadian immigration history course, suggested we might write our own family's immigration history for our term paper. That academic history could actually be about my own life was a new concept; years of high school and other university courses had never prepared me for this. What an exciting idea! Armed with a tape recorder, a bit of newly acquired knowledge of the history of Canadian immigrants in the early twentieth century, and a vague sense of the outlines of Baba's life story gleaned from family lore and gossip, I set out to interview her. I should add that I was also armed with what I considered my best, most engaging feature, which I thought would get Baba to open up and spill the beans of her life instantly: my feminist passion and politics. I thought my commitment to excavating the history of women would provide a sisterly connection with this old lady who, despite her presence at most of the special occasions of my life, I didn't actually know very well. All I had to do was tell her that her life was important, worthy, noble, and in need of recording. I was right, and I was wrong.

Baba, it turned out, already knew that her life was important and worthy. As a woman who had raised her brothers almost singlehandedly from the age of nine, lived through the Russian Revolution and two World Wars, immigrated to Canada on her own at age 18, raised three children in Fort William through the Depression, and was a politically active Communist in Canada, she required little sisterly validation from me. She was more than willing to talk about these and a host of other aspects of her life, and I was transfixed. I learned more about her life in that one afternoon than I had in over 20 years of family dinners. Over the course of my friendship with my Baba (which began that afternoon in 1982 and lasted until her death in 1993), my studies in Canadian women's immigration history and labour history came alive.

The project was a smashing success: I loved the research, I wrote a good paper and received one of my first As. I'm probably romanticizing a bit, but I've always thought of that project as one of the important turning points in my education. It helped change me from a politically active but intellectually lazy B student to an engaged, critical, and hard-working A student – the kind I now cherish as a professor. The only thing that mars this otherwise happy story is the moment I fell into what I think of as the pit of feminist arrogance.

Of all of the stories that Baba told me that day in her kitchen, the ones that engaged me the most were the tales of her political life. I had no idea how central politics had been to her throughout her life. My parents were fairly politically active social democrats, and I had some sense that Baba leaned towards the left too. I knew, for example, that they went to "the Hall" – the Ukrainian Farmer Labour Temple Association – and not "the Church." Communism and Christianity split my hometown down the middle, a binary opposition no one would dare deconstruct.

I listened to Baba's stories of entertaining Communist Party meetings at the small restaurant she and her husband ran when the Hall (and "the Party") had been made illegal during World War II. I laughed with her as she recalled washing a banner – emblazoned with hammer and sickle – after a demonstration and hanging it in the back yard to dry; her Christian neighbour had the priest over for lunch at the very same time. After many such stories, I gathered my courage to ask her the questions uppermost in my mind: how did you feel as a woman, spending so much time working for such a male-dominated organization as the Communist Party? Didn't it bother you that all of the really important leadership decisions were made by men?

I'm not quoting myself here, because I cannot, of course, actually remember my exact words. But they were close to being this blunt. This interview took place well before the publication of the many fine studies that now exist in Canada of the history of women's involvement in left-wing politics, and women in immigrant communities generally.[1] I had only the vaguest sense of the history of the Communist Party at that point, much less about women's

Miners' Mothers'Day collection

Women cooking, 1940s or 1950s.

involvement in the Canadian left. But as a politically active socialist feminist, I "knew" that Baba and her sisters in the party must have been marginalized. Again, I was right and I was wrong.

Her response was a little more than I expected. She blew up at me: "Who do you think did the cooking? When [Communist Party leader] Tim Buck came to town, when [Communist activist] A.E. Smith came to town, who do you think cooked? Isn't the cooking important?"

This version of Baba has come to class with me many times since that day. Remembering the way my third-year oral history project sparked my historical passion, I have used this same teaching device since I began teaching women's history. I call it the "Baba project." The assignment asks students to interview an "older woman." Many select their mothers; others choose to interview aunts, friends, and even strangers. My angry, indignant Baba plays a useful role when I introduce students to the work of oral history, for she illustrates one of the central tensions surrounding feminist oral history.

I still quite fully support the claims made by many historians for bringing oral history into the "canon" of historically respectable sources: it gives voice to the powerless, to those left out of the traditional historical record, to those who do not have their papers filed and preserved in acid-free archival boxes, and indeed, to those who left no "papers" at all. But recent debates among historians, anthropologists, and others have complicated the approach. The whole concept of "giving voice" suggests a power relationship between those who had the experiences and those in a position to "use," write, and theorize about those experiences. This is a power relationship that sisterly presumptions of solidarity cannot wish away, and ought to be recognized.

Folklorist Katherine Borland has recounted her own story of interviewing her grandmother, in which the pit of feminist arrogance loomed for her as well. Her grandmother was quite resistant to Borland's feminist appropriation of an incident from her grandmother's life, prompting Borland to ask the difficult question, who controls the text? "How," she asks, "might we present our work in a way that grants the speaking woman interpretive respect without relinquishing our responsibility to provide our own interpretation of her experience?"[2] Furthermore, what happens when the "voiceless" don't like the voice we have "given" them or when the listeners don't like what they hear?

These are vexing questions, for they are about the subtleties of power relationships. They certainly complicate what was for me as a student, and for my own students now, one of the most appealing aspects of oral history projects: the chance to "give voice," to encourage an individual woman to see herself as a player on the historical stage, and to record the results for posterity. Over the years, the essays that come in have a familiar ring. They often begin by reporting the woman's initial reluctance to talk ("Why are you asking me? I haven't done anything important"); and then they proceed to tell tales that clearly keep the students riveted. The stories are about raising children in a Northern Ontario mining town with no running water, about immigrating to Temiskaming without knowing a word of English, and sometimes even about sexual adventure or violence. It is hugely instructive for younger students to think about the everyday realities of women's lives in the past, particularly through the eyes of one individual.

But, as my own experience with my Baba suggests, there are certain tensions inherent in this process. If I have been successful in my job as a teacher of women's history, students begin the interview process armed, as I was, with a healthy feminist respect – if not passion – for the accomplishments of women. This, ironically, might be enough to set them on the sort of collision course with their "subject" that Borland has described, and that I experienced. In telling them my Baba story when I introduce the assignment, I hope to illustrate the "wrong" way to interview – a point well made also by Kathryn Anderson and Dana Jack, who suggest that listening is as crucial a skill as asking questions.[3] Yet even the most skilled, sensitive interviewer may well encounter the sort of interpretive conflict described by Borland, conflicts made more complicated when they occur among family members.

I also request that students write their essays using existing relevant historiography. If their "subject," for example, worked in an Inco smelter during World War II, students should know something about what historians have written about this topic. This makes the project more "work" (as students often point out), but it ultimately helps students to see the connections the assignment is designed to draw out: how individual lives are shaped by social forces.

I'm never sure, at the end of each year when I have used this assignment, if I have been successful in encouraging students to consider the important methodological, political, and ethical questions involved in barging into another person's life. If undergraduate students participate in and reflect on the power dynamics inherent in probing an individual's life, then perhaps, I reason, this might temper their use of power later in life, for most of them are headed into the middle class anyway. Similarly, especially for those who choose to interview family members, their lives as mostly middle-class university students are altered a bit when, in listening to the stories of their immigrant great-aunts, they learn how important their Jewish-ness, French-ness, or Italian-ness once was to their family, or when they discover their grandmother had once been involved in a union. Some have "discovered" a lesbian great-aunt, a grandmother who found herself pregnant and unwed in the 1930s, and many stories of violence and heartbreak.

While I'm unsure whether the methodological and political issues involved receive proper attention when students invite Baba to the classroom, I'm certain that most students also find her delightful company. I also know that some students experience a "conversion process" similar to what I felt in my immigration history class. History begins to look much more interesting after you have tried to see it through the eyes of someone else. I often joke to my students that "this class will at the very least make them love and appreciate old ladies." Of the various pedagogical goals we teachers set for ourselves, that's not, on the whole, such a bad one.

Part Three

Daily Stresses

The women's movement has raised women's consciousness about the feminization of poverty and the violence that colours the lives of many women. The chapters in this section examine the major stresses northern women deal with, and the impact that such tensions can have on their lives.

In Ontario, mining is synonymous with the north, but seldom do we think of the way in which mining creates anxiety in women. Nancy Forestell examines the lives of women and their families as they dealt with accidents, disease, and even the death of the men in their lives. One of the issues raised in that chapter, women's poverty, is dealt with further in the chapters by Carol Kauppi and Marge Reitsma-Street and by Marie-Luce Garceau. Kauppi and Reitsma-Street have found that low income and high cost of living mean that many women, especially single mothers and older women, live in poverty. Garceau writes specifically about older francophone women: while they take pride in their domestic contributions, most live in dependent situations and have few options due to low levels of education.

Economic isolation is just one factor identified by Marian Beauregard as leading to lives defined by abuse and even violence. The women she interviewed speak of the resulting impact on their mental heath; they also identify ways they have found to break the cycle of violence faced by so many women.

Stresses created by poverty, isolation, and violence can have a profound effect on women's health. Health issues are central to the concluding chapters in this section. Roger Pitblado and Raymond Pong use the Ontario Health Survey to show that women in Northern Ontario have slightly higher rates of both health problems and chronic diseases than women in Southern Ontario. After reviewing the health practices of 177 women, Carole Suschnigg identified barriers to care: attitudes of doctors to women's health concerns, the pressures of work and home demands, low income, and poor working conditions.

16

"You Never Give Up Worrying": The Consequences of a Hazardous Mine Environment for Working-Class Families in Timmins, 1915–1950

Nancy M. Forestell

On the early morning of 10 February 1928, a fire started in a refuse pile on the 550-foot level of the Hollinger mine. Within minutes, dense smoke began to spread throughout the network of interconnecting passageways in the mine. Most of the 921 men on dayshift were quickly alerted and managed to escape, but 59 miners were unable to make their way out or were incapable of doing so and found themselves trapped underground. Intensifying the crisis, the company lacked the necessary equipment – respirators and masks – to stage a rescue attempt. Unlike coalmines, where fires were a recognized problem, such incidents were so rare in goldmining that Hollinger had considered these materials an unnecessary expense. By the time the closest source of rescue equipment arrived from the coalfields of Pennsylvania a day later, 39 men had died. The tragedy of this event was compounded by the fact that a disproportionate number of the miners who perished in the fire had been married men with wives and children to support. Even among the single men, moreover, many had been the primary wage-earners for their parents and siblings.[1] The magnitude of the "Hollinger Disaster" underscored to the goldmining community of Timmins in general, and to the working class in particular, the hazardous nature of goldmining and the precarious position of all workers in this occupation on whom so many depended. At the same time, this event also highlighted the emotional and financial losses incurred by individual families as a result of these types of accidents.

Although historians have long recognized and documented the hazards of mining, few have extended their analysis beyond the narrow confines of the workplace to explore the implications of disability, disease, and death for miners' families.[2] In a Northern Ontario goldmining town such as Timmins, the limitations of health and safety in the mines had long-term repercussions in the household. Drawing upon both oral interviews and written documents, this chapter will explore how the emotional, physical, and financial consequences

were especially burdensome for the female spouses of miners.[3] The chapter
will further explore how the assistance received by widows and their children
in the event of job-related accidents and disease often depended on an inter-
play of ethnicity and marital status, and on occasion, even a twist of fate.
Rarely, however, was this assistance sufficient.

The existence of large, capital-intensive mines in the Porcupine district of
Northern Ontario from 1909 onward (when gold was first discovered in the
area) spurred the development of the nearby town of Timmins. This community, which was first established in 1911 with a population of several hundred,
grew to a peak population of over 41,000 by the early 1940s. The multi-ethnic
labour forces in the district mines – which included substantial numbers of
European immigrants, as well as both anglophone and francophone Canadians
– would be replicated in the composition of this developing single-industry
community.

Throughout the three and a half decades covered by this study, the ability
of Porcupine goldminers to provide for their families was never jeopardized
by the large-scale layoffs, imposition of part-time work, or seasonal patterns
of employment that so adversely affected workers in other industrial sectors.[4]
Although mineworkers in this district were not confronted by these difficulties, they faced continued problems with dangerous and unhealthy working
conditions, which seriously diminished and frequently extinguished the wage-
earning capacity of many.

Accident rates were extremely high during the early decades of goldmining development in the Porcupine and improved only marginally thereafter.
Prior to 1930 approximately one-third of the mining labour force sustained
some form of workplace injury on an annual basis. In over half of these cases,
the injuries were serious enough to warrant more than a week off work. After
that point, the accident rate declined somewhat, but still did not drop below the
level of 25 percent until the late 1940s. Although the majority of injuries were
often temporary, a substantial proportion of men were left with permanent disabilities. Large fatal accidents rarely occurred, yet hundreds of mineworkers
died in these goldfields between 1910 and 1950. From the 1930s onward, the
goldmining industry actually had a disproportionately higher fatality rate than
other sectors of the mining industry in Ontario.

With alarming frequency, miners in this area also developed the debilitating lung disease silicosis, which resulted from the inhalation of fine silica dust
in the workplace. Miners here were particularly susceptible to this occupational disease as the density of silica particles in district mines was the highest in
Ontario. A medical survey of Porcupine miners with over five years of work
experience conducted by the Ministry of Health in the late 1920s discovered
that 19.5 percent had some degree of this lung ailment.[5] Despite the preventive
measures subsequently introduced, this incurable disorder remained a serious
health problem for goldminers. In its earliest stages, mineworkers observed

little discomfort, but as the disease progressed, they endured a noticeable decrease in muscle strength and an increase in shortness of breath. Of even greater consequence, silicosis predisposed men to tuberculosis, which in combination led to quite rapid physical decline and early death. This "double jeopardy," as Gerald Markowitz and David Rosner have termed it, was prevalent among silicotic miners throughout the period.[6] There were still others who contracted tuberculosis without the complication of silicosis, although still as a direct consequence of the mine environment. Labouring underground weakened lungs generally and therefore significantly reduced miners' ability to ward off such a communicable disease. Later research studies would also demonstrate that working conditions directly contributed to an extraordinarily high rate of lung cancer among goldminers.[7] Whereas mining accidents could strike men indiscriminately of age and work experience, these particular occupational diseases were linked directly to length of service. Every additional year spent underground increased the likelihood of developing such afflictions. The projected "incubation" time gradually increased, but even by the end of the period, workers who started in the mines as teenagers faced the likely prospect that they would contract these lung ailments while still relatively young men in their forties. In the Porcupine, mineworkers were more likely to die from an occupational disease than an injury.

Miners' wives here were keenly aware of the dangers of the workplace. These women lived with the constant fear of accidents and chronic diseases that might befall the family breadwinner and they were the ones who had to deal most directly with the consequences of such misfortune. As a second generation reached maturity in this community during the interwar period and kin networks became more intricate and interconnected, numerous women endured the added anxiety of having sons and other close male relatives employed at the mines. In many of the interviews, miners' wives revealed that they worried daily about whether their men would make it safely through another shift.[8] Peggy Boychuck expressed a common sentiment: "John worked at the Hollinger for over 30 years, and during that whole time I never gave up worrying. I would keep myself busy, but from the time he left until he came home I was always tense…. You see, John's brother was killed in an accident."[9]

The regularity and unpredictability of serious mishaps in the goldmines reinforced to all wives that no worker was exempt. As one woman wrote in a 1938 letter to the *Union News:* "Every time I see the Hollinger ambulance I almost drop in my tracks for fear it is my husband."[10] Tragedies on the scale of the 1928 Hollinger fire, and the 1945 Paymaster accident in which 16 mineworkers were killed when the cable to their transport cage suddenly snapped, only served to further substantiate women's concerns.[11] Moreover, a miner's wife also lived with the uncertainty of whether he might become one of the unfortunate to develop silicosis; or worse, that the silicosis would be complicated by tuberculosis. The following 1937 letter by a "Miner's Wife" articulated the fears of many women: "You hope and trust that somehow your husband will be luckier than the others when right down in your heart you are uneasy and constantly dread the approaching years knowing disruption of domestic calm is usually the reward for long service in the mining game."[12] Yet the majority of women realized that their husbands and sons would be hard pressed to find jobs in the vicinity that offered the same wages and as steady a source of employment as goldmining. For the most part they accepted that "the worrying and the waiting was just something you had to put up with."[13] While this sentiment reflected a certain amount of fatalism, paradoxically it also demonstrated a determination to confront adversity.

In the event of a debilitating accident or illness, most wives assumed the onerous responsibility of taking care of the incapacitated worker. In addition to all of their other domestic duties, many women performed a variety of labour-intensive tasks in tending to their husbands, such as cooking special meals, bathing them, changing dressings, and massaging strained muscles.[14] Individual situations varied tremendously, but even a temporarily disabled husband created substantially more work at home. Although paid nursing care was provided through Workmen's Compensation from 1917 onward and through the company medical plans, once they were introduced in the late 1930s, the bulk of this labour was still left to wives.[15] Injuries and ill health meant that women also had to carry out those household chores normally done by their husbands. When Steve Deveschuk sprained his back while mucking ore at the McIntyre, his wife Natalia chopped wood and shovelled snow throughout an entire winter.[16] While some of these women must have felt overwhelmed by the physical and emotional demands of ministering to an ill spouse, and resentful about running a household on their own, there is a noticeable silence in the interviews on this issue. The silence can be attributed in part to the gendered expectations of being a "miner's wife," which dictated that women take on these additional obligations but precluded any emotional space for them to complain about it. Moreover, in a mining community such as Timmins, these burdensome tasks were not viewed as extraordinary measures; instead they represented necessary work that most wives performed at some point in their husband's working life. Somewhat surprisingly, feminist scholars have largely overlooked this type of unpaid female labour as an integral aspect of caring for working adults. For many working-class women, in Timmins at least, this labour often proved to be critical in getting men back to work.[17]

Of course, the wives of male breadwinners permanently incapacitated by injuries and disease were confronted by the even more daunting responsibility: they had to look after a disabled spouse on a long-term basis. These situations were especially difficult not only because of the substantial commitment of time and effort required, but also because there was so rarely any hope of improvement. Men afflicted with silicosis or tuberculosis or both could enter a sanatorium; yet with the nearest facility located over 150 kilometres away in Haileybury, most were reluctant to go because of the expected long-term "separation from their families and friends."[18] Since hospital care could do little to arrest the progression of these diseases anyway, many preferred to remain at home. For four years Eva Bijakowski nursed her silicotic husband and, as her daughter remembered, "tried to preserve what health he had left." During the final months of his life, the disease had advanced to the stage where Eva could do little but "make him as comfortable as possible," as he fought for each additional breath. Similar tragedies were played out over and over again in homes throughout this community.[19]

The frequent occurrence of tuberculosis among mineworkers had additional implications for their families. Both women and children were placed at physical risk from the numerous miners who also developed this communicable disease. As noted already, weakened lung capacity that resulted from mining work made goldminers in this area highly susceptible to tuberculosis. In some instances these men passed on this communicable disease to family members. Although tuberculosis was not a serious problem in the community initially, by 1935 Timmins had the highest rate in the province.[20] While the rate of tuberculosis elsewhere declined sharply in the 1930s and 1940s, this mining centre experienced only a marginal reduction. Even by the end of the period, the incidence of this disease in Timmins continued to be almost double the provincial average.[21] Reports to the provincial Board of Health in the 1930s reveal that local health officials were well aware that hazardous working conditions in the mines were having a deleterious effect not only on the health of miners, but also on their families.[22] Concerned with the situation, the district health nurse approached local mining companies in 1933 about donating funds for tuberculosis prevention work, and with their assistance, a public health nurse was subsequently hired for this sole purpose.[23] Mine executives refused to admit publicly, however, that the mine environment contributed in any way to this ongoing health problem in the area. They took the position that silicotics were not the ones principally responsible for the spread of the disease; instead, "contacts" in the community, particularly family members, were infecting the men. They further suggested that a poor "home environment" rather than an unsafe workplace was the main cause of the high tuberculosis rate.[24] Although overcrowded housing conditions and inadequate sanitation in some areas of Timmins certainly exacerbated the situation, the mining companies chose to ignore current literature on public and industrial health, which made links between the mine and the household.

The financial consequences of disease and accidents were just as serious. Most households depended solely on a single male breadwinner, and if he was seriously injured or killed, families were left without any wage-earner. Even the brief cessation of income could hasten a financial crisis, as many lived from paycheque to paycheque. In temporary situations, it was normally left up to the wife, as the manager of the household budget, to deal with the family's financial predicament by cutting back on expenses and by asking local store owners to extend their credit,[25] but these measures were not always sufficient. In those cases where miners suffered long-term injuries, other family members usually attempted to find employment, and if the children were young, this almost always meant the wives. Securing paid work could be especially difficult for these women. As documented elsewhere, the female labour market in Timmins remained quite restricted throughout the first half of the twentieth century. While in principal women with permanently disabled husbands were viewed as deserving of employment, individually they had to confront local reticence to hire any married woman. Even the Workers' Co-operative, a progressive working-class organization that operated a store in town, rarely suspended its preferential hiring policy of single females over married women in straitened circumstances. On one specific occasion, a woman whose husband had been hurt in a mining accident at the McIntyre wrote to the executive board of the co-op asking that an exception be made in her case, but since her husband's injuries were not permanent the request was denied.[26]

Widows found themselves in an even more vulnerable financial position. When municipal officials investigated the finances of families who lost a relative in the Hollinger disaster, they discovered that while a few of the widows had some savings, most possessed only the money left over from the previous payday, with bills still owing for groceries and other expenses. Some owned their own homes, but in almost every instance mortgage payments were outstanding.[27] One positive finding of the investigation was the fact that most of the men who perished in the fire left behind some form of life insurance. As Suzanne Morton has noted, however, many working-class widows spent a sizeable portion of the insurance payment on funeral expenses. In this instance, the widows were entitled to $100 each from Workmen's Compensation for the burial of their husbands, but this amount did not cover all the costs.[28] As with married women, widows often discovered that job opportunities were scarce.

Workmen's Compensation

With the implementation of the Workmen's Compensation Act in 1915, the Ontario government established the first comprehensive scheme of income protection against job-related disability, disease, and death in the country. For widows and children of deceased workers, this state program instituted a set of formal procedures that accorded payments to them regardless of the circumstances of the accident or illness. Prior to this act, the relatives of a deceased worker had to initiate a court case and prove employer negligence in order to obtain compensation.[29] In order for widows to be considered "deserving" of Workmen's Compensation benefits, however, they were expected to prove legal and moral worthiness for benefits, and even thereafter, they were subject to continued surveillance of their private, including sexual, lives.

The widows of miners had to meet stringent criteria and provide detailed documentation to support their eligibility for pensions. Not surprisingly, the policy clearly stipulated at the outset that only the legal spouse of a deceased worker would be recognized.[30] To confirm this status, applicants were required to present copies of their marriage certificates. While this request proved to be simple enough for most women married in Canada, it sometimes presented a serious obstacle for European immigrant women who were not in possession of such a document and because of economic or political upheaval in their country of origin found it difficult, if not impossible, to obtain the certificate. Widows who were non-residents of Ontario had to further establish that the deceased wage-earner had been providing continued financial aid to his family. In many instances, the necessary evidence was either insufficient or non-existent, as few women retained the necessary records, and on the other side, their husbands rarely left behind more than scattered traces of the money they had been sending.

Lone working-class men in Timmins, especially immigrants, seldom opened bank accounts or established formal procedures for transferring sums "back home." After Vincent Grenko was killed in an explosion at the Buffalo Ankerite mine in 1933, his widow in Jugoslavia, Maria, submitted a claim for herself and two children. The Workmen's Compensation Board (WCB) would not accept the four money order stubs included by Maria as adequate proof that Vincent had been assisting in their upkeep on an ongoing basis, and thus made inquiries with the mine and local banks in Timmins to ascertain "the extent to which the workman contributed towards the support of his family." The board received assurances from his Jugoslavian friends that Vincent sent money home, but failed to uncover any record of such transactions in the form of a bank draft or registered mail. Unfortunately for Maria, the board subsequently determined that lacking any tangible corroborating evidence, the claim could not be approved.[31]

The strict application of the legal provision in this policy excluded countless women in common-law relationships and the children produced from such unions. Regardless of the length or circumstances of the relationship, "extralegal" spouses were not covered at all by Workmen's Compensation until the early 1940s, and then only in restricted situations. Having transgressed accepted moral boundaries, these women were not entitled to the same kind of "protection" from the state, nor were their children. Protests were occasionally waged on their behalf, as in the aftermath of the Hollinger disaster in 1928, when it was discovered that five of the widows were actually common-law wives and therefore ineligible for compensation. All five were the wives of Finnish immigrant men who perished in the fire; two of the women had chosen not to legally sanction their marriages on political grounds, while the other three had no other option since the men already had a legal spouse back in Finland. At a meeting of the Northern Ontario District Women Workers soon after the accident, Finnish women from Timmins introduced a motion that called for immediate changes to the Workmen's Compensation Act so that all women and children would be covered. In an open letter that appeared in the Woman Worker, the executive committee of the Canadian Federation of Women's Labour Leagues offered support to the Timmins group in demanding that the women receive pensions:

> We desire to bring to your attention the fact that already a question has been raised concerning Compensation and the right of our Finnish women comrades to this Compensation because their marriage form is not recognized by Canadian law. We ask your League to take this matter up immediately with the Union representatives in Timmins and ask them to see to it that our Finnish women comrades are not put on one side because of this. They have a right to full Compensation and must dispute any decision that is made by the authorities which would rob them of that right.[32]

In the months following the mining disaster, a variety of local and national groups pressured the government to alter the policy to include these women, but all to no effect. In 1943, the province passed an amendment to the Workmen's Compensation Act that permitted some common-law wives to collect benefits. Limiting the pensions to mothers with young children, the amendment took great pains to distinguish these women from other recipients by stating explicitly that they qualified for benefits only on the basis of their position as the "mother of a dependent illegitimate child," not as a "widow" worthy of compensation. Once the children reached 16 years of age, the payments ceased abruptly.[33] The amendment also stated that these women were additionally required to maintain their households "in a manner which the Board deems satisfactory." What conditions the board considered to be "satisfactory" have not yet been determined precisely. This policy provision was principally intended to extend financial assistance for the care and upbringing of this particular group of children without appearing to condone common-law relationships.

With the exception of pensions for "extralegal" spouses, widows were granted monthly stipends until they remarried or died. Once a "morals clause" was appended to the act in 1925, however, the WCB had the power to rescind benefits if a woman contravened the new guidelines of sexual chastity. The clause specifically stipulated that "[w]here it is found that the widow to whom compensation has been awarded is a common prostitute or is openly living with any man in relation of man and wife without being married to him, the Board may discontinue or suspend compensation payments."[34] It is not entirely certain how many women lost their benefits for such violations, but it is evident that this rule was used to justify ongoing moral scrutiny of all widows. Unlike recipients of Mothers' Allowance, these women were not subject to visits by social workers inquiring into their living arrangements, but as several cases in Timmins demonstrated, community surveillance could be just as effective. A local union newspaper reported in May 1938 that the WCB had recently cut off the pensions of two widows on grounds of "moral delinquency." The article indicated that the board had taken such action after receiving letters about the women from community residents.[35] Interestingly enough, the article further suggested that the women were innocent of the charges, but had not been given any opportunity to defend themselves.

The widows of silicotics and tuberculo-silicotics had to fulfil one additional requirement. The policy clearly stipulated that they were entitled to a pension only if silicosis proved to be the primary cause of their husband's death.[36] The narrow interpretation of "primary" by medical officials at the compensation board disqualified numerous women in Timmins. Although a silicotic miner may have received a full pension for this industrial disease during his lifetime, if he died from a heart attack or stomach cancer his widow was refused benefits.

The Workmen's Compensation policy also established a quite separate and inequitable benefit structure for widows and other dependents than the one established for injured and diseased workers. While the benefits for incapacitated (mostly male) workers were based on a proportion of their individual earnings, those for widows and children were set at a flat rate.[37] In the original legislation, all women were entitled to $20 per month and an additional $5 for each child under 16 years of age up to a total maximum of $40.[38] The policy also initially outlined that the pension could not exceed 55 percent of the deceased workmen's earnings. However, except for the widows of extremely low-paid, seasonally employed, unskilled workers, pension entitlements very rarely reached this limit. For the widows of goldminers, these pensions turned out to be a fraction of the amount they might have received if the benefits had been assessed in relation to the wages of the deceased breadwinner. To give an example, the pension of $30 allotted a mother with two children in 1917 could have easily reached over $50, given the average earnings of goldminers reported that year.[39] Thus from the beginning, Workmen's Compensation offered widows much lower benefits on the whole than the already insufficient amounts granted injured or diseased workers. There was no balancing act when it came to these women – the policy treated them as dependents and paid them accordingly.

Another distinction between the two benefit structures was that regardless of the date of disability, workers' pensions automatically rose along with increases to the proportional compensation rate. This proportional rate was initially 55 percent, rose to 66 2/3 percent in 1918, and was increased in 1949 to 75 percent. In contrast, a widow's pension was "locked in" at a specific amount from the time of her husband's death. This stipulation proved to be especially restrictive for the women who qualified for benefits during the initial years of the policy, and then continued as a pensioner for an extended period of time.

The province did make some adjustments to dependents' pensions in 1920 by augmenting the monthly stipend of newly eligible widows up to $40, and up to $10 for their children.[40] The government also eliminated the provision that imposed a specific limit on all pensions. Still, the women who gained the most from these changes – widows with large families – represented only a small proportion of those collecting benefits. Several years after these new rates were implemented, an investigation by the Workmen's Compensation Board into the conditions of "death pensioners" determined that on the whole they were "living average lives of normal activities without [a] general lowering of standards." Even evidence contained in the report, however, would appear to refute such a contention. Almost one-fifth of the widows surveyed were unable to maintain a household on their own, and one-third required additional income from paid work in order to keep their families together. Perhaps most revealing, 98 percent of these women were using their pensions for basic living expenses.[41] Not surprisingly, given the positive (although one would argue erroneous) conclusions of this report, benefits remained unaltered for some time afterwards.

Although it is difficult to chart precisely the financial situation of widows on Workmen's Compensation pensions in Timmins, there is some indication that women in this community were further disadvantaged. The benefit structure, which applied rates uniformly across Ontario, penalized women in northern resource towns such as this one. Because of the persistently high cost of living here, compensation payments bought fewer basic necessities in Timmins than in Southern Ontario communities, which generally had lower consumer prices and household expenses. To illustrate this point another way, it has been estimated that a family of three required approximately $60 per month in 1939 to achieve the provincial minimum living standard – coincidentally, the same amount granted a widow with two children from Workmen's Compensation.[42] Yet an identically sized family in Timmins needed $75 to reach the same level. These figures substantiate not only that widows in this community, along with other residents, faced higher costs, but also that their Workmen's Compensation pensions were clearly inadequate to meet even minimal standards of comfort.[43] In effect, such province-wide benefit rates ignored known regional differences in the cost of living to the detriment of women and children in the north. Also given the higher accident and disease rates throughout this region, such an oversight had adverse consequences for a disproportionate number of women receiving widows' pensions.

Throughout the interwar period, labour groups lobbied the government to enhance Workmen's Compensation benefits for widows and other dependents, but new measures were not introduced until the early 1940s. Minor increases were instituted for pensions in 1943 and again in 1947. Perhaps of equal long-term significance, during this decade policy changes were enacted that extended coverage to children who remained in school up to 18 years of age and brought the monthly payments for all widows up to the same rate irrespective of when their claims were activated.[44] As to standardizing the pensions retroactively, some women whose benefits had been established decades earlier were still collecting as little as $20 per month. The delay can be attributed in part to ongoing concerns by government and business that such changes threatened to transform Workmen's Compensation policy from a "social insurance" to a "social assistance" scheme. As a brief on compensation by the Ontario Mining Association noted:

> We cannot deny that a widow originally pensioned at $20 per month in 1917 finds herself in difficult circumstances today, but no more so we submit than a person who had at that time purchased an annuity deemed adequate to take care of him in his old age. In the case of the annuitant it would hardly be suggested that the Government or the insurance company who financed the annuity should, with no further recompense, bring the amount of same up to a "living wage" scale.[45]

For a time this type of logic justified more parsimonious benefits for some women and children on Workmen's Compensation than they would have received from other less socially legitimate welfare state policies. In the end, it would appear that the provincial government acceded to these alterations, over the objections of the corporate sector, because the situation had become politically embarrassing. Even with all these improvements, by the end of the 1940s the gulf between widows' and workers' pensions had, if anything, grown larger. With specific reference to the local situation, a widow with two children in 1950 was entitled to less than half the amount allotted to the average injured goldminer with full benefits. In addition, with a newly imposed maximum of $100, the policy now financially supported only up to four children.[46]

Neighbourly Support and Company Assistance

While the scope and level of benefits from Workmen's Compensation generally improved over the period for the widows of mineworkers, serious limitations obviously still remained. Working-class women in Timmins thus continued to draw upon traditional sources of support – family, friends, and community organizations in various combinations – in ways that were sometimes ethnically specific and that were adapted to the particular conditions of a mining community in flux. In addition, the benefits offered through corporate welfare schemes by the local mining companies became another source of financial assistance for families temporarily or permanently without a male breadwinner, albeit with notable conditions attached. And finally, often as a last resort, women in dire financial circumstances relied upon municipally funded relief. Private and municipal initiatives were not superseded by provincial and federal welfare state policies, but proceeded to exist alongside them.[47]

Mutual emotional and financial support offered between friends and among members of extended families was often crucial for the working class of this community when misfortune occurred. Extended family members were rarely resident during the early decades of this community, and thus friends played a far more central role. By the mid-1930s when a second generation began to reach maturity, family assumed its traditional importance. Theresa Del Guidice offers one of the best examples of this point. She recalled that during the mid-1920s when her mother became ill at the same time as her father was on a trip back to Italy, a couple who lived close by looked after Theresa and her three siblings for several months. Over a decade later when she left an abusive husband, Theresa turned to her parents for assistance.[48] Working-class women often relied upon informal support networks within their own ethnic groups of friends, and later family, during crises.

With the exception of Catholic and Protestant women's church groups, relatively few philanthropic organizations existed in Timmins throughout the period. This mining town did not have a sizeable middle class to fill the ranks of various charitable organizations as they did elsewhere. Instead, middle-class women joined church groups along with working-class women in the community to raise money for congregation members "in need" and for "the poor." At least for some of the working-class women in these organizations, the boundaries between mutual assistance and philanthropy were blurred at times. The numerical and political importance of the Catholic church in Timmins determined that one of its organizations, the Ladies of Charity, would play a dominant role in philanthropic work. By hosting large euchres and bazaars, this organization secured enough funds to buy food, clothing, and household goods for financially strapped families throughout the community regardless of denominational affiliation.[49] The Protestant women's groups tended to operate on a smaller scale. Raising money from teas and bake sales, the Ladies' Aid of First United Church offered food and clothing and, in extraordinary cases, emergency funds to members of the congregation.[50]

On an informal basis, selective mine officials in the Porcupine had always dispensed aid to employees' families. In the aftermath of the disastrous fire in 1928, the company provided $200 to the family of each accident victim for living expenses.[51] Yet this type of financial support was certainly not accorded to the relatives of every employee. A noticeable shift in corporate practices occurred at many of the goldmines during the mid-1930s when they introduced comprehensive benefit schemes that included not only medical coverage, but also life insurance. With few exceptions the mining companies assumed the expense of life insurance for their workers. The McIntyre life insurance plan, inaugurated in 1936, offered initial coverage of $500 to workers after three months of service. Thereafter, the company increased benefits incrementally each year until they reached a maximum amount of $1,500 after seven years. Given the transient nature of mining work, however, relatively few employees achieved that length of company service. And even at the maximum amount, the insurance payment represented less than one year's earnings for the average goldminer.

As in most newly developed communities, the town government of Timmins initially lacked the administrative procedures and institutional structures to deal with individuals or families in financial crisis. As it turned out, this municipality faced ongoing difficulties in developing social services because of severe financial constraints. The tax structure in place for this type of mining town restricted revenues, and as a consequence limited the money available for welfare. The municipality received some funds from the province, but these represented only a fraction of the amount needed by the town for relief payments. Far removed from other population centres, this municipality could also not pool its meagre resources with other communities, a common practice in rural southern counties in Ontario, in order to build publicly funded institutions for the poor such as a house of refuge, a home for the elderly, or an orphanage. The absence of such institutions could be viewed as a positive development because the impoverished in this area were not institutionalized; yet it should also be kept in mind that unlike poor families in other areas, residents here did not have the choice of using such institutions as a temporary or permanent measure for alleviating their financial distress by placing elderly parents or young children in care.

Municipal relief remained the sole form of local, publicly funded assistance. At first, applicants had to appeal directly to members of the town council who considered the merits of each case. Having exhausted other options, many turned to relief as a last resort. The council initially issued relief in kind rather than in cash by paying directly for recipients' food, fuel, and sometimes rent. In most instances the total amount fell well below benefit levels for provincial social assistance plans. The council offered the equivalent of $30 a month to a woman with four children in 1925, or $20 less than she would have received as a beneficiary of Workmen's Compensation. More standardized guidelines were drawn up once the council hired a relief officer to oversee cases in 1932. That same year, however, the municipality imposed new restrictions on public aid, disqualifying any applicant who had been resident in the community for less than a year.[52] These regulations were rescinded only with the onset of World War II. Soon afterwards the municipal government began offering relief in the form of cash payments, although citing financial considerations, it did not make any alterations to the amount.[53]

In this mining town where so many working-class families depended on a sole male wage-earner, an unsafe mine environment had dire consequences not only for the individual worker, but also for his wife and children. While Workmen's Compensation offered assistance to some families, still many others failed to qualify for benefits. Friends, kin, companies, and the local municipal government offered assistance in certain circumstances, yet a great deal of distress still remained.

Epilogue

Since 1950, accident rates in the Porcupine district have declined, due in part to the persistence of labour representatives in Timmins to ensure a safer work environment for miners. Nonetheless, scores of workers have been seriously injured and several dozen have been killed during these decades. Silicosis rates have also decreased, but it has become apparent that hazardous working conditions have directly contributed to a disproportionately high rate of death among miners from lung cancer and other lung diseases as well as other cancers. Victims of Mining Environment, a group organized in the fall of 1986 and composed principally of widows of former mineworkers, has been instrumental in drawing attention to the long-term consequences of accidents and disease. The "search for justice" by these women has also involved ensuring that surviving spouses received pensions from Workers' Compensation. This organization has raised much-needed public awareness in Timmins and among the labour movement in Ontario to the ongoing plight of working-class families in this community.

17

Women and Poverty in Northern Ontario[1]

Carol Kauppi and Marge Reitsma-Street

I do without to give to my children. I feel really bad when I have to constantly say no to my kids. They don't ask for much when they do ask, but I'm always having to explain "no" to them. And it's not things that they don't need. I feel so badly, I just want to go work, work, work all the time, non-stop. I wish I didn't have kids sometimes because it hurts me that I can't get a job and provide for my kids properly. – Sudbury mother on social assistance[2]

There is no money to save; we just make it month by month.... You seem like you're always owing – always, always – and when I get my child tax credit, I always owe. – North Bay mother under poverty line[3]

My son even said that the kids at school said he had germs because he was poor. And he asked me if he had germs. I had to tell him he didn't and those kids were being cruel. It hurts when your kids come home hurting because we are poor.[4]

These excerpts from interviews with northern women living below the poverty line suggest we need to be as concerned about the levels of poverty within our own Canadian borders as we are about poverty in the developing nations of the world. The emergence and rapid development of a system of food banks in Canada during the 1980s following a severe recession drew public attention to the issue of poverty. Research has demonstrated the vulnerability of Canadian women to poverty within industrial societies,[5] but little work has been done to examine how women in the northern regions of Ontario have fared.

After the invasion of white men and industrial capitalism, single-industry towns and male-dominated occupational structures developed, limiting employment opportunities available to women. Men outnumbered women in the north until relatively recently, drawn to job opportunities offered by rail, mining, and lumber industries [see Chapter 1].[6] Today, the economy is still dominated by the mining industry in the northeast, while in the northwest the core economic activity stems from the pulp and paper industry.[7] The economic situation in the smaller communities is strongly affected by seasonal variations in employment patterns as well as by cyclical changes in industry. Changes relating to technology and environmental practices have affected industries in the primary sector and suggest that Northern Ontario faces long-term problems stemming from decreased primary industry activity.[8] The lack of diversity in northern economies further restricts types of jobs for women. In all Census Districts of Northern Ontario, employed women work predominantly in clerical, sales, and services occupations that are poorly paid and often provide only part-time positions; men are employed in a much broader range of occupations and dominate in the highly paid, unionized, and secure fields.

In this chapter, we present evidence on indicators of poverty and lack of access to financial resources among women in Northern Ontario.[9] As we will show, women who live in the north are more likely than northern men, and even their southern sisters, to be affected by low income, dependency, and second-class status in the workplace. The analysis focuses first on the incidence of low income for selected northern cities and towns, sources of income and dependency for women in Northern Ontario. Evidence on poverty is presented for two particularly vulnerable groups: single mothers and elderly women. We then present a comparison of the employment trends and average earnings for women in all Census Districts of Northern Ontario to examine the gender gap in incomes and the persistence of gender inequality over time.

Incidence of Low Income in Northern Ontario Cities and Towns

Over one-third of the women living in Northern Ontario cities and towns reported annual incomes under $10,000 in the 1991 census. Even without considering other factors, such as the number of dependents, this level of income was below all of the 1990 poverty lines (the year on which average income was based in the 1991 census).[10] The variations by city presented in Table 1 show that the 1991 incidence of income below $10,000 for women is higher in all but one (Kenora) of the five northern cities and selected smaller towns than the provincial rate of 31.5 percent. The communities in which the highest incidence of low income for women occurred were the northern cities of Sault Ste. Marie and Timmins, where 40 percent of women had annual incomes under $10,000.

Contrasting the male and female rates for incomes under $10,000 indicates that northern women are considerably worse off than are northern men. With the exceptions of North Bay and Kirkland Lake, the proportion of men in these northern communities with this low level of income was either less than the provincial average or very close to it (that is, within 2 percent).

Table 1. Incidence of Income Under $10,000 for Women and Men in Selected Northern Ontario Cities and Towns, 1991

CITIES AND TOWNS	PERCENTAGE OF WOMEN WITH INCOME < $10,000[a]	PERCENTAGE OF MEN WITH INCOME < $10,000[a]	RENT AS A PERCENTAGE OF WOMEN'S TOTAL INCOME[b]
North Bay	37.7	20.1	43.0
Sault Ste. Marie	40.1	18.6	39.4
Sudbury	35.8	19.5	37.0
Thunder Bay	34.4	16.4	37.8
Timmins	40.2	18.7	42.4
Parry Sound	33.0	18.7	44.4
Kirkland Lake	36.9	22.2	36.2
Kapuskasing	38.5	16.6	33.4
Kenora	30.9	16.8	39.7
Fort Frances	33.1	17.3	33.9
Ontario	31.5	17.7	40.9

[a] The percentage of women and men with low income is based on 1991 census data for individuals 15 years and over with income under $10,000.
[b] This ratio is based on average total incomes for women and the average rent in each community in 1991, as reported in census data.

Although women may have access to more money if they live in a household with one or more other adult earners, this is not necessarily true. Commonly accepted measures of poverty such as Statistics Canada's low-income cut-offs are based on the number of family members and total family income. Such definitions implicitly assume that the total family income is available to all family members on an equal basis. Unfortunately, this assumption is not always valid. According to the Canadian Advisory Council on the Status of Women, there is evidence that "women who live in families where the total income may be adequate are individually deprived because they do not control family resources or have adequate personal spending money."[11] The census data indicate that many northern women do not have access to or control over money in amounts sufficient to support themselves or their families independently. An analysis of women's total annual incomes in relation to the gross rents in the northern communities listed in Table 1 indicates that, on average, Northern Ontario women do not have access to sufficient income to maintain a household without slipping under the poverty line. If dependent on her salary alone, the average woman in eight of the Table 1 northern communities would be living under the poverty line when paying the average rent in her community. Hence, without even considering the additional costs of shelter that are typically not included in rent (for example, utilities) as well as food

and clothing, the average woman in these communities could not live independently without falling far below the poverty line. When the additional costs of
food, clothing, and shelter are considered, women's average incomes place
them substantially below the poverty line in all of these northern communities.[12] This basic fact explains why poverty is a reality for most women who
are the sole heads of households or who need to leave two-adult families due
to abuse.

Sources of Income and Dependency for Women

The vulnerability of women to low income and dependency on others in the
cities and towns of Northern Ontario is reinforced by 1991 tax filer data.
Women report one-half the amount of income that men do: $4,333,000 versus
$8,587,000. Most women and men who filed tax returns in 1991 derived the
majority of their income from work-related sources (see Table 2). Of the 1991
income accessible to women, however, 16.7 percent was derived from their
status as mothers, senior citizens, or consumers below the poverty line who
were eligible for some income credits or supplements compared to 5.5 percent
for men. Women in Northern Ontario were three times more likely than men to
receive government transfer payments and the rate of dependency on government transfers for northern women was greater than that for Ontario women as
a whole. Northern Ontario's women are disadvantaged and more dependent
not only relative to men in the north and but also relative to women in other
parts of the province.

**Table 2. Percentage of Income Derived by Women and Men Tax Filers
from Work or Status Sources in Northern Ontario and Ontario, 1991**

GROUPS	TOTAL INCOME (in millions)	PERCENT OF INCOME	
		FROM WORK SOURCES[a]	FROM STATUS SOURCES[b]
Northern Ontario			
Women	$4,333	83.3	16.7
Men	$8,587	94.5	5.5
Ontario			
Women	$62,598	88.8	11.2
Men	108,851	95.3	4.7

[a] Jobs, UIC, CPP, Pensions
[b] Family Allowance, Child Tax Credit, consumer, Old Age Pension, needs-tested welfare programs

Another way to assess poverty and dependency is to look at an area's economic dependency ratio (EDR). According to the Northern Ontario Regional
Economist's Office (1995, 2), the "EDR is effectively a measurement of how

poor an area is."[13] Comparisons of the EDR for Northern Ontario with the province as a whole show clearly that dependency rates are higher in the north than they are in the southern and central areas. These ratios also provide an indication of the extent to which northern women are at greater risk of poverty than are men. For example, the EDR rate of 40.5 percent for women in the northeast was higher than the 24.5 percent rate for men in 1991. The 40.5 percent EDR for northeastern Ontario women is even more alarming when it is compared with the 28.1 percent rate for all women in Ontario.

Vulnerable Groups

Poverty of mothers. Canadian women who are parents caring for children are particularly vulnerable to poverty, especially if there is not another adult in the household working in the labour market.[14] Canadian (and American) single female parents are three to four times at greater risk for experiencing poverty than are their European counterparts.[15] The poverty rate for single-parent mothers in Canada has been reported to be 52 percent for those who were previously married and 75 percent for those who were never married.[16]

Data were not available for all cities in Northern Ontario, but special tabulations of 1981, 1986, and 1991 census data on child poverty in Sudbury indicate that poverty rates were higher in Sudbury than in the province as a whole: 21.4 percent of all children under the age of 18 in the City of Sudbury were poor compared to 14.7 percent in Ontario during the 1991 census year.[17]

Oderkirk reported that 47 percent of all low-income families in Canada with children were single-parent families.[18] In contrast, the proportion of poor families that is made up of single-parent families was 70 percent in the City of Sudbury and 62 percent in the Region of Sudbury in 1991. Fifty percent of all the families headed by female parents were below the poverty line in 1991 in the City and Region of Sudbury, compared to less than 15 percent of male single parents. Considering only the 3,960 poor children in single-parent families living in the Regional Municipality of Sudbury, fully 95 percent were in families headed by women.

The census data also showed that the trend towards the concentration of child poverty in lone-parent families in the Sudbury area had accelerated in the last decade: 57 percent in 1981 and 56 percent in 1986, rising to 66 percent in 1991.

Poverty among elderly women in Northern Ontario. Returning to information on all of Northern Ontario, and looking into the future, we ask whether the situation is likely to improve for women who reach retirement age. Can older women expect that after a life of work inside and outside the home there will be some security and an adequate income? The answer, unfortunately, appears to be no.

Elderly women are particularly likely to experience low income and to require government assistance. Figure 1 clearly indicates that Northern

Ontario men received far more than women when three major sources of income for the elderly were considered: Old Age Security (OAS), Canada Pension Plan (CPP), and private pensions. Elderly women and men received almost equal amounts from the Old Age Security, which is to be expected, given that this program is a right of all citizens aged 65 and over. The slightly higher amount going to women reflects the fact that there are more older women than men in the population. Men, however, received approximately two-thirds of the income from CPP and over three-quarters of the income from private pensions.

The most striking contrast between men and women is in regard to the amount received from private pensions: northern men received $477,495,000 in total compared with only $143,671,000 for women. The lost income from fewer years of labour force participation due to child bearing and rearing as well as the lower average earnings for women continue to affect them throughout their lifespan. Women over age 65 averaged $13,000 per year in 1991 based on their right to Old Age Security and income from work-related pensions or savings, while, on average, elderly men had access to twice that amount of money.[19]

Figure 1. Sources and Distribution of Income to Senior Women and Men Tax Filers in Northern Ontario, 1991

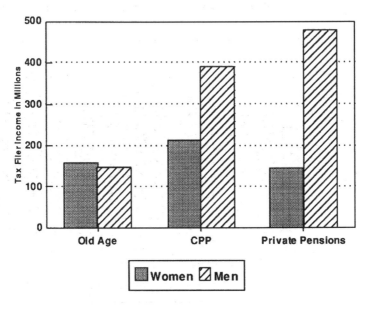

Women's increasing vulnerability to low income as they age is part of the legacy of traditional gender roles for women and their place in the traditional family. Even those elderly women who had been employed in the labour force receive lower incomes than elderly men after retirement, because most were not consistently employed full time during their working lives. Hence, their income from private pensions and from CPP (or Quebec Pension Plan in Quebec) is typically lower.

The Gender Gap in Average Incomes

Serious consequences follow from the limited access to adequate income that is the reality for many northern women, especially those who are mothers. As was noted above, dependency on incomes from male partners or the government is one of these consequences. Women who live in Northern Ontario are less able than Southern Ontario women to earn good incomes, in part because of the large gender gap and continued inequality in wages.

Women's average employment incomes are substantially below those for men in the north whether they worked full- or part-time. The 1991 census data showed that, overall, Northern Ontario women who were employed full-time earned just two-thirds of the salaries of their male counterparts. For the majority of Northern Ontario women who worked part-time, the situation was much worse: they earned substantially less than two-thirds of the corresponding male salaries (56 percent). Furthermore, the census data on women employed part-time shows that the gender disparity in wages is substantially higher in Northern Ontario compared with Ontario as a whole (see Figure 2).

Figure 2. Female Income as a Percentage of Male Income

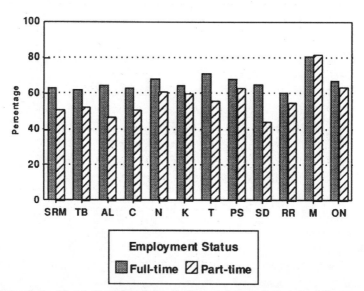

SRM=Sudbury Regional Municipality; TB=Thunder Bay; AL=Algoma; C=Cochrane; N=Nipissing; K=Kenora; T=Temiskaming; PS=Parry Sound; SD=Sudbury District; RR=Rainy River; M=Manitoulin Island; ON=Ontario.

An examination of variations between the Census Districts of Northern Ontario presented in Figure 2 shows that the gender gap in wages is the largest for the Sudbury District (i.e., in the smaller communities outside of the Regional Municipality), where women working part-time earned only 43.8 percent of the salaries of men employed part-time. The Districts of Nipissing, Timiskaming, Parry Sound, and Manitoulin appear anomalous with regard to the gender gap in wages: for women working full-time in these districts, average incomes were closer to those of their male counterparts. What is also common to all these districts, however, is that men's average incomes were substantially below the provincial average. Hence, women's earnings in these areas appeared to be more equal to men's, but this is only because the men in these areas earned much less than the average salaries for men in both Northern Ontario and Ontario as a whole.

A comparison of Northern Ontario women's salaries with those of Ontario women shows that women in all the northern districts earn substantially less than their southern sisters. Average earnings for full-time women employees in Northern Ontario were $24,780, compared with $27,862 for Ontario women.[20] Similarly, the corresponding averages for women working part-time were $9,987 in the north and $11,814 in the province as a whole. There were considerable variations in the average incomes for women employed full-time in different Census Districts of the north. Women's incomes were generally higher in the districts that contain the north's major urban centres; women earned more in Sudbury, Thunder Bay, Sault Ste. Marie, North Bay, and Timmins than in the other districts. The patterns in average incomes for women employed part-time were similar, with part-time earnings being lower in the districts that do not contain major urban centres.

An essential condition of self-sufficiency in industrial society is participation in the labour force. Traditionally, industrial capitalism enhanced male control over resources through the creation of wage labour and the "breadwinner" family. By reinforcing the distinction between male and female labour, devaluing women's work in the domestic or informal economy, and introducing labour laws that increased women's dependency on men, conditions were established that restricted women's access to the means of their livelihood. Social and economic changes in recent decades that increased the demand for female employees have led to steady increases in labour force participation. Having access to employment is obviously a prerequisite for participation; however, employment opportunities are likely to be distributed differentially in the Ontario economy.

The 1991 census data indicated that women in all parts of Northern Ontario were less likely to participate in the labour force on either a part-time or full-time basis than were southern women. A comparison of female participation rates in different northern districts showed that the participation rate for women was lower than the female provincial rate in every Census District in Northern Ontario. On average, the female participation rate combining full- and part-time work for northern districts was 7 percent lower than the corresponding provincial average. There was also considerable variation between regions in the north with regard to women's labour market participation as participation rates ranged from 2.3 percent (Thunder Bay) to 11.7 percent (Manitoulin) below the provincial average.

Only a minority of women were employed full-time in all districts of Northern Ontario. When considered in relation to the Ontario rate, the proportion of northern women participating full-time in the labour force was 20 percent lower than the provincial rate. In 1991, northern women were most likely to work at full-time jobs if they lived in the Regional Municipality of Sudbury and the Thunder Bay or Nipissing Districts; they were least likely to work full-time if they lived in the Sudbury, Algoma, or Timiskaming Districts. Hence, women were least likely to participate in the labour market if they lived in non-industrial settings. The low participation rates in smaller communities in the Sudbury, Manitoulin, and Parry Sound Districts probably reflect less access to employment opportunities: the occupations in which women are employed in larger urban centres (i.e., service and clerical jobs) do not exist in the same proportions. In addition, women in northern communities also have more restricted access to full-time jobs. These structural barriers along with the lower average earnings of northern women are major factors contributing to poverty for women in the north.

One question that can be raised is whether the situation has improved for women over time. Is the gender gap in wages decreasing and does a higher level of educational attainment make a difference in wage disparities? Unfortunately, data were not available on all of Northern Ontario. We know that female income as a percentage of male income in Sudbury was at a low of 31 percent in 1971, increased to 51 percent by the mid-1980s, and then stayed at this level for the last two census years (1986 and 1991). Census data for Sudbury also indicated that the difference between men's and women's average incomes was substantially smaller for women under age 39 than it was for older women. Younger women with university degrees had made significant gains in income as compared with women who had only high school diplomas. Yet a comparison of women with the same levels of education in 1991 suggests that older employed women who had attained university degrees have benefited less than younger women from the moderate improvements in the status of women in Sudbury's labour market.[21]

Hence, there have been some positive changes in the last 20 years, but the improvements have not been constant for women of all ages. In addition, the gradual trend towards decreases in gender inequality seems to have slowed in the last few years, with increases in education benefitting younger but not older women.

Discussion

Our analysis of the census and tax files information on poverty and work indicate the following:
- northern women have far less income than men, and their level of economic dependency on men and government transfers is high;
- northern women are more disadvantaged than their sisters in Southern Ontario;
- women in smaller towns have less access to employment and lower income than those living in the larger northern cities;
- single mothers and unattached older women are especially vulnerable to low income and poverty; and
- Canadian women have been making slow progress in achieving equity in the labour market, particularly in the last decade, but progress has been slower for women in Northern Ontario.

These basic facts about northern women reveal that the social and economic structures as well as cultural values in Northern Ontario have made independence and self-sufficiency a virtual impossibility for most women. The reality is that most northern women do not have access to a level of income that allows them to support themselves and their families – despite some positive changes in the last 20 years and a substantial increase in the hours women work outside the home.

Women's low wages and poverty have been more persistent in northern communities than in southern ones because of the resource-based economies and the more limited employment opportunities available to women. Historically, women have had less access than men to employment in the single-industry communities of the north. The lingering effects are manifested in the continued lower labour force participation rates, higher rates of part-time employment, the lower wages for women, and higher degree of gender inequality in wages. Our findings also showed that women who live in Northern Ontario's smaller towns experience even greater disadvantages than those living in the larger urban centres.

For women, as for men, work generates the major source of income as over 80 percent of their income is generated from work sources, including jobs, unemployment insurance, or private pensions. Despite northern women's high participation in the labour force, their average salaries consistently place them below the poverty line when measured against the average rents in their communities. Inadequate childcare, seasonal employment patterns, and higher costs of transportation compound the poorer employment opportunities of women who live in the small towns of Northern Ontario. Furthermore, a substantial minority of women and their children depend on families, male incomes, universal programs such as medicare and Old Age Security, as well as needs-tested programs like Family Benefits, for some income during a part of their lives. This dependence is greater than that of northern men and greater than women (or men) in Southern Ontario.

Women take great pride in their ability to care for others – at times against immense odds – yet they are blamed if they are perceived not to do these jobs well or to put other interests first.[22] The "rewards" that are reaped by women for the sacrifices they make in nurturing family members to ensure financial independence and social maturity for the latter are too often economic and social dependency for themselves. Moreover, women who must rely on social assistance are seen as a drain on society, costing the government millions of dollars to maintain. Economic structures and social processes continue to limit opportunities for women and keep their incomes low. Yet when they are forced to rely on social assistance, they face derogation and humiliation.

Poverty rates would be much higher for families and children if women had not increased their labour force participation in the last 25 years.[23] In the early 1970s, less than 40 percent of women and mothers worked in the labour force, and now over 50 percent do so in Northern Ontario. Women have increased their working hours outside the home without a significant reduction in their responsibilities for work inside the home [see Chapter 12]. Thus northern women are working longer hours than before, without a substantial increase in control over income or hope for security in the future.

18

La pauvreté des Franco-Ontariennes de 45 à 64 ans du Nord-Est de l'Ontario

Marie-Luce Garceau[1]

Le riche tire gloire de sa richesse, parce qu'il sent qu'elle attire
naturellement sur lui l'attention du monde .... [En revanche] ... Le
pauvre, au contraire, a honte de sa pauvreté. Il a conscience qu'elle le
met hors de la vue des hommes, ou bien que s'ils prêtent attention à
sa personne, ils n'ont guère de commisération pour son malheur et sa
détresse ... Le pauvre entre et sort sans qu'on le remarque.[2] (Smith,
cité par Heilbroner 1986)

C e n'est pas un hasard que la Fédération des femmes canadiennes-
françaises de l'Ontario (FFCFO) ait entrepris une vaste enquête de type
recherche-action, en 1990-91, sur les Franco-Ontariennes de 45 à 64
ans. En effet, cette organisation regroupe majoritairement des femmes de cette
tranche d'âge.

Par cette enquête, la FFCFO voulait sortir de l'indifférence sociale qui
stigmatise les femmes de 45 à 64 ans vivant dans le Nord-est et ailleurs, en
Ontario. Elle voulait mettre spécialement l'accent sur la fragilité économique
des femmes de ce groupe d'âge.

Pour comprendre l'importance de cette enquête, il faut d'abord considérer
l'ensemble des écrits sur l'Ontario français. Lorsqu'on procède à l'examen de
la recherche sociale effectuée sur cette population, on est rapidement décon-
certé par le long silence qui entoure la vie des femmes de 45 à 64 ans, et en
particulier de celles qui sont dénuées économiquement. En fait, la majorité des
études font fi de la condition des femmes francophones de cette province. Les
travaux de recherche, souvent axés sur la définition d'une identité collective
de cette population minoritaire, se conjuguent au masculin. La fonction identificatrice[3] des structures sociales, culturelles ou politiques franco-ontariennes
s'énonce au masculin. Les Franco-Ontariennes sont les éternelles absentes.
L'indifférence dont sont l'objet les Franco-Ontariennes de 45 à 64 ans est
exemplaire à ce titre.

S'inscrivant dans la foulée du mouvement des femmes de l'Ontario
français, ce projet de recherche provincial, dirigé par la FFCFO, a permis d'at-

tirer l'attention du public sur cette génération de femmes et la spécificité de leurs conditions de vie: économique, historique, culturelle et linguistique, éducationnelle, sanitaire, familiale, et de bénévolat.

À l'origine de ce projet, le besoin de reconnaissance sociale de ces femmes, soit de ne plus passer inaperçues ni d'être l'objet d'indifférence, cherchait à légitimer leur contribution sociale. De l'exécutif, en passant par les directions locales, aux membres du comité spécial mis en place pour effectuer cette recherche-action, toutes les membres de la FFCFO ont oeuvré à la réalisation de l'enquête. Non seulement souhaitaient-elles cette reconnaissance pour elles, au niveau politique, mais elles désiraient aussi qu'elle s'étende à l'ensemble des Franco-Ontariennes de 45 à 64 ans, en se faisant leur porteparole. Prenant conscience de leur enfermement, il s'agissait donc d'un mouvement massif de femmes, d'un phénomène collectif cherchant la reconnaissance d'autrui, des détenteurs de pouvoir.

Par la participation intense des femmes au projet de recherche-action, la FFCFO a mis à jour leur contribution à la société actuelle, en développant un nouveau savoir par, avec, sur, et pour les Franco-Ontariennes de 45 à 64 ans. Particulièrement, les femmes ont dénoncé le sacrifice de leur vie passée à prendre soin de celles et ceux qui les entourent, souvent au détriment de leur avancement personnel en termes de carrière professionnelle ou de situation économique. Elles attribuaient une grande importance à une forme de reconnaissance de leur travail domestique, de leur contribution sociale.

Pour réaliser le désir de tourner le regard sur elles, nous avons situé les sujets de l'enquête dans leur rôle d'actrices sociales. Nous avons tenté de rendre explicites leurs points de vue, de prendre les expériences des femmes comme point de départ de la recherche. D'une part, l'inclusion de leur propre perspective, du lieu où elles se placent, la reconnaissance et la validation de leur vécu et leur participation au projet permettent la conscientisation et la création de nouvelles connaissances, ayant pour objectif le changement ou l'amélioration de leurs conditions. D'autre part, elle permet aux femmes d'avoir un contrôle sur leur propre situation.

Produit d'une époque et d'une société données, quant au contenu de leur identité sexuelle et ethnique, cette génération de femmes a reconnu, au moyen de la recherche-action, les déterminants sociaux de leur situation, c'est-à-dire une position subordonnée dans les rapports sociaux de sexe, comme dans les rapports ethniques. Les résultats de la recherche-action démontrent largement les inégalités sociales affectant les Franco-Ontariennes de 45 à 64 ans. Vivant en français dans une province où elles sont minoritaires, les destinées de ces femmes ont été tracées à la fois par une socialisation différenciée entre les sexes, et par les importantes luttes ethniques. Il s'agit là d'un double phénomène d'infériorisation: comme femme et comme femme francophone.

Fortes de ce nouveau savoir, les Franco-Ontariennes de 45 à 64 ans du Nord, de l'Est ou du Sud ont elles-mêmes pris la parole et entrepris des actions

afin que les conditions de vie des femmes de cette tranche d'âge puissent être
améliorées,[4] tout particulièrement en ce qui a trait à leur situation économique.
Définitivement, elles voulaient percer l'indifférence qui les accablent.

Collection Miners' Mothers' Day

*Sophie Lagacé Belanger assise sur son balcon —
avec le gros lot (une chaise et une radio), fin des
années 1940.*

Pauvreté des Franco-Ontariennes de 45 à 64 ans du Nord-est

Parler de pauvreté, c'est prendre en considération à la fois l'insuffisance de
revenu (manque de ressources financières qui empêche de combler les besoins
fondamentaux: nourriture, vêtements, logement, etc.) et le manque d'accessibilité à des ressources qui limitent la capacité des femmes de pourvoir à leurs
besoins. Dans le premier cas, il s'agit de la pauvreté objective. On la reconnaît
par l'utilisation d'une mesure établissant l'incidence de la pauvreté et servant
à vérifier l'ampleur du phénomène. Dans le second, il s'agit davantage de la
pauvreté entendue comme la manifestation concrète de situations de personnes ou de groupes de personnes marquées par l'insuffisance ou le non-accès à
des ressources disponibles ou des moyens pour contrer la pauvreté. Cette
dernière inaccessibilité engendre la dépendance économique, la précarité du
statut social, et l'exclusion d'un mode de vie (matériel et culturel) dominant.[5]

À partir des données rassemblées au cours de l'enquête recherche-action sur les Franco-Ontariennes de 45 à 64 ans habitant le Nord-est, nous notons les phénomènes qui suivent quant au manque d'accessibilité aux moyens et aux ressources et son lien avec la pauvreté.[6] Pour l'essentiel, nous analyserons le travail et l'éducation.

L'enquête a été effectuée à partir des données rassemblées sur un échantillon représentatif de la population des Franco-Ontariennes (862 femmes). De ce nombre, 267 d'entre elles vivent dans le Nord-est de l'Ontario.

Pauvreté objective

Un regard sur les statistiques recueillies en cours d'enquête montre des populations particulières de femmes et de familles pauvres. Dans l'ensemble de l'échantillon, comme le montre le tableau 1, 20,3 pour cent des femmes du Nord-est déclarent un revenu familial sous le seuil de pauvreté.[7] Pour l'année 1992, dans l'ensemble de la population ontarienne, le taux de pauvreté des personnes âgées de 45 à 64 ans ne s'élevait qu'à 14 pour cent, soit un écart de 6 pour cent.[8] Cette différence importante nous amène à constater que le taux de pauvreté est plus importante qu'on ne le croît.

Dire que la pauvreté affecte davantage les femmes que les hommes est un truisme. La structure familiale s'étant modifiée suite à une séparation ou un divorce, les taux les plus élevés de pauvreté, chez les Franco-Ontariennes de 45 à 64 ans, se situent dans les familles monoparentales dirigées par une femme, dont deux (66,6 pour cent) ou un enfant (50,0 pour cent) sont actuellement aux études. En outre, les femmes vivant seules sont aussi largement affectées par la pauvreté (50,0 pour cent). En Ontario, pour l'année 1992, le taux de pauvreté chez les personnes seules est de 11,2 pour cent. Cette différence s'explique par l'âge avancé des femmes, et nous doutons fort que la situation vécue puisse changer dans un proche avenir. Pour elles, la pauvreté est durable, tout particulièrement dans les cas des femmes qui sont actuellement veuves.

Pour les couples n'ayant plus d'enfants à la maison, on trouve 13,3 pour cent de familles pauvres. Dans ces cas, c'est particulièrement chez les familles dont l'un des deux conjoints est à la retraite que la pauvreté frappe. De plus, 19,6 pour cent des couples ayant un enfant et 20,0 pour cent des couples ayant deux enfants actuellement aux études vivent sous le seuil de pauvreté. Encore ici, compte tenu de l'âge avancé des femmes, comme de celui de leur conjoint, leur situation de pauvreté est fort probablement durable.

Finalement, la pauvreté personnelle touche particulièrement 22,5 pour cent des femmes du Nord-est qui travaillent à temps plein, et 78,7 pour cent de celles qui travaillent à temps partiel. Le taux est aussi particulièrement élevé chez les femmes à la retraite (48,0 pour cent) et les travailleuses au foyer (94,2 pour cent). De plus, chez les couples dont le conjoint est retraité, 28,6 pour cent d'entre eux vivent sous le seuil de pauvreté. La pauvreté des femmes, comme celle de leur conjoint, étant fonction de leur faible rémunération de travail, elle se perpétue à la retraite, parce que les pensions gouvernementales sont établies en fonction de cette rémunération.

Tableau 1. Taux de pauvreté des familles franco-ontariennes dont la femme est âgée de 45 à 64 ans, selon les types de familles

Types de familles	Taux de pauvreté (%)
Familles monoparentales - 1 enfant	50,0
Familles monoparentales - 2 enfants	66,6
Femmes seules sans enfant	50,0
Couples sans enfant	13,3
Couples - un enfant	19,6
Couples - deux enfants	20,0
Total de pauvreté dans l'ensemble des familles de l'enquête	20,3

Valeurs présentes: 77,5%

Pauvreté et inaccessibilité aux ressources

En prenant pour objet d'analyse le travail féminin, les données confirment la division sexuelle qui s'opère dans la sphère domestique comme dans la sphère du travail, et la place subalterne qu'occupent les Franco-Ontariennes de 45 à 64 ans dans la première comme dans la seconde. La structure discriminante de la répartition des tâches dans la famille fait porter en totalité le poids des responsabilités domestiques et familiales sur les femmes. Leur intégration prolongée dans la sphère domestique les disqualifie largement lorsqu'elles veulent intégrer la sphère du travail salarié, limitant de ce fait la participation d'une large proportion de femmes de cette tranche d'âge à la sphère productive. Par ailleurs, la structure et l'organisation du marché du travail est aussi discriminante à l'égard de ces femmes. Elles prédisposent les Franco-Ontariennes de 45 à 64 ans à occuper une place précise dans la structure professionnelle des emplois. L'analyse de leurs activités professionnelles permet de voir qu'elles sont majoritairement confinées dans les emplois peu qualifiés, moins rémunérés, et moins valorisants. Concentrées dans des ghettos féminins d'emploi, dans des professions à prédominance féminine, qui prolongent leurs activités domestiques, leur participation reflète les besoins et l'évolution du marché du travail actuel: souplesse, prédisposition aux horaires partiels, discontinuité de longue durée, faible rémunération, absence d'avantages sociaux, et faible syndicalisation, etc.

Il est donc facile de comprendre l'inégalité économique saillante des Franco-Ontariennes de 45 à 64 ans et leur pauvreté personnelle compte tenu de leur assignation prioritaire à la sphère domestique, et de leur accès limité dans la sphère du travail. Elles ont pour la plupart des revenus nettement inférieurs à ceux de leurs conjoints. Ceci entraîne leur dépendance économique et, par conséquent, leur incapacité d'atteindre une certaine autonomie financière. De ce fait, les femmes doivent négocier au quotidien la volonté de redistribution du conjoint.

Or, la pauvreté personnelle des Franco-Ontariennes du Nord-est âgées de 45 à 64 ans est plus élevée qu'ailleurs en province. Ainsi, 65,1 pour cent de ces femmes gagnent moins de 15,000$ par année, alors que dans l'ensemble des autres régions étudiées dans l'enquête, ce pourcentage est de 59,0 pour cent. En outre, dans cette même tranche de revenu, on retrouve 37,9 pour cent des femmes du Nord-est qui déclarent n'avoir aucun revenu personnel.

De plus, l'incidence annuelle de revenu de moins de 10,000$, dans l'ensemble de la population féminine, dans certaines villes du Nord de l'Ontario, varie entre 40,1 et 30,9 pour cent [voir le chapître 17] . Dans l'ensemble de la province, il se situe à 32,5 pour cent. Dans l'enquête, 53,2 pour cent des femmes de 45 à 64 ans habitant le Nord-est de l'Ontario déclarent un revenu personnel de moins de 10,000$ pendant l'année de l'étude. C'est donc dire que dans la population des femmes de 45 à 64 ans, l'incidence annuelle de revenu de moins de 10,000$ est beaucoup plus élevée que dans la population féminine en général.

Mais qui se soucie de la pauvreté personnelle d'une femme mariée, comme de ses conséquences quotidiennes? Après tout, dira-t-on, elle a un conjoint qui peut subvenir à ses besoins comme à ceux de ses enfants. Et qui se préoccupe réellement des femmes pauvres du Nord-est de la province qui vivent seules, ou qui sont chefs de famille monoparentale?

L'analyse du niveau de scolarité des Franco-Ontariennes de 45 à 64 ans du Nord-est ontarien est aussi en lien avec leur pauvreté. Dans la tradition franco-ontarienne, le niveau de scolarité primaire ou secondaire suffisait amplement aux femmes destinées à travailler au foyer. C'est pourquoi la plupart des femmes de cette région n'ont pas dépassé le niveau de scolarité secondaire (72,5 pour cent). La sous-scolarisation est un facteur important dans la décision de ces femmes de travailler toute leur vie au foyer. L'équation est fort simple: pour la majorité, un faible niveau de scolarité, combiné à la composition de la famille, notamment le nombre d'enfants, font qu'elles ne peuvent se distancier du modèle familial traditionnel de travail au foyer. Peu scolarisées, ces femmes ont choisi d'exercer leur profession de travailleuse au foyer. Travail non reconnu et effectué sans aide, il impose par dessus tout la dépendance économique aux femmes qui l'exercent. Pourtant, dans leurs aspirations, elles veulent une forme de valorisation sociale ou économique de ce statut. À l'opposé, celles qui ont atteint une scolarité de niveau postsecondaire, se distancient du modèle traditionnel du travail au foyer afin d'intégrer le marché du travail à temps plein ou à temps partiel. Mais, malgré leur large participation à la sphère du travail salarié, ces femmes sont conscientes des limites qu'impose la structure du marché du travail. Pour nombre d'entre elles, malgré certaines compétences académiques, cela signifie des interruptions de travail en fonction du modèle ambiant de vie familiale, et une structure de marché du travail discriminante envers les femmes. Par ailleurs, le système éducatif n'est pas réellement accessible à l'ensemble des femmes francophones de cette génération. En Ontario français, les établissements d'enseignement ne déploient pas beaucoup d'énergie pour rejoindre les femmes de ces âges. Il n'est pas réellement accessible, à cause de l'étendue du territoire et du peu d'accessibilité à l'éducation en français dans certaines régions éloignées, mais surtout parce qu'il représente une course à obstacles infranchissables, tout particulièrement pour les femmes moins scolarisées.

Ces deux exemples d'inaccessibilité aux moyens et aux ressources afin de contrer la pauvreté permettent de comprendre rapidement la situation économique personnelle, très précaire, de la majorité des Franco-Ontariennes de 45 à 64 ans, comme de celles des femmes du Nord-est de la province. Dans de telles circonstances, elles ne peuvent, pour la plupart, subvenir à leurs besoins et doivent faire appel à la générosité de leur conjoint. Or, cette inaccessibilité, ou l'insuffisance de ressources et de moyens, sont exacerbées lorsqu'il s'agit de la pauvreté objective des femmes.

Commentaires

Les trajectoires sociales et uniques de chacune des femmes de 45 à 64 ans qui vivent dans le Nord-est ontarien ne sont pas à négliger dans l'explication de leur situation de pauvreté. Mais, même si ce groupe social n'est pas unifié, il existe des réalités collectives qui permettent d'expliquer leur pauvreté: transformations des formes familiales, transformations du marché du travail, et faible niveau de scolarité.

L'insuffisance de revenu de travail est une cause importante de pauvreté des femmes comme de leur famille. Ces bas salaires sont une conséquence des modifications de la structure de l'emploi survenues au cours de la dernière décennie: tertiarisation du marché du travail, accroissement du secteur des services, précarité, flexibilité, féminisation de l'emploi, ou faible syndicalisation, etc.

Quant au faible niveau de scolarité, combiné à l'âge des femmes, ils ont des effets déterminants sur la situation de pauvreté. Or, les Franco-Ontariennes du Nord-est indiquent ne pas avoir la possibilité, ni le goût de parfaire leurs études. Elles n'en voient pas la réelle utilité, l'âge y étant pour beaucoup. Pourtant, celles qui l'ont fait, malgré leurs inscriptions dans les filières traditionnelles d'éducation réservées à leur sexe, certaines ont pu réussir à se tailler une meilleure place dans la sphère du travail rémunéré.

La pauvreté des Franco-Ontariennes de 45 à 64 ans du Nord-est a des conséquences majeures sur leur mode de vie, marqué par la précarité, l'exclusion, et l'inquiétude face à l'avenir. Ce mode de vie influe sur leurs comportements individuels et collectifs: honte, perte d'estime de soi, humiliation, solitude, isolement et problèmes de santé.[9] Depuis la dernière campagne électorale ontarienne, les réformes entreprises par l'État ontarien, comme entre autres et à titre d'exemple, la réforme de l'aide sociale, vont dans le sens d'associer aux revenus de transferts gouvernementaux, ceux qui étaient jadis un instrument de soutien à la consommation, une forme ou l'autre d'activités d'éducation, de formation ou d'utilité sociale. Face au discours actuel et aux coupures qu'il entraîne, celles qui sont ou seront touchées par ces mesures, les plus démunies, n'ont pas droit au chapitre. L'indifférence qu'on porte à leur situation n'a d'égal que le désir des riches d'améliorer leur propre situation.

Certes, les femmes de l'Ontario français ont depuis longtemps déjà préconisé les valeurs d'entraide et de partage, dans leur travail domestique, leur entraide intergénérationnelle, ou leur bénévolat. Pourtant, ces valeurs ne sont jamais reconnues socialement. Et si aujourd'hui on leur accorde de l'importance et une centralité, il faut dire que les femmes et leurs valeurs n'accepteront plus de passer inaperçues, dans l'ombre.

Les femmes de l'Ontario français, et plus particulièrement celles qui font partie de la Fédération des femmes canadiennes-françaises de l'Ontario, ont compris que la solidarité envers les plus démunies visent plus qu'une simple prise de conscience d'une situation de pauvreté. Elles ont compris que sans reconnaissance sociale pour les sortir de l'indifférence, toutes seront plus pauvres.

19

A Study of Violence and Isolation Experiences of Northern Women

Marian Beauregard

This chapter is based on interviews with 18 abused women living in areas in Ontario that are primarily northern and rural.[1] Physical isolation was a common experience for the majority of the women interviewed. Most of them had at one time been in a shelter for abused women or in a mental health clinic. Their stories show that isolation contributed to the women's mental health problems and perpetuated abusive behaviour. While the focus of the conversations with these women was the way isolation contributed to abuse, the interviews also revealed the strategies the women used to cope with their isolation.

Isolation

Chalmers and Smith discuss three ways in which women can be isolated: social, psychological, and geographical.[2] I will argue that as well as the three factors cited, economic isolation also contributes to women's isolation, particularly in the context of rural Northern Ontario. While social isolation or isolation from the mainstream of Canadian society can affect Ontario women regardless of where they live, it is most prevalent among minority women. This was evident in the interviews conducted. A lesbian living in an abusive situation expressed concern over the loneliness she experienced while "living closeted in a straight community.... I was afraid to be open with anyone.... I used alcohol to avoid dealing with my fears." For socially isolated women like herself, seeking help meant disclosing her sexual orientation and the risk of discrimination.

"Psychological isolation finds its roots in the more general isolation experienced by all women."[3] The expectation that women will protect the privacy and honour of the family demands silence on certain issues such as family violence. Loyalty and family unity separate individual women from understanding the common experiences they share regarding inequalities and violence within the home. Silence means the violence goes unreported and the abuser goes unpunished. The abuse is not counted in official statistics and both the violence and victim remain invisible.

Geographic isolation is a problem for many people in Northern Ontario. Most of the area is rural with wide expanses of forests and lakes between towns and dwellings. While individuals are geographically isolated, the region itself is cut off from the centre of political decision making in the southern part of the province. Policies made by a centralized government are often difficult to execute in northern areas and sometimes exact heavy penalties on women who live there. For example, the policy of laying charges in domestic assaults as described by Billson is difficult.[4] Because of the time needed to respond to a crisis, the police seldom witness either the violence itself or its result. The police might arrive hours after the dispute; by this time the woman might be severely injured or the partners reconciled. If the man is charged, the woman may face considerable pressure from the community as a result of calling the police. The authorities often find that an abused woman does not want to testify against her partner; she knows her circumstances may worsen if her partner is jailed or fined. The next time the abuse occurs, the woman finds it more difficult to call police, causing the problem to go "underground."[5]

Economic isolation is likely to handicap women at both ends of the economic scale. While it may be easier to understand the isolation of a woman living in poverty without a telephone, car, or access to public transportation, the isolation of the middle- and upper-class woman is often invisible. A professional woman living in a rural community may feel isolated from her peers and have few friends in the community. The nature of either her job or her husband's employment may further impede her attempts to seek help: the policeman's wife cannot turn to her husband's co-workers for support; the doctor has no one else to tend to her injuries but her own staff and colleagues.

Chalmers and Smith point out that a violent man can isolate his partner by preventing her from working outside the home, controlling the number and frequency of contacts with friends and family, and monitoring her activities.[6] He may move her to a remote area where services are inaccessible and support unavailable. This allows the abuser to have an exclusive relationship with his partner. Cut off from others, the abused woman begins to rely on her abusive partner for all her needs. When the abuser discovers the responsibility he has assumed, he begins to feel suffocated and becomes violent.

Stories of Isolation

Amelia spoke of the isolation she and her children endured with her husband – a professional man who was both abusive and alcoholic – when they lived on an island. At another stage in their marriage, they lived "in an isolated place in the country where it was hard to have people visit." He sabotaged her efforts to see her friends and did not allow her to achieve her personal goals. She was, however, eventually able to make friends with other parents in the community and this was how she was able to overcome her depression.

Irene's husband moved her to an isolated area where most of her neighbours were her in-laws. Her husband's violent behaviour led to the death of her first child. Both his abuse and the family's isolation contributed to her inability to get assistance in times of crisis. She said the violence always began "at home when there was nobody around." Living at least 30 minutes from the nearest police detachment, Irene had no hope that they would get there soon enough to witness the abuse. She felt her family was afraid to come and see her in case her husband "was drunk and in a rage." When her husband discharged his shotgun at her children, the neighbours dismissed the incidents as target practice. Medical care was virtually unavailable for Irene. She turned to drinking with her husband as a means of coping with the abuse that continued for more than 30 years. With the assistance of her daughter, Irene was eventually able to leave her husband and quit drinking, but by that time she was in her sixties and physically disabled from the abuse.

Amy stated that "as soon as we were married, I was totally isolated from my friends." The family moved to a reserve where, as a non-native, she was made to feel that she had no rights. A Native woman, Mary, felt that because she herself was from another reserve, the neighbours always took her husband's side. At one point he dragged her by the hair from the office where she worked and beat her; her co-workers witnessed the abuse but did nothing.

Some women felt that they could never tell if their husband's family would help them and their children during a family crisis; accepting and charitable one day, they could turn their backs the next rather than get involved. One abused woman often commiserated with her sister-in-law, who was also an abused woman. Both felt they put each other at risk if they provided certain kinds of help, such as a drive into town or assisted with a long distance call, if there was any chance that it could be traced back to either woman.

Karen connected her acceptance of the abuse she suffered to her social isolation. "I think the reason I stayed so long was that I had so few people to turn to; he was all I had." Her partner's friends were of little help: "He only had one friend and I had to put up with him even though he had spent ten years in prison for killing his wife. I didn't like him." Karen mentioned feeling like she was in a prison because she had no privacy and no control over her life. Her partner was charged after he stabbed her. She was then able to get away from him and soon left the area to create a new life for herself.

Diane spoke of how her husband alienated one of the few friends she could turn to when she was abused. "I had this girlfriend at work, and one night when he abused me I ran to her place. The next time she called me, he cursed at her and told her not to call me again." Elizabeth lived 25 miles out into the country. "I wasn't even supposed to go to a Tupperware party. If I did, there was always a 'payback' and I learned to stay at home." Suzette learned that she could contact her family only once a month. If she took too much time with anyone outside the home, even her doctor, she would have to face abuse of some kind. Many of the women mentioned that they were allotted a certain amount of time to go to appointments, shop for groceries, get back and forth to work, or visit family. To go beyond the prescribed time meant risking a beating.

Michelle had been an outgoing community-minded person before she became involved with her partner. "It was like he kept me like on a chain. He even prevented me from leaving the house."

Responsibility for childcare was seldom shared in these families, and some men would keep the women home by refusing to watch the children or pay a babysitter. However, limited family resources or issues around the care of the children never controlled how often the men could go out. Many of the women complained of the long hours their partners took for hunting and fishing, leaving the wives alone with the children and without transportation into town.

When Josie was most depressed she would shut all the curtains, lock all the doors, and seldom go out. She had no phone and lived down a country road where the only neighbour was an old man. She said, "My husband moved me into the bush. He took my car keys to work with him so I had to stay home. I wasn't allowed to visit my family." He was so jealous that she risked a beating if another man looked at her or spoke to her.

Sunny, a badly abused woman with a psychiatric history, tried for years to leave her husband. She visited many shelters in her attempts to disappear. Her religious friends would tell her partner where she was and he would then force her to go back with him. He tried to fire her doctor, interfered with her psychiatric care, and threatened her family members if they hid her from him. She learned to avoid her family in case he harmed them. Sunny credited the shelters for giving her a place to stay and with helping her come out of her depression. At the shelters she met people with whom she could talk. After each period of isolation, Sunny said that when she arrived at the shelter she would talk until she was "blue in the face."

Stories of Abuse

Although all the women I interviewed were physically abused, four were battered to the point that their lives were endangered. Of the 18 women, 11 had had something thrown at them; 17 were pushed, grabbed, or shoved; 12 were slapped or kicked; and 10 were beaten. Eight women were choked; three were stabbed or cut; 12 were punched with a fist; 17 were knocked to the ground; two were burned; 10 were forced into sex; and 11 had their property destroyed. Elizabeth said, "My husband grabbed my glasses and broke them, shredded my nightgown off me, pulled hair, flipped me off the mattress when I was sleeping." Sue's husband forced her to have sex with his friends to pay for his drugs.

Seven women were threatened by guns, three by knives, one with an axe. Evelyn's husband, a police officer, quit beating her after he stopped drinking. Later she discovered he was drinking again and also having an affair. She discovered that he was plotting to kill her. "Twice … I thought he was going to get his gun…. He was always drunk." Michelle reported, "Once when I was going to call for help, he took the cord of the telephone and threatened to choke me with the darned thing." Three of the women admitted that they also tried to kill their husbands. Marie served time in jail on a charge of dangerous use of a firearm when she tried to shoot her husband. Irene tried to shoot her husband but the gun misfired. Sue stabbed her husband through his leather jacket.

Some of the women were severely abused during pregnancy. Three women reported that they went into premature labour because of abuse, two lost premature babies, and one woman had three miscarriages as a consequence of violence. Two women had abortions rather than carry the baby to full term after they terminated the relationship. Karen explained her experience: "I would have ended up losing it from getting beat up. I didn't think it would develop normally."

While most women seek help because of physical abuse, some women reported less physical abuse but more emotional abuse. Three women were aware that their partner had sexually abused their children. Michelle describes the catalyst for the last incident of violence. "He wanted to kill the dog in front of my son. I got rid of the dog by chasing him down the street. Nobody'd help."

Mary's husband put an unloaded gun into her vagina and pulled the trigger. He also threatened to harm her with scissors. Generally speaking, the pattern was of emotional abuse that escalated into physical abuse. Sunny's case is somewhat different: the physical abuse started early in the marriage. "The first day he hit me was the day after the wedding. I had to go to a shelter five weeks after we were married; I had been sent there from the emergency ward. In three years, I left 13 times."

Many of the women continued to be abused by their partners after they separated. Josie's husband not only abused her after they separated but also molested her son and sexually assaulted the child of a social worker who assisted her to leave him. In trying to escape from their partners both Sunny and Karen adopted new identities. Many of the women had to move to a new community to escape the abuse, leaving their homes, friends, and jobs behind. Elizabeth's husband continued to threaten her by phone from across the country, forcing her to move every few months out of fear. Three husbands threatened to kill themselves if their wives did not return to them, and one did commit suicide. Many women complained of the lack of protection by the police, the legal system, neighbours, and family. Some men, mostly those from the middle class, were able to manipulate psychiatrists and judges to take their sides.

Consequences to Mental Health

Evidence from the interviews supports the theory that social connection is important to women's mental health and that abuse and isolation are predictors or even precipitants of depression. Of the 18 abused women, 16 suffered from clinical depression during the time they were being abused or when they left their partners. Those who had a history of childhood sexual abuse suffered from more extreme depression than the women who had not gone through such abuse. In fact, only two of the 18 battered women interviewed for this study did not meet clinical criteria for major depression. Features of anxiety disorders – notably post-traumatic stress disorder – and panic attacks were common in this group. Indeed, with only one exception, the women who had the most extensive psychiatric histories also had the most extensive histories of abuse.

The profile of the depression suffered by these abused women is similar to that of other persons who are depressed. The difference is that abused women have the added dimension of fear. Problems with sleep, loss of appetite, low energy levels, and lack of enjoyment of daily activities were commonly reported. The women's increased irritability and displaced anger sometimes resulted in mistreatment of their children and guilt because of the harm they might have done. However, some women sought solace in their children and made a special effort to compensate them for having witnessed the abuse.

Three of the women interviewed found temporary relief from their abuser by having themselves admitted to a psychiatric hospital. However, the stay in a psychiatric ward provided another kind of isolation. Abused women who have had to stay in a psychiatric ward often feel ashamed of having had to seek such help, which leads to further depression and more isolation. Left alone to dwell on their problems without support or validation, some women became fearful, agoraphobic, and even psychotic.

One man played on his wife's fears by telling her that her neighbour was a rapist and left her with a loaded gun and a guard dog to protect herself. He called her at various times during the day or night to "check on her," made their home unwelcome to anyone who came to visit, and made it impossible for her to go out or talk to friends on the phone. After she became psychotic, she was a danger to all those who lived around her, since she had come to believe that everyone was "out to get her." Grinell describes this as "folie à deux," where dependence on a crazed dominant person distorts the subordinate person's reality.[7] When isolation prevents one from checking with others and correcting one's reality, an induced depression or anxiety with psychotic features can develop.

Attempts to Overcome Isolation and Abuse

Women in Northern Ontario have found a number of ways to cope with isolation. These include the social networks that have spawned such organizations as the Women's Institutes, various women's auxiliaries, quilting groups, horticultural clubs, and so on. Native women have initiated women's healing circles and craft groups. Some other cultural groups have active social networks that endeavour to offer ethnic heritage events and to break the isolation of new members and immigrants in the community.

It is only by breaking out of the isolation that women can stop the abuse and regain their mental health. Social connections can help women recover from depression, a phenomenon that is regularly seen in women's shelters. When abused women come together in shelters or self-help groups, many are astounded at how common their experiences are. "We could have been married to clones," commented Elizabeth. Low self-esteem, low self-worth, shyness, and lack of confidence are common features in the mental health of isolated women. Yet reaching help is made difficult by women's isolation in the north. Abusive men who live in cities may be court-ordered to attend batterers' groups as part of their sentencing. However, few communities in Northern Ontario have the agencies or trained staff to offer such programs. Instead, the abusers may be placed in addiction programs where their violent nature is not addressed.

Seldom are the efforts of women to improve their lives and the lives of other women noted in the recorded history of the north. For most women in Northern Ontario, their isolation has decreased through the years. However, for abused women, the depth of isolation is similar to that of their grandmothers, and the effects on mental health draw women in abusive situations to drugs, psychiatric hospitals, and private despair.

Women in Northern Ontario have made outstanding contributions to the fabric of community life as they cope with the isolation endemic to the north. If women in Northern Ontario are to overcome the isolation and the abuse and enjoy positive mental health, they must have control over their daily lives.

20

Women's Health in Northern Ontario: An Introductory Geographical Appraisal

J. Roger Pitblado and Raymond W. Pong

The shortage and maldistribution of qualified health professionals is a problem of long-standing concern to the providers and consumers of health care in the north, as well as to the provincial government. Consequently, the Northern Health Human Resources Research Unit (NHHRRU), a conjoint undertaking of Laurentian and Lakehead universities, was established in 1991 to undertake and foster multi-disciplinary research that addresses health personnel issues. Components of the research activities of NHHRRU include the examination of the complex interactions between health status, health behaviour, and the utilization of health care resources.

More than 50 percent of health care consumers are women. Given both the objectives of NHHRRU and the nature of this volume, it is appropriate that we focus our attention on women's health.

The primary objective of this paper is to examine the health status of women, their health behaviours, and how they use the services of health care providers. Selecting a limited number of measures from the Ontario Health Survey (OHS) and using a descriptive overview approach, we are particularly concerned about the character of regional variations. The focus is on women in the north, with additional comparisons made with women's health either in Southern Ontario or in Ontario as a whole.

The Ontario Health Survey

The Ontario Health Survey is a population-based health survey designed to be representative of each of the province's 42 Public Health Units (PHUs). Statistics Canada was contracted by the Ontario Ministry of Health (MOH) to design the survey, select the PHU samples based on population numbers from the 1986 Census, and to conduct the survey.[1] The target population within the PHUs consisted of all Ontarians who were residents of non-institutional dwellings during the survey period from January through December 1990. A major disappointment of the OHS sampling design, especially for those of us dealing with health issues in the north, was the fact that First Nations people living on reserves and residents of extremely remote locations were excluded.

The OHS was conducted in two stages. Part 1, a 22-page questionnaire, was completed by interviewing one member of a sampled household who was knowledgeable enough to answer questions pertaining to everyone within the household. Questions dealt with recent or current health problems, disability days, accidents and injuries, health status, chronic health problems, use of health services, and demographic information. The 26-page Part 2 questionnaire was administered within each sampled household to each member aged 12 years or older. The latter questionnaire was self-completed and dealt with such issues as self-rated health, use of medicines and drugs, smoking, alcohol use, and nutrition.

The geography of health care administration and program planning in Ontario is reflected in the OHS, as all cases are identified by Ministry of Health planning region, district health council, and public health unit. The large MOH planning regions sometimes mask the significant intra-regional differences of OHS responses.[2] In this paper, therefore, we not only present data on the northeastern and northwestern planning regions, but also look at some important variations among the smaller public health units. For scale and reference purposes, the PHUs have been outlined in Figure 1 with the Northern Ontario public health units identified by name.

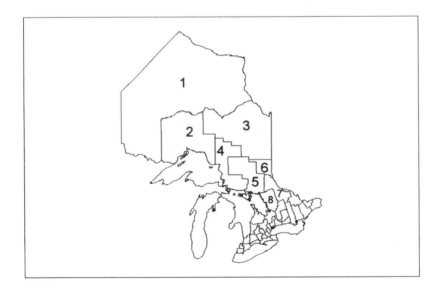

Figure 1

Outlines of Ontario's Public Health Unit areas. Northern PHUs are identified by numbers: 1 - Northwestern; 2 - Thunder Bay; 3 - Porcupine; 4 - Algoma; 5 - Sudbury; 6 - Timiskaming; 7 - North Bay; 8 - Muskoka-Parry Sound

There are 61,239 cases in the OHS sample. Using the survey's weighting scheme, this represents 9,743,720 people in Ontario, of whom slightly more than 4.9 million are female. Under the three headings listed earlier, we have chosen to highlight only a very small number of the 1,200 variables in the OHS data-set: smoking, mammogram screening, number of health problems, chronic health problems, and contacts with physicians and dentists.[3]

Health Status

In the 12 months preceding the survey, a majority (67 percent) of women in Ontario experienced one or more health problems. Of these women, 43 percent reported having only one health problem, while close to 50 percent experienced two to four problems. Regional variations in the numbers of health problems are not striking. However, there is a tendency for women in the north to have slightly higher numbers of health problems than their counterparts in the south or in the province as a whole. For example, just over 9 percent of the women with health problems in northeastern Ontario reported having five to eight (the maximum number included in the OHS) problems. For northwestern Ontario and Ontario as a whole, the comparable figures are 10 percent and 8 percent, respectively.

In its initial review of the OHS data, the Ministry of Health noted that the major categories of the most prevalent chronic health problems of Ontarians were: muscle/skeletal (25 percent), respiratory (23 percent), injuries and poisoning (12 percent), and circulatory (12 percent).[4] These disease or morbidity patterns are similar for women. Unfortunately, the figures for women in the north often tend to be higher than those for the whole province. Indeed, of the 20 categories of long-term health problems reported by the OHS, the highest proportions in 15 of these are reported by women in either the northeast, the northwest, or Northern Ontario as a whole.

Compared with women in Southern Ontario, northern women suffer slightly higher percentages of skin diseases and back pain and significantly higher proportions of arthritis/rheumatism, circulatory, and heart disease problems. The regional variations are illustrated for these chronic illnesses in Figure 2.

Health Behaviour

Both health professionals and public health advocates have urged people to practise or avoid certain behaviours. These are activities that are considered to be beneficial for promoting health and prevent illness or lifestyles that are seen as detrimental to health and well-being.[5] The OHS dealt with these activities through a large number of questions and derived indices. One group of derived variables may be considered measures of health risks: driving patterns, use of bicycle helmets, substance use and abuse, activities that increase the exposure to sexually transmitted diseases, and workplace risks. The second group con-

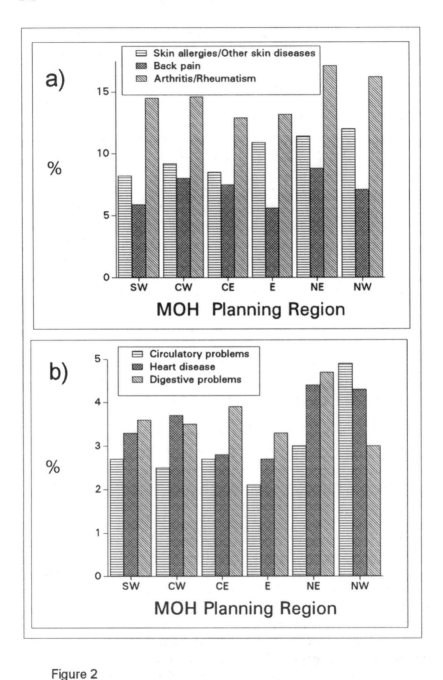

Figure 2

Chronic illness patterns for women by planning regions:
SW - South West; CW - Central West; CE - Central East;
E - Eastern; NE - North East; NW - North West

sists of preventive activities in the areas of nutrition, weight gain or loss, physical activity, and screening/monitoring. Because of space limitations we have chosen to examine only one measure from each of these two groups of factors: smoking and mammogram screening.

Smoking. In Ontario today it is estimated that prolonged disease, suffering, and 20 percent of all deaths can be attributed to smoking. This is the case despite the fact that over the past 25 years tobacco use by the adult population of Ontario has declined from approximately 40 percent to well under 30 percent.[6]

Unfortunately, northerners continue to be relatively heavy smokers: 29.9 percent and 28.6 percent of women in the northeast and northwest, respectively, are regular smokers. And to these figures could be added the 5 to 6 percent of women in these regions who are occasional smokers. The picture is worse than this, however, if one examines women's use of tobacco by a smaller unit, the Public Health Unit. As illustrated in Figure 3, there is only one northern PHU (Algoma) where the proportion of women who are daily smokers is similar to that of the overall Ontario rate (23 percent). The proportions are particularly high in the Sudbury-Manitoulin area and the two most northerly PHUs, Northwestern and Porcupine. It is also important to point out that all PHUs which fall into the Figure 3 mapping class of 30 to 34 percent are located in Northern Ontario. By contrast, all the PHUs in the 15 to 19 percent mapping class are located only in Southern Ontario (not shown in Figure 3).

Mammogram screening. In a recent front-page article, the Globe and Mail highlighted the results of a major study undertaken by the Ontario Cancer Institute in Toronto.[7] That study shows that the density of women's breasts is a major risk factor for breast cancer. Of particular note in the context of this paper is the fact that a mammogram is required for measuring breast density.

The Canadian Task Force on the Periodic Health Examination and the Ontario Cancer Treatment and Research Foundation recommend physical examinations of the breast for women aged 40 to 49 and both physical examinations and annual mammograms for women aged 50 to 69. These recommendations are not being followed. "Unfortunately, 64 percent of women between the ages of 50 and 69 report either never having been screened (51 percent) or having been screened more than two years ago (13 percent)."[8]

Very striking regional variations of mammogram screening exist when proportions are disaggregated to the level of Public Health Unit areas (Figure 4). In the majority of these areas women do not follow a regular screening program. In Northern Ontario, women living in or near Sudbury and Thunder Bay do not seem to have had much difficulty in following a regular screening regimen. However, the proximity to major centres where health care facilities exist cannot be cited as the major determining factor in this particular screening behaviour. It would not, for example, explain the relatively high propor-

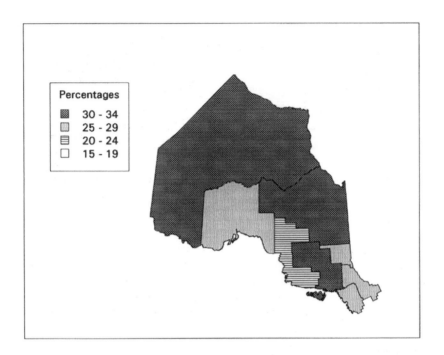

Figure 3

Proportions of women (by northern PHUs) who are current daily smokers

tions of women who do not follow a regular screening program in the Hamilton, London, or even Toronto areas, where health facilities exist; or, conversely, the low proportions (indicating that women are obtaining regular mammograms) in the more rural areas of southwestern Ontario, Grey-Bruce, or the Peterborough and Hastings areas.

These initial patterns are difficult to explain. Failure to undergo regular screening is not associated with levels of income or education nor is it associated with generalized (urban-rural) location of residence. The OHS is unable to tell us whether poor access to childcare, greater distances, or minimal public transportation facilities make it more difficult for northern women to obtain a mammogram.

Utilization of Health Care Resources

Visits to doctors. Communities across the north (as well as many in rural areas of Southern Ontario) are clamouring for increased health services, notably for more and better access to general practitioners/family physicians and physician specialists. The Ontario Ministry of Health has responded with many programs and initiatives. For example, the Underserviced Area Program is designed to encourage physicians, as well as other health care

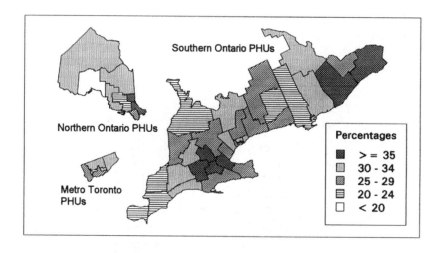

Figure 4

Proportions by Public Health Unit of women who have had a mammogram and whose last screening was more than two years prior to the Ontario Health Survey

providers, to locate in communities where practitioners are in short supply. The Northern Ontario Family Residency Programs in Sudbury and Thunder Bay were established in the hope that physicians who have received training in the north will stay in the north. The Northern Health Travel Grant provides financial assistance for northerners who must travel long distances to have access to medical care.

These and other programs have helped a great deal, but have not entirely solved the problem. One only has to skim headlines or letters to the editor in local or national newspapers to determine that problems still persist.

How often do northern women see doctors? As shown in Table 1, in the 12 months preceding the survey, 82 to 84 percent of northern women saw or talked to a general practitioner about their health problems. This is slightly less than for the Ontario average of approximately 85 percent. The variation from one region to another was relatively small. There was slightly more regional difference with respect to contacts with specialists, as 35 percent (ranging from 29 to 37 percent by region) had used the services of a physician specialist in the one-year period. The women who did not see or talk to a physician reported having no or very few health problems (57 percent with no health problems, 28 percent with only one problem, and only 15 percent with two or more health problems).

By disaggregating the regional figures into proportions by PHU (Figure 5), one can observe much more substantial regional variations in the use of physician services. For Northern Ontario women and, in many instances, for women living in rural areas of the province, those maps also suggest that general practitioners and family physicians may serve as substitutes for physician specialists where the latter are in short supply. However, these are areas where the former are also in short supply and access is often difficult.

Table 1. Proportions (percent) of Women by MOH Planning Region Who Saw or Talked to General Practitioners (or Family Physicians) and Physician Specialists in Preceding 12 Months

MOH PLANNING REGION	WOMEN WHO SAW GENERAL PRACTITIONERS		WOMEN WHO SAW PHYSICIAN SPECIALISTS	
	YES	NO	YES	NO
South West	82.6	17.4	28.6	71.4
Central West	86.9	13.1	35.3	64.7
Central East	86.1	13.9	36.3	63.7
Eastern	83.9	16.1	36.5	63.5
North East	84.4	15.6	30.7	69.3
North West	81.9	18.1	32.9	67.1

Differences in geographic locales (for example, rural/urban dichotomies) and distances (whether measured by kilometres, hours travelled, or various measures of travel difficulty) to physicians' offices have long been considered prime influences on health care access. However, the authors who identify those geographic influences also cite socio-economic factors as major contributors to differential access to and utilization of health care services.[9] The OHS is well suited to the generation and testing of hypotheses of the social, economic, and demographic determinants of physician utilization. The resulting spatial patterns, as shown in Figure 5, are complex. There are no simple north-south or east-west trends in utilization rates. It is the explanation of these complex patterns that forms part of the current research work of NHHRRU.

Visits to dentists. Compared with the use of physicians, regional differences in the use of dentists (Figure 6) are strongly evident. With the exception of those in the Algoma Health Unit area (72 percent), women in Northern Ontario see dentists much less frequently than women in Southern Ontario, where the proportions are commonly from 60 to 80 percent. In the Porcupine PHU, only 49 percent of women visited a dentist at least once in the past year, while in the rest of Northern Ontario the proportion is in the range of 50 to 60 percent. It has been observed that people "with dental insurance are more likely to have seen a dentist in the last year, whereas those with no insurance are more likely to have seen a dentist either three or more years ago or can't even remember how long it has been."[10] While this may be true for Ontario as a whole, having some form of dental insurance does not explain the comparatively low utilization of dentists' services in Northern Ontario. In fact, the proportion of women with dental coverage is the same or slightly higher in the northern planning regions (NE - 68 percent, NW - 69 percent) compared with those in the south (SW - 67 percent, CW - 69 percent, CE - 67 percent, E - 63

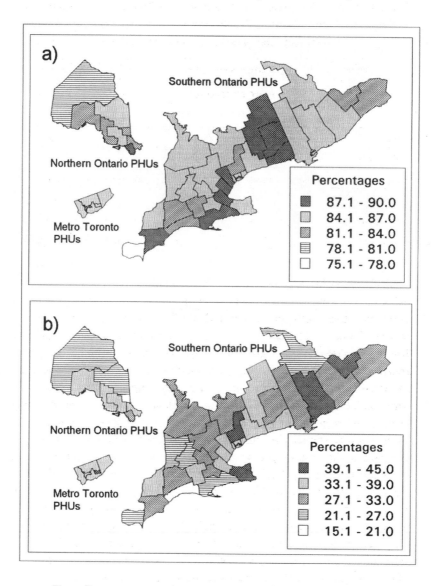

Figure 5

Physician utilization patterns for women, by Public Health Unit:
a) general practitioners/family physicians; b) physician specialists

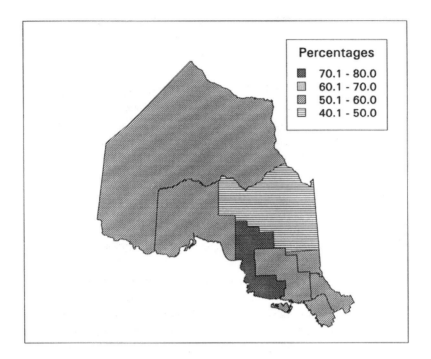

Figure 6

Proportions of northern women, by Public Health Unit, who used a dentist's services during the 12-month period prior to the Ontario Health Survey

percent). Explanations for these regional variations, other than insurance coverage, must be sought.

Implications and Future Research

In 1987 the Premier's Council on Health Strategy proposed five broad health goals for Ontario. These were subsequently adopted by the Ministry of Health.[11] Two of these goals are particularly relevant to the present discussion.

"Shift the emphasis to health promotion and disease prevention."[12] The OHS is very well suited to assisting the advancement of this goal because it provides information about health behaviours that can be used to target characteristic individuals or groups and geographical areas.

With respect to smoking, for example, we have already demonstrated that Northern Ontario should be targeted for anti-smoking campaigns. While more and more northern women aged 45 and older are quitting, what is worrisome are the high proportions of 12- to 19-year-olds who are regular or occasional smokers. The proportions of women in this age group who are daily smokers are again higher in Northern Ontario (18 to 20 percent) than in the south (8 to 14 percent). The conclusions of Blackford and colleagues, from a limited study of tobacco use by teenagers in Sudbury, are particularly relevant here:

Reduced tobacco use in this Northeastern Ontario population may be achieved when: 1) the particular conditions and consequences of adolescent tobacco use are identified within the context of teenagers' everyday lives; 2) the market and political forces of tobacco manufacturers are sufficiently taken into account; and 3) public messages focus accurately on issues of current relevance to teens in this locale.[13]

Clearly these conclusions have wider relevance than just to the Sudbury locale, but they are particularly appropriate for those geographical areas where smoking rates are high.

It is also evident that health screening recommendations are not getting through to a large number of women. OHS data for Ontario suggest that targeting women by education levels would not be fruitful, as screening does not vary significantly by education attainment categories. However, the Ministry of Health suggests that there is a tendency for screening to be related to income: higher proportions of women living in households reporting incomes of $50,000 or more (21 percent) report having had a mammogram within the last two years than in low income households (15 percent).[14] Similar figures for the Northeast and Northwest also indicate that 50- to 69-year-old women from low income households tend not to follow regular mammogram screening. But the low figures for various income groups indicate that there are no clearcut associations between mammogram screening and income. It would seem to be much more appropriate to target all women in this age group for health screening campaigns.

The second goal of the Ministry of Health that we would like to highlight is to "provide accessible, affordable, appropriate health services for all."[15] It is patently obvious that the provision of medical and dental insurance – either by the state or through private corporations – can have a significant impact on health care utilization. But it is also clear that neither medical nor dental insurance coverage alone can explain the spatial variations that have been highlighted in this paper. Northern women have slightly more regular and chronic health problems than women in Southern Ontario. They also use physicians somewhat less, and dentists far less, than southern women. What implications does this have for their quality of life and for access and affordability of health of health services?

These questions and implications allow us to introduce what is – for some social scientists in general and for many feminist authors in particular – a somewhat controversial issue. With respect to women, should studies of the social and cultural impacts on health and health care utilization focus attention on male-female differences or on analyses of commonalities, differences, and concerns among women?[16]

In preparing for this paper, we were struck by the fact that very little has been written about the determinants of women's health care use per se. As one author has pointed out, "There is a relative lack of work offering anything more than description of the provision and consumption of health care for and by women."[17] Where more detailed work appears, it is contained in the considerable body of literature dealing with gender differences.[18]

In her review of 20 years of research on medical care utilization, Muller characterizes research on male-female differences as the "gender agenda."[19] It appears that the gender agenda has been pursued at the expense of research efforts to examine differences among women, as relatively little research is devoted to identifying factors influencing women's health status and their use of health care.[20] Twenty years ago it was stated that "one of the most consistent observations in health survey research is that women report symptoms of both physical and mental illness and utilize physician and hospital services for these conditions at higher rates than men."[21] That was 20 years ago! Now, however, an increasing number of researchers[22] are moving away from that research agenda to focus on what Nathanson referred to in 1975 as differences in morbidity and the utilization of health services "among women." It remains, however, important to remember the question raised by Coburn and Eakin:

> Epidemiological-like studies view the various factors examined in isolation from one another, as separate factors torn out of the broader social structure within which they are located. How can the health status of women, for example, be understood without examining those aspects of women's lives which produce and reproduce gender inequalities?[23]

21

Health Issues for Women in Northeastern Ontario

Carole A. Suschnigg[1]

During 1990 and under the auspices of the Manitoulin-Sudbury District Health Council, a women's health needs assessment was conducted by 15 members of the Women's Health Research Steering Committee.[2] The committee's mandate was to examine how local health services could become more effective, and how women's access to those services could be improved. While conducting the needs assessment, however, committee members came to understand that access to good quality health services is an important but not sufficient condition for improving the health status of women in the north: a more fundamental precondition is the elimination of economic, social, and political inequities between men and women.

Unlike most research committees, this one was extraordinarily diverse in race, ethnicity, formal education, occupation, mother tongue, income level, employment status, family status, and age. In part, it was this very diversity that contributed to the members' understanding of health determinants for women in the north. Notably, members reached decisions by consensus throughout the project.

The committee adopted a feminist participatory research approach in order to carry out the needs assessment.[3] With this approach, women (not just academic or professional women) learn to investigate their own reality through cycles of action and reflection. Collectively, women are enabled to define their own research problem, to design their own research instrument, and to collect and interpret their own data. In however small a way, this research approach is emancipatory: women are transformed from research objects into research agents; they become more aware of conditions that undermine their well-being as women; they see opportunities for changing those conditions; and they become motivated to promote women's rights as human beings.[4]

Because the majority of committee members initially lacked confidence in their own abilities, I took every opportunity to demystify the concept of "scientific" research. As research co-ordinator, I saw it as my job to offer suggestions to the committee with regards to the research design and implementation. These suggestions included an assessment of the strengths and weaknesses of various approaches. On every occasion that we met, committee members enthusiastically debated the questions at hand and often ended up reframing my definition of a problem as a consequence of their own life experiences and accumulated knowledge. Through this process, committee members developed more confidence in their own critical faculties. And as they made informed choices with regards to the research design, they began to change their earlier belief that only "professionals" are qualified to conduct research on women's health.

Committee members examined literature on women's health. They studied government statistics on major causes of sickness and death among women in northeastern Ontario. They developed a directory of health and social services for women. They interviewed people who work in Sudbury's "formal" health care system. And they consulted members of workplace health and safety committees. Most importantly, the committee consulted diverse groups of women who live in and around Sudbury. The rest of this chapter focuses on the way in which local women were consulted and the valuable information they contributed with regard to health planning for women in the north.

Our Research Methods

When we contemplated how we would elicit information from women in the community, we realized that we did not have enough resources to interview a "random" sample of the female population.[5] Nevertheless, we wanted to ensure that our research report represented local women's diverse opinions and experiences. Most importantly, we wanted to provide a voice for women who tend to carry a higher burden of ill health, or women who experience greater difficulty gaining access to health services. Such women – non-anglo immigrant women, women with low literacy skills, First Nations women, women with disabilities, lesbians, women with low incomes, and sole-support mothers, for example – rarely have an opportunity to participate in the health planning process in the north.

We aimed to consult with many women across the district, but due to limited resources, we decided to organize focus groups rather than individual interviews. We aimed for proportionate representation in these focus groups based on the region's urban/rural distribution, its anglophone/francophone distribution, and its age distribution for female adults. While adhering to this general demographic framework, we asked women from the above mentioned target groups to participate as research respondents.

Eleven members of the committee agreed to "adopt" particular focus groups; they agreed to approach contacts in the community, to set up their own focus group(s), to conduct their own interviews, and to write up the results of their interviews. These women used a variety of methods to bring their focus groups into being. One member of the committee, for example, drew on her friendship network to set up interviews with groups of rural women in their homes. Another member used her position as a public health nurse to inter-view a group of teenaged women and a group of older adult women. Another used a contact at the Literacy Hotline to get in touch with a teacher at a local school who, in turn, asked her adult, female, low-literacy students if they would agree to be interviewed. One member of the committee approached two local organizations – the Native Friendship Centre and Key North – to arrange focus groups with First Nations women, while another invited a diverse group of contacts to a series of discussions on health and spirituality.

The committee decided to divide the two-hour focus group session into four parts. The first part would consist of a simple exercise in which each respondent would be asked to identify and rank her main health issues in writ-ing.[6] By participating in this exercise, respondents also would get some sense of how their group ranked women's health issues. Finally, when all the focus group interviews had been completed, the research committee would be able to pool the responses for the whole sample and get a sense of how local women identified and ranked women's health issues.

During the second part of the focus group session, respondents were to be asked to complete a self-administered, structured questionnaire. The purpose of this formal questionnaire was to elicit information on who provides health care in the home, and what kind; the quality of the respondent's relationship with her physician; problems with the respondent's health; the respondent's self-treatment activities; the respondent's disease prevention activities; the respondent's interest in alternative health care; the respondent's rating of the importance of various health and social services; the respondent's knowledge of local health and social services; and demographic information such as age, mother tongue, and household income.

The third part of the focus group session was to be an open discussion on respondents' experiences with the health system. The interviewer was to try to elicit responses from all participants in the focus group and not allow any one person to dominate the discussion. The interviewer was to note the kinds of experiences that were mentioned, as well as the extent to which particular experiences were shared by other members of the group.

The fourth and final part of the focus group session was to be a guided discussion on women's vision of health services for the future. Women were to be asked to imagine that they could start from scratch – to imagine that they had a fairy wand. What would their health facility look like? What kinds of services and resources would be available at no charge to the public? What kinds of health personnel would they like to consult? What would be the gen-eral attitude of health personnel towards their clients ? And so on. Women were to be asked whether they wanted a health facility that served women only, that served women and children only, or that served all members of their community. First Nations women were to be asked whether they would prefer a facility that was run by and for First Nations people. Most importantly, women were to be asked whether they thought local people should have a say in the planning of health services, or whether such decisions should be left in the hands of health professionals.

For some women, we decided to modify our original focus group format. We quickly realized that women with low literacy skills or with certain physical disabilities would not be able to participate in any activities that required writing. For these groups of women, interviewers were asked to modify the opening, written exercise and to ask respondents just to say what the major health issues were for them; interviewers were instructed to record how many women in the group supported any major issue that was raised. The second part of the focus group session – the formal questionnaire – was dropped altogether. The third and fourth parts were retained as originally planned. This modified format also proved to be a more culturally sensitive way to consult with First Nations women who participated in focus groups.

Finally, there were women whose voices we wanted to hear but for whom focus groups could not be arranged. In order to give these women an opportunity to participate, the guidelines for the focus groups were used to create a four-part, self-administered question package in both English and French. In the case of the French packages, two francophone contacts who were familiar with our project distributed these packages within the community, bearing in mind our desire to hear from women from diverse backgrounds. The English packages were distributed to contacts via committee members.[7]

Prior to conducting the survey, committee members participated in three training sessions during which they discussed the kinds of problems that might arise during focus group sessions and decided on policies for dealing with such problems. Ethical issues such as anonymity, voluntary participation, and the importance of feedback to survey respondents were addressed.

All told, we succeeded in hearing from 177 women in our community. Statistically speaking, of course, our results cannot be generalized to the whole population because they are not based on a random selection of respondents. Nevertheless, based on the subsample of 111 women who completed the formal, written questionnaire, we know that the majority of our respondents were well matched to the population in language distribution, quite well matched in age distribution, and somewhat biased towards urban women.

Major Health Issues Identified During the Opening Exercise

The first exercise in the survey revealed respondents' concerns about health issues. In decreasing order of priority, these issues included:
  • barriers that limit women's access to medical services, particularly waiting lists to see physicians, the need for more female general practitioners, language barriers, and physical barriers for people with disabilities;

- concerns about physicians' professional competence, and especially physicians' attitudes and behaviours towards female patients;
- concerns about women's physical health, particularly breast cancer;
- concerns about women's mental health, particularly stress and depression;
- concerns around support services for childbearing women;
- concerns around lifestyle education, particularly nutrition;
- concerns around reproductive control, particularly access to abortion and birth control;
- concerns around the vulnerability of women on low incomes;
- concerns about various forms of male violence against women.

Also mentioned were the need for more home support services, particularly for the frail elderly and people who are chronically sick; the need to improve people's access to accommodation; the need for alternative health care services; the need for more preventive medical services; concerns around substance abuse; the need for respite services for caregivers; and the right to euthanasia.

The results from the opening exercise revealed an interesting contradiction. On the one hand, respondents were highly critical of medical practices, and especially of physicians' attitudes towards their female patients; for many women, interaction with the health system itself is a source of stress. On the other hand, respondents were extremely concerned about the difficulties they experience gaining access to medical services and to particular kinds of medical personnel. More importantly perhaps, the results indicated that – for our respondents – access to medical services is only one determinant of health. Other determinants include things like good nutrition, economic security, and the elimination of male violence.

Results from the Formal Questionnaire

a. Respondents' main health ailments. In Canada, most health status reports are based on government statistics that list the main reasons people are admitted to hospital and the main reasons people die. While these reports are very useful, they by no means provide an accurate profile of the type, severity, and frequency of ailments that people experience. For this reason, in the formal questionnaire, we asked local women about the kinds of physical and mental ailments they had recently experienced. The most common complaints were backache, headache, swollen or painful joints, coughs and colds, menstrual problems, allergies, foot problems, constipation, chronic fatigue, difficulty sleeping, stress, anxiety, and depression. These results reinforced our suspicion that women in our area suffer from ailments that often are not captured by conventional health status data.

b. Respondents' relationship with their physician. Increasingly, people are advised to take responsibility for their own health care. Part of this responsibility includes making an informed decision about the medical treatment one receives. In this regard, the following information was elicited from our respondents:

- When asked, "Do you usually have time to fully discuss your health concerns when you visit your doctor?" nearly a third of the women who answered this question said no.
- When asked, "Does your doctor usually explain the possible side effects of drugs she/he prescribes?" over a quarter of the women said no.
- When asked, "Can you talk to your doctor in the language you usually speak at home?" nearly a fifth said no.

From these results we concluded that a large minority of our respondents did not have the opportunity to make an informed decision about the medical treatment they received.

c. Respondents' self-treatment and provision of unpaid health care for others. In our community, we tend to believe that health care consists mainly of medical treatment and that physicians and nurses are the main providers of health care.

The results from our formal questionnaire, however, suggest that local women take a lot of responsibility for treating their own health problems; many of our respondents said that they take vitamins or minerals, painkillers, antihistamines, cough syrup, and laxatives in order to deal with their ailments. It is worth noting that these over-the-counter remedies are not covered by provincial medical insurance.

In addition, the results from our formal questionnaire suggest that many essential health care services – food preparation and attention to hygiene, for example – are mostly provided by unpaid workers in the home. Moreover, these unpaid workers are far more likely to be women than men. As researchers, we concluded that this little-recognized and uneven sharing of health care responsibilities may be a source of stress for women in our community, particularly women who are sole-support parents and women who have paid employment.

d. Respondents' disease-prevention activities. Currently in Canada, the major causes of death for non-indigenous peoples are cardiovascular disease and cancer. The medical establishment has had little success in either preventing or curing these chronic diseases. Nevertheless, federal legislation guarantees people's access to medical services regardless of their ability to pay. This fundamental commitment to human rights is recognized and admired by people all over the world.

While access to medical services is very important, it is not the only factor that determines people's health. Other factors include people's lifestyle habits (regular exercise, a healthy diet, not smoking, and so on); occupational hazards such as chronic stress or exposure to chemical toxins; environmental hazards such as air and groundwater pollution; poverty; and systemic discrimination based on gender or race. Thus, a comprehensive approach to health promotion must include a number of non-medical, disease-prevention initiatives. For this reason, we asked local women what they do to prevent disease.

A large majority of the respondents reported that they ate healthy foods, used alcohol in moderation, and did not smoke. A majority of respondents reported that they did things to protect the environment. Notably, however, half the respondents said they usually did not get enough sleep; over half said they were unable to avoid stressful or unhealthy work conditions; over half said they lacked time to relax. It would seem, then, that while our respondents had the freedom to pursue some healthy behaviours – sensible consumption patterns, for example – they lacked the freedom to pursue other healthy behaviours; the majority of respondents lacked the opportunity to recuperate from work, or to choose work that did not take a toll on their health.

e. Respondents' priorities regarding health and social services for women. The results from our formal questionnaire indicated that women place services related to control over their own bodies at the top of their priority list, that is, services related to birth control and to sexual assault.[8]

f. Respondents' knowledge of local health and social services for women. Our respondents showed a surprising lack of knowledge about local health and social services for women – even for services they had rated as most important in the previous section of the questionnaire. The committee concluded that lack of public information is probably one of the main barriers to women's access to existing health and social services in our community.

Women's Experiences with the Health System

During the third part of the survey, women told us about their encounters with the health system; most of those experiences were negative. Some of their accounts are presented here; names have been changed in order to protect women's identities.

In particular, respondents complained about their physicians' condescending attitudes and sometimes rude behaviour. Leanne wrote, "Un spécialiste m'avait examinée d'une façon très brusque et je suis sortie de son bureau très frustrée et en colère."

Amy described how her doctor was very rude to her during her pregnancy and told her she was fat. When her baby was born prematurely, the doctor accused her of carelessness and of causing early labour. After the baby was born, he was critical of the way she was caring for her child. When Amy asked the doctor to explain things to her, he responded, "What grade of education do you have?"

Yvonne confided in her doctor that she was feeling tired and depressed. He recommended that she quit her job, that she didn't have enough of a social life. He spent very little time talking to her and said that even though her problem was just nerves, he would send her for blood tests and other tests anyway.

Yvonne left in tears, feeling that her doctor had no idea about her circumstances if he assumed she could just quit her job.

In a focus group with six non-anglo, immigrant women, four women claimed that their doctor refused to prescribe birth control for them because of his own cultural/religious beliefs.

Women from groups that are the most disadvantaged and the least often heard in our community – those with physical disabilities, those with low literacy skills, lesbians, and First Nations women, for example – felt doubly victimized and were particularly vocal about physicians' lack of sensitivity to their situations.

Barb is a young woman in a wheelchair. She has muscular dystrophy. For three years, she had a rod in her back that poked down into her hipbone and caused a great deal of pain. Her doctor claimed that the pain was all in her head and that, since Barb was unable to walk anyway, there was no point in investigating the problem.

Another woman with a physical disability, Jane, mentioned that she found it difficult when she has to deal with a new doctor or specialist – someone who is not familiar with her condition. A new person has to go through all her medical history; the problem is compounded due to Jane's almost incomprehensible speech.

Pam is a young woman in her twenties; she has cerebral palsy and is in a wheelchair. Because of her disability, her conversation is slow, laboured, and difficult to follow. She said that she was at a doctor's office once, and that she needed to use the washroom. These facilities were inaccessible, so she had to use a bedpan; she found this experience very embarrassing.

Jean, a lesbian, said that she has always had a hard time getting pap tests; she finds them extremely uncomfortable. She said that doctors have made little or no effort to put her at ease. Instead, they have attributed the problem either to her small body size or to her not having had intercourse. She has been told to do things to make herself "larger."

Women complained about the lack of birthing options open to them, about the medicalization of childbirth, and about the power of the medical system over childbearing women. Leslie, for example, spoke about her first pregnancy. When labour began, she went to the emergency department at her local hospital. She was treated in a very patronizing manner, was told that the lower back pains she was experiencing were not labour pains, and was instructed to go home. Leslie's pains intensified and after eight hours she returned to the hospital. She was made to sit up in a wheelchair even though such a position was especially uncomfortable. The situation ended up with a breech birth taking place in the labour room rather than in the delivery room. Leslie had negative memories of this whole experience. She felt that doctors failed to take her seriously when she reported on her own condition; they told her husband that she knew too much for her own good.

Nancy said that her first birthing experience took place in a hospital. She felt a loss of personal power because the hospital staff did not allow her to make decisions; they insisted on using their technology in the birthing process. Nancy felt that she was treated in a humiliating manner by the nurses. This negative experience prompted her to seek out information on birthing alternatives.

Lisa, a First Nations woman, said that the lack of midwives was a serious problem in the north. There were no midwives in the area between Thunder Bay and Hudson's Bay, and women had to travel far to get to the nearest hospital to have their babies. There was no place at the hospital for husbands to stay and no one to take care of other children in the family while the mother was away having a baby.

Women questioned the number and value of hysterectomies being performed by physicians; some respondents who had had a hysterectomy complained that they had not been told about the possible side effects of surgery; others complained that they had not been presented with any other options. In a focus group with five low-income women, three had had hysterectomies. One of these women felt that she had been too young when she had undergone surgery. She would like to have known about possible alternatives to surgery, but her doctor did not discuss these with her.

Women had some favourable comments to make about their experiences with the health system. Fay, for example, was in a wheelchair, which she operated via a stick held in her mouth. She said that she had been very lucky to get a doctor who was concerned and who was willing visit her where she lived. Dawn had been a cancer patient for ten years; she said she appreciated the care she had received at Laurentian Hospital – that staff there had the personal touch and a positive attitude.

Women's Vision for Future Health Programs

In the fourth and final part of the survey, women told us about their vision of health services for the future. The vision they mentioned most often was a health facility that had a warm, non-intimidating atmosphere, where people were treated with respect and as partners in their own health care. Women wanted this facility to take a holistic approach to health care. As well as housing a medical clinic, women wanted this facility to have spaces for childcare, a health lending library, a meditation room, a pharmacy, and a community seminar room. Rural women expressed their desire for a birthing centre to be attached to the facility. Respondents stressed the importance of such things as multilingual signs, wheelchair accessibility, access to public transportation, parking for the disabled, and so on.

The health care professionals to whom women most wanted access included a physician (especially a female general practitioner), a mental health counsellor, an affordable dentist, a nurse (especially for preventive health care), a chiropractor, a physiotherapist, a nutritionist, a chiropodist, an acupuncturist, a masseuse, a native healer, a naturopath, and a herbalist. As well as the various clinical and therapeutic services available from such workers, respondents wanted access to self-help groups, to healing circles, to spiritual health retreats, and to health seminars.

Few women wanted a health facility for women only; the majority of respondents wanted their vision of health services made available to the whole community. Interestingly, only one respondent thought that health service planning should be left to professionals, and one respondent wanted health care professionals excluded from health planning altogether. The rest of the respondents thought that both professionals and ordinary people should have a say in the planning of health services.

Conclusion

The catchwords of the participatory research approach are "participation, education, and transformation." Regarding participation, the approach that was used to carry out the needs assessment on women's health gave local women far more opportunity to get involved in an investigation of women's health issues than a conventional approach to research would have done. As for education, the participatory research approach helped women discover the power relations that exist within the local community, in the health system, and between male and female in our society.

As a result of my experience co-ordinating the needs assessment on women's health, "community participation in health planning" has taken on a specific meaning for me. By "community," I mean those people who have relatively little economic or social power and who have a vested interest in challenging the status quo. By "participation," I mean an opportunity for those people to exercise control in the planning process, not merely an opportunity for them to be included in a public opinion poll. By "health planning," I mean a collective effort to eliminate biological, behavioural, environmental, social, economic, and political factors that undermine health.

Discussing individual transformation, women on the committee began to believe – or deepened their belief – that they, themselves, are experts on their own health. They began to recognize that knowledge gained through their own experience has as much to contribute to the planning process as does knowledge gained through formal education; each type of knowledge complements the other.

In the area of the transformation of social conditions, the committee chose to locate its recommendations for health planning within a broad social context; the committee advised that significant improvements in women's health will not occur until women have achieved economic, social, and political equality with men.

On all these points, the participatory research approach provided congruence between means and ends. My overall assessment of the project can best be summed up using the words of Maguire – words that sustained me throughout the project:

Participatory research is time consuming, demanding, and troublesome. The accomplishments and rewards are often small in scale. Perhaps the primary lesson for me is that redistribution of power and empowerment are not events, but rather long haul struggles. These processes require both tangible and intangible resources, including determination, respect, and a profound belief in people's ability to grow, change, and create change.... The challenge is to celebrate our collective accomplishments, however small, and nurture ourselves as we move, however slowly and imperceptibly, in the direction of change for social justice.[9]

Part Four

Sources of Change

Many women still recall the Northeastern Ontario Women's Conference (NEOWC) of 1984 held in Sudbury. The energy generated at this conference re-emerged a decade later at the symposium that led to this anthology. Joan Kuyek and Gayle Broad recalled the early conferences and how women learned to identify issues and organize for change.

The activism talked about by Broad and Kuyek has a long history in Northern Ontario. The chapter by Linda Ambrose describes the work of the Women's Institutes in Northern Ontario since the early part of the century. She argues that the northern branches found creative ways to address the needs of women as they dealt with the realities of life in New Ontario. Contemporary efforts to meet the needs of women are dealt with by Kitty Minor, whose chapter surveys six northern Women's Centres and suggests the important role these centres play in improving women's lives. Organizing for change is also shown in Ginette Lafrenière and Barbara Millsap's description of the co-operative housing movement.

The issue of education as an agent of change is set out in the chapter by Johanne Pomerleau. Pomerleau describes how concerns with the overall lower level of education among francophone women in Northern Ontario, the needs of older women, and the issue of violence against women of all ages led the Collectif des femmes francophones du Nord-est ontarien to concentrate since 1988 on reducing barriers to education for this particular group of women. The importance of university courses offered by distance education is discussed in the chapter by Anne-Marie Mawhiney and Ross Paul. Access to such programs can significantly improve women's lives. Similarly, Douglas Goldsack et al. look at factors in a northern faculty of science that may have increased the number of female science graduates.

The final chapter, by Susan Vanstone, suggests that the history of activism evident throughout this section continues in the lives of young women. Young women who have chosen to champion women's issues develop both their own understanding of feminism and their own avenues of change.

22

The Women's Institutes in Northern Ontario, 1905-1930: Imitators or Innovators?

Linda M. Ambrose[1]

Recounting her experience of a 1914 Women's Institute convention in the Rainy River District of Northern Ontario, Miss S. Campbell of Brampton told her Toronto audience:

> I arrived early at Emo the day of the convention, but had scarcely taken a little rest, when I saw lumber wagons coming in, filled with women. But I saw more – a class of brave, intelligent women.... The District Secretary walked four miles the evening before the convention over trail, logs, water and brush with rubber boots and raincoat, and on Monday morning drove the remainder of the way – eight miles – in a lumber wagon – a mode of travelling which has to be experienced to be understood. And all this inconvenience that she might not miss the convention! She spoke of the special requirements of the pioneer country and ventured the opinion that the Institute can meet these needs in a way that is not required of the Institute in the older districts.[2]

Miss Campbell was raising two important themes about Northern Ontario women, which she wanted her southern audience to understand: first, Women's Institute members in Northern Ontario faced particular hardships; and second, they used the Institute branches to meet needs that were specific to their northern context.

The roots of the Women's Institute movement are traced back to the first branch established in Stoney Creek, Ontario, near Hamilton, in 1897. Adelaide Hoodless, credited with founding the WI, has been dubbed "the domestic crusader" because of the tremendous energy she expended in working to establish domestic science education for women throughout Ontario. Through the vehicle of the Women's Institutes, she was anxious to see that kind of education extended to the women of rural Ontario particularly.[3]

After a few years of struggle and setback, the WI grew at a phenomenal pace from the early 1900s through the first three decades of this century.[4] The growth was remarkably fast in Northern Ontario. As Figure 1 illustrates, 28 new branches were created in Northern Ontario between 1905 and 1910, and by 1930, 50 more had been added.[5] That growth is partly explained by the government's campaigns in the summers of 1905 and 1906 to establish WI branches. Female lecturers, employed by the provincial Department of Agriculture, travelled by train to hold 130 meetings for the purpose of organizing WI branches in Northern Ontario.[6]

Figure 1. Growth In Branches (Northern Convention Areas)

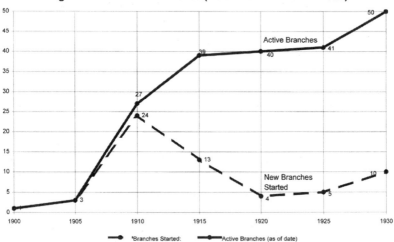

The lecturers were warmly welcomed, and the idea of establishing WI branches proved to be very popular. In 1905 there were only 172 Institute members in the north, but seven years later, in 1912, more than 1,600 women took out memberships throughout the 13 districts across Northern Ontario. By 1922, the northern members numbered well over 3,000. This is a tremendous rate of growth. After 1906, women in the northern parts of the province consistently accounted for approximately 10 percent of the total provincial membership.[7] This consistency is particularly noteworthy considering that the population of the north represented just over 10 percent of the total population. It is even more impressive though, given the fact that women in Northern Ontario made up only 8.5 percent of the total female population of the province in 1911. The statistics demonstrate that northern women's participation in the Institutes was slightly higher than that of women in the southern part of the province.[8]

With the expansion of Women's Institutes throughout the province, but particularly because of the popularity of the organization in Northern Ontario, the head office in Toronto was forced to provide regional annual conventions for the convenience of the members, rather than holding only one meeting in Toronto:

The rapid development of the work led to the opening up of other areas as it soon became evident that to journey from Kenora to Toronto, was as prohibitive as previously it had been undesirable to travel from Glengarry to Guelph. In 1915 a temporary centre was chosen at North Bay, and in 1921 convention gatherings were held in Algoma, Kenora, Temiskaming, Thunder Bay and on Manitoulin Island.[9]

On the issue of why the WI appealed so much to women, recent research confirms that the Women's Institutes served a variety of purposes, including educational, social, and community development roles throughout rural Ontario.[10] This chapter concentrates on the WI branches located in Northern Ontario. It explores the ways in which the Women's Institutes in the north "branched out" from their southern roots. In doing so, the northern branches did imitate their sister branches in the south, but they also acted in innovative ways that set them apart from the southern branches.

Writing about social development in Northern Ontario, Baldwin argued in his 1979 article, "Imitation vs. Innovation: Cobalt as an Urban Frontier Town," that the north imitated the south in fashion, infrastructure, and fraternities. Baldwin included a photograph of a Cobalt garden party to help make his case, urging his readers to "notice the Japanese lanterns, the flower pots, and the fancy clothes." He invoked a maternal metaphor when he characterized the railroad as a "massive steel umbilical cord" linking the northeast to Toronto.[11]

Although Baldwin's examples did not specifically include any women's organizations, I was curious to explore whether his thesis holds true in the case of the Women's Institutes of the north. The umbilical cord metaphor seemed to be a particularly appropriate one to adopt in exploring women's history. Is the idea of fetal dependence on the mother in the south an accurate representation of women's experiences in the WI movement in Northern Ontario during the period 1905 to 1930? Or did the WI, when it came north, cut the ties to the mother and begin an independent existence? To use Baldwin's terms then, were northern Women's Institute members "imitators" of the women in the south, or were they "innovators"?

Certainly, there are important ways in which the branches of WI in Northern Ontario imitated the southern branches. The constitution of the organization, the official symbols, the handbook, the procedures, the aims, and the motto were all adopted without revision.[12] The first branch at Stoney Creek is referred to as the "Mother Institute." After 1904 the northern branches also received financial support from the Ontario government in the same way as their sister branches in the south. This monetary support was a very important incentive for the formation of new groups, especially in New Ontario.[13] At first glance, it seems plausible then to argue that women simply reconstructed the movement, according to Baldwin's model, with no conscious attempt to adapt to the differences a northern context would present. In other words, it could be argued that WI groups in Northern Ontario were imitators rather than innovators.

Yet one must be careful not to ignore the particular historical context of WI branches in Northern Ontario. From very early on, reports of northern branches were set apart from those in the south by tales of hardship. In a very real sense it was the hardships that the members of the northern branches faced and their pioneering spirit that shaped the branches there and caused the members to seek innovative ways of using the WI branches to improve the lives of women in Northern Ontario. Southerners were told that they would never understand the particular northern context without experiencing it themselves. In a 1915 report, Mrs. Parsons from Cochrane reported on the tenacity and determination demonstrated by northern WI members in making transportation arrangements for the annual convention.

For many Women's Institute members in Northern Ontario, transportation was a challenge. Pictured here are some of the delegates who attended the 1912 Area Convention in Rainy River District.

I heard one little incident that may interest. A small party of busy women rose early on Convention day and walked five miles over a bush road with skirts tucked up and heavier shoes than one sees on Yonge Street. At the end of their little walk they met the wagon that was to take them the seven remaining miles to their destination. They took their part ably on the programme of the day without hint of fatigue, and when the National Anthem closed the day's programme at 11 p.m. these undaunted ones climbed into the friendly wagon and recounted happy experiences for seven miles. Then with lanterns in hand the last five miles was made, and the general opinion was: "I wouldn't have missed it for anything."[14]

This is a classic report of the heroism, stamina, and energy exhibited by pioneer women. While women in the south undoubtedly knew the isolation of household routines and rural living, their experiences did not compare with those of northern women in the backwoods. "You people here do not know anything about being lonely," one woman told the delegates to a Toronto convention, "about living in a place where you do not see another woman twice a year."[15] One elderly WI member from Thunder Bay district recalled her early experiences as a member who joined the local WI in 1906:

In the early days when I came to this district, I was very lonely as I had never lived on the farm and only my love for animals kept me from depression. When the WI came [in 1906], it filled a long-felt project for farm women especially and I wonder sometimes at how it has broadened out from the very small beginning of a recipe for a salad or a batch of cookies shared with the members in the early days. It has shouldered many problems since those early days....
Always a lover of horses, I could handle them before coming to the farm and in the old days gathered many a sleigh or democrat load of members for a distant meeting.[16]

"Are women of the North any different?" Margaret MacAlpine asked rhetorically in 1912. "I think you will agree with me," she continued, "that nobody can be among big rocks and wide expanses of water and not grow visionary, idealistic, and more or less spiritual."[17] Women of the northern Institutes were indeed different. But idealistic? The "big rocks and wide expanses of water" that Mrs. MacAlpine spoke about did not make WI members more idealistic; if anything, it made them more pragmatic. Members of Women's Institutes valued their contacts with other women, and they were determined to put the organization to good use.

Two themes in particular provide case studies about the things to which northern Institutes began to turn: the practice of mutual aid and the politics of women's issues. Northern experiences of practical assistance and political activism were both different from those in the south, and in each case northern innovation is evident.

The innovative way in which the northern branches practised mutual aid is the first theme to be explored. Mutual aid was a component of WI experience throughout Ontario, where branch members helped one another both formally as fellow members and informally as neighbours and friends. The

Women's Institutes became known as groups that "establish a spirit of neigh-
bourliness throughout the community"[18] by caring for one another in times of
need. Local record books show that members made layettes and held baby
showers for new mothers, provided bed linens for victims of house fires,
raised money for medical facilities, and gave expressions of sympathy in times
of bereavement.[19] Summing up this kind of mutual aid activity in one branch
in the Thunder Bay district, the O'Connor Women's Institute Tweedsmuir history book records:

> Theirs has been a record of unselfish service in the good Samaritan
> line; the rallying point of successful efforts in raising money and sup-
> plies for distressed neighbours; in cases of fire, accident or lack of
> necessities. No afflicted family ever appealed in vain to the Institute;
> a combination of the qualities of the Red Cross, the Salvation Army,
> and the Saintly Dorcas of the Scriptures. The O'Connor Institute has
> to their credit an everlasting list of good deeds and those who can
> well be thankful for the alleviating assistance they received through
> the medium of the Women's Institute.[20]

The Ontario WIs were a very important agency for social welfare
throughout the province in the years before government agencies were in
place to fulfil those roles. In 1927, a report to the Minister of Agriculture concluded that "in fact, the Institutes may be considered the recognized medium
through which relief work is carried on in many sections of rural Ontario."[21]
The WI was noted for the quality of its service; as one observer remarked,
"There is that personal touch and neighbourly spirit which is often lacking in
many welfare undertakings in the larger centres of population."[22] That neighbourly aid was particularly important to northerners.

In part, it was the Northern Ontario experience that first pushed the WI
towards a systematic, province-wide relief effort. Throughout the years of
settlement in New Ontario, risk from forest fires was a constant one. The
fires that raged through different parts of Northern Ontario were a rallying
point for the WI across the province to send aid to their fellow members in
the north. In 1922 Premier Drury came by train to Englehart after the great
fire at Cobalt. "On Saturday when I arrived back in Toronto," he recalled,
"Mrs. Drury informed me that all Women's Institutes … over the province
had been alerted and were gathering winter clothing. Much of this arrived in
two weeks in the north."[23] The WI could certainly boast a very efficient
delivery of services!

Similar assistance was reported in 1929, this time because of crop failures. "Great quantities of supplies are sent each year by the Institutes of old
Ontario to the north, where the poor crops of a year ago had resulted in more
than usual want among the settlers."[24] The fires, the crop failures, and the

hardships serve to remind us that women in Northern Ontario were still pioneers. The precarious nature of the frontier experience gave a new mandate to
the southern branches of the WI as they shared in the prosperity of their established communities.

The challenges of the northern frontier and the hardships of pioneering
also shaped the northern Women's Institutes themselves. While their more
comfortable sisters in the south set up systems for sharing from their cast-off
clothing, members in the north worked on ways to overcome their poverty. At
the Marter WI in Temiskaming District, the members allowed themselves to
dream a little in 1916 as they responded to a roll call, "If you had a dollar, how
would you spend it?"[25] The year before, the same branch had carefully considered a motion on spending money before they finally agreed "that there should
be a gallon of coal oil bought out of the funds to light the school at the
Delegates meeting." They agreed to spend 75 cents for the fuel.[26]

However, in 1915 when the women of Marter WI received a letter from
George Putnam, Superintendent of Institutes, asking for contributions for
relief, charity, and patriotic work, the women had to refuse his request. The
struggling northern branch's reply gave the superintendent a picture of their
economic reality, stating that "the Marter branch has not been able to directly
contribute to any of these things, as, it is all we can do to stay here at all and
clear land."[27]

Another branch in that same district established an innovative system
of distributing groceries to community members who were in need – but
the needy included women from their own Institutes. In 1932, records of
the Dane WI relief committee show that the members purchased several
food items with money that was not from a local source. The minutes
reveal that "Groceries and Merchandise ... was [sic] purchased by money
sent by the Wexford WI [in York County] which came in handy at the
time." The more prosperous southern branch had sent $30 for these pur-
poses.[28] Members from the local northern branch administered the distribution of these foodstuffs among their neighbours' and fellow members'
families. Clearly, the women in the north had to be creative in their mutual
aid. Economics dictated that they could not match the cash donations of
their southern counterparts.

These stories of women struggling with the poverty of frontier living and
the consequences of natural disasters are not the activities usually associated
with middle-class women's organizations in the early twentieth century. They
are very different from the experiences of WI members in the south and also
from the more fortunate in the north. What seems unique about the WI, particularly in Northern Ontario, is that this organization included women with a
wide variety of means. Branches claimed to include all the women in a community, and in the remote areas of the north this appears to have been the rule
rather than the exception.[29] For example, Island Falls (50 miles north of

Cochrane) produced twelve members for a local Women's Institute in 1935 from "a community of twelve log cabins."[30]

Although it is impossible to perform a detailed demographic analysis of the members of the WI branches, some tentative conclusions about membership can be drawn. First, there was regional variation among the branches. Those in more prosperous areas of the south shared with those who were experiencing hardships in the north. Second, when natural disasters struck, whole communities became needy at the same time, and members shared with one another and practised mutual aid among their members. Finally, although the more isolated communities were the least financially secure, it was there that the Women's Institutes flourished. A partial explanation is the fact that the WI was not in competition with other groups, for in most communities there was no other organization for the women to join. The economic realities presented by the northern frontier caused the WI to branch out into a variety of forms of relief work and to become innovative in the distribution of money and goods and in the definition of mutual aid.

Another theme to explore in comparing the northern and southern branches of the WI is the relative political activism of members in the two regions. In addition to purposes of mutual aid, the Women's Institutes became a political vehicle for northern women. While these members were not as economically advanced as their sisters to the south, they were more progressive politically. Evidence suggests that northern Institutes were overt in their support for female suffrage even though the authorities in the south ordered them not to be.

Officially, the discussion of political questions at Institute meetings was forbidden. At the Toronto convention in November 1914, Superintendent George Putnam answered a question submitted by one of the delegates asking why the WI did not work actively on behalf of women's suffrage. In response, he said, "We do not want to take up these questions as an Institute." He explained that the tremendous growth of the WI could be explained in part by the fact that such issues were not discussed. He urged the members to avoid all questions of a controversial nature and, specifically, to avoid offending any members of the provincial legislature. "We are as an organization supported liberally by the Provincial Government," he explained, "and it may be that there are some men connected with the Government or who will be members of Parliament who are not in favour of Women's Suffrage, and if it were known that the Women's Institutes stood for Women's Suffrage, we might lose the influence of some members of Parliament." For emphasis he added, "I hope I have made myself quite clear."[31]

He was very clear. The superintendent's position on the issue, and that of his department, was unmistakable. Yet the members of the Institutes in Northern Ontario did not comply with his advice. Several branches reported boldly to the next annual meetings that they had taken the question up in a light-hearted manner through comic dramas (one entitled "Should Men

Vote?") [32] while others had addressed it through a more formal debate format. One branch reported, "Three of our ladies visited [another community] and debated the question, 'Should Women Vote?' Needless to say the women won. The gentlemen said that the best argument we could use was our presence there and our way of taking up the subject."[33]

Branch record books reveal that many of the Northern Ontario branches took up this question and discussed it in some depth. The Monteith WI in Cochrane District serves as a good example. In that branch, the members took up the question on four different occasions during the fall and spring of 1916-17. Although the minute books do not give a full report of the discussions, one entry reported that at one meeting, Mrs. Clark read a paper on the subject which "gave many of us a little food for thought."[34]

Some branches took the issue beyond discussion and decided to act on their convictions. At the 28 September 1916 meeting of Kentvale Institute on St. Joseph Island in Algoma District, this motion was presented: "That we undertake the work of canvassing for names of those in favour of women of Ontario receiving the franchise." The motion carried, and at the next monthly meeting, members followed through by ordering "one dozen blank forms to canvass for names." Presumably they were working in co-operation with some formal suffrage organization from which they ordered their supplies. By December of that year, the women resolved to have each member "take a petition form and get the granting of the Franchise to Women."[35]

The issue gathered momentum among the members and was continuously brought to the annual conventions in Toronto, much to the chagrin of the provincial superintendent. Mr. Putnam urged the women to avoid these controversial questions and assured them that if they did not do so, they were sure to "antagonize" some people. Assuring the women that he was not personally opposed to the idea of women voting, he pleaded with them to join him in pursuing "the greatest good [for] the Institutes."[36] But the question would not go away. It continued to surface, and Putnam held firm to his original position: no questions of a political or controversial nature were to be entertained at Institute meetings. His only compromise was to suggest that if members decided to discuss these issues, they should find a different forum for doing so. "Deal with these questions if you wish, but do not deal with them as an Institute."[37]

But Institute members who had discussed the question of suffrage and had even campaigned and petitioned for it were not about to go along with Putnam and his reservations. His suggestion that they should do their political work through some other organization was not realistic for women in Northern Ontario. A member from Rainy River explained, "Whereas, in the small villages and towns there are other organizations – ladies' aids and so on – there are in many cases no women's organizations in the further back settlements other than the Institute."[38] Without access to any other women's organizations, Putnam's advice to join a temperance group or a franchise league fell on deaf ears in the north. The isolation of northern locations did not afford the same variety of organizations from which to choose. Politically minded WI members in the north could not simply turn to a local franchise league, even if they had wanted to.

Members had no intention of stopping their discussions of suffrage. A member from the Lee Valley Women's Institute just outside Massey defied the head office when she reported to their 1917 annual meeting in Toronto that she and her fellow northern members had no intention of complying with Putnam's directives.

> There was a strenuous effort to keep suffrage out of the Institute. However, it was of no avail. We have got the suffrage microbe in our District, and we are hopelessly infected. Headquarters may give all the orders they like, but when women get interested in anything, it is going to come out in the Institute, and indirectly our Institute, although officially opposed to suffrage, has been the best medium we have had to spread the suffrage doctrine.[39]

For Putnam, the prognosis was not good – the Institutes were infected with the suffrage bug, and the symptoms were developing at a rate beyond his control.

Other Institute officials who reported on the north confirmed that there was definitely something different about the northern membership. "Shall I be misunderstood if I say there is a "Western air [up] here?" Mrs. Parsons mused.[40] Drawing the parallel with women who worked actively for the franchise in the prairie provinces, this woman emphasized that WI members who were pioneering in the north had a different approach to Institute work than their more southerly peers.

A special guest representing the newly formed Alberta Women's Institutes echoed the same theme, but from a different perspective. Coming from the west, Mrs. J. Muldrew addressed the Toronto Convention in 1917, where she told the WI members of southern Ontario that their close proximity to other branches and their long-established community life set them apart from the experience of western women. By inference, one concludes that Institute members from the Prairies did indeed have much in common with Northern Ontario women. Mrs. Muldrew reported further on the issue of women and the vote:

> At the passing of the Equal Franchise Act, it just so happened that it was to be passed on the afternoon of one of our meetings, so we adjourned and went to the Parliament Buildings and were able to have seats in the gallery in order to see the passing of that remarkable Act which gives to every woman in Alberta absolutely the same privileges that the men have."[41]

Evidently, on the issue of suffrage, Mrs. Parsons had been correct to assume that the Northern Ontario Women's Institutes had a certain affinity with those in the West.

Ontario women were soon to enjoy the same rights as their western sisters when they achieved the vote federally and provincially in 1918. Yet in Institute work, Ontario was the only province that continued to be dominated by male leadership. George Putnam served as Superintendent of the Ontario Women's Institutes from 1904 to 1934. Dr. C.C. James, Dominion Commissioner of Agriculture, pointed out this anomaly in 1915 when he remarked:

I mentioned the Women's Institutes of the other Provinces. Go to Quebec, and work is carried out by a lady on the staff of Macdonald College. Go to Fredericton, and you meet the lady superintendent; go to Prince Edward Island and you meet the lady superintendent; go to Nova Scotia and you meet the lady superintendent; go to Manitoba, Alberta or Saskatchewan or British Columbia and it is the same thing. You ask, where is the man? You have to come back to Ontario to find the man. This is the only Province where the Women's Institute work is wholly directed by a man. But Mr. Putnam has called to his help and assistance and direction you women, and he was wise enough to know he could not do it of his own accord.[42]

Putnam did indeed consult with women in running the Institutes, but he changed his position on suffrage only slightly. Not until after the vote had been granted and the press had questioned his rigid stance did he concede that he had no real power to control the content of Institute meetings.

At the 1919 annual convention, he faced the issue directly and admitted that the relationship between the Institutes and the Department of Agriculture needed to evolve. As a concession, he admitted, "If you wish for the best results you must allow every latitude for the development of individuality. In the case of an organization such as the Women's Institute, of the people and for the people, the very life of the society depends upon the development of individuality in the members and the societies." But at the end of his remarks, he reiterated his original preference, that "if you will discuss party platforms and controversial questions, you should, of course, belong to the Institute, and also join some other organization where these matters can be discussed freely and frankly, but let us keep the Institutes for the whole people."[43]

Putnam had conceded to the new political status of women, and the northern WI members had helped to force the issue by their defiance of the Toronto directives. When they became interested in questions of a political nature, they used the WI as a vehicle for promoting those interests and for working towards their goals. They did not imitate the Institutes in the south, and they did not comply with southern directives. On the question of political activism, women in the northern branches of the WI were innovators, not imitators.

Conclusion

In many ways the northern branches resembled their sister branches in the south. At the same time, evidence suggests that it was not a simple case of imitation. There were innovative differences between the northern and southern branches of the Women's Institutes.

Despite incredible hardships of distance and primitive conditions, Institutes were developed in 13 northern districts. The context and needs of new settlement areas saw the WI branch out into social welfare campaigns to support the members who were battling against specific northern problems such as recovering from forest fires. The northern branches let the south know that because of their pioneer experience and unstable economy, they could not afford to participate in southern fund-raising drives. Furthermore, the northern branches defied instructions from the south to avoid political involvement in the suffrage debate, in part because they did not have a variety of women's organizations at their disposal. When northern women established an organization, they used it for a variety of purposes. When women adopted the Women's Institute movement for the north, they also adapted it and pragmatically put it to new uses.

The Institutes that sprang up across Northern Ontario were undeniably the daughters of southern branches. However, they were not so closely tied to the mother in the south as to follow her every move or to mimic her exactly. There was a family resemblance, but there was no slavish dependence on southern directives and mandates. There were definite ties to the mother organization, but when the Women's Institute was adopted by and adapted to its new northern context, the umbilical cord tying it to the south was definitely cut.

23

The Northeastern Ontario Women's Conference 1981–1984: A Conversation on Learning to Act

Gayle Broad and Joan Kuyek

We have put on five conferences in northeastern Ontario and created a network of 50 or so women who share a common vision of the world they want to create. The women who participated went on to work on several additional Northern Ontario women's conferences. Over the span of these five conferences, we came to understand why there is such an enormous gap between the world as it is and how we would like it to be. Because we believe that the key to developing social change lies in a participant's own life experience, we wanted to create a conference environment where such experience could be expressed, examined, and allowed to flower.[1]

These five conferences (see Table 1) changed the way women who attended them thought about and organized around issues such as labour, the environment, health, education, and the women's movement in the north.

Table 1. Northeastern Ontario Women's Conferences

DATE	TITLE	PLACE
October 16-18, 1981	"Women and Multinationals"	Sault Ste. Marie
May 16-17, 1982	"Who's Screwing You?"	Sudbury
November 7-9, 1982	"More than Bandages: Healing for People, Not for Profit"	Camp Wakonda
May 13-15, 1983	"Bread and Roses: Alternatives to Despair"	Timmins
April 12-14, 1984	"Through the Looking Glass"	Sudbury

What happened at these conferences? What made them different from other conferences? Why were they so successful at developing and energizing women activists? This chapter is written as a conversation between the authors as they searched for answers to these questions.[2]

Joan: Women were crucial to the success of the lengthy Inco strike of 1978-79 in Sudbury. During that time, we learned a lot about the ways in which large multinational corporations organized our lives in Northern Ontario, and we desperately wanted to make changes. Some of us felt that unless we understood how these companies "disorganized" us, we would never be able to create the kinds of changes that women really wanted and needed. We began to look for opportunities to do this work in a collective setting. When Marylou Murray, co-ordinator of the Sudbury Women's Centre at the time, and I attended a conference called "Women and Well-Being" in Toronto in March 1981, the idea of a conference presented itself.

Miners' Mothers' Day collection

Wives Supporting the Strike, 1978.

Gayle: My son Nathan was nine months old when I had a chance to go to the conference on health in Toronto entitled "Women and Well-Being." I wasn't able to socialize with the other participants because daycare ended when the conference workshops ended, and as Nathan was one of those all-night-long breast-fed babies, I didn't have much energy to go out in the evenings, anyway. I missed quite a bit because of this. On the last day, we had a "Northeastern Ontario caucus" meeting – I remember wondering what exactly a caucus was. Many of the women already knew each other. The discussion eventually moved to having a conference closer to home, where we could get together again and find a way of working as a group. I supported this idea and suggested that a small grant that the women – all six of us who called ourselves feminists – in Sault Ste. Marie had obtained for a local conference could perhaps be used to host a larger conference. Joan and Marylou agreed to find speakers, and the first Northeastern Ontario Women's Conference (NEOWC) was born.

Joan: Marylou and I couldn't believe how fortunate we were to have this opportunity to put a conference together. Gayle and Lavera Crack, co-ordinator of the Sault Ste. Marie Women's Centre at the time, came from the Soo for a planning meeting. They wanted to look after all the physical arrangements, but said that Marylou and I should take care of the conference design. We called the conference "Women and Multinationals." It was to be held in Sault Ste. Marie at the Ramada Inn, although – due to limited funding – everyone was billeted; meals were provided at a chain restaurant (Smiley's) next door.

We spent hours trying to figure out how we could design a conference that really changed the behaviour of participants. We felt that we had often attended conferences and workshops where people were overwhelmed with information. This took away their ability to act and made no real difference in how they conceptualized the world around them. We looked at what we wanted to gain from the conference; we re-examined successful learning experiences; we consulted with others. What we came up with were some simple basics. At the outset, we needed to create an atmosphere of trust and intimacy, so that women could feel safe to examine new ideas and to say "I don't know." We needed to find resource people who could speak in ways that the participants could readily understand and who would respect those attending the conference enough to see themselves as only one expert among many. We also wanted to find ways for participants to translate the information they learned at the conference into actions that were related to their daily lives and their home communities, without creating more commitments for them at home (too many of us went to conferences and came home with new commitments that only "disorganized" the work we were already doing).

We looked around for a resource person who could talk about women and multinationals and settled on Kari Levitt. But the week of the conference Levitt informed us she was unable to come. We called everyone we could think of and ended up with Marguerite Cassin, a graduate student working with Dr. Dorothy Smith at the Ontario Institute for Studies in Education. Smith was a sociology professor at OISE and a leading theorist on women, class, and the state.

Marguerite: I got a call from a woman asking me if I could come to Sault Ste. Marie that weekend to speak for about a half-hour on women and multinationals. I was also invited to stay around and participate in the discussion for the rest of the weekend. I was so excited, I stayed up all night working on my presentation.

Joan: Finding Marguerite and the work of Dorothy Smith was crucially important to the future usefulness of these conferences. There were many reasons for conference participants and planners to be enthusiastic about Marguerite's participation, not least her understanding of what that first conference was trying to do and the analysis of societal organizing principles.

Marguerite: I can say at the end of the third conference that I learned much more from the women at the conference than I contributed to them.... Also my work is such that it must be taken up by people like yourselves in order to be useful.... The organizers offered the resource people something very special ... an opportunity to enter into a very exciting process.

Gayle: As always, we learned from our mistakes as well as our successes. Some of the important lessons for us from this first conference related to physical arrangements, and they were incorporated into future planning. People need decent food to eat and some opportunities for exercise. Billeting is a wonderful way to connect with one another and provides more opportunities for the processing of information.

Lavera and I felt totally responsible for the small turnout at that first conference – very few women from Sault Ste. Marie and surrounding area attended. I myself was not captivated by the idea of learning about multinationals and went only out of a sense of duty. Joan introduced the discussion on Saturday by stating that we could look at the turnout as a great disappointment or as a great opportunity – here were 25 women activists who were willing to give up a weekend out of their busy lives to begin to build a network for change. Suddenly we felt like we were being adventurous, that we had strength, and that we were in this thing together. By the end of the weekend, I had fundamentally shifted many of my values – for the first time in an educational setting, I had an opportunity to analyze my own personal experience in the context of a world driven by organizational imperatives that conflicted with the organizational imperatives of people.

I learned on a cognitive level, but more importantly, I had the opportunity to take this information and integrate it with my own life. By the end of the weekend, I realized that the material security I had been clinging to had actually been controlling my choices, that I would have to "let go" of financial security, if I wanted to take charge of my life. Within weeks I was working part-time at the Women's Resource Centre for $100 per week and was certain that this was the work I wanted to do.

That first conference had several ingredients that are now recognized as crucial to the later success of the other conferences: a dynamite analysis in language we could understand and that was located in our daily lives; significant amounts of time set aside for simulated problem solving, a technique introduced to the group by Joan and refined at later conferences; an opportunity to "play" and be entertained, a skill that Lavera encouraged to flower; and a wrap-up discussion that focused on reflecting what we had learned and when we could get together again, instead of on resolutions or plans of action.

Joan: During and immediately after this first conference in the Soo, we formed a core collective to work on future conferences: Gayle and Marylou Murray (who worked at the Women's Centres in the Soo and Sudbury), Cathy Cervin (a doctor in Timmins), Katherine Fournier (a homemaker and community worker from Hearst), Cathy Ingwerson (a homemaker and peace activist from New Liskeard), and myself. This group struggled with the process and content of the workshops in the conferences, trying to make them better each time. From time to time other women participated in the collective, depending on where the conference was to be held.

Between conferences we would meet for a weekend every two months or so, usually in Sudbury because it was the most accessible. These meetings were intense experiences for all of us. We would arrive on Friday night and catch up with each other's busy and active lives. All of us were engaged in demanding projects in our own communities and had many responsibilities at home. We made sure our planning for the conference took these contexts seriously.

Gayle: When we came to Sudbury for a planning meeting, Cathy and I usually slept on the mattress on the floor of the spare bedroom of Marylou's house. We talked until 3 or 4 a.m. about our lives, our parents, our partners, our emotions. At the planning sessions, we listened and we talked, and then went away until the next meeting two or three months later, giving ourselves time for reflection and understanding of how our lives were being transformed by the process of planning these conferences. If there is one memory that stays with me more than any other it is the thought of the hours spent grappling with issues in these planning sessions, both individually and in a group. It developed a level of trust with the other women who worked with me. This is something I have rarely experienced with any other group of people.

We explored the issues affecting our lives: poverty, children, food, work, violence, loneliness. As our trust with one another grew, so did our ability to analyze the issues and connect them with one another. We didn't need to compete with one another because there was nothing to be won or lost. We built on one another's ideas and visions, expanding, revising, revisiting, until we all felt we had found the root that was the basis for our next step in the learning process.

Marguerite: This dialogue shows how you organize conference work. It reflects how I see you working. The process begins with an observation – we often get things wrong and don't see how it happened and the same goes for getting things right. There is nothing wrong with that. We learn by trial and error, we learn what works and what doesn't. However, I have heard all of you talk about how well you work together and how it just works mysteriously for you. Of course the work you do shows that it isn't magic, but a set of working practices – you respect one another, listen, and are prepared to have disagreements, you have a lot of experience, and in most ways you all want the same things.... You have strong understandings about how to take up different work and bring it together.... So your work brings the conferences into being. But it also depends on the women who come and work while they are there. The two parts bring off the conferences.

The conferences have the character of praxis. By this I mean a way of learning that is connected to real life. You begin in the north, where you live and see the problems and issues of women. You work to bring together women who share the problems. You use "resource people" to help you present the issues of your lives and the lives of the women who come in a framework, an analysis. You learn as you go and so do the conference participants. The work presented by your resource people is taken up if it can be used in getting the work done.... It gets left behind if it is not useful.

Conference work is evolving. It is educational. It develops women's skills and capacities. It connects women who are active and brings women who are not active into a setting where they can learn about what other people are doing.

It is important for me to see that the strength of the conference and of the steering committee is that they both function quite similarly. There is no division between the steering committee and participants in the conferences in their concerns, working style, and life situation. Your organizational work teaches women at the conferences how to work.

Gayle: Over time we improved our work on these conferences, paying more attention to the participation of the women who came. Because everyone had to travel on Fridays, sometimes for as long as eight hours (we had no money for airfares), we knew that people could not spend much time being "talked at." We did have Friday speakers at our "More than Bandages: Healing for People, Not for Profit" conference in November of 1982 at Camp Wakonda and deeply regretted it; no one had the energy to absorb what they had to say, and the speakers felt marginalized and angry. Because of this, Friday night became a time for arrival, a time to be greeted by friendly faces and assigned a comfortable billet. We tried to provide some opportunity for those who arrived early to "get into" the conference right away though – sometimes with a selection of films, making sure they were not too intense, and later with the "Game of Life." This game was developed by Joan and Marylou for one of the early conferences and used thereafter with great success. Resembling the "Poverty Game" that was later developed and popularized, the "Game of Life" allowed people to enter and leave the game at will, but always forced the players to make choices that would benefit themselves, their community, or some other not so benevolent group.

Joan: The "Game of Life" proved to be a good way to start a conference since women arrived at different hours and had to wait around for billets. We didn't want this time to be "wasted" and we wanted to find some way to get strangers talking about important issues with one another as soon as possible.

The "Game of Life" has no winners or losers. It is to be played in groups of five or six. A little "person" goes around a board landing on squares labelled "money," "education," "community," "decisions." For each of these, there is a pile of cards. Written on each card is a decision – for example, "you decide to live in a co-operative house," "you decide to spend $350 on an antique vase," and so on. The person who draws that card then has to discuss the decision with the other players and they collectively decide "who profits" from the decision: "I," "we," or "they" ("they" is defined by the group). On the "Decision" squares, a problem is presented for group solution: "Your best friend comes to visit and brings her favourite porn film," etc. It worked like magic.

Gayle: As the conferences evolved and there were many new women each year, we had to find as many opportunities for meeting and getting to know each other as possible. Meals became a time when we often had both informal and formal sharing of what we were doing in our different communities. Long unstructured breaks, numbering off into a variety of small groups, silly physical games, charades, and doing chores together also provided time for participants and organizers to talk. This sharing served many purposes: we were able to get to know each other better; it also helped us realize we were working on many different issues – environment, health, community economic development, violence against women, to name a few; it helped us make connections with others who were involved in the same things we were doing or wanted to do.

Real change in the way we work, transformation, can come about only when there is an atmosphere of trust. Again, many of the exercises and activities at the NEOWC were designed to ensure that the women present were comfortable and felt safe enough to talk about and explore their own values. Several of the underlying assumptions of the conference were based on values that significantly contributed to this atmosphere.

The conferences numbers were limited to 80. Initially, of course, there was no necessity to limit numbers, but by the final conference, we did reach 80 participants. This limit allowed the planning committee to attend to personal needs of conference participants and also allowed participants to recognize speakers and develop friendships. To increase the intimacy of the group, participants were encouraged to spend the whole weekend together, rather than dispersing to shop or be entertained outside of the conference. The "playtime" of Saturday nights reinforced this further, as did the small group work that was a part of every conference.

The planning committee also accepted that there would be wide variation in participants' previous exposure to some of the issues: not everyone would know and understand why we tried to avoid fast foods and styrofoam cups; not everyone would use language or conduct themselves in a manner that was "politically correct." Instead, the planning committee concentrated on ways in which women could share their knowledge and understanding of issues, sensitizing one another to different issues, and helping them realize that they were all part of a larger whole. Thus it was important to select speakers who could help with this analysis, and to ensure that all participants felt respected, and respected others.

Marguerite: The point of developing an analysis is to be able to use it to reveal how features of our lives are organized outside us and how we can begin to control our lives more. Because of the complex character of our world, this is a big task, since both economics and politics are bound together.

Gayle: Our growing analysis was deepened and made useful to participants by our trying to use it in action. We used a number of techniques like simulation games and popular theatre to allow this to happen in the conference format. The simulations were designed by the conference planning committee and involved real people and real problems. A written statement in a paragraph or two set the context for a small group of women to develop a strategy for working through a simulated community problem. The issue might be drinking water polluted by the town's major employer. The group working on it would be assigned the roles of people found in a northern community – an environmentalist busy with two young children, a stay-at-home mom who depends on her husband's employment by the polluter for the family's livelihood, and so on. The people in the group would adopt their roles and work out a strategy for dealing with the issue, drawing on their own knowledge and experience and using resource people to help. This activity developed analysis skills and strong bonds among the participants. They learned different ways of looking at the problem by listening to each other and by using the analysis provided by speakers; they learned to look for allies in their communities – people whom they could work with and whom they might not have thought to ask before; they began to realize the extent of their own expertise.

For example, at the fourth conference, "Through the Looking Glass," in Sudbury in 1984, Dorothy Smith and Marguerite spoke about the media and how a "story" in the news reports is organized. They used several examples to illustrate what is made invisible and unworthy. Then we used "newspaper theatre" to explore a news report about a demonstration by a community group trying to draw attention to an issue. The participants used body sculpture to show what the news did not say. What the news story left out, of course, was all the telephone calls and letters that were sent out trying to get people to attend; the preparation of the news releases and then the telephone calls to the media to get them to report on the event; the picking up of coffee urns, cups, etc., so that the demonstrators could be given a hot cup of coffee; and the scrounging for funds to pay for the coffee. Then there was the agonizing over who should speak, what they should say, and making sure the police were okay with the location of the demonstration. In fact, what the news item reported was a very minor part of what had really happened. Dorothy and Marguerite spoke about how one small word could create a completely different perception of the event – stating "only" 40 people came out makes the event look small and unrepresentative, whereas "at least" 40 people makes it sound like a large gathering. I have never read or listened to a news report since with an uncritical eye or ear, and whenever I hear of an event, I think about the people and the energy behind it. Whenever I am involved in organizing an activity that will be reported, I try to think of ways of conveying to the public what this event is really about and what our group is really doing, and I have come to realize that news reports are only one very limited form of communication.

Joan: In the third conference in Timmins, the planning committee acknowledged that it was despair that often kept us from dealing with issues like war and the nuclear industry. We organized "Bread and Roses: Alternatives to Despair." This conference included dance and theatre workshops that helped us to work the tensions out of our bodies and minds and talk about those issues that made us feel the most helpless. This workshop later inspired the central theme for my book on community organizing.[3]

To my mind there were key lessons about our reality as women in Northern Ontario that I took away from these conferences:

• That when we characterize the difficulties in our reality as issues, instead of as themes, we fragment that reality and exhaust ourselves. In NEOWC, we consciously tried to build a way of seeing reality that sought our common themes and root causes. All issues are different windows on the same reality.

• Our lives are organized by forces outside ourselves and in a set of interests different from our own. Our reality is shaped by bus routes, work, recreation, and by the food we eat and the way we raise our children. When we see the common patterns in these forms of organization, we can better see how to resist and change them.

• Information we need in order to get control of our lives is often located in language and forms we cannot access in the halls of academia and in the media.

• The holistic approach we adopted enabled us to understand what our Native sisters had been trying to tell us about the role of women in the community and to begin to learn from them about building healthy communities.

• Resistance to the corporate agenda for our lives can begin in our daily lives and our communities. We will heal ourselves by mutual aid, by circles of strength, and by creating alternative economies and social forms.

Gayle: After three and a half years of intense work, planning, organizing, and sponsoring conferences, many planning committee members made choices that took the strategies learned in the conferences into other venues. Marylou went to work for the National Action Committee in Ottawa; Cathy Cervin left the north and now teaches community-based medicine in Halifax; Kathy Ingwerson became active involving women in the environmental movement; Katherine Fournier moved to Toronto; Marguerite completed her Ph.D. and began a teaching career at Dalhousie University; and Joan and I, in different jobs, remained active in our home communities.

Joan: Over time we began to realize just how much the conferences influenced the style and direction of many women's meetings. We were constantly consulted about format for conferences. Women had begun to take on economics as a women's issue, challenging definitions and concepts of a "job," and seeing corporate structures themselves as relevant to women.

Gayle: In fact, we have all continued to work in the community. Here are just a few examples. In the fall of 1982, a phone call from Sudbury and a show of support from women who had participated in NEOWC enabled Soo women to take advantage of an opportunity for action to call the government to account. Russ Ramsey, then Minister of Labour and MPP for Sault Ste. Marie, publicly stated that equal pay for work of equal value would be "the straw that broke the camel's back" of the Ontario economy. Although the women from the Women's Centre in the Soo were outraged, it wasn't until the Sudbury Women's Centre called us asking what we intended to do that we were spurred to action. We hastily sent an invitation to Russ Ramsey to join us at the Women's Centre for lunch so we could tell him through the media what we thought of his comments. No one expected that the Minister of Labour would actually attend. Then someone came up with the idea of granting him the "Pacifier Award," an idea that came from the annual meeting of the National Action Committee (NAC). Merle decided to write a poem. The media jumped on the idea. On Wednesday afternoon, within a few days of Ramsey's ill-chosen remark, about 40 women and newspaper reporters, along with television cameras and radio microphones, jammed into the small living room of the Women's Centre to present Russ Ramsey with a giant soother and show all of Ontario that feminists do indeed have a sense of humour.

Several conference planners and participants went on to take an active role in politics – as municipal councillors and school trustees, as candidates at the provincial and federal levels, as policy advisors; several took on employment that involved teaching others what they had learned, at universities, in national organizations, in local community-based non-profits; others began or continued active community development at the grassroots level, developing services for abused women, people in conflict with the law, children's programs.

Joan: Another example of the way in which our conferences contributed to women's activism occurred in Sudbury. In 1983 Inco shut down for six months, and the consequences were terrible in the community. A group of union activists asked the women to get involved in protest actions around this issue. However, because of the work we had done in NEOWC, the women's movement understood that work to change Inco's activity in Sudbury had to be taken up in the realities of women's daily lives. The Nickel Alliance was organized on the basis of NEOWC practice: working in small groups, collective decision-making, bringing our whole lives to the meeting, and starting from the problems and concerns of women. The traditional male leaders were outraged and proceeded to take the group apart. The women shifted their focus and worked with issues around increasing homelessness, neighbourhood action, and welfare rights. We were able to see these more effective ways to take on the company at that time because we had learned to trust our own experience.

Gayle and Joan: We found people who believed us and believed in us and, at a time when there were no feminist therapists, we provided therapy to one another. We listened to each other's stories – I'll never forget Susan Hare talking about her experience of racism – and we were forever changed by them, because these stories had happened in our communities and now we were seeing them from a different side. The stories brought us to a place where we could no longer hide, because it was in ourselves and our families.

As organizers we trusted the women who came to the conferences to explore new worlds, new ways of seeing and being. Most conference organizers want to be certain of "outcomes"; most funders want reports that show "plans of action." What we were doing at the Northeastern Ontario Women's Conferences was building energy – energy that the women took back into their own communities in order to make change.

24

Northern Ontario Women's Centres: Women of Vision, Women of Change[1]

Kitty Minor

There have always been meeting places for women, regardless of culture, race, or geographical location. The meeting place has often been in a kitchen where a few women gathered to discuss how politics, parenting, and both paid and unpaid work shape their lives and order their priorities. These informal meetings often take place amid the rush of wiping noses, preparing meals, and answering phone calls. Some of these encounters have led to the realization that women needed a place of their own, a women's centre. Creating women's centres in Northern Ontario has evolved through an unselfish desire on the part of some women to improve the lives of all women. In spite of opposition to their efforts, Northern Ontario women have much to be proud of. Their efforts have profoundly changed the lives of many individuals involved in the women's centre movement.

This chapter will review some of the accomplishments of northern women in establishing women's centres in six Northern Ontario communities over the past 20 years. Gathering the stories of the women's centres discussed here was accomplished through an interview process. In keeping with a feminist research perspective, the women who agreed to be interviewed were given a list of prepared questions. They were asked to address the questions that interested them and that they felt comfortable answering. Once completed, the transcript of the interview was sent to the woman for corrections.

The North Bay Women's Centre

Developing the story of the North Bay Women's Centre would not have been possible without the assistance of Kathy Kilburn, who in 1989 began documenting the "herstory" of the North Bay Women's Centre.[2] Although still unpublished, her account is particularly valuable since the North Bay centre, opened in 1974, closed it doors in June 1990.

Kilburn recounts how four women – Meg Purdy, Jay Costello, Bette Morton, and Marea Mainer – gathered in Meg's kitchen in what was at first an informal support or consciousness-raising group as they were known at the time. They called themselves EQUALS and they were "the first feminist organization in North Bay."[3] EQUALS later underwent a transformation when it became the North Bay Women's Centre in April 1976 and was renamed the North Bay Women's Resource Centre shortly after. The name change signalled a new direction for the centre, which came about as a result of declining resources of both money and women's energies. In an attempt to save the centre, it was moved into the basement of Emmanuel United Church.[4] The lack of consistent funding has made the staff and volunteers in many women's centres familiar with church basements and small rooms in dilapidated buildings that are often located in a section of town that is less than desirable. In North Bay the women's centre relocated many times because of funding difficulties.

As in other women's centres, the need to find the money to maintain the North Bay centre meant that considerable time and energy was diverted from the needs of women in crisis as staff and volunteers applied for government grants. However, the women in the North Bay centre raised funds by collecting newspapers, IGA stamps, Canadian Tire money, Dominion Store cash slips, and so on.[5] But even these efforts were inadequate. By 1990, centre finances were in such straits that replacement staffing could not be contemplated. In spite of these difficulties the members of the centre's Women's Culture Committee developed an exciting program for International Women's Week.[6] Although the week itself was a success, the centre closed in June of that year.

Regardless of the demise of the North Bay Women's Centre, the organization is known for its childcare advocacy and for the fact that it was instrumental in starting three parent co-operative childcare centres – Tot Town, Big Bird, and Child's World. It was also a leading force behind the Rape Crisis Centre, Big Sisters, and the Nipissing Transition House. The centre also did a retrospective of women's lives in Nipissing in the early part of the century. It produced an education and support package for use in schools to deal with child sexual abuse, a home daycare-givers' registry, and a women's health needs survey. The centre was also responsible for establishing the Mayor's Committee on the Status of Women. Besides these activities, the centre also held numerous conferences and workshops, including one on creative play and several specifically aimed at teen women.[7]

The women involved in the North Bay Women's Resource Centre can take pride in the fact that their struggles have resulted in positive gains for women in the North Bay area. Kathy Kilburn writes: "Although it closed its doors, the centre has not actually disbanded. There are those of us who intend to see it open again and efforts to see this come about should begin next year."[8]

The Sudbury Women's Centre

In the early 1970s the women who were interested in discussing issues arising from the women's movement usually met in someone's home. Although these gatherings were loosely organized, they often resulted in direct political action. Karen Dominick writes that "Sudbury women lobbied for abortion referral services, a birth control centre, the acceptance of working women into unions, and demanded that politicians take up issues of concern to women."[9]

In 1978, when Local 6500 of the United Steel Workers of America decided on strike action, few Inco workers were prepared for the battle that followed. For eight and a half months, strikers and their families struggled to hang on to what they had. In the ensuing struggle a group emerged who called themselves "Wives Supporting the Strike."[10] These women provided support to one another and also to the families of the strikers. This strike and the women's groups that supported the families effectively provided a nucleus of women who called themselves "Women in Action." When the group decided that community interest was sufficient to support a women's centre, they petitioned the federal government for funding and were successful in obtaining $17,000 to found the Sudbury Women's Centre.[11]

In January 1981, the Sudbury Women's Centre opened its doors at 86 Ignatius Street. Like the North Bay centre, the Sudbury Women's Centre moved several times, and even closed temporarily more than once because of limited funds. The centre specifically addressed issues women struggled with in their daily lives: employment rights, health issues, and child-rearing were just a few of the topics on which the centre provided information and counselling. The centre also supported the Sudbury's Rape Crisis Centre when it was experiencing difficulty. The Sudbury Women's Centre has a long history of recognizing and supporting striking workers. Bringing women together for conferences and workshop is only one of the accomplishments of the Sudbury Women's Centre. However, limited financial resources and shortages of volunteers have taken their toll over the years. In fact, the centre has had only one full-time staff position since 1982, even though the demand for services continues to increase.

Today the centre is administered by a steering committee. Its mission is to support women in difficult situations by giving them access to information, public education, and outreach programs as funding allows. It also makes referrals through community and social service networks in a non-threatening environment that reflects and respects the woman's needs. Despite limited financial resources, internal conflicts, and a shortage of women-power, the Sudbury Women's Centre has much to celebrate in its accomplishments. Throughout the years it has been operating, the centre has established an anti-pornography group, a homemakers' committee, and a free legal clinic, which it continues to operate today. It produces a monthly newsletter and sponsors workshops on various topics. Although the accomplishments are many, the members of the centre are always hopeful that they will be able to expand their services more as resources permit.

Phoenix Rising Women's Centre and Non-profit Homes Inc., Sault Ste. Marie

The Phoenix Rising Women's Centre and Non-Profit Homes Inc. was opened in Sault Ste. Marie in 1986. Originally, the centre hoped to establish a child-care centre and have an in-service program component that would include support for mentally ill women. Although the centre works as a collective, a board of directors was formed in 1986 in order to achieve incorporation. Construction of an apartment building with five units set aside for women with a psychiatric diagnosis finally began in 1991. The women who envisioned the project managed "to provide permanent, affordable, and safe homes for mentally ill women and to provide programs that would empower women to gain control of their lives."[12] In addition to the apartment complex, Phoenix Rising has a women's centre that functions as a drop-in centre and houses a resource library, and it sponsors support programs for women and a play area for children. When funds allowed for an outreach component to be added to the program, it was decided that it would be located in Elliot Lake. All these community resources are testimony to the courage, perseverance, and determination of a few dedicated women in Sault Ste. Marie.

Phoenix Rising-Women's Drop In Centre, Elliot Lake

With the support of both its sister centre Sault Ste. Marie's Phoenix Rising, and the provincial government, the Phoenix Rising-Women's Drop In Centre opened in Elliot Lake in October 1990. Functioning as a working collective, its mission is "to offer support to women; to provide a safe environment for women and children; and to offer programs that support the empowerment of women."[13] The Elliot Lake Centre is a young centre with great potential. It will be interesting to observe its growth and development over the next few years.

Northern Women's Centre, Thunder Bay

In 1972, the Women's Liberation Group invited women from the community to attend a meeting that would consider the feasibility "of organizing a regional women's conference" in Thunder Bay.[14] Organizers expected about 60 women to attend. In fact, close to 600 showed up. The conference provided the impetus for a women's resource centre, which began with a grant from the Secretary of State in April 1974.[15] Its mission was to provide a meeting place for women, to advocate on behalf of women's issues, and to provide support and education to women.

The core funding the group received in 1980 disappeared in 1987. The centre managed to survive by relying on grants, donations, and fund-raising, and with the help of a small number of dedicated volunteers. In 1993, a $50,000 grant from the provincial NDP government ensured the continuation of the centre for at least two more years. Its mission statement, developed in 1987, states that "the Northwestern Ontario Women's Centre is a meeting place that provides a strong feminist voice for women in northwestern Ontario."[16]

Today, the centre continues to advocate on behalf of women, provides community education, and provides women with a place to meet. It produces a newsletter and has established an impressive resource library of historical and current documents on women's issues.

Women's Place Kenora

After a survivor of a sexual assault became upset with the treatment and lack of support she had received within the traditional social service system, she organized a group of volunteers to operate a crisis line.[17] The line was established in 1976 and signalled the beginning of the Kenora Women's Crisis Intervention Project. The centre opened its doors in June 1979. With funding from a Canada Works Grant, the centre was able to house a small number of women and their children. Some of the women were escaping domestic violence; others had been sexually assaulted and required a safe, supportive environment.

Faced with the persistent problem of finding operational funding, the crisis centre submitted a proposal to the Kenora Town Council in March requesting "hostel" status. This qualified the centre for ongoing per diem funding. The proposal was rejected on the grounds that the proposed crisis centre was a duplication of a service already offered by the town. In fact, the "service" that was in place provided only one night's accommodation in a transient hotel and a $3.50 food voucher. Subsequently, the centre lost its right to provide shelter on the basis that it did not meet fire and safety regulations.[18]

In 1981, continuing funding difficulties caused the Kenora Crisis Intervention Project to reassess its mandate. Following this, it incorporated as Women's Place Kenora with a vision to provide a 24-hour crisis line, to advocate for services for women in the District of Kenora, and to network with women and women's groups to bring change on behalf of women at all levels of government.

The centre has since received both federal and provincial funding as well as private donations. Additional funds come by way of a nominal membership fee from those who can afford to pay. Women unable to afford the fee are given the option of supporting the centre in other ways. Members are kept informed of scheduled events through the centre's newsletter. Although the centre has an executive committee, all decisions are made collectively by the membership. Members also sit on various committees that help oversee general centre operations and programming.

Although Women's Place Kenora began with the goal of providing a support service for women who have been sexually assaulted, it was soon apparent that other services for women were needed. Today, the centre attempts to fill those gaps in services for women. It operates a 24-hour rape crisis line, has worked with the community to establish a transition house, advocates on behalf of victims of crime, and has worked to establish special needs housing.[19] Kenora will never be the same, and the women in Kenora will never again have to stand alone thanks to the efforts, strength, and courage of a few women.

Commentary

In examining the herstories of women's centres in Northern Ontario, the theme that emerged time and again is that centres are constantly struggling to meet the financial obligations that arise from trying to deliver services. Although most centres raise a portion of their operating expenses from nominal fees and from private donations, core funding comes from some branch of the provincial government. As well as the core funding, centres can also apply for additional funds for a special limited-time project.

The endless conditions attached to government funding are a constant problem. Application for funding requires that a centre be incorporated and have a board of executive officers with proper signing authority responsible for all program proposals and disbursement of funds. In order to obtain funding, the centre is forced to conform to a prescribed hierarchical structure that does not lend itself to the concept of collective work or to egalitarian relationships that are central to feminist organizations.

As well, if the centre is to receive government money it must agree to maintain records according to prescribed standards. Considerable resources are diverted away from the real work of the centre as time and energies of staff and volunteers are consumed with record keeping that will satisfy funders. Receiving funds from more than one funder can mean that several different kinds of records must be kept. Such requirements can exhaust and frustrate those who most need the services as well as those who provide the services.

In order for women's centres to escape this cycle, they will need to find new and less time-consuming ways to meet funders' requirements. Women's centres need to explore different avenues of funding sources. Whether women's centres like it or not, they may have to become less dependent on government. Certainly the election of the Harris Conservatives will mean there will be less money for publicly funded social welfare groups. Women's unpaid labour has always been exploited by the state, and funders have no qualms about continuing this lucrative practice, particularly when they have tapped it successfully for decades. The lack of long-term funding for women's centres will result in confusion and exhaustion, both for women who seek services and for those who provide care. But we need to continue sitting around kitchen tables and struggling in order that the needs of women will be addressed.[20]

25

Getting It Together: Women and Co-operative Housing in Northern Ontario

Ginette Lafrenière and Barbara Millsap

Almost daily one hears of the consequences of structural unemployment in this province. Layoffs, downsizing, and child poverty are all familiar to the average person. The impact of the current economic situation that faces many people is nowhere more noticeable than in the struggle to find affordable housing in the north. This problem is of particular concern to women. According to a recent study conducted by the Sudbury Women's Housing Network, women who needed affordable housing cross all barriers, including age, ethnicity, and circumstance.[1] A number of reasons have been identified to explain why so many women needed access to affordable housing in the north. First, their accommodation at the time was inadequate. It was either too small for the size of the family or was in a state of disrepair. Second, breakdown in family relationships meant that the woman and her children had to seek new, cheaper living arrangements. Finally, changing circumstances were a factor caused by the need to live closer to an urban centre where services and employment were more accessible.

While the reasons women look for affordable housing varies, the biggest barrier they face is discrimination based on socio-economic status, race, age, marital status, or the fact that they have children. In a study on women's housing needs, Wekerle points out that in every city she visited women complained of landlords who were prejudiced against single mothers, women living on social assistance, visible minority women, and lesbians.[2] Intolerance, however, is not the only problem women face in their search for housing. Findings in Sudbury indicate that even during a period when vacancy rates were high, affordable housing was still in very short supply.

Co-operative housing can make a difference for women. Sixty percent of those participating in co-op housing projects are women.[3] Over the years we have witnessed hundreds of women regain control over their lives by channelling their creative and intellectual energy into participating in the management and social development of their housing environment. Both of the authors have worked for years initiating and developing co-operative housing projects in Northern Ontario and in educating anyone who would listen to the philosophy of the co-operative movement. The quotes in this brief overview are the voices of four women whose lives have been changed as a result of being accepted as members in a co-operative housing complex.[4]

The roots of the co-operative movement can be traced back to Rochdale, England. It was there that the first consumer co-operative was initiated in 1844 by a group of 28 people known as the Rochdale Pioneers. John Craig has argued that "the principles that distinguish co-operative from non-co-operative organizations are a translation of the philosophical values of the movement, rather than a literal statement of the values themselves."[5] He claims further that co-operation has as its foundation three basic value sets: equality, economic justice, and mutual self-help.

It is important to understand the philosophy of the co-operative movement because its inherent values help to explain why the lives of so many women have changed once they became active in the movement. Co-op housing works for women because of the nature of these housing projects. There is a sense of ownership among the members that is not the case in state-owned housing projects. Even though members cannot own their units on an individual basis, they own the housing projects collectively, with financing by the government. There is a tremendous sense of responsibility, which members recognize as important in order to effectively run the co-op.

Members try to achieve a balance in the socio-economic make-up of co-op projects so that a healthy community can develop. Students, recipients of family benefits, both blue- and white-collar workers, and people with disabilities often live in the same complex. Data collected nationally in the early 1990s suggest that 66 percent of households in co-op projects have incomes below $30,000; families in co-ops are twice as likely to have incomes below the poverty line; close to 57 percent of adult co-op residents are women, whereas women make up 52 percent of the general population; women as heads of single-parent families living in co-op housing have a higher rate of labour force participation than do women living elsewhere (79 percent compared to 61 percent); and a much higher proportion of older adults in co-op housing are women. In fact the proportion of older women living in co-op housing is 50 percent higher than those living in other forms of housing. Also, co-op housing has a greater representation of immigrants than do other forms of housing (24 percent compared to 16 percent).[6]

Wekerle has argued that single parents are often attracted to co-operative housing not just because of the diverse nature of the population but because co-operatives do not have the same stigma that public housing has.[7] Because co-ops tend to emphasize equality and mutual self-help, they do not appear to practise the discrimination that is prevalent elsewhere against women as heads of families.

Co-operative housing is a non-profit, community-based form of housing that has been developed under various federal and provincial government programs. Co-ops are owned and operated by resident members within a democratic structure. More than 85,000 units have been built in this country over the past 27 years, and co-op housing projects tend to be located in urban areas, with families apparently the major target group. Households pay housing charges (rent) based on a percentage of their income, up to the level of the market value for their unit.

A volunteer board of directors is elected by the membership at the annual general meeting. Here, members put forth their names for election for the board of a co-op project. Once elected, the board meets regularly to manage and to set policies for the project. Given the intense pressure on the board to decide on issues such as noise level, ownership of pets, landscaping, and repairs, there are various committees for which residents volunteer for various committees that are formed to participate in the decision making. A significant difference that exists between co-op housing and state-owned housing projects is that the right to vote is not based on the unit of housing but is granted to anyone residing within the co-op who is at least 18 years of age.

There are few studies that examine the impact that co-op housing has on women and their children. We have found that the co-op housing project allows them to take control of their lives by participating in many of the decisions regarding how they will live. One avid member stated, "For the first time in my life, I have a say in what my rent should be like, what colour my walls should be painted, and what type of playground equipment could be useful to my children."

Women can also develop skills as they become active in co-op work. Deborah, a co-op member from Sudbury, told about coming to co-op housing from a basement apartment where she spoke to no one. At the co-op, she says, "I had to attend a general membership meeting the second night I had moved in. I was very shy and … wondered what I had gotten myself into, but living in the co-op is the best thing that has happened to me."

Women such as Deborah have little choice but to speak out at meetings where decisions are made concerning their environment. They often gain the public-speaking skills needed to contribute effectively to committee work. As well, women develop abilities in areas such as bookkeeping, parenting, and conflict resolution. In addition to the practical experience women receive through their volunteer activities, they also develop social networks. One co-op resident stated, "Making friends was a big deal for me when I lived in a housing co-op. After living with an abusive husband for five years, I finally had friends I could call my own."

Participation in the movement has shown many women that they have a talent for leadership. Many northern women are voting delegates to the national organization. Canada's national co-op housing movement is the only co-operative organization in the country that has a woman as the executive director of the national organization and a woman as president of the national board. In fact, the majority of elected leaders at the local, regional, and national levels of co-op housing are women. Thus the co-op experience gives many women the opportunity to develop networks, teaches them the value of lobbying, and often allows them to become politically involved in the movement. One woman shared her thoughts on the subject: "When I saw myself drawing up posters and going door-to-door to ask my neighbours to vote for me, I knew I had come a long way from the shelter I was in three years ago. Living here has made me a very different person. I'm not afraid any more."

Co-op housing also helps women to meet their basic need of a safe, secure, and affordable environment. Once they have access to affordable housing, stress levels diminish and enthusiasm emerges for goals that once seemed unattainable. It is not uncommon to witness women on social assistance gain the confidence to complete high school or finish a degree. In fact, education is central to the co-operative movement. Resource groups that have worked with founding boards of directors have realized the importance of education for housing members. Many critics of the co-op housing structure have argued that while it is noble to provide affordable housing, it is imperative that education in co-op principles prepare members for the challenges that accompany the responsibility of being a co-op member. A co-op is only as strong as the level of education its members receive. Because we live in a society where many decisions are made for us as renters, the thought of running a multi-million dollar corporation collectively is frightening to many. Therefore, many women and men in northeastern Ontario have benefited by attending various workshops offered by the local resource group or regional federation.

Educational workshops are designed for an adult population. The method of teaching is experiential, and most participants seek to take courses offered in management, conflict resolution, bookkeeping, maintenance, and other topics relevant to a housing co-operative. Many women take advantage of the workshops that are usually offered at the co-op's community centre. Childcare is often less of a problem in a co-op setting because the women have the option of bringing their children to the centre with them. Often a neighbour is willing to barter childcare during the course.

During such sessions, women frequently think about returning to school. The process of education is often demystified in co-op courses taught in a supportive and nurturing environment. One women stated: "I had never even thought of becoming a bookkeeper, but after taking two courses offered by the finance committee at the co-op, I thought that it wasn't so hard after all."

Co-op housing has also taken the initiative to speak out on current issues. Many co-ops have declared themselves "Domestic Violence-Free Zones" to provide a safe and secure environment for women. Some housing co-ops have designated units for women in need of emergency shelters. While the number of units is not adequate, the co-op acknowledges that emergency housing is imperative for victims of domestic violence.

As practitioners working within the Canadian Co-operative Movement, we want women in northeastern Ontario to know the impact co-operative housing projects can have on the daily lives of women seeking comfortable and reasonably priced housing. Today there are many examples of women in co-op housing who have been able to get their lives together, develop new skills and confidence, and go on to become leaders in the broader community.

26

Le Collectif – un médium pour améliorer la condition des femmes francophones

Johanne Pomerleau et collaboratrices[1]

Voici notre histoire comme femmes et membres du Collectif des femmes francophones du Nord-est ontarien (désigné par le «Collectif» dans la suite du texte). Cette histoire s'est tissée à partir du vécu des femmes qui ont géré des projets et de celles qui y ont participé. La mission du Collectif est de favoriser l'avancement des femmes francophones par le biais de l'éducation post-secondaire ou par la mobilisation collective autour d'un projet commun. Les membres du Collectif veulent aider les femmes francophones à compléter leur éducation ou à faire reconnaître les expériences qu'elles ont acquises au travail, que ce travail soit rémunéré ou non. Il est connu que les francophones n'ont pas un niveau de scolarité élevé.[2] C'est pourquoi le Collectif a choisi d'écouter et de répondre aux besoins d'éducation des femmes francophones, en facilitant leur accès aux études post-secondaires ou encore en obtenant du financement pour mettre sur pied des programmes de formation sur mesure.

Depuis sa naissance en 1988, le Collectif a géré plus de quinze projets à plus ou moins long terme, ciblant des femmes de tous les âges et de divers niveaux de scolarité. Croyant fermement que l'autonomie des femmes est reliée à leur éducation, les femmes du Collectif ont mené à terme des projets en utilisant une idéologie féministe et une approche de développement communautaire. Cette vision a permis de mettre sur pied des programmes d'éducation, d'information et de développement personnel adaptés aux besoins spécifiques des femmes. Aujourd'hui la réputation du Collectif, dans ce type de dossiers est établie et reconnue. Comme organisme, il bénéficie et entretient des relations de partenariat avec d'autres organismes de la région dont la vocation est éducative, scientifique ou communautaire.

Une des premières actions entreprises par un noyau de femmes en 1988 a été de rejoindre les femmes francophones de la région et d'identifier leurs besoins. Deux rapports ont été publiés à la suite de ces projets: «Le répertoire des femmes francophones du Nord-est ontarien» et «Ouvrir les portes du secondaire aux Franco-Ontariennes.» Il est devenu très évident que les besoins en éducation pour les Franco-Ontariennes étaient grands et que peu de ressources étaient disponibles. Afin de combler certains de ces besoins, le Collectif a entrepris des projets tels que l'«Université au féminin,» la «Violence,» «Le réseau d'entraide des femmes aînées,» «Harmonisation travail-famille,» et le «Colloque sur l'intervention féministe» pour n'en nommer que quelques-uns. Nous présentons ici quelques projets et activités en ordre chronologique, sans pour autant donner tous les détails qui démontrent le bien fondé de ces projets ou les démarches nécessaires pour qu'ils deviennent réalisables. Nous avons aussi inclus des témoignages de femmes qui ont eu un impact ou mobilisé d'autres femmes francophones vers l'atteinte d'un but commun.

L'université au féminin

Ce programme a été conçu par une équipe pour faciliter le retour aux études des femmes francophones et leur intégration aux programmes d'études post-secondaires. Quatre fils conducteurs ont servi de trame au programme: information, formation, orientation, et réseautage.

Le programme a été offert une première fois à titre d'essai à l'été 1992 à l'Université Laurentienne. Nous savons que des treize femmes inscrites au projet pilote et qui ont complété le programme, deux poursuivent leurs études au niveau universitaire avec succès et deux autres viennent de terminer le programme «Éducation des petits» au collège. L'une d'entre elles a l'intention de suivre des cours à l'École de service social à l'université et l'autre vient de réussir avec succès le test de compétence linguistique. Trois femmes terminent leur première année, soit deux en Service social avec une option en gérontologie et une en Administration des affaires; deux suivent des cours de formation générale au collège; une termine un programme de secrétariat informatisé au Centre de l'Assomption; une autre complète sa 12ième année dans un programme alternatif pour adultes; et deux sont sur le marché du travail.

En 1993, douze femmes de 22 à 62 ans se sont inscrites à la première session officielle du programme et neuf d'entre elles l'ont complétée avec succès. Après une semaine de cours, deux femmes ont abandonné pour des raisons de santé et l'autre parce qu'elle n'était pas suffisamment motivée. Des neuf graduées de ce groupe, quatre ont l'intention de poursuivre des études universitaires, quatre autres veulent entreprendre des études au niveau collégial, et une dernière considère prendre quelques cours comme auditrice libre ou à l'éducation permanente.

Voici le témoignage d'une finissante du premier groupe:

> Le mot «éducation» semble quelquefois vouloir prendre différentes définitions et même intimider certaines gens. N'ayant pas complété mes études secondaires et étant mère de trois enfants, le besoin d'apprendre ou d'élargir mes connaissances ne faisait que hanter mes rêves quotidiens. Cet appétit d'élargir mon degré éducationnel semblait cependant s'entre-mailler avec un certain degré

d'incertitude, de doute, et de peur. Les mots tels que «collège» et «université» me semblaient être irréels et trop difficiles à atteindre.

Peu à peu, j'ai d'abord entrepris certains cours offerts dans ma communauté, pour finalement m'aventurer au Collège Cambrian dans le but de me recycler. Suite à une session d'information du programme université au féminin, j'ai décidé de m'y tremper les pieds.

Ma participation au programme université au féminin m'a donné la chance de me familiariser avec l'environnement universitaire, tout en me permettant d'élargir certains échanges sociaux avec d'autres femmes étudiantes francophones de ma région.

Cette expérience m'a aidé à développer un certain sentiment d'appartenance au milieu de l'éducation et m'a encouragée grandement dans l'expression de mes talents. L'aide professionnelle en orientation scolaire qui m'a été donnée, m'a apporté une plus grande assurance et le goût de vouloir continuer à me découvrir davantage en tant que femme francophone.

Les femmes aînées

Le programme de formation «Réseau d'entraide des femmes aînées» a été créé afin d'offrir à ces dernières des occasions de formation personnelle et de promouvoir leur développement quant à leur capacité d'aider d'autres personnes âgées. Il s'agit en fait de permettre aux femmes aînées de réaliser leur potentiel ainsi que de compléter ou de parfaire leur apprentissage personnel.

Le programme «Réseau d'entraide pour personnes aînées» est la version française du projet initial de Samuels et Cole, intitulé «Senior Connection.»[3] Ce programme innovateur comporte trois volets. Les femmes aînées doivent tout d'abord s'inscrire au premier volet connu sous l'appellation «Découverte de soi» (DDS). Par la suite, certaines d'entre elles, désireuses de poursuivre et démontrant une capacité de diriger d'autres aînées, pourront passer au deuxième volet, qui est la «Formation d'animatrices communautaires» (FAC). En dernier lieu, les animatrices communautaires pourront s'inscrire au troisième volet, qui est la «Formation des coanimatrices communautaires» (FCAC), dans le but de diriger les aînées de leur communauté à compléter le premier volet.

Une animatrice a la responsabilité de veiller au bon déroulement du programme afin qu'il réponde aux besoins des participantes. Les commentaires de cette dernière sont résumés à la fin de la description du programme de formation.

Les réactions des femmes qui ont suivi le premier volet ont permis de justifier le bien-fondé de ce projet. En effet, les commentaires émis par les participantes nous laissent croire qu'elles redécouvrent leur richesse personnelle et leur capacité personnelle. Ces réalisations nous permettent de croire que les objectifs d'apprentissage de ce programme sont atteints. De plus, même si les commentaires mentionnés font davantage référence aux conséquences sur la personne, il est important de souligner que l'opportunité d'interaction sociale s'offre aux participantes et qu'elles semblent contribuer à l'établissement de nouvelles amitiés.

Les fondements théoriques d'une telle démarche ainsi que les nouvelles politiques gouvernementales soulèvent l'importance de poursuivre de telles activités de formation afin de favoriser l'autonomie maximale des aînées.

L'avenir de tels projets est à privilégier. En effet, la prise en charge par les personnes aînées de leur propre réseau peut sans aucun doute permettre à ces dernières de reconnaître leur valeur et ainsi de partager avec d'autres le fruit de leur découverte. Cette réalisation peut avoir lieu dans un environnement qui leur est propre et qui répond à leurs besoins d'expression et de partage.

Ce qui suit est le témoignage d'une animatrice du programme de formation «Réseau d'entraide»:

> J'ai commencé à oeuvrer au sein du Collectif en décembre 1991 dans le cadre du projet «Réseau d'entraide pour femmes aînées francophones». Avec ce projet, j'ai appris à me faire confiance et à être patiente. Ce programme était un projet pilote à l'intérieur duquel je devais offrir aux femmes francophones de 55 ans et plus des sessions qui leur permettraient d'améliorer leur communication et leur qualité de vie. J'ai donc traversé toutes les étapes qu'implique un projet pilote: c'est-à-dire, concevoir un pamphlet qui donnait un bref aperçu des sessions, faire du recrutement, et établir des contacts avec des personnes-ressources susceptibles de m'aider dans un tel projet. La résultante de tous ces efforts s'est concrétisée de la façon suivante: deux groupes à Hanmer ont débuté les 10 et 11 février 1992.
>
> Depuis le début, onze groupes ont bénéficié des sessions «Découverte de soi» et quatre groupes ont choisi de s'inscrire au deuxième volet, la «Formation d'animatrices communautaires.» Deux participantes, qui ont terminé le FAC ont choisi de devenir co-animatrices du programme (troisième volet).
>
> Qu'est-ce que les participantes ont pu recevoir de ces sessions? Tout d'abord, elles sont d'accord pour affirmer qu'elles ont une meilleure estime d'elles-mêmes, des vraies amies, et un moyen pour répondre à un besoin d'appartenance. Elles ont appris à écouter leurs paires de même qu'à les aider efficacement à faire des choix, à prendre des décisions pour elles-mêmes, à prendre conscience de leurs forces, et à connaître les ressources existantes dans leur communauté respective. Finalement, tout cela fait qu'elles sont en mesure d'organiser leur vie de façon plus satisfaisante.
>
> La majorité des participantes ont gardé contact entre elles et plusieurs me téléphonent régulièrement pour me donner de leurs

nouvelles. Un groupe m'appelle une ou deux fois par année afin que l'on se rassemble pour se souvenir des bons moments vécus dans les cours et pour discuter devant un bon souper. Un autre groupe veut reprendre les cours du début à la fin dans le but de devenir de meilleures animatrices communautaires. Une des participantes, victime d'abus psychologique de la part de son conjoint depuis près de 40 ans, a choisi de divorcer et de reprendre sa vie en main. Je vois cette dame régulièrement et elle ne cesse de s'affirmer et de s'épanouir de jour en jour.

Personnellement j'avoue que j'ai, par la force des choses, élargi mes connaissances religieuses et spirituelles. J'ai appris à écouter avec le coeur et non seulement avec les oreilles. Je me prépare sagement pour ma retraite future. Je me suis fait de très bonnes amies et j'ai appris à faire des conserves et comment transformer les tomates vertes du jardin en tomates rouges pour une bonne partie de l'hiver.

Le Collectif m'a permis par l'entremise de ce projet de me créer une carrière qui correspond à mes diplômes collégiaux et communautaires et qui répond surtout à mes aspirations personnelles. J'ai même commencé à enseigner ou à superviser des stages de formation pour des étudiantes et des étudiants inscrits à un programme de gérontologie offert dans un collège communautaire.

Bref, j'ai le sentiment très clair d'apporter plein de belles choses à des femmes qui ont un très grand besoin d'apprendre et qui veulent s'accomplir! Cela est aussi valorisant pour moi que pour ces femmes. Ma plus belle et ma plus grande acquisition est que je me suis découvert des talents dans l'animation. Je me sens bien là-dedans, les gens m'apprécient, et je suis très fière de moi. Toutes ces expériences, j'ai réussi à aller les chercher à travers les projets que le Collectif m'a offert en toute confiance. Je suis heureuse de faire partie d'un groupe qui travaille à promouvoir la qualité de la vie des femmes en commençant par ses membres.

La violence contre les femmes

«La violence, il faut que ça finisse.» Le Collectif travaille le dossier de la violence depuis plusieurs années. Nous avons abordé cette problématique en traitant différents volets: réseautage, information, partenariat et collaboration, banque de ressources, et formation.

Ce projet nous a permis de nous rendre compte que les domaines de la sensibilisation, de l'éducation, et de la prévention avaient été complètement laissés pour compte dans la grande région de Sudbury. La plupart des organisations, groupes, ou agences offrent des programmes et des services de première ligne aux victimes. Par contre, nous avons identifié des besoins quant à la conscientisation, à l'information, et à la sensibilisation. Nous nous sommes donné les objectifs suivants:

- tester les outils d'intervention que nous avons développés et les utiliser
- intervenir sur une plus grande échelle
- continuer notre intervention
- sensibiliser le milieu francophone à la prévention de la violence faite aux femmes
- augmenter le nombre d'intervenantes en prévention de la violence et offrir une formation sur mesure à celles qui interviennent déjà mais qui n'ont pas eu la possibilité de se former à la prévention.

Nous espérons qu'à la suite de ces interventions, les domaines de la sensibilisation, de la prévention, et de la conscientisation à la violence faite aux femmes seront organisés et feront partie des activités régulières des groupes et des organismes qui oeuvrent en violence. En plus, nous aurons formé des intervenantes communautaires et mis en place des activités qui se dérouleront régulièrement dans la région de Sudbury. Les liens que nous aurons tissés avec les groupes, les agences, et les intervenantes seront suffisamment solides et ils pourront se maintenir sans autres interventions majeures. Nous aurons aussi monté une banque de ressources imprimées et de vidéos. Nous croyons que les intervenantes communautaires pourront identifier et intervenir auprès des femmes au premier cycle de la violence et ainsi briser l'engrenage et soutenir certaines femmes dans leur cheminement vers l'autonomie.

Notre démarche s'inspire des modèles de conscientisation qui ont déjà fait leurs preuves. Il est impossible de changer les attitudes et les comportements s'il ne se produit pas d'abord des changements profonds au niveau de la connaissance des éléments de la problématique de la violence faite aux femmes: connaissance des causes, des dynamiques, du cycle, et de l'escalade.

Depuis 1992 plusieurs organismes régionaux – dont le Collectif ainsi que plusieurs femmes de la communauté – travaillent à la mise sur pied d'un centre francophone d'aide aux femmes aux prises avec des agressions à caractère sexuel. C'est ainsi que le Centre Victoria a vu le jour à l'automne 1993. Depuis le 8 mars 1995, ce centre est en mesure d'offrir des services tel qu'une ligne d'écoute, du soutien immédiat, de l'accompagnement, des services d'éducation et de sensibilisation.

Le Collectif, le Centre Victoria, ainsi que la Fédération des femmes canadiennes-françaises de l'Ontario ont maintenant établi un partenariat qui permet à ces trois groupes de s'épauler dans leurs démarches d'intervention, de prévention, et de sensibilisation dans ce dossier.

Sensibilisation dans les écoles. En octobre 1995 le Collectif décidait d'offrir des ateliers de sensibilisation sur la violence dans les écoles. Ce projet voulait rejoindre les jeunes adolescents des milieux ruraux et urbains. Le but était de sensibiliser, d'informer, et de prévenir la violence dans tous les milieux: familial, social, scolaire et au sein de la relation «Chum/blonde.»

Quatre écoles francophones de la région de Sudbury ont participé – 291 étudiantes de 11, 12 et 13ième années ont pris part à cette activité. Deux animatrices et cinq bénévoles étaient présents lors des sessions. La direction et les professeures et professeurs des écoles ainsi que les conseillères et conseillers en orientation étaient invités à assister aux présentations et étaient disponibles, si le besoin se présentait, pour aider les étudiantes et les étudiants après les rencontres.

Comme animatrices ou bénévoles, nous étions sensibles à ce qui se passait dans les ateliers. Nous passions à travers toute une gamme de sentiments: d'excitation en allant rencontrer ces jeunes, à la satisfaction en notant les connaissances des adolescents sur le sujet, ou encore à la frustration lorsque certains jeunes refusaient de participer ou ne prenaient pas le sujet au sérieux, à la peine en écoutant les partages des participants.

La durée de chaque atelier était d'environ 90 minutes et se subdivisait en trois phases consistant à: 1) discuter des valeurs et connaissances des adolescents sur ce sujet, 2) corriger les mythes et sensibiliser à la violence, et 3) encourager et aider les adolescents à développer un programme de sensibilisation pour leur école. À la fin des rencontres, les animatrices remettaient aux participants une trousse d'information concernant les formes de violence, les mythes, les stéréotypes, les conseils aux victimes et aux aggresseurs, et une liste d'endroits pour aider les victimes.

Suite aux lectures des évaluations après les ateliers, il fut étonnant de constater que les adolescents avaient une soif d'information et de sensibilisation au phénomène de la violence. De plus, plusieurs ont demandé un suivi à cette présentation. Pour assurer un suivi, nous avons fait parvenir un rapport des ateliers à chaque école participante ainsi que la liste des ateliers d'information que les jeunes aimeraient recevoir à travers leur programme scolaire. Le témoignage d'une animatrice suit:

> Parfois ça nous faisait mal de réaliser que beaucoup de jeunes filles vivaient de la violence. Tout comme les autres membres du groupe de travail, je trouve cela satisfaisant de donner espoir à ces jeunes en les aidant et en leur donnant accès à des ressources. Notre équipe de travail croit fermement que c'est raisonnable de penser que ces sessions de sensibilisation aident nos jeunes filles à réaliser qu'elles sont capables de s'en sortir et qu'elles n'ont pas à subir de violence provenant des faits et gestes d'une autre personne.
>
> Personnellement, ces ateliers sont enrichissants parce qu'ils permettent de travailler avec des jeunes qui ont un vécu similaire au mien. J'estime qu'il ne faut pas lâcher, il faut continuer de lutter et d'informer les gens afin que chaque personne ait la possibilité de

mettre fin à ce cycle de violence. J'aimerais, comme mère, être capable de respirer sans peur pour l'avenir de mes filles.

Modèles-à-imiter

La journée «Modèles-à-imiter» est une entreprise conjointe du Collectif, du Conseil des écoles séparées catholiques du district de Sudbury, et du Conseil de l'éducation de Sudbury (écoles publiques). Cette journée offre aux étudiantes de la région de Sudbury des modèles de femmes francophones qui ont une expérience dans différents types d'emploi. Elle permet aux femmes qui ont opté pour des professions ou des métiers plus ou moins traditionnels de parler de leur expérience, plus particulièrement de leurs qualifications, des avantages et désavantages du métier ou de la profession, de leurs compétences, aptitudes, et qualités particulières à mettre en jeu, ainsi que le chemin parcouru et les obstacles à franchir pour se tailler la place qu'elles occupent actuellement.

À chaque année depuis 1991, environ 200 étudiantes des écoles primaires et secondaires de la région de Sudbury ont participé à la journée «Modèles-à-imiter.»

Le programme «Modèles-à-imiter» fonctionne selon le principe d'apprentissage fondamental soit l'identification à une personne qui a réussi. Les jeunes filles écoutent les femmes parler de leur expertise. Ces présentations leur permettront de réfléchir sur ce qu'elles veulent devenir et sur la place qu'elles veulent occuper dans la société. Ce programme vise à encourager ces jeunes étudiantes à élargir leurs horizons quant à leurs choix de carrières. Ainsi, chaque fois qu'elles ont l'occasion de s'entretenir avec une femme occupant une profession ou un métier différent, une nouvelle porte s'ouvre ainsi qu'un nouvel éventail de possibilités sociales, économiques, et culturelles.

Selon les évaluations, les étudiantes trouvent cette journée très profitable. Étant donné que les jeunes filles ont encore tendance à se limiter dans leurs choix de carrières, les conseillères et conseillers en orientation ressentent le besoin de continuer une telle activité. Il est important que cette journée aide à mettre fin aux stéréotypes et permette de faire réaliser, non seulement aux jeunes filles mais aussi aux personnes pouvant les influencer, que les femmes d'aujourd'hui ont le droit et les capacités de choisir, tout autant que les hommes, un métier ou une carrière dans quelque domaine que ce soit. C'est pour ces raisons que nous demandons la participation des conseillères et conseillers en orientation et du personnel enseignant dans la préparation et le déroulement de cette journée.

En plus de faire réaliser aux étudiantes que les femmes peuvent aussi entreprendre efficacement des carrières non-traditionnelles, nous voulons souligner aux étudiantes l'importance du bilinguisme. Jusqu'à tout récemment, le français était la langue des pauvres et des «petits peuples.» Aujourd'hui, ce sont, pour une bonne part, les personnes bilingues qui grimpent les échelons et occupent les postes de direction. Il est donc important de faire comprendre aux jeunes Franco-Ontariennes qu'elles ont un atout que bien des professionnelles unilingues leur envient. Elles ne doivent surtout pas le perdre.

En résumé, la journée Modèles-à-imiter veut tout simplement démontrer aux jeunes filles qu'elles ont la possibilité d'avoir accès à un métier qui leur assure une vie décente et indépendante et qu'elles peuvent occuper la place qu'elles ont choisie à titre de membre à part entière de la société.

Colloque sur l'intervention féministe

Favoriser l'avancement des femmes de l'Ontario français par l'éducation ou par la mobilisation collective autour de projets, c'est ouvrir grandes les portes des savoirs théoriques et pratiques qui les concernent. Voilà pourquoi s'est déroulé le colloque sur l'intervention féministe dans le Nord-est de l'Ontario en février 1992. Cette rencontre de plus de 300 femmes provenant de tous les milieux démontre que le mouvement féministe en Ontario français, et plus particulièrement dans le Nord-est, est très actif, multidisciplinaire, et multidimensionnel. Le colloque a été une des nombreuses manifestations du besoin des femmes de discuter de leurs pratiques féministes, de s'organiser, de travailler individuellement et collectivement la transformation des conditions discriminantes envers les femmes et à l'amélioration de leur qualité de vie.

C'est à partir d'une large définition de l'intervention féministe que les organisatrices du colloque ont lancé les invitations aux chercheures et aux intervenantes de tous les milieux, à présenter leurs pratiques auprès des femmes. Par intervention féministe, on désigne tous les discours, toutes les approches et les pratiques qui questionnent et dénoncent les conditions discriminatoires envers les femmes et qui préconisent des modalités de transformation de ces conditions.

Nous avons tenté de poser un regard sur certaines des problématiques contemporaines qui touchent les femmes francophones du Nord-est, à partir de deux axes principaux et complémentaires sur lesquels se fondent les débats et les contributions récentes des féministes de l'Ontario français.[4] D'abord un pôle analytique et réflexif qui définit l'univers conceptuel et théorique autour duquel s'articule le discours féministe. Les femmes engagées dans ce travail ne sont pas nécessairement impliquées dans les actions menées sur le terrain par les divers organismes sociaux. Elles jouent plutôt un rôle d'informatrice auprès des groupes directement impliqués dans des mouvements de revendications. Le second pôle met l'emphase sur les perspectives d'actions intégrées, sous-tendues par ce cadre théorique.

Lors des discussions sur l'intervention féministe, les conférencières ont touché son histoire, ses définitions, les liens entre les théories et les pratiques féministes, et la complexité des interventions et des expériences. Les textes présentés lors des tables rondes et les ateliers offerts lors de cette rencontre de trois jours font état du savoir collectif des femmes du Nord.

Celui-ci regroupe quelques grands thèmes: l'intervention féministe, les images de femmes, les femmes et la santé, la place des femmes dans la société et les perspectives d'avenir de l'intervention féministe en Ontario français. Certaines, à partir de leurs recherches ou de leurs pratiques, ont parlé d'une démarche mettant l'accent sur la réalité, l'originalité d'une construction collective de l'intervention féministe en Ontario français. D'autres, à partir d'expériences personnelles, ont parlé du mouvement des femmes dans le Nord-est ontarien et de l'impact de la double minorité des Franco-Ontariennes, comme femmes et comme francophones dans leur vie quotidienne. À partir du terrain comme de la théorie, les femmes ont discuté de l'inceste, des agressions à caractère sexuel, du harcèlement, de la violence conjugale, de la pornographie, du suicide, de l'épuisement ou de la victimisation.

Finalement, le colloque s'est terminé sur les perspectives d'avenir de l'intervention féministe. Les éléments qui en émergent sont liés à des valeurs sociales fondamentales: vérité, complicité, entraide malgré les embûches et les obstacles qu'il reste aux femmes à surmonter afin d'atteindre l'égalité de droit comme de fait.

Certes, ces journées mémorables n'ont pas épuisé le sujet de l'intervention féministe, ni touché toutes les problématiques. Toutefois, elles ont été stimulantes à maints égards. D'une part, elles ont permis d'avoir un premier aperçu des pratiques féministes qui traversent le Nord-est de l'Ontario français. D'autre part, elles ont contribué au mandat du Collectif de favoriser l'avancement des femmes par l'éducation. Cet objectif important s'est réalisé par la publication du document Relevons le défi! Actes du colloque sur l'intervention féministe dans le Nord-est de l'Ontario.[5] Ce document est maintenant entre les mains de plusieurs femmes, d'hommes, d'organismes féminins et féministes, de services sociaux et communautaires, d'institutions collégiales et universitaires. Il constitue, dans tous ces milieux, un instrument de travail utile et stimulant afin de maintenir l'élan des changements amorcés lors du colloque.

Projet de recherche «harmonisation travail-famille»

Depuis la fin des années '80, une des préoccupations centrales de certains groupes de femmes en Ontario est l'étude de la conciliation travail/famille du point de vue des femmes. Cette préoccupation pose la question des conditions de vie des femmes, des familles dans une société en changement et de l'importance de la proportion de plus en plus grande de femmes sur le marché du travail. Le Collectif a choisi de se pencher sur cette question en analysant les façons dont les femmes qui occupent un emploi rémunéré concilient les contraintes imposées par le travail à l'extérieur du foyer et les multiples obligations familiales. Ce projet a pour but ultime de développer de nouveaux modèles d'harmonisation du travail avec la famille.

Le choix d'emploi des femmes est en général limité par de multiples facteurs dont la préparation académique, la socialisation, et la situation familiale. Holder et Anderson soutiennent que 80 pour cent des femmes travaillent dans des emplois traditionnellement féminins qui se situent presque toujours au bas de l'échelle salariale.[6] Des études ont démontré que la femme franco-ontarienne, à l'instar des autres femmes francophones du pays, est en général moins scolarisée que ses consoeurs anglophones.[7] Il est donc plausible de penser qu'elle est défavorisée au niveau des possibilités offertes par le marché du travail. L'emploi qu'elle choisira sera souvent celui traditionnellement réservé aux femmes soit les emplois de bureau et les emplois dits de service.

Cette recherche-action dans laquelle l'intervention se mêlait à l'étude empirique avait comme objectif la sensibilisation des participantes. Les outils de recherche choisis, le questionnaire et le «focus-group» ont permis aux participantes de réfléchir sur leur situation, d'identifier les carences ainsi que les changements nécessaires pour la satisfaction de leurs besoins et de ceux de la famille. Le point de départ de l'étude était d'abord l'expérience des femmes; elle nécessitait une attitude empathique de la part des chercheuses et de l'animatrice des «focus-groups»; elle visait la majorité des Franco-Ontariennes dans sa finalité et elle implique une hiérarchie horizontale entre les participantes et les chercheuses.[8]

La question de recherche était la suivante: Quelles sont les stratégies utilisées par les femmes francophones employées de soutien d'une institution d'enseignment postsecondaire du nord de l'Ontario pour concilier les exigences reliées au travail et aux responsabilités familiales?

Un questionnaire fut distribué à 149 femmes employées de soutien d'une institution d'enseignement postsecondaire du Nord-est de l'Ontario, 55 questionnaires ont été retenus, ce qui correspond à un taux de réponse de 37 pour cent. L'échantillon est composée de Franco-Ontariennes de 35 à 44 ans. Parmi ces femmes, 18 ont participé à une rencontre de l'un des quatre «focus-groups.»

Les résultats démontrent que les participantes détiennent encore en grande partie la responsabilité des tâches familiales. Le partage entre les hommes et les femmes s'effectue comme suit: la femme s'occupe des travaux ménagers à l'intérieur de la maison tandis que son partenaire vaque aux travaux extérieurs et à l'entretien de l'auto [voir aussi le chapître 12]. Ces résultats sont conformes aux autres études où les femmes accomplissent les tâches les plus routinières et répétitives, alors que les hommes conservent leurs spécialités saisonnières et occasionnelles, comme les poubelles, pelouse, pelletage, etc.[9] Les conjoints participent aux soins des enfants, mais leur contribution se situe surtout au niveau des soins psychologiques (42,8 pour cent), des activités (40.7 pour cent), et de l'éducation (39 pour cent).

Ces femmes passent en moyenne de 11 à 25 heures par semaine aux travaux ménagers et de 11 à 25 heures aux soins des enfants. Elles sont donc légèrement plus accaparées par les travaux domestiques que par le travail salarié (33,75 heures). En général, les femmes consacrent beaucoup plus de temps aux travaux ménagers et aux soins des enfants, qu'à la relation de couple et à leur vie personnelle, ces deux dernières occupant chacune moins de 10 heures par semaine. Pour rattraper le temps qui leur manque, elles effectuent les coupures dans leur temps personnel et leurs loisirs. Les principales contraintes au niveau familial et personnel sont le manque de temps et la culpabilité ressentie du fait de ne pas pouvoir être avec les enfants.

Au travail, l'inflexibilité des heures de travail et des horaires et le manque de compréhension de l'employeur sont les principales contraintes rencontrées. Ces répondantes réussissent à améliorer l'utilisation de leur temps en adoptant les stratégies suivantes: un horaire de travail, qui leur procure une sécurité financière et leur permet de planifier; ou encore, elles sacrifient leur pause pour partir du travail plus tôt de façon à pouvoir accomplir plus de tâches à la maison.

La garde des enfants constitue une préoccupation chez au moins la moitié de nos répondantes, puisque 42 pour cent d'entre elles ont des enfants âgés de moins de dix ans. Les stratégies utilisées par les femmes se situent davantage aux niveaux personnel et familial, milieu qu'elles contrôlent plus facilement, qu'aux niveaux social ou gouvernemental où elles ne voient pas leur pouvoir. Une des stratégies utilisées par les répondantes consiste à impliquer les enfants et le conjoint dans les responsabilités familiales. La famille élargie est également sollicitée pour apporter du soutien. Les femmes ont besoin de ces appuis. Elles ont dû apprendre à déléguer les tâches, à être tolérantes et à établir des priorités c'est-à-dire, à passer plus de temps avec les enfants et à consacrer moins de temps aux autres responsabilités.

Les résultats se comparent à l'étude de Corbeil et al. où les stratégies utilisées sont plutôt au niveau personnel que social parce que les femmes se sentent responsables de la vie familiale: implication du conjoint, réduction des travaux ménagers, accent sur la qualité plutôt que la quantité d'heures passées avec les enfants, recherche d'un travail offrant des conditions flexibles.[10] Nos résultats se comparent également à la recherche de Higgins et al. qui mentionne que les deux stratégies les plus utilisées par les femmes sont: établir des priorités et diviser les tâches familiales.[11]

Il sera donc intéressant de rencontrer les répondantes de notre étude afin de partager les résultats et les stratégies déjà utilisées et de pousser la réflexion plus loin afin d'amorcer des pistes d'intervention pour mettre en fonction des stratégies ou modèles que ces femmes aimeraient adopter pour harmoniser le travail et la famille. Des rencontres de sensibilisation sont planifiées afin de communiquer les résultats aux femmes et discuter de stratégies. Lors de ces rencontres, nous mettrons l'emphase sur les stratégies fonctionnelles adoptées par les femmes et nous pourrons également explorer les avenues non utilisées par nos répondantes mais qui pourraient faciliter l'harmonisation du travail et de la famille.

Conclusion

En prenant un recul, il est évident que ce travail de rédaction ne raconte pas toutes les activités du Collectif mais plutôt quelques-uns des projets qui ont atteint une certaine maturité. Comme organisme communautaire à but non lucratif, le Collectif à réussi à faciliter ou à accélérer des changements sociaux par des actions collectives de mobilisation communautaire dans des secteurs et dans une région bien précise. Car si le mandat de l'organisme est de promouvoir l'autonomie des femmes par l'éducation, cette tâche n'est pas simple si on travaille avec une population qui est minoritaire et dispersée sur un territoire relativement grand. Cela signifie qu'il faut avoir une bonne communication entre les membres et s'adapter à une membriété qui change selon les types de projets entrepris. Toutefois, même si les membres changent – certaines s'a-joutent et d'autres nous quittent – un noyau de personnes ressources demeurent disponibles pour assurer le suivi des dossiers et offrir du support à celles qui veulent démarrer ou développer de nouveaux projets. Il faut aussi reconnaître que les membres qui composent le Collectif sont beaucoup plus nombreuses que l'énumération des collaboratrices pour ce chapitre.[12]

L'organisme semble avoir un effet positif sur ses membres en fournissant un appui mutuel et en créant une atmosphère de solidarité. Les témoignages inclus dans ce texte supportent cette constatation. En effet, plusieurs de ces femmes, qu'elles soient membres ou participantes, ont eu peu d'occasions de travailler en français ou de se mobiliser pour améliorer leurs conditions de vie en tant que femmes francophones. Le Collectif a ainsi servi de catalyseur aux femmes pour revendiquer des services en français et pour développer d'autres services ou projets pour répondre à leurs besoins.

Les succès et le mode de fonctionnement de l'organisme n'étant pas menaçant, cela a eu pour effet d'apprivoiser des femmes non-familières avec cette approche et de les aider à sortir d'un rôle de dépendance. Les réalisations de ce groupe de femmes ont permis à l'organisme d'obtenir une reconnaissance pour le travail accompli et d'avoir un groupe d'appartenance francophone. Aujourd'hui, certains projets s'orientent définitivement vers des activités de «lobbying», par le biais de la concertation, afin de faire entendre le point de vue des femmes et de revendiquer des changements socio-politiques.

27

Women and Distance Education in Northeastern Ontario

Anne-Marie Mawhiney and Ross Paul

In this chapter we look at the participation and completion rates of women in northeastern Ontario who have taken courses from Laurentian University during the period 1970 to 1994. We review the opportunities, participation levels, and retention rates of women taking distance education courses, and the factors that promote high participation rates of women are explored.

Canada stands out as a world leader in women's participation in university distance education.[1] In other countries, participation of women in distance education is between 15 percent (in the Correspondence Institute of Tanzania) and 35 percent (in the University of South Pacific).[2] In contrast, at Alberta's Athabasca University, for example – an open university dedicated entirely to distance learning – two-thirds of the students are female.[3] Laurentian has an even higher rate: women pass 74 percent of its distance education courses; 67 percent of those students who earn a complete degree through distance education are women.

It seems Canadian, and northeastern Ontario women, have taken advantage of the opportunities posed by distance education to pursue university studies. It is commonly accepted that distance education, with its provision of opportunities for home study, caters to the needs of many women. For example, in her interviews with female distance learners, May found them to place the highest value on being able to study from their homes, where it was more convenient to their personal schedules.[4] It is interesting to note the relatively high participation of Aboriginal women in university distance education in Canada. Our experiences of working with some of these women suggest that they have looked to education as the springboard for adapting their cultures to the modern world and for regaining control over their own destinies. Spronk and Radtke found Canadian Aboriginal women to be directed towards "self determination and tribal sovereignty over land."[5] While acknowledging that family and communal responsibilities create problems, these women have also been able to recognize that they provide support groups for facing such common problems as poverty, violence, and inadequate transport and childcare.

Distance Education at Laurentian University

Three of the main historical barriers to participation in postsecondary education for people in northeastern Ontario have been geography, culture, and class. Northeastern Ontario consists primarily of single-resource communities scattered throughout the eastern part of the Canadian Shield. Four larger communities – Sudbury, Timmins, North Bay, and Sault Ste. Marie – are surrounded by many small, rural, and relatively isolated communities. Prior to the establishment of Laurentian University in 1960, it was impossible to obtain postsecondary education on a full- or part-time basis without travelling to the southern part of the province.

Participation in postsecondary education by those living in northeastern Ontario shows a significant under-representation, historically, by francophones and Aboriginal people. Traditional barriers to entry into universities have included structural racism, lack of role models, and lack of programs and courses that are culturally relevant or in the appropriate language, as well as class barriers.

Historically, northeastern Ontario has been populated by working-class people who are not oriented to formal education because it has seemed irrelevant to their own circumstances and work-related realities. Those working in stores and offices, in mines, lumbering, and pulp and paper mills have not needed any formal education beyond basic literacy to do their work. As well, many of these workers had poor experiences in elementary and secondary schools and lacked the confidence and interest to pursue postsecondary education. It was usual for young men to quit school at the legal age and to start to work in the local company. Likewise, working-class women were actively discouraged from becoming "too" educated, not only by their husbands but by their parents as well. Those families for whom postsecondary education was important have had a tradition of "going away" to university. Until recently, many of those who have chosen to study at Laurentian have been the first generation to attend university.

In the late 1950s, part-time ("extension") students living close to Sudbury travelled to Sudbury for evening classes offered by the University of Sudbury, Thorneloe University, and Huntington University. However, those for whom such a commute was difficult found it impossible to obtain a university degree on a part-time basis, unless they were able to attend summer sessions in Southern Ontario. Prior to the establishment of Laurentian University (and the federation with these three existing universities), students studied at the three universities on letters of permission from southern universities like the University of Western Ontario and the University of Toronto. Courses were held in the early evenings so that "regular" and "extension" students would take classes together. The vast majority of extension students were teachers, and most were women.[6]

Off-campus programs at Laurentian University started in the mid-1960s. Until the mid-1980s, these courses were primarily offered either by television or in person, in various communities throughout northeastern Ontario. The university's outreach to students in communities outside the Sudbury area was impressive, especially in the early "pioneering" days of adult learning. Student counselling, admission, and registration of off-campus students was done in these communities prior to each session by a team that included administrators and staff from the Centre for Continuing Education, Treasury, and Admissions. Because of the large geographical territory that was involved, these itinerant registration teams often drove from one community to the next for as long as two weeks, twice annually. Professors, who were most often university-based, would drive or, when possible and distance required it, fly (or, in one famous instance, go by snow machine) to the learning centre every second weekend and hold six hours of classes over Friday evening and Saturday morning. Students, who were all studying on a part-time basis, would take from seven to twenty years to complete an undergraduate degree in arts, science, or social work.

Studying on a part-time, off-campus basis required highly motivated, independent learners. From about 1970 to 1984, the majority of such students were elementary and secondary school teachers upgrading their credentials.[7] During this period, a total of 10,745 off-campus courses were taken, 7,715 (71.8 percent) of them by women. Of these women, 24 percent took courses in French and 76 percent in English. Of all students taking courses in French, 79.5 percent were women; of all students taking courses in English, 69.7 percent were women.

From 1975 until 1981, in addition to the courses offered towards a BA, the School of Social Work offered its Bachelor of Social Work (BSW) program, in English only, to off-campus students in Timmins, Kirkland Lake, Sault Ste. Marie, Bracebridge, and Parry Sound. In the period from 1982 until 1987, a second round of the BSW program was offered in Timmins, Pembroke, Hearst, and Kapuskasing. In the latter two centres, courses were offered in French. A total of 100 graduates finished this program between 1975 and 1987; of these, approximately 85 percent were women.

In 1985, Laurentian's Centre for Continuing Education started to concentrate its resources on the development of distance education courses, using primarily print format. Courses were written by a course team comprising an instructor or instructor team, a designer, two reviewers, and an editor. In all cases, the course designer was female, as were most of the editors; this may be significant for our later discussion. In 1987, with the establishment of Contact North/Contact Nord, the development of teleconference and mixed-media courses started.[8] At present, Laurentian University offers 21 teleconference courses, 14 in English and 7 in French.

In 1987, the School of Nursing initiated its post-RN (registered nurse) program as a teleconference and on-site program, and the Native Human Services Program started to develop its BSW (Native Human Services) using a primarily print-based format. Programs leading to a Bachelor of Arts have also been developed using print or multi-media formats. In total, six BA concentrations in the English language and four in the French language are offered: in Law and Justice, Psychology, Religious Studies, Native Studies, Sociology, Women's Studies; psychologie, sciences religeuses, folklore, administration des affaires. For the 110 courses offered in these concentrations, 37 (30.8 percent) had a woman and 83 (69.2 percent) had a man as the senior author.[9] For French-language concentration courses, 21.2 percent had a woman and 78.8 percent had a man as the senior author; for English-language concentration courses, 38.2 had a woman and 61.8 percent a man as the senior author. As of 1995, there are a total of 235 courses available to off-campus students, including those that offer a complete degree concentration and those that are offered as electives. In print format there are 119 in English, including 21 targeting Aboriginal students, and 116 in French.

Many of the women studying at Laurentian throughout the period from 1970 until the late 1980s may have been motivated by financial and career considerations. For instance, in the late 1960s, the Ministry of Education started to require an undergraduate degree as a prerequisite for a teaching certificate. Those already teaching were given a set time period during which they were expected to obtain a degree; there were also significant incentives for upgrading existing degrees. Social workers without formal credentials were motivated to obtain a social work degree in the late 1970s and early 1980s for the purposes of promotion and mobility. By 1982, the Ontario Association of Professional Social Workers had established the College of Certified Social Workers, a voluntary college that required a degree from an accredited school of social work. Likewise, a change in education requirements by the Ontario Nursing Association in the late 1980s led to the development of the post-RN program at Laurentian. Perhaps these provincial changes in the standards of professional organizations are connected to the large number of women who have taken off-campus courses from Laurentian University and help explain why completion rates seem relatively high in comparison with those in the literature.

Participation and Completion Rates of Women at Laurentian University

We examined off-campus student records by gender and language for the period from 1970 until 1994.[10] In total, 24,593 off-campus students from northeastern Ontario registered in 24,593 distance education courses for this period. Of these, 20,897 courses (85 percent) were completed successfully.[11] As shown in Table 1, three times as many women as men took distance education courses in the 25-year period. Four-fifths of both female and male students who registered in a course, not only completed but passed the course; the rate of women who passed was slightly higher than the rate for men.

Table 1. Total Registrations and Passed Courses 1970-1994
Off Campus, Excluding Sudbury

SEX AND LANGUAGE	REGISTRATIONS		PASSED		PERCENT PASSED	
Female	18,162		15,701		86.5	
English		13,335		11,304		84.8
French		4,827		4,397		91.1
Male	6,366		5,148		80.9	
English		5,124		4,069		79.4
French		1,242		1,079		86.9
Total	24,528*		20,849		85.0	
English		18,459		15,373		83.3
French		6,069		5,476		90.2

* Excludes those of unknown sex from the total of 24,593 registrations.

In the 25 years, 5,761 students graduated using off-campus distance education courses. Table 2 presents a breakdown of those who earned their degree in this manner. Although women made up nearly three-quarters of those registered off campus, the female-to-male ratio narrowed by graduation. Of the distance education graduates, 66.8 percent are women, suggesting again the importance of distance education to women in Northern Ontario.

Table 2. Number of Off-Campus Graduates, 1970-1994 Including Sudbury

SEX AND LANGUAGE	NUMBER WHO GRADUATED	
Female	3,843	
English		2,314
French		1,529
Male	1,918	
English		1,399
French		519
Total Female and Male	5,761	

Looking at the language of students in Tables 1 and 2, we see another pattern. One-third of the population of the university catchment area is French, and 32.8 percent of those registered in off-campus courses were French. The percentage passing was definitely higher among the French than the English, in both female and male students. As for the graduates, 35.6 percent of them were French.

One of the surprising findings of this study is the extent to which women are retained in off-campus courses. It is especially remarkable that 91.1 percent of francophone women – doubly marginalized by gender and language – completed courses successfully for the period from 1970 until 1994.

Unfortunately there is no information in the database on students of Aboriginal descent, even though the catchment area has significant numbers and Laurentian University has made a commitment to serve this group. This omission is now being corrected, and some Aboriginal faculty members are interested in examining the factors that affect completion rates of Aboriginal students, especially in Native Studies and Native Human Services programs.

Recommendations for Further Study

Drop-out rates in distance education are usually very high, and the authors know of no other studies that have produced the completion rates we have found: 84.8 percent for English women and 91.1 percent for French women. The findings are surprising when one considers that Laurentian University has paid less attention to course design and student support than many institutions elsewhere in the world or other programs in Canada. Not more than one-quarter of the courses have been written by women at Laurentian. Further study is needed to determine reasons for the much higher completion rates in northeastern Ontario and to understand better the factors that have produced such significant differences in completion rates. These can be divided into factors affecting the nature of the student body, and factors related to programming.

The nature of the student body in the courses surveyed. It is possible that factors such as social class, race, and student maturity help explain the high completion rates. For example, it would be important to examine the extent to which working-class, Aboriginal, and younger people participate in distance education and to compare completion rates with the aggregate one presented here. Laurentian University's high completion rates by women can be accounted for at least in part by the significant numbers of professional women – nurses, social workers, and teachers – who are highly motivated to take distance education courses for career reasons. The extent to which Laurentian's distance education students are first-generation postsecondary students needs further analysis, especially in light of Robb and Spencer's finding that the education experience of the student's parents is an important factor in participation rates in distance learning.[12] Given Laurentian's history of educating first-generation students, we would expect to find results that conflict with Robb and Spencer; however, this warrants more attention. It is difficult to determine to what extent class barriers are present. Do course fees, geography, the types of courses that are offered, and the content of these courses constitute barriers for working-class women? Further study is needed to determine the extent to which class barriers remain in our current system at Laurentian.

Motivational factors and personal qualities particular to this group of students. Social workers, nurses, and teachers have been required and encouraged to take courses for promotion or financial reward. Distance education provides the most flexible conditions under which to take university-level courses. Some anecdotal information suggests that mature students are more highly motivated to complete distance education courses than are full-time, young students on-campus who take distance education courses. Completion rates for the on-campus, younger students need to be examined in order to determine the extent to which this might be true. Qualitative interviews of both student populations would allow researchers to understand other qualities and factors – for instance, sheer determination in spite of barriers – that are involved in the completion of these courses.

Factors related to the way courses are delivered at Laurentian University. Some studies have shown a strong correlation between "pacing" and course completion. Pacing refers to an approach where a student finishes a course according to timelines set by the institution rather than at "her own pace" (self-pacing). Laurentian University's distance education courses are all paced, whereas Athabasca uses a self-paced approach. If no other significant variables can be identified, this study may present evidence of the impact of pacing on course completion in distance education. Although Laurentian University has lacked resources to provide extensive student support, individuals within the Centre for Continuing Education and some faculty members work closely and regularly with students. Perhaps there are elements in this part of course delivery that would help explain completion rates.

Mixed-gender course development teams. The vast majority (over 95 percent) of print-formatted courses have had women designers and women editors, and therefore courses may be more sensitive to gender than would be the case for courses developed by all-male teams. Further study is needed to compare completion rates by women for courses by mixed or all-women development teams with their completion rates for courses by all-male development teams.

Courses offered are traditionally taken by women. Another explanation for our high completion rate could be the fact that the degree programs that are offered to off-campus students are mainly those that have been traditionally of interest to women students. There is perhaps a selection process that occurs prior to registration. If programs in more traditionally male-dominated disciplines were developed, perhaps more men would participate and complete courses successfully. We would need to study those potential students who never did register for courses as well as those students who withdrew from courses, in order to determine the extent to which different course subjects, more woman-centred courses, and courses of more interest to non-professional women would increase enrolments with different target groups than we have reached to date. We would also need to survey those women who have completed courses successfully, to determine the extent to which we could retain and attract more women students by improving opportunities for peer contact and by making women more visible in course content.

Concluding Comments

This chapter suggests that Laurentian University's distance education courses have high participation and graduation rates of women – seemingly higher than those in other places – especially for minority francophone women. Factors promoting participation are reviewed.

Closer scrutiny reveals some irony in this largely positive development, however, in that distance education is viewed as having both advantages for women – by providing a convenient and flexible mode of study – as well as disadvantages – by confining them to this limited form of education, one that is often considered "second-class" and susceptible to traditional one-way methods of learning.[13] The undoubted impact of distance education in providing study opportunities for women must be tempered somewhat by an appreciation of its limitations. Faith has drawn attention to this paradox, saying that while "distance education ... on the one hand ... encourages individual development and choice, on the other hand it colludes with traditional gender roles and expectations by facilitating women's confinement to the home."[14]

Given this concern, while Laurentian University can be proud of the very high retention rates experienced by its women students, it must continue to ensure – through course design, student support services, and innovative delivery systems – enhanced degrees of interactivity among students studying at a distance. Sensitivity to the limitations that much of distance education may have for women studying at home is the first step in helping them to overcome these.

28

Women in Science at a Northern Ontario University: A 35-Year Perspective

Douglas Goldsack, Cindy Ives-Bigeau, and Roy Kari[1]

Over the past decade, concerns have been raised about the participation of women in science and related technical programs in postsecondary institutions. It is important to understand why women are not as involved in these areas as they are in others. Recent studies have looked at how to retain women in science programs and how to minimize the drop-out rate.

The report of the National Advisory Board on Science and Technology points out, among other things, that an efficient labour force will be realized only as both women and men are encouraged to pursue careers that maximize their abilities.The report states that "every sector of the population must be carefully utilized and valued for the diversity it contributes. Innovation thrives in a climate which nurtures diversity."[2] Change will come, the report argues, only as both the education and employment systems challenge existing structures and policies that act as barriers to women within science and technology. A gender-sensitive approach must involve women in the process of change, and the goals set must reflect realistic time frames to allow progress to be monitored.

Gilbert and Pomfret followed 2,000 University of Guelph students between 1986 and 1988.[3] Their study was undertaken because 46 percent of women withdrew from the Canada Scholars Program after only one year in university. This program was established in 1988 to enhance Canada's international competitiveness by producing more scientific and technologically literate individuals. Their purpose was to look at student departure rates with respect to transfers to other programs, forced withdrawals, stopouts, and system leaves. A number of interesting issues emerged from the study. It was discovered that women entered science on the encouragement of teachers and because they had attained good grades in the subject in high school. Many entered science hoping to continue to get those high marks while at university and assumed that those grades could be used as a stepping-stone to another field of study. Thus, the study suggests that for women, more so than for men, science was a means to an end. Women's career goals appear to be "more practical, applied and more oriented to helping, curing and healing"[4] such as in nursing. The report states that women may be leaving science "partly in response to pressures created by a 'poor fit' between their value orientations and expectations, and the practices, realities and values of the educational environment." The report concludes that if women had more support in their first year of a university science program by being better informed as to what they could expect from the social climate they were entering, the dropout rate would be considerably reduced.

Highlights of a research project by O'Driscoll and Anderson in the United Kingdom provide some clues as to why women neglect careers in science.[5] For example, women perceive the length of the work day to be excessive, dislike the isolation demanded of scientific research, and have problems with the notion of working on projects that are defence-funded or that involve animal experimentation. Women, it appears, prefer to work on projects that have a practical application.

Tobias, in *They're Not Dumb, They're Different – Stalking the Second Tier,* suggests a number of themes that relate to female students' decisions to drop out of science programs: the competitive culture, the desire for a "well-rounded liberal education," and the anticipated conflicts they perceive will emerge between family and a career in science.[6] A recent article by Pat Shipman, a senior scientist, in American Scientist, reflects on the effects of negative reactions to her career in science by male colleagues and indicates clearly the need for changes in attitudes that are necessary before women will feel comfortable in the science field.[7]

Participation of Female Students in Science Programs at Laurentian University

Laurentian University in Sudbury, founded in 1960 to serve northeastern Ontario, is a small bilingual university with 5,100 full-time and 2,300 part-time undergraduate students, as well as 160 full-time and 180 part-time graduate students. Programs are offered in arts, science, and professional schools.

By 1994, nearly one-half of the students enrolled in biochemistry, biology, environmental earth science, kinesiology, and neuroscience programs were female. Female students constituted 22 percent of the students in chemistry, 36.3 percent in mathematics, and 27 percent in geology. The lowest rates were in computer science and physics, with 16.2 percent and 22.9 percent respectively in 1994.

Trends over time are presented in Table 1, with data available for the winter academic sessions from 1985 to 1994. There are only two clear trends: in computer science the rate of participation by females was 23.6 in 1987, fell drastically the following years to a low of 3.0 percent in 1991, and climbed slowly back to 16.2 percent in 1994. In geology, there was a steady increase of female students, from a low of 13 percent in 1985 to a high of 39.9 percent by

1992 and falling a bit thereafter. In the other science programs, rates went up in some years and slipped in others.

Table 1. Percentage of Students Who Were Female in Laurentian University Science Programs (1985–94 winter sessions)

Session	BICM %	BIOL %	CHMI %	COSC %	ENES %	GEOL %	KINS %	MATH %	NSCI %	PHYS %	Other %
85W	43.9	51.2	40.0	13.4		13.0		27.0	50.0	8.4	41.7
86W	45.1	47.2	34.4	17.5		16.0		34.2	65.5	12.2	60.7
87W	51.9	47.3	35.8	23.6		21.6		26.6	61.2	12.3	49.7
88W	50.2	52.2	30.5	21.5		33.0	50.0	17.7	80.4	1.1	50.8
89W	45.0	59.8	33.0	8.5		28.8	53.6	18.5	86.6	19.8	43.2
90W	49.1	59.3	27.8	7.8	69.8	28.4	60.0	24.5	69.5	26.0	31.7
91W	46.0	51.0	33.6	3.0	55.4	27.8	42.2	32.0	75.0	13.0	39.6
92W	60.9	53.1	29.0	4.5	44.3	39.9	50.0	36.8	48.4	12.2	68.6
93W	57.4	56.3	40.5	5.9	44.2	35.9	49.7	41.7	61.7	17.2	54.4
94W	61.5	50.2	22.2	16.2	43.3	27.0	43.9	36.3	54.0	22.9	44.8
Ave	51.1	52.8	32.7	12.2	51.4	27.1	49.9	29.5	65.2	14.5	48.5
Median	50.2	52.2	33.0	12.2	47.9	27.8	49.9	29.5	65.2	13.0	48.5

BICM biochemistry	ENES environmental earth science	NSCI neuroscience
BIOL biology	GEOL geology	PHYS physics
CHMI chemistry	KINS kinesiology	Other 3-year general and liberal
COSC computer science	Math mathematics	science programs

Looking at just the female students enrolled in science programs for the decade of 1985–94, it appears that biology was the preferred choice for one-third of the students. This preference was steady over time with 36.9 percent enrolled in biology in 1985, 36.7 percent in 1990, and dipping to 24.4 percent in 1994. Over one-half of the women enrolled over the decade in Laurentian's science programs selected either biology or health-related programs such as biochemistry, environmental earth science, neuroscience, and kinesiology. Fewer than 20 percent selected either chemistry, geology, mathematics, or physics. These trends fit the pattern observed generally at other universities in Canada and complement the conclusion of Gilbert and Pomfret concerning the present pattern of female science students being involved in programs perceived to be more caring and practically oriented.[8]

Do female students in the sciences graduate? We do not have information on those who began in science but either dropped out or transferred out before completion. There are data, however, on numbers of graduates. In 1963, 12 students graduated from Laurentian University science programs; of these, only two were women. Both the number of science graduates and the proportion who were women increased over the next three decades. Throughout the 1970s and 1980s, the number of science graduates climbed steadily, up to 108 in 1995; of these, 52 were women. The proportion of graduates who were women started at 17 percent in 1963, climbing to 46 percent by 1995.

Survey of Graduates

In 1995 the Alumni Office had addresses for 440 of the 573 female science graduates over Laurentian's 35-year existence and sent out a short question-naire asking for information on jobs, further education, aspirations, and satis-faction with their Laurentian education. Of particular interest to this chapter are factors such as mentoring that have helped or hindered the careers of these women. Of the questionnaires sent out, 185 were completed and returned. Caution must be exercised in interpreting the following results, as 68 percent of the original 573 graduates could not be contacted or did not return their questionnaires.

Of those who responded, the majority had work, with 55 percent working in science-related jobs as summarized in Table 2.

Table 2. Distribution of Female Science Graduates by Type of Job

JOB TYPE	NUMBER OF GRADUATES	PERCENT
Science-related	102	55.2
Teaching	40	21.6
Non-Science*	43	23.2
Total	185	100.0

*includes unemployed and retired

Ninety-seven graduates went on to complete further degrees: 33 finished Bachelors in Education; 46 completed Master's degrees, mostly in science; and 18 have been awarded doctorates. Those in science and teaching careers were far more likely to earn additional degrees than women who reported working in non-science jobs or were retired or unemployed. As Table 3 indi-cates, those women graduates of science who were in science-related careers, including teaching high school, perceive their education as more relevant than those in non-science careers. However, the perception of the Laurentian University education experience is still positive even when the graduate is not in a job or career directly related to science.

A large number of women responded to the question about career impedi-ments, suggesting that there are strong feelings among women regarding prob-lems they face as scientists or in their science-related careers. Some of the bar-riers women identified were as follows: "glass ceiling," "family commit-ments," "being female in the early 70s," "spousal employment," "intimidating unsupportive thesis advisor," "lack of relevant work experience," "getting married and being female," "limited rapport with professors at the graduate level, I believe I could benefit from more female role models," "two children and mobile husband," "three small children!" "marriage, motherhood, gender issues," and "macho culture in business in having to outperform to get acceptance." This suggests that besides the problems of family commitments – which are common to the vast majority of working women – there are other issues such as the male environment of university graduate-level science departments and gender discrimination in the workplace that must be addressed if women are going to make real progress in science careers.

Table 3. Perceived Relevance of Laurentian University Education to Job and Job Satisfaction

CAREER TYPE		WELL PLEASED %	NEUTRAL %	NOT PLEASED %
Science	Relevance of LU education to job	69	19	12
	Satisfaction in job	72	13	15
	Satisfaction with LU education	81	15	4
Teacher	Relevance of LU education to job	69	17	14
	Satisfaction in job	86	7	7
	Satisfaction with LU education	83	17	0
Non-science	Relevance of LU education to job	35	12	53
	Satisfaction in job	50	19	31
	Satisfaction with LU education	69	23	8

The results of the survey also indicate that the mentoring process – implying help in career counselling or encouragement in continuing in a particular career – makes a difference for women graduates who wish to pursue a career in either pure or applied science, but it does not matter whether the mentor is male or female. Slightly more than half of the respondents working in science-related careers had been mentored while a student in a science program; 61 percent of those with mentors reported the person was not from the university. Only one-third of the women in teaching or non-science-related jobs spoke of mentors. These data would suggest that an improvement in the mentoring system at the undergraduate level of a science program might be a useful steering mechanism to increase female entry into pure and applied science careers.

Concluding Comments

The fact that the total number of female students and graduates in science programs at Laurentian University has increased to nearly 50 percent of the student population bodes well for the future. The increase, however, is mostly in biology and health-related science programs. The participation and graduation rates of women in mathematics, chemistry, physics, and computer sciences remain far below that of males. Anecdotal evidence suggests that once women made up half of the graduates in disciplines such as law and medicine, it took only one generation for them to be accepted as an integral part of those professions. It is expected that the same pattern will follow for women in science careers in the twenty-first century.

The survey of 185 female Laurentian science graduates (of the 573 women who graduated from science programs between 1963 and 1994) indicates three-quarters of the respondents worked in science-related jobs including teaching. Over one-half went on to complete additional degrees. Those women who worked in science-related careers and teaching felt that their educational experience was relevant to their work, and they were very satisfied with their education and careers. It is not known to what degree these positive results would be changed by the many graduates who could not be reached or did not complete the survey. Many of those who did respond, however, reported that they continued to face impediments on the job that arose either from the male culture of the workplace or from the problems they faced in juggling a career and a family.

The study results also suggest that mentoring female science students while they are in university and when they begin their careers will have a positive impact on women's entry into jobs in pure and applied science. In their book, *Women, Mentors and Success,* Jeruchim and Shapiro indicate that successful career-oriented women should not feel alone.[9] It is not clear yet who is best suited to serve as mentors, or what the process looks like.

The future is optimistic, given the growing numbers of women in science-based programs at small universities like Laurentian and in other centres of higher learning.[10] A more supportive culture, and the use of mentoring, may well help to attract and keep women in the sciences and increase their numbers in mathematics, physics, chemistry, and computer sciences.

29

Young Women and Feminism in Northern Ontario[1]

Susan Vanstone

Young women – those under age 30 – constitute a significant source of activism and efforts for change in Northern Ontario. I interviewed 15 women between the ages of 17 and 28 from Sudbury, Val Thérèse, Markstay, Thunder Bay, Kenora, and Chapleau about their views of feminism and their involvements in political, social, and feminist causes and organizations. As young women, all born during the resurgence of feminism in the 1960s and 1970s, they represent new voices in the contemporary women's movement and thus are part of the future of feminism. Their backgrounds as activists are both impressive and varied: some have been involved with feminist organizations (women's centres, sexual assault crisis centres and phone lines, lobby groups); others with student associations, unions, political campaigns, task forces, community coalitions; and some have contributed to a combination or all of these efforts.

This chapter cannot be considered a definitive statement about young women and their experiences in Northern Ontario. Indeed, there can be no such statement, as young women have varying opinions and experiences, shaped considerably by race, ethnicity, sexuality, location, class, and ability, as well as their individual life situations. Furthermore, it is vital to note the limitations of this research; all the women whose thoughts are reflected in this chapter are white, most are university-educated (or plan to be), heterosexual-identified, non-disabled, anglophone, and middle-class. Thus, this chapter does not comprehensively address racism, ableism, classism, cultural and linguistic barriers, homophobia, and other oppressions experienced by young women.

Young Women's Views of Feminism

A considerable amount of literature suggests that young women are less likely to identify with feminism and are less concerned about issues of equality than are older women.[2] However, a comparison of studies does not confirm this claim.

A 1989 Time magazine-Cable News Network (CNN) survey of 1,000 American women of all ages showed that 33 percent considered themselves to be feminists;[3] a couple of years later, the same pollsters found 29 percent to be feminist-identified.[4] A separate survey in 1993 of 600 U.S. women put this percentage at 41.[5] The few surveys that consider exclusively young women's views of feminism do not suggest drastic differences in their attitudes when compared with these more general polls. In a study of 398 female university undergraduates conducted in the U.S. in the late 1980s, 27 percent identified themselves as feminists, and about two-thirds refuted stereotypical views of feminists (disagreeing with, for example, the notions that they are "unhappy misfits" and are "trying to turn women into men").[6] The survey also identified a growth in support for feminist ideas as students advancing through their university years experienced a "liberalization of attitudes" and personal encounters with sex discrimination. The only available Canadian data was a 1989 survey of over 1,600 female high school students in Nova Scotia.[7] Here, the question of identification was not directly addressed, but 49 percent of respondents held positive views of feminism.While it is problematic to draw definitive conclusions from separate studies, these statistics do not suggest that young women are dramatically more complacent and resistant of feminism, as claimed by some older writers.

Young women interviewed for this paper expressed varying views about the nature of feminism and their personal identification with the term.[8] For example, one young woman stated the following:

> For me, feminism is a way of living. I try to support women and women's issues whenever I can. Feminism is not just the [Beijing] conference of women studying women's issues. It's also about the woman who has no clue that that conference is going on and lives in a subsidized house and has been knocked around by this system all the time.

For some young women, the demand for a simple response of "yes" or "no" to the question "Are you a feminist?" frames thought too narrowly, and does not allow for more complex responses. According to one woman, "I'd say yes, I agree with everything feminism stands for and upholds. But I say no to the label because I've always made a point never to pigeonhole, stereotype, or label myself in any way, shape, or form in terms of any kind of political activity." Nor do simple questions allow for the fact that the nature of feminism, as an abstract, lived experience, might defy definition:

> There are so many different interpretations, as many as there are women. Feminism can be as simple as two women getting together for lunch or to go shopping. There is a female bond and sense of autonomy in that. But I think true feminism means not only talking the talk but, most importantly, walking the walk: practising what you preach about equality, oppression, surviving, and supporting women who experience difficulty.

Young Women as a Source of Change

Young women have been an important force throughout contemporary North American feminism. A number of the early "liberationist" groups that emerged in the late 1960s were formed by students who experienced sexism from men in leftist movements. As well, community-based women's liberation groups drew considerable support and membership from students and other young women.[9] By the mid-1970s, female students successfully established numerous campus women's centres in Canada.

In Sudbury in the 1970s, many young women were involved with grass-roots groups like Women's Liberation Movement and Women Helping Women. The latter was closely associated with the establishment of the Sudbury Women's Centre, which opened in January 1981 [see Chapter 24]. In 1978 and 1979, wives of striking Inco workers in Sudbury, both young and old, formed Wives Supporting the Strike (WSS), a volunteer organization which undertook a number of charitable activities to help the thousands of people affected by the United Steelworkers of America Local 6500's job action. The women of WSS raised money, collected donations of clothing, food, and other necessities, organized recreational events, ran a crisis hotline, published a newsletter, and marched at rallies to champion the union. All of these endeavours contributed to the workers' success in negotiations that ended the strike. WSS's support work taught the labour movement about the power of alliances and that women, as partners and domestic co-workers with strikers, are important contributors to union efforts. Many of the young women involved with WSS were irreversibly politicized by this experience, and once the strike ended, could not accept returning exclusively to their household roles after working as activists in the public domain.[10]

Canadian culture, politics, and public discussion continue to be significantly affected by young women. Vancouver writer Evelyn Lau came to national attention in 1989, at age 18, with the publication of her autobiographical *Runaway: Diary of a Streetkid*.[11] She has since written numerous additional works and received a Governor-General's Award for *Oedipal Dreams*.[12] Hélène Jutras, a 20-year-old law student, has established a presence in the politics of Quebec separatism. Her book, *Le Québec me tue,* provides a critical analysis of indépendantistes and provincial education, as well as an argument that separatist discourse is controlled by an older "elite."[13] Goalie Manon Rhéaume became the first female to play professional hockey in 1992. Ever-present opposition to the *Toronto Sun's* "Sunshine Girl" page continues thanks to the Bitch Brigade, a self-described "subversive" group of high school feminists who set fire to or deface the Sun's newspaper boxes with messages like "The Sunshine Girl has a gun."[14] Women from the Ontario Federation of Students (now Canadian Federation of Students – Ontario) developed an anti-date rape campaign that gained international recognition and helped promote the fact that "No means no." Shelley Martel became a member of provincial parliament for Sudbury East at age 24 and a cabinet minister at 27. Tammy Gulati and Nancy MacLean, two Toronto-area women in their early twenties, unionized retail clothing outlets for the first time in Canadian labour history in 1991, and 17-year-old Sarah Inglis attempted to organize workers at an Orangeville McDonald's restaurant in 1993. These three young women turned the attention of the union movement at last to the youth-dominated "McJobs" segment of the low-wage service sector.[15] And Gwen Jacob, a student at the University of Guelph, expelled a "whole mindset, that whole patriarchal definition of body" when she removed her T-shirt in public and walked topless on a humid summer day in 1991.[16] Her charge and conviction of committing an "indecent" act spurred women to organize a number of shirtless rallies in support of both Jacob and the "choice to take our shirts off when we feel like it."[17]

Clearly, young women are capable of creating change and influencing political and public agendas in efforts aimed at individual achievement and wide-scale social reform. One young woman stressed the strengths of a youthful outlook and her frustration with the slow pace at which change often takes place:

> I'm not sure that society realizes the uniqueness of the perspectives of young people. We haven't yet had the opportunity to be co-opted into the institutional or status-quo mindset.... People have often said to me that I'm naive and idealistic. But it never ceases to amaze me how willing people – especially those older than me – are to accept the way things are, even if these things are so obviously wrong.

Young Women's Efforts for Change in Northern Ontario

While many young women in the north participate in organizations with feminists of all ages, some are also involved with youth-oriented activist projects. This section of the chapter will outline three endeavours by young women aimed at determining and addressing their own needs.

Womyn Rhythms Conference, Kenora. In 1993, members of the feminist community in Kenora became concerned that issues affecting young women were not being adequately addressed in the north, particularly in rural areas, and decided that a conference was necessary. The intent was to attract young women between the ages of 14 and 21 and to "empower them and provide them with more options, information, and emotional tools that will allow them to make more informed, healthy decisions regarding their present and future."[18] Forty-five young women from a number of centres in the northwest attended Womyn Rhythms, which took place on the May long weekend in 1994. The organizing committee of six young women planned the conference, which included sessions on sexuality, dating violence, mask making, the history of the women's movement, prostitution/women in the sex trades, visualization and meditation, sexual harassment, dating violence, and "what do you have to do to be a woman?" Those who attended Womyn Rhythms identified the experience as positive: "It was an introduction to feminism for young women in Kenora … which is hard to do because people are so nervous about the whole feminism thing." Another participant concluded in a written personal recollection: "Even though we are all leading different lives, I find it most important to remember that we have a common bond in the fact that we are young women. We should now use that bond to continue supporting each other."[19]

Women's Place, Kenora

Participants of the Womyn Rhythms Conference, Kenora, May 1994. Standing, left to right: Irshad Manji, Tammy McMahon, Natacha Boulton, Teika Olson, Erika Olson, Kike Roach, Bernice Korzenoski, Sandy Loucks, Meghan Blackburn. Kneeling: Allyson Donnelly.

It is clear that something as seemingly simple as a conference can be an immensely empowering experience for young women. Indeed, it is rare that youth are allowed to discuss issues affecting them in a relatively free manner, uncontrolled by authority figures such as parents or educators.

Campus centres for women: Lakehead and Laurentian universities. Another approach taken by young women has been to organize student-oriented groups or services for women at colleges and universities. Although efforts to establish campus women's centres in Canada first started in 1919 at the University of Toronto, they have been in existence only since the mid-1970s.[20] As more females undertook postsecondary education and the presence of feminism permeated campuses, women began to address their marginalization in the male-dominated tradition of higher learning. While not necessarily exclusive to students, many campus women's centres attempt to ensure that young women are well represented in their membership. Since universities failed to ensure healthy environments for all students, and existing student organizations and administration-run services did not adequately address issues and problems faced by females, women needed meeting places that would provide female- and student-positive environments within male-dominated institutions.

Women's centres act as a populist means for feminist activism, where the principles of feminism – which may or may not have been learned in classrooms – can be applied to student life. They provide work space for political action, collection of resources, and organization of programs and events. This

Feminist activism on campus: Pamela Alexander of the Laurentian University Women's Centre/Centre des femmes de l'Université Laurentienne.

function is important, as few rooms at most institutions are reserved for student use, and access to equipment such as computers, telephones, and fax machines can be difficult. While they are usually far from adequate in their size, funding, and resources, women's centres give students access to the necessary organizational tools that many others on campus take for granted. Most fundamentally, a women's centre is a gathering place. Many of the women I interviewed who have been involved in these centres said they have established close and lasting friendships with like-minded women they would not have met otherwise.

When discussing campus women's centres, it is important to distinguish three types: those run independently by student volunteers and staff, those with differing degrees of association with or control by student governments, and those operated by institutional administrations. According to these arrangements, the women involved have varying abilities to determine a centre's internal organizational structures, political orientations, services, and programs.[21]

Universities in Northern Ontario have been the slowest in the province to establish centres for women. While York's and Carleton's were founded in 1975 and 1976 respectively, Lakehead did not establish the Gender Issues Centre (GIC) until 1991, and Laurentian its Women's Centre/Centre des femmes until 1994.[22] No comparable organization yet exists at Nipissing University in North Bay. One Lakehead student pointed out that despite its title, the GIC was originally intended to be a women's centre:

> I guess it was quite a fight. I wouldn't want to say the Gender Issues Centre was watered down [from being a women's centre], but it was a compromise, the idea being you can't have a place just for women because women would have too much of a corner on the market. But the goal was to have something offered for women, to have the resources, to have someone there to do crisis intervention, to do education and awareness, and expand the services.

Compromise is an unfortunate reality for many campus women's centres. Lakehead's GIC is relatively well funded – its total annual budget is about $22,000; its annual library fund alone is over $6,000, more than the entire budget of other campus women's centres – but it is accountable to the university's student government. The GIC's director "reports to the Lakehead University Student Union Vice-President Student Issues ... [and] all [GIC] activities must follow the Lakehead University Student Union Constitution, Policy, and By-Laws."[23] As well, the GIC recently established a Lesbian, Gay, and Bisexual Centre that reports to the GIC, and consequently in turn, to the student government. This denial of autonomy reinforces hierarchies of gender and sexuality and does not fundamentally alter institutional structures and processes.

Further east, women students have also been dissatisfied with campus culture and extracurricular opportunities:

> There were religious groups at [Laurentian's] colleges, and having just left Marymount [an all-female Catholic high school in Sudbury], that was really something I wanted to stay away from. Then there was athletics, but except for this renegade group of women who wanted a field hockey team, and women's basketball, that was it. It just seemed there was so little for women to do.

A campaign to establish a women's centre/centre des femmes at Laurentian University began in 1992, an effort in which I was very much involved. Having completed a degree at York University in Toronto, which is often considered to be the most politically active campus in Canada, I was disappointed by what I saw as a lack of community at Laurentian, particularly for women, when I started a second BA program there. One young woman described her Laurentian experience this way:

> The university had a [Presidential Advisory] Committee on the Status of Women that did nothing for students. We heard of many instances of horrible things going on in classrooms and the residences, and there were pimps in the Great Hall saying, "We've got women for you, so you can't be charged with date rape." There was such a low awareness. There was no place to go. There was no culture other than pub night.

Siobhan Kari, another student, and I spread the word around campus that we were looking for other interested women to form a group aimed at establishing a women's centre. Calling ourselves the Laurentian University Women's Centre/Centre des femmes de l'Université Laurentienne (even though we didn't yet have a physical space, we figured we'd show that we meant business by using this title), the 15 or so of us who formed the group conducted a survey that showed that 85 percent of 125 women questioned wanted such a centre. We collected about 1,000 signatures on a pro-women's centre petition and flooded administrative and student association offices with letters of support demanding space for a centre. The goals in forming a women's centre/centre des femmes, we explained, included:

> Establish[ing] programs ... that will contribute to the intellectual culture outside of the classroom ... with an emphasis placed on women's experiences; ... [to] build up resources and referral services;... [and to create] a safe and comfortable environment for women at Laurentian.... We believe that by focusing on education and support, the [women's] centre will help women in terms of awareness, positive self-images, and pursuit of goals – all immensely empowering tools against which females often encounter considerable barriers.[24]

After four attempts at securing a permanent location, we were finally successful, although we didn't get any of the rooms that we had requested.

We may have been guilty of toning down external communication regarding our raison d'être in attempts to win over conservative decision-making bodies, but our internal process reflected more progressive strategies. Traditional organizational structures based on hierarchical power and survival-of-the-fittest philosophies are seen by many feminists as oppressive to women and contradictory to the goals of feminism.[25] We leaned towards the more egalitarian methods of process developed in the second wave of feminism, seeking to maximize each woman's ability to contribute to decision making. We adopted a collective model of organization – which was eventually modified to include two co-ordinators to carry out the decisions of the collective – in which individual authority was rejected in favour of valuing each woman as a leader who shared equally in managing the centre's affairs. Decisions were made only when consensus was reached; thus each woman had a direct role in formulating policies. Compromises were frequent. Despite attempts at direct democracy, though, a few upper-year students with strong personalities dominated discussions and appeared to be looked at as leaders. Indeed, some students with backgrounds in feminist activism or who majored in Women's Studies overlooked the fact that not all members were at their level of familiarity with certain issues.

One key reason for students' involvement with campus women's centres is that some older women connected with feminist organizations hold negative views about young people. While working for change in the community, many of the young activists I interviewed experienced hostility, exclusion, and a relegation to subordinate roles because of their age. One young woman stated her experiences this way:

> It's happened to me many times where I've felt really marginalized and really put down because of my age and I had a lot to say, maybe too much for my age. What I keep getting told by other women I've confided in is: "You're a threat to them because you're younger and you have perhaps come to the same place they have and you can work alongside them, but they have this ideology that if you're younger you shouldn't have as much knowledge or as much to say." It's like if you [know] something, there's an anger or resentment about it. It makes a younger woman feel the same way an older woman must when a man discriminates against her.

Thus some young women prefer to be involved with campus centres, where their youth does not deny them acceptance.

Other young women take exception to feminism's history of emphasizing unity and assuming a commonality of women and their experiences. Feminism, they argue, has failed to address the concerns of those excluded by the white, mainstream women's movement. These criticisms were expressed by one young woman in her analysis of feminism:

> My problem with the feminist tradition is the racism, ableism, and the middle-class heterosexism of it. I'd prefer to be part of a new era of difference and inclusion, and I don't see a move towards that in many older-dominated organizations, so I feel like I have to distinguish my efforts from this tradition of exclusion by previous feminist generations. And that's why I prefer being involved with the group on campus.

According to some women I interviewed, university women's centres, while not perfect or unproblematic, at least provide a more youth-friendly environment where young women, less constrained by age-based stereotypes and hierarchies, might more effectively identify their concerns and initiate efforts for change.

Critical views of the feminist movement are only part of the rationale for campus centres for women. The refusal of university administrations and student associations to adequately combat sexism on campuses has resulted in the need for women's centres. In response to the patriarchal nature of postsecondary culture, some young women see the need to create spaces accepting of progressive ideas where their feminism can be validated and nourished. Whether called a Gender Issues Centre or Women's Centre, whether semi-autonomous or independent, the aims remain similar: support of women, political action, accumulation of resource materials, and development of awareness campaigns, to name a few. They also provide valuable extra-curricular opportunities through which young women can develop skills and learn outside of classrooms. These centres bring together women from varying backgrounds, enriching the lives of those involved, as well as the cultures of their host institutions.

Concluding Comments

The much-overlooked voices of today's young women are now surging to the surface of feminism. As these voices mark a point of departure in basic assumptions and ideas, they constitute a fresh wave of feminist activism.

It is clear that young women have insightful views about society, feminism, and methods for change. Our contributions to feminist activism are important and impressive. When young women are able to overcome obstacles that isolate us or attempt to keep us "in our place," we can accomplish personal goals and work towards social change.

Younger and older women share an interest in the preservation of the movement to end sexism. Older feminists may wish to ensure that the struggle continues because of their concern for women, and that the extraordinary gains they accomplished are not eroded in the years to come. Younger feminists want to maintain the rights they now have and continue to work for a future of improved social conditions.

Notes

Introduction

1. Ashley Thompson, Gwenda Hallsworth, and Lionel Bonin, eds., *The Bibliography of Northern Ontario/La Bibliographie du Nord de l'Ontario 1966-1991* (Toronto: Dundurn Press, 1994).

2. "Women of the North," in *Canadian Woman Studies/Les cahiers de la femme* 14, 4 (1994).

3. Joy Parr, ed., *A Diversity of Women: Ontario, 1945-1980* (Toronto: University of Toronto Press, 1995).

4. Joanna Dean, "Mothers Are Women," in *Limited Edition: Voices of Women, Voices of Feminism*, ed. Geraldine Finn (Halifax: Fernwood, 1993); Imelda Whelehan, *Modern Feminist Thought: From the Second Wave to "Post-Feminism"* (Edinburgh: Edinburgh University Press, 1995); Wendy Weeks, in collaboration with women in Women's Services, *Women Working Together: Lessons from Feminist Women's Services* (Melbourne, Australia: Longman Cheshire, 1994); Jeri Dawn Wine and Janice L. Ristock, eds., *Women and Social Change: Feminist Activism in Canada* (Toronto: James L. Lorimer, 1991).

5. Eleanor Leacock, "Women in Egalitarian Societies," in *Becoming Visible: Women in European History*, ed. Renate Bridenthal, Claudia Koonz, and Susan Stuard (Boston: Houghton Mifflin Company, 1987), 27.

6. Mercedes Steedman, Peter Suschnigg, and Dieter K. Buse, eds., *Hard Lessons: The Mine Mill Union in the Canadian Labour Movement* (Toronto: Dundurn Press, 1995). See also *Women Challenging Unions: Feminism, Democracy and Militancy*, L. Briskin and P. McDermott, eds. (Toronto: University of Toronto Press, 1993).

7. Karen Shaw, "Women and Municipal Politics," speech delivered 18 May 1995 to the INORD symposium at Laurentian University, Sudbury, "Changing Lives: Women and the Northern Ontario Experience."

Chapter 1

1. Prior to the Province of Canada taking the first census in Northern Ontario in 1861, the territory north of Lakes Huron and Superior had been divided into two large districts – Algoma and Nipissing. Following Confederation, the government of Canada initiated census-taking every ten years, beginning in 1871. For the first national census after Confederation, statisticians divided Northern Ontario into eight districts – West, Centre, and East Algoma; Manitoulin; North and South Nipissing; Muskoka; and Parry Sound. For the 1881 Census, Northern Ontario was reduced to two districts – Algoma and Muskoka – which subsumed the eight districts of ten years before. For the 1891 and 1901 censuses, the statisticians expanded the number of districts to three – Algoma, Nipissing, and Muskoka-Parry Sound. In 1911 statisticians further expanded the number of districts, to six: East and West Algoma, Manitoulin, North and South Nipissing, and the combined District of Thunder Bay and Rainy River. Population increases in Northern Ontario between 1911 and 1921 encouraged census bureaucrats to alter the number and size of the districts again. For that year statisticians counted people in ten districts: Algoma, Kenora, Manitoulin, Muskoka, Nipissing, Parry Sound, Rainy River, Sudbury, Thunder Bay, and Timiskaming. For 1931 the same ten districts plus Cochrane provided the designations with which the enumerators worked. These eleven districts prevailed until the 1981 Census when the Sudbury Regional Municipality was added. For 1991, the number of districts continued to be twelve.

2. Peter C. Newman, *Company of Adventurers* (Markham: Penguin Books, 1985), 110. G. E. Thorman, "Sergeant, Henry," *Dictionary of Canadian Biography*, 1 (Toronto: University of Toronto Press, 1966), 605-06. Hudson's Bay Company factor Henry Sergeant brought his wife, her companion (a Mrs. Maurice), and a female servant to his post on Hudson Bay in 1683. These were the first English women known to have wintered in Northern Ontario. They remained until 1687 when the company ordered Sergeant and the women to return to England.

3. Derived from *Census Report of the Canadas, 1861*, and from *Census of Canada, 1871, 1881, 1891, 1901*.

4. Derived from *Census Report of the Canadas, 1861*, and from *Census of Canada, 1871, 1881, 1891, 1901*.

5. Census enumerators adhered to a political-geographic definition of nationality. For example, since most of the Polish population in Northern Ontario had emigrated from German-held provinces of Poland, they were classified as Germans. The same rationale applied to Finns, whose country had been annexed by Russia early in the nineteenth century. Census enumerators counted them as Russians rather than Finns. Most of the Ukrainian population of Northern Ontario had emigrated from that part of the Ukraine controlled by the Austro-Hungarian Empire. Hence, they were counted as either Austrians or Hungarians.

6. The Manuscript Census for 1861 and subsequent years designated Aboriginals, who did not claim allegiance to main-line churches, as Heathens and Pagans.

7. Derived from *Census Report of the Canadas, 1861*, and from *Census of Canada, 1871, 1881, 1891, 1901*.

8. Dr. Helen Ryan advertised her specialty in the *Sudbury Journal*, 21 May 1891, 1.

9. *Ontario Statutes, 1871*, Chapter 33 (School Improvement Act). *Ontario Statutes, 1881*, Chapter 30 (Compulsory School Attendance Act).

10. *Census of Canada, 1901. Ontario Statutes, 1871*, Chapter 33, Paragraph 3. *Ontario Statues, 1881*, Chapter 30, Paragraph 1.

11. Derived from *Census of Canada, 1911-1951*.

12. Derived from *Census of Canada, 1911-1951*.

13. Derived from *Census of Canada, 1911-1951*.

14. *Ontario Statutes, 1919*, Chapters 77, 78.

15. Derived from *Census of Canada, 1961-1991*.

16. Derived from *Census of Canada, 1961-1991*.

17. Derived from *Census of Canada, 1961-1991*.

Chapter 2

1. Different spellings of the word Ojibwa, Ojibway, and Ojibwe appear in this chapter. There are different orthographies by which this word is written. I choose to use the spelling "Ojibwa" in this article when referring to the Ojibwa people and "Ojibwe" when referring to the spoken language. However, as a matter of courtesy to others who choose to spell it differently, I have included other orthographies.

In reference to the explanation of the definition of the word *Anishinabe* as it appears in Eva's biography, *Anishinabe* is the word that the Ojibwa people use to refer to themselves. It means "original people" or "original man." However, it is not uncommon today to hear other people use the word *Anishinabe (Anishinabeg)* in reference to the Ojibwa (Ojibway) cultural group as well.

2. "Wiki" is the short name used by residents of the community of Wikwemikong on Manitoulin Island to refer to their hometown.

3. *Cassot* is a French-Canadian word used to describe the basket-like birchbark container used to collect maple sap in the spring.

Chapter 3

1. James Morrison, "Upper Great Lakes Settlement: The Anishnabe-Jesuit Record," *Ontario History* 86, 1 (1994), 61.

2. Morrison, "Upper Great Lakes," 62.

3. Morrison, "Upper Great Lakes," 62.

4. Morrison, "Upper Great Lakes," 62.

5. Carol Devens, *Countering Colonization: Native American Women and Great Lakes Missions, 1630-1900* (Los Angeles: University of California Press, 1992).

6. David Nazar, Personal communication, May 1995.

7. Edward Benton-Banai, *The Mishomis Book* (Wisconsin: Red School House, 1988).

8. See Benton-Banai, *The Mishomis Book.*

9. Wynne Hanson, "The Urban Indian Women and Her Family," *Social Casework: The Journal of Contemporary Social Work* 61 (1980): 478.

Chapter 4

1. For further information see, in addition to the works referenced elsewhere in this chapter: Marguerite V. Burke, *The Ukrainian Canadians* (Toronto: Van Nostrand Reinhold Ltd., 1978); Anne Kmit et al., *Ukrainian Easter Eggs and How We Make Them* (Minneapolis, MN: Ukrainian Gift Shop, 1979); William Kurelek, *Lumberjack* (Montreal: Tundra Books, 1974); Manoly R. Lupul, ed., *Visible Symbols: Cultural Expressions Among Canada's Ukrainians* (Edmonton: Canadian Institute of Ukrainian Studies, 1984); Jaroslav Rozumnyj, ed., *New Soil – Old Roots: The Ukrainian Experience in Canada* (Winnipeg: Ukrainian Academy of Arts and Sciences in Canada, 1983); "Sudbury's People," *Polyphony* 5, 1 (Spring/Summer 1983); and "Ukrainians in Ontario," *Polyphony* 10 Double Issue (1988).

2. Mary Stefura, "Ukrainians in the Sudbury Region," *Polyphony* 5, 1 (Spring/Summer 1983).

3. C.M. Wallace and Ashley Thomson, eds., *Sudbury: Rail Town to Regional Capital* (Toronto and Oxford: Dundurn Press, 1993).

4. The organizations contacted are as follows: St. Olga's Ukrainian Women's Association; Ukrainian Catholic Women's League; Ukrainian Canadian Culture Centre; Ukrainian Professional and Business Club of Sudbury, Inc.; League of Ukrainian Canadian Women; Association of United Ukrainian Canadians; Ukrainian Seniors Centre; and Sudbury Branch of the Ukrainian Women's Organization of the Ukrainian National Federation.

5. Myrna Kostash, *All of Baba's Children* (Edmonton: Hurtig Publishers, 1977).

6. Statutes of Canada (Chapter C-18.7, 1993): 3, 5.

7. Christopher Guly, "Canada's Multicultural Policy under Debate," *The Ukrainian Weekly* 25 (1993): 8, 18.

Chapter 5

1. There is much controversy about the usage and appropriateness of the terms "Hispanic" and "Latino" to describe Spanish-speaking peoples. See Suzanne Oboler, *Ethnic Labels, Latino Lives: Identity and the Politics of (Re)Presentation in the United States* (Minneapolis, MN: University of Minnesota Press, 1995); Louise Fiber Luce, ed., *The Spanish-Speaking World: An Anthology of Cross-Cultural Perspectives* (Lincolnwood, Illinois: NTC Publishing Group, 1992).

2. "The culture of Latin America is the result of a complex process in which the popular tradition of local, Catholic, Americanist, and populist thought has interacted with the cultural trends which reflect international influences." Andrew Machalski, *Hispanic Writers in Canada: A Preliminary Survey of the Activities of Spanish and Latin-American Writers in Canada* (Ottawa: Department of the Secretary of State, Multicultural Sector, January 1988).

3. The Spanish language has both a familiar and a polite form of address for "you." The general rule has been the automatic use of the polite form of *usted* to show respect when speaking to strangers, older people, or those in authority. Increasingly, in Latin America, one

encounters the familiar *tú* in place of *usted*, and this change in language and social custom is the example offered as one of the more disconcerting and uncomfortable experiences one woman had during a recent visit to Latin America. See Carmen García, "A Cross-Cultural Study of Politeness Strategies: Venezuelan and American Perspectives," in Luce, *The Spanish-Speaking World*, 146-63.

4. For further exploration of this kind of experience see *Crucero/Crossroads*, "a complex look at notions of identity and representation. It focuses specifically on the position of Latin Americans and their culture in North America and uses this specific to examine a sense of otherness or cultural displacement." Screenplay by Guillermo Verdecchio. Produced and directed by Ramiro Puerta. Videocassette. (Toronto: Snake Cinema, 1994).

Chapter 7

1. Becki Ross, *The House That Jill Built: A Lesbian Nation in Formation* (Toronto: University of Toronto Press, 1995), 230.

2. Throughout this chapter, we have included excerpts from stories collected during interviews with women who identify themselves as lesbians. While not all of the lesbians we spoke with requested anonymity, those who have been quoted in this chapter did. Their voices, along with those of the authors, have not therefore been individually referenced.

    The excerpts were drawn from two sets of interviews. The first set of interviews was conducted in 1994 during a research project investigating accessibility of social services to lesbians and gays. The second set of interviews was conducted in 1995; they were specifically related to the writing of this chapter.

    The discussions we refer to are those that occurred at conferences, workshops, community organizing meetings, and informal lesbian gatherings.

3. Susan E. Gentry, "Caring for Lesbians in a Homophobic Society," *Health Care for Women International* 13 (1992), 175.

4. Ross, *The House That Jill Built*, 9.

5. See J. Ross Eshleman and S. J. Wilson, *The Family* (Scarborough: Allyn and Bacon Canada, 1995), 25; Carol Allen, "Who Gets To Be Family: Some Thoughts on the Lesbian and Gay Fight for Equality," in *And Still We Rise: Feminist Political Mobilization in Contemporary Canada*, Linda Carty, ed.(Toronto: Women's Press, 1993), 102; and Margrit Eichler, *Families in Canada Today*, 2nd ed., (Toronto: Gage Educational Publishing Company, 1988), 3.

6. See Adrienne Rich, "Compulsory Heterosexuality and Lesbian Existence," in *Feminist Frameworks*, Alison M. Jaggar and Paula S. Rothenberg, eds. (Toronto: McGraw-Hill Book Company, 1984), 416-420.

7. Anne Bishop, *Becoming an Ally* (Halifax: Fernwood Publishing, 1994), 130.

8. Suzanne Pharr, *Homophobia: A Weapon of Sexism* (Inverness, CA: Chardon Press, 1988), 18.

9. The American Psychiatric Association; Diagnostic and Statistical Manual of Mental Disorders (DSM-IV) is the authoritative clinical guide used by mental health practitioners for the assessment and diagnosis of mental health disorders.

10. See Linda Garnets et al., "Issues in Psychotherapy with Lesbians and Gay Men: A Survey of Psychologists," *American Psychologist* 46 (1991): 964-72; Margaret S. Schneider, "Attitudes and Beliefs" in *Often Invisible: Counselling Gay and Lesbian Youth* (Toronto: Central Toronto Youth Services, 1988), 41-47; and Debra L. Tievsky, "Homosexual Clients and Homophobic Social Workers," *Journal of Independent Social Work* 2, 3 (1988): 51-62.

11. Marie Cumming Steel, "Identifying and Meeting the Needs of Gay and Lesbian Adolescents in Family Therapy," *Canadian Journal of Human Sexuality* 2, 1 (1993): 1-12.

12. Sophie Freud Loewenstein, "Understanding Lesbian Women," *Social Casework: The Journal of Contemporary Social Work* 61, 1 (1982): 32.

13. For a list of resources, see *The Rainbow Book: An Ontario Directory of Community Services for Lesbians, Gay Men, Bisexuals, Transsexuals, Transgenderists, and Transvestites* (Toronto: Ryerson CopyPrint, 1995); and *Toronto Pink Pages* (Toronto: Pink Pages, 1995).

14. In this context, the word "gays" refers to gay males.

15. See Michel Foucault, "The Perverse Implantation," *The History of Sexuality: an Introduction* (New York: Vintage Books, 1978), 36-49.

16. Legislative Assembly of Ontario, Third Session, 35th Parliament, Official Report of Debates (Hansard) (138), Monday 6 June 1994, p. 6659.

17. Legislative Assembly of Ontario, Third Session, 35th Parliament, Official Report of Debates (Hansard) (141), Thursday 9 June 1994, p. 6789.

18. This information was received during a telephone interview with Ms. Donaldson in April 1995.

19. See *The Rainbow Book.*

Chapter 8

1. Interview with Aina Mackie by Varpu Lindström, Vancouver, B.C., 1982.

2. Varpu Lindström-Best, *The Finns in Canada* (Ottawa: Canadian Historical Association, 1985), 7, 16; Varpu Lindström, *Defiant Sisters: A Social History of Finnish Immigrant Women in Canada* [Toronto: Multicultural History Society of Ontario (MHSO), 1992], 34-39.

3. Finnish emigration patterns have been discussed in Reino Kero, *Migration from Finland to North America in the Years Between the United States Civil War and the First World War* (Turku: The Migration Institute, 1974); in Keijo Virtanen, *Settlement or Return: Finnish Emigrants (1860-1930) in the International Overseas Return Migration Movement* (Turku: The Migration Institute, 1979); and in Lindström, *Defiant Sisters*, 1-39. On chain migration, see for example: Franc Sturino, *Forging the Chain: Italian Migration to North America 1880-1930* (Toronto: MHSO, 1990); and Franca Iacovetta, *Such Hardworking People: Italian Immigrants in Postwar Toronto* (Kingston: McGill-Queen's University Press, 1992), 3-51.

4. Ian Radforth, *Bushworkers and Bosses: Logging in Northern Ontario 1900-1980* (Toronto: University of Toronto Press, 1987), 101.

5. Interview with Martta Laitinen by Varpu Lindström and Börje Vähämäki, Petroskoi, Russia, 1988.

6. *Vapaus*, 21 August 1923; Lindström, *Defiant Sisters*, 86.

7. Interview with Martta Laitinen, 1988.

8. Interview with Impi Kanerva by Lennard Sillanpää, Schumacher, Ont., 1977. MHSO ILF 1925.

9. Nelma Sillanpää, *Under the Northern Lights: My Memories of Life in the Finnish Community of Northern Ontario*, ed. Edward W. Laine (Ottawa: Canadian Museum of Civilization, 1994), 24.

10. Interview with Reino Keto by Varpu Lindström, Toronto, 1978. MHSO ILF 5187.

11. Interview with William Eklund by Lennard Sillanpää, Sudbury, 1977. MHSO ILG 2222.

12. American Letter Collection (ALC), University of Turku, KAR:CXXXI, Hilja Rantala, 2 March 1929, AC Ry. Mile 198.

13. Interview with Alva Korri by Lennard Sillanpää, Porcupine, Ont., 1977. MHSO ILG 1164.

14. Radforth, *Bushworkers and Bosses*, 33.

15. Radforth, *Bushworkers and Bosses*, 101. Quote by Buzz Lein.

16. Radforth, *Bushworkers and Bosses*, 92-93.

17. Interview with Linne Korri by Lennard Sillanpää, Timmins, 1977. MHSO ILF 1921. See also the interview with Alva Korri, 1977.

18. Nelma Sillanpää, *Under the Northern Lights*, 9.

19. Wm Eklund, *Canadan Rakentajia: Canadan Suomalaisen Järjestön Historia* vv. 1911-1971, (Toronto: Vapaus Publishing, 1983), 106.

20. Interview with Yrjö Kyllönen by A-M Lahtinen, Sudbury, 1978. MHSO ILG 2904.

21. Interview with Linne Korri, 1977.

22. Interview with Yrjö Kyllönen, 1978.

23. Interview with Martta Laitinen, 1988.

24. Interview with Mary Erickson by Raili Nieminen and Helena Doherty, Nolalu, Ont., 1979. MHSO ILF 7458.

25. ALC, University of Turku, Finland, Eura:XXI, Aino Norkooli to A. Hägerman, 15 December 1925 in "dense forest."

26. ALC, University of Turku, Eura:XXI Aino Norkooli to her mother in Finland, 27 October 1936 in "at the camp."

27. Radforth, *Bushworkers and Bosses*, 255.

28. Eklund, *Canadan Rakentajia*, 109.

29. ALC, University of Turku, LOIM:XXXIII, Artturi Saari, 17 September 1929, at a bush camp.

30. ALC, University of Turku, MER:CCVIII, Raakel Vanhala, 30 May 1946, Sault Ste. Marie, Ont.

31. Nelma Sillanpää, *Under the Northern Lights*, 6.

32. *Vapaus*, 12 August 1922.

33. ALC, Aino Norkooli, 1936.

34. Nelma Sillanpää, *Under the Northern Lights*, 26.

35. Nelma Sillanpää, *Under the Northern Lights*, 14.

36. Interview with Alva Korri, 1977.

37. Interview with Irene Hormavirta by Varpu Lindström, Toronto, 1978. MHSO ILF 4985.

38. Nelma Sillanpää, *Under the Northern Lights*, 7.

39. Nelma Sillanpää, *Under the Northern Lights*, 12.

40. Interview with Alva Korri, 1977.

41. ALC, Hilja Rantala, 1929.

42. ALC, University of Turku, Eura XXII, Minni Lahtinen, Hearst, Ont., 1961.

43. Nelma Sillanpää, *Under the Northern Lights*, 25.

44. Varpu Lindström, *Uhmattaret: Suomalaisten siirtolaisnaisten vaiheita Kanadassa 1890-1930* (Helsinki: WSOY, 1991), 132.

45. *Daily Times Journal,* 30 September 1930 as quoted by Nancy Chong Johnson's unpublished undergraduate research paper "Finnish Immigrants in Thunder Bay: Representation in the English-Language Press 1875-1878,1903-1906, 1930" (Toronto: University of Toronto, Finnish Studies Program, 1995).

46. Lindström, *Defiant Sisters,* 86-87; for additional information on children in the lumber camps, see Lindström, *Uhmattaret,* 131-33.

47. *Vapaus,* 2 February 1928.

48. Radforth, *Bushworkers and Bosses,* 102.

49. Interview with Aina Mackie, 1982.

50. Interview with Alva Korri, 1977.

51. Ian Radforth, "Finnish Lumber Workers in Ontario, 1919-1946," *Polyphony* 2 (Fall, 1981), 26; Nelma Sillanpää, *Under the Northern Lights*, 10-11.

52. Interview with Toivo Tienhaara by Lennard Sillanpää, South Porcupine, Ont., 1977. MHSO ILF 1161; Radforth, "Finnish Lumber Workers," 26.

53. ALC, Hilja Rantala, 1929.

54. Interview with Martta Huhtala by Varpu Lindström, Parry Sound, Ont., 1983. Author's Collection.

55. Radforth, *Bushworkers and Bosses*, 108.

56. Radforth, "Finnish Lumber Workers," 29.

57. Radforth, "Finnish Lumber Workers," 29.

58. Interview with Gertie Gronroos by Helena Doherty, Port Arthur, Ont., n.d. (1978?). MHSO ILF 7198.

59. *Metsätyöläinen* 8 (1932): 15.

60. *Industrialisti*, 11 October 1934.

61. Interview with Mary Erickson, 1979.

62. Unidentified Finnish language newspaper clipping, 17 October 1934.

63. Unidentified Finnish language newspaper clipping, 29 October 1934.

64. *Vapaus*, 26 February 1921; Lindström, *Defiant Sisters*, 87.

Chapter 9

1. This chapter is based on interviews with Elva Pellerin (formerly Elva Sullivan) that I conducted with Donna Mayer, co-ordinator of the Sudbury Women's Centre in 1991.The interviews were done as part of the Sudbury Women's Centre's Women and History Project, and I am grateful for Donna's co-operation with this project. I want to thank Elva Sullivan Pellerin for sharing her story of teaching in Northern Ontario and also Elizabeth Griffin, who provided her reminiscences of life as a student in Biscotasing.

2. H. Smaller, "A Room of One's Own: The Early Years of the Toronto Women Teachers' Association," in *Gender and Education in Ontario: An Historical Reader*, ed. Ruby Heap and Alison Prentice (Toronto: Canadian Scholars' Press, 1991), 103-27.

3. D.J. Frantila, "'Back to the Land' Land Relief Settlement in Northern Ontario." Honours Thesis. (Sudbury: Laurentian University, Department of History, 1986).

4. *Sudbury Star*, "Strips of Birch Bark Serve as Blackboard in Settlers' Schools," (October 1933): 1-2.

5. A. Prentice, "From Household to School House: The Emergence of the Teacher as Servant of the State," in *Gender and Education*, Heap and Prentice, 25-49.

Chapter 10

1. Some of the material for this chapter first appeared in Susan Kennedy and Jennifer Keck, "Every Miner Had a Mother," *Our Times* (September-October 1985): 28-30.

2. From the Introduction, "Every Miner Had a Mother" Photographic Exhibit, May 1983.

3. Keck and Kennedy are founding members of the Sudbury Women's Centre.

4. C.M. Wallace and A. Thomson, eds., *Sudbury: Rail Town to Regional Capital* (Toronto: Dundurn Press, 1993).

5. M. Steedman, P. Suschnigg, and D. Buse, eds., *Hard Lessons: The Mine Mill Union and the Canadian Labour Movement* (Toronto: Dundurn Press, 1995).

6. See also the 16mm/vhs (73 min.) film, "A Wives' Tale," produced by S. Bissonnette, M. Duckworth and J. Rock (1980), distributed by Fullframe Film and Video Distribution of Toronto.

7. See "Women's Centre Unveils Alternative Centennial Logo," *Northern Life*, April 1983; "Mining Town Mothers to Share the Limelight," *Sudbury Star*, 27 April 1983.

8. Women had been working at production jobs at Inco's Sudbury operations since 1974. The miner's hard hat was a bit misleading, however, as no women were working underground until the early 1990s.

9. See D.R. Roediger, *The Wages of Whiteness* (London: Verso Books, 1991).

10. As cited in Roediger, *Wages*, 6.

11. For example, see Wallace and Thomson, *Sudbury: Rail Town*.

Chapter 11

1. This project has been supported by the Institute for Northern Ontario Development and Research, Local 6500 of the United Steelworkers of America, District 6 of the United Steelworkers of America, Inco, and Marion V. Royce Memorial Grant, Women's Bureau of Human Resources Development Canada. As authors, we gratefully acknowledge this financial support, but we alone are responsible for the content and for the views expressed.

We thank the women of Local 6500 for their participation in the project and acknowledge in particular the women on the research advisory committee who have contributed support, advice, and enthusiasm for the project.

We would also like to acknowledge the excellent work of our research assistants, Tammy Roy, who worked on the project in 1994, and Tricia Leduc, who worked on it in 1995. Ron Orasi and Lorenzo Mariega at the Inco Archives were extremely helpful and we thank them for sharing their knowledge of the company and its records. Gerry Rogers, manager of public affairs for Inco, provided comments on an earlier version of the paper and made available photographs from the *Inco Triangle*. We also appreciate the thoughtful advice and insight contributed by David Leadbeater.

2. These differences are based on data for the City of Sudbury. If we look at data for the Regional Municipality of Sudbury, there remains a very small lag in 1981 and a smaller lead in 1991 than evidenced by the City of Sudbury/Canada comparison.

3. *Statutes of Ontario*, 1890, Chap 10, s. 4.

4. Graeme Mount, "The 1940s" in *Sudbury: Rail Town to Regional Centre,* ed. C.M. Wallace and Ashley Thomson (Toronto and Oxford: Dundurn Press, 1993), 175.

5. PC 7032. A second order-in-council, PC 8063, was issued on 23 September 1942 extending the right to employ women to Inco's Port Colborne operations. *Labour Gazette* 42 (September 1942): 1026. Cited in Sandra Walton, "Women at Work in Industry during World War II: Inco a Case in Point," Honours Paper, History 4185, Laurentian University, 25 March 1986, 6.

6. *Sudbury Star*, 28 August 1942. "Seventeen Women Accepted as Inco Employees," cited in Walton, "Women at Work," 7.

7. Walton, "Women at Work," 7-8.

8. This figure comes from research being done by Sandra Battaglini, who is examining the wartime records at the Inco Archives. It is almost double the previous estimate of 877, prepared by Sandra Walton on the basis of operating reports and newspaper accounts.

9. Graeme Mount, "The 1940s," 171-72.

10. Mike Solski and John Smaller, *Mine Mill: The History of the International Union of Mine, Mill and Smelter Workers in Canada Since 1895* (Ottawa: Steel Rail, 1984), 124.

11. Solski and Smaller, *Mine Mill*, 109.

12. Solski and Smaller, *Mine Mill*, 171.

13. *Labour Gazette* 45 (7-12), 1945, 1603 cited in Walton, "Women at Work," 9-10.

14. Walton, "Women at Work," 8.

15. Average nickel production for Canada as whole, not just Inco, was 238 million pounds between 1946 and 1949.

16. *Statutes of Ontario*, 1948, Chap 56, s. 151 (2).

17. J.A. MacMillan, G.S. Gislason, and S. Lyon, *Human Resources in Canadian Mining* (Kingston: Queen's University, Centre for Resource Studies, 1977), xiv, cited in Wallace Clement, *Hardrock Mining: Industrial Relations and Technological Changes at Inco* (Toronto: McClelland and Stewart, 1981), 84.

18. The decline in staff has been only slightly less dramatic. From 4,135 in 1971, the staff complement has declined by 60 percent to 1,644 in 1994.

19. The very first women production workers at Inco were hired in January 1974 in Inco operations at Thompson, Manitoba, and by October 1974, "there were over sixty women working [at Thompson] in various surface jobs – including the Pipe Mine." See Clement, *Hardrock Mining*, 92.

20. *Statutes of Ontario*, 1970, Chap 79, s. 2.

21. The end to the prohibition against women underground came when Part IX of the Mining Act, which contained the section in question as well as other provisions regarding the operation of mines, was repealed. We have not yet been able to establish if this was a deliberate decision, or merely a by-product of legislative housekeeping. The repeal of Part IX was one of a list of similar provisions at the end of the new Occupational Health and Safety Act (*Statutes of Ontario*, 1978, Chap 83, s. 42).

22. News Brief: "Female Miners," *The Labour Gazette* April 1974, 240. Some mining companies had responded to the labour shortage by hiring "women for jobs other than office and clerical."

23. "May Welcome Women in Area Mines," *Sudbury Star* 25 January 1974, 1.

24. "First Ladies," Inco *Triangle* August 1974.

25. Inco, Ontario Division, *Inco Report of Operations*, 1974, 33.

26. In late 1992, as part of its restructuring, Inco proposed transferring 86 office and technical workers (roughly half of them women) to jobs underground. Put forward unexpectedly, the proposal was met with consternation and controversy. Inco then agreed to company-union consultations, which resulted in only 38 workers (18 of them women) being transferred, some to surface jobs and some to jobs underground. Mick Lowe, "Women of the Mines," *Financial Post Magazine* January 1995, 20-27.

27. See Karen D. Hughes, "Trading Places: Men and Women in Non-Traditional Occupations, 1971-1986," *Perspectives on Labour and Income* (Statistics Canada Catalogue 75-001E), 2, 2 (Summer 1990): 58-68; and "Women in Non-Traditional Occupations," *Perspectives on Labour and Income* (Statistics Canada Catalogue 75-001E), (Autumn 1995):14-19.

28. We have used company records, union lists, and newspaper articles to document layoff and end dates for the 80, but the bulk of the data come from employment records of 72 women, which contain information about the worker's length of service and benefits entitlement as well as some personal background, including level of education, former occupation, date of birth, marital status, and language. These records are a valuable source, but they have some limitations. First, records were usually filled out at the time of hiring and updated by the Personnel Office; employment-related matters are well documented but changes in personal information (birth of children, marriage, separation, or divorce) may not be always noted. Second, information is not always complete. For example, although some records note that the worker spoke French or Finnish, many records contain no mention of language and it is possible that the question was not asked of every worker. Finally, some information is ambiguous. In the case of education, records may indicate a grade, but it is not clear whether the worker completed Grade 10 (for example) or left school during Grade 10.

29. Clement, *Hardrock Mining*, 88.

30. This is consistent with the observations made by Fran Cherry, Nancy McIntyre, and Deborah Jaggernathsingh, who noted that women in trades and technology they interviewed stressed the importance of "being confident, assertive, and unintimidated by men when working with them." Cherry et al., "The Experience of Canadian Women in Trades and Technology," *Women's Studies International Forum* 14, 1/2 (1991): 25.

31. These categories were defined by company records, not by the authors. For most of the women, their civil status was noted at the time of hiring. It was not always clear when or if this status changed.

32. Although the women still employed had been on the jobs for 20 calendar years, their actual time on the job is reduced by shutdown and in some cases layoff.

33. The remaining eight are women whose exit was of an undetermined type.

34. Clement, *Hardrock Mining*, 338.

Chapter 12

1. P. La Novara, *A Portrait of Families in Canada: Target Groups Project* (Ottawa: Statistics Canada, 1993).

2. C. Bernier, S. Larocque, et M. Aumond, *Familles francophones: multiples réalités* (Sudbury: Institut franco-ontarien, 1995), 117.

3. Meg Luxton, "Two Hands for the Clock: Changing Patterns in the Gendered Division of Labour in the Home," in *Through the Kitchen Window: The Politics of Home and Family.* 2nd ed., ed. Meg Luxton, Harriet Rosenberg, and Sedef Arat-Koc, (Toronto: Garamond Press, 1990), 39-56.

4. Statistics Canada, *General Social Survey*, 1992.

5. M. Baker and D. Lero, eds. *Families: Changing Trends in Canada* (Toronto: McGraw-Hill Ryerson, 1996).

6. See Ann Oakley, *Housewife* (London: Allen Lane, 1974). The number of studies on housework has grown enormously since that time.

7. Statistics Canada, *Profile of Census Divisions and Subdivisions in Ontario, Part A* (Ottawa: Industry, Science and Technology Canada, 1994). *1991 Census of Canada.* (Catalogue Number 93-338).

8. L. Thompson and A. Walker, "Gender in Families: Women and Men in Marriage, Work, and Parenthood," *Journal of Marriage and the Family* 51 (1989): 845-71.

9. Respondents were asked to check whether they were working full-time or part-time.

10. Statistics Canada, *Women in the Labour Force.* Catalogue 75-507E. (Ottawa: Statistics Canada, October 1994).

11. La Novara, *Portrait*, 29.

12. N. Pupo, "Balancing Responsibilities: The Part-time Option," in *Few Choices: Women, Work and Family*, ed. A. Duffy, N. Mandell and N. Pupo (Toronto: Garamond Press, 1989); H. Krahn and G. Lowe, *Work, Industry and Canadian Society* (Toronto: Nelson Canada, 1993).

13. B. Shelton, *Women, Men and Time: Gender Differences in Paid Work, Housework and Leisure* (Westport, CT: Greenwood Press, 1992).

14. M. Townson, *Women's Financial Future* (Ottawa: The Canadian Advisory Council on the Status of Women, 1995).

15. Vanier Centre for the Family, *Profiling Canadian Families* (Ottawa: Vanier Centre for the Family, 1994).

16. N. Pupo, "Balancing Responsibilities: The Part-time Option," p. 74-100 in *Few Choices*, Duffy et al.

17. N. Pupo, "Balancing," 77.

18. M. Ferree,"Negotiating household roles and responsibilities; Resistance, conflict, and change," paper presented at the annual meeting of the National Council on Family Relations, Philadelphia, 1988.

Chapter 13

1. Financial assistance in the form of a research grant from INORD is gratefully acknowledged. We wish to thank J.-C. Cachon for help in the initial stages of the project and Jo-Anne Palkovits and Trudy Dussault for their able research assistance.

2. Lois Stevenson, "Some Methodological Problems Associated with Researching Women Entrepreneurs," *Journal of Business Ethics* 9 (1990): 439-46; and Kathryn Campbell, "Researching Women Entrepreneurs: A Progress Report," *Canadian Woman Studies/Les cahiers de la femme* 15, 1 (1994): 8-14.

3. See Robert D. Hisrich, and Candida G. Brush, "The Woman Entrepreneur: Implications of Family, Educational and Occupational Experience," in *Frontiers in Entrepreneurship Research* (Wellesley, MA: Babson College, 1983): 255-70; Sandra Honig-Haftel and Linda Martin, "Is the Female Entrepreneur at a Disadvantage?" *Thrust: The Journal for Employment and Training Professionals* 7 (1986): 49-64; and Linda Neider, "A Preliminary Investigation of Female Entrepreneurs in Florida," *Journal of Small Business Management* 25, 3 (1987): 22-29.

4. See David J. Brophy, "Financing Women-Owned Entrepreneurial Firms," in *Women-Owned Businesses*, ed. O. Hagen, C. Rivchun and D.L. Sexton (New York: Praeger Publishers, 1989), 55-75; Robert D. Hisrich and M. O'Brien, "The Woman Entrepreneur as a Reflection of the Type of Business," in *Frontiers in Entrepreneurship Research* (Wellesley, MA: Babson College, 1982), 54-77; and Candida G. Brush, "Local Initiatives for Job Creation," in *Enterprising Women* (Paris: OECD, 1990), 37-55.

5. See Robert D. Hisrich and Candida G. Brush, "The Woman Entrepreneur: Management Skills and Business Problems," *Journal of Small Business Management* 22, 1 (1984): 30-37; and Carole E. Scott, "Why More Women Are Becoming Entrepreneurs," *Journal of Small Business Management* 24, 4 (1986): 37-44.

6. See Candida G. Brush, "Research on Women Business Owners: Past Trends, a New Perspective and Future Directions," *Entrepreneurship Theory and Practice* 16, 4 (1992): 5-30; and Honig-Haftel and Martin, "Female Entrepreneur."

7. See Brophy, "Financing Women-Owned Entrepreneurial Firms"; Robert D. Hisrich, "Women Entrepreneurs: Problems and Prescriptions for Success in the Future," in *Women-Owned Businesses*, O. Hagen et al., 123-45; and Brush, "Local Initiatives."

8. See Richard Cuba, David Decenzo, and Andrea Anish,"Management Practices of Successful Female Business Owners," *American Journal of Small Business* 8, 2 (1983): 40-45; and Nieder, "A Preliminary Investigation."

9. A. Baker Ibrahim and Willard H. Ellis, *Entrepreneurship and Small Business Management: Text, Readings and Cases* (Dubuque, IA: Kendall/Hunt, 1990).

10. Amar Bhide, "How Entrepreneurs Craft Strategies that Work," *Harvard Business Review* (1994): 150-61.

11. Peter Rosa, Daphne Hamilton, Sara Carter and Helen Burns, "The Impact of Gender on Small Business Management: Preliminary Findings of a British Study," *International Journal of Small Business* 12, 3 (1994): 25-32.

12. Cuba et al., "Management Practices."

Chapter 15

1. Studies that would have helped me understand my Baba with more nuance include Joan Sangster, *Dreams of Equality: Women on the Canadian Left, 1920-1950* (Toronto: McClelland and Stewart, 1989) and Francis Swyripa, *Wedded to the Cause: Ukrainian Canadian Women and Ethnic Identity, 1891-1991* (Toronto: University of Toronto Press, 1993). Useful studies of immigrant women's history also include Varpu Lindström, *Defiant Sisters: A Social History of Finnish Immigrant Women* (Toronto: Multicultural History Society of Ontario, 1988); Ruth Frager, *Sweatshop Strife: Class, Ethnicity, and Gender in the Jewish Labour Movement of Toronto 1900-1939* (Toronto: University of Toronto Press, 1992); and Franca Iacovetta, *Such Hardworking People: Italian Immigrants in Postwar Toronto* (Montreal: McGill-Queen's University Press, 1992).

2. Katherine Borland, "'That's Not What I Said': Interpretive Conflict in Oral Narrative Research," in *Women's Words: The Feminist Practice of Oral History*, ed. Sherna Berger Gluck and Daphne Patai (New York: Routledge, 1991), 64. See also Ann Oakley, "Interviewing Women: A Contradiction in Terms," in *Doing Feminist Research*, ed. Helen Roberts (London: Routledge, 1981), 30-61.

3. Kathryn Anderson and Dana C. Jack, "Learning to Listen: Interview Techniques and Analyses," in *Women's Words*, Gluck and Patai, 11-26.

Chapter 16

1. PAO, RG 18, Government Commissions, B-82, *Report of the Hollinger Mine Inquiry*, 1-5. For detailed information about the age, marital status, number of children, and nationality of the miners killed in this accident, see TIM, 985.61, Municipality of Timmins, File Hollinger Disaster, 1928.

2. In the Canadian context, see for example, Donald MacLeod, "Colliers, Colliery Safety and Workplace Control: The Nova Scotia Experience, 1873 to 1910," CHA, *Historical Papers, 1983*, 227-53; Doug Baldwin, "A Study in Social Control," 79-107. One notable exception is the work of anthropologist Elliot Leyton that presents the life histories of fluorspar miners and their spouses in St. Lawrence, Newfoundland. See Elliot Leyton, *Dying Hard: The Ravages of Industrial Carnage* (Toronto: McClelland and Stewart, 1975). There is a growing American literature on labour and health in mining. See, for example, Alan Derickson, *Workers' Health, Workers' Democracy: The Western Miners' Struggle, 1891–1925* (Ithaca, N.Y.: Cornell University Press, 1988); Barbara Ellen Smith, *Digging Our Own Graves: Coal Miners and the Struggle Over Black Lung* (New Haven, Conn.: Yale University Press, 1987); and David Rosner and Gerald Markowitz, *Deadly Dust: Silicosis and the Politics of Occupational Disease in Twentieth-Century America* (Princeton, N.J.: Princeton University Press, 1991).

3. In order to ensure the privacy of those individuals interviewed and those referred to in the documentary sources, pseudonyms have been used.

4. For example, see: Ian Radforth, *Bushworkers and Bosses: Logging in Northern Ontario, 1900-1980* (Toronto: University of Toronto Press, 1987), 25-45; and Franca Iacovetta, *Such Hardworking People: Italian Immigrants in Postwar Toronto* (Montreal: McGill-Queen's University Press, 1992), 64-71.

5. PAO, RG 13-21-0-40, Silicotic Hazard in Ontario, 27 February 1931. This figure concurs with the estimate provided by Alan Derickson for North American metal miners. See Alan Derickson, *Workers' Health*, 52.

6. See Gerald Markowitz and David Rosner, "'The Street of Walking Death': Silicosis, Health and Labor in the Tri-State Region, 1900–1950," *The Journal of American History* (September 1990): 532. On the incidence of tuberculosis in silicosis for Ontario miners, see Ontario, Department of Mines, *Silicosis in Hardrock Miners in Ontario* (1958), 53.

7. Ontario, Ministry of Labour, Workers' Compensation Board and Atomic Energy Control Board of Canada, *Study of Mortality of Ontario Gold Miners, 1955–1977*, July 1986.

8. See, for example, interviews with Kathleen Beauchamp, born 1927; Jeanne Carver, born 1910; Irene Hamilton, born 1901.

9. Interview with Peggy Boychuck, born 1913, married 1934. For similar views of wives in a British Columbia coalmining community, see Lynne Bowen, *Boss Whistle: The Coal Miners of Vancouver Island Remember* (Lantzville, B.C.: Oolichan Books, 1982), 120-21.

10. *Union News*, January 1937.

11. For details of the Paymaster accident, see *Timmins Press*, 3 February 1945.

12. *Union News*, 10 February 1937.

13. Interview, Grace Woodward, born 1912.

14. See, for example, interviews with Jeanne Carver, born 1914; Kathleen Beauchamp, born 1923; and Anne Ritchie, born 1915.

15. Ontario, *Annual Report of the Workmen's Compensation Board, 1917*, 18.

16. Interview with Steve Deveschuk, born 1905.

17. In an otherwise comprehensive discussion of domestic labour, Meg Luxton fails to mention these tasks. See Meg Luxton, *More Than a Labour of Love: Three Generations of Women's Work in the Home* (Toronto: Women's Press, 1980), 117-59. See also Veronica Strong-Boag, "Keeping House in God's Country: Canadian Women at Work in the Home," in *On the Job*, ed. Craig Heron and Robert Storey (Montreal and Kingston: McGill-Queen's University Press, 1986), 124-51. Even Susan Kleinberg, who details the effects of dangerous conditions in Pittsburgh steel mills on working-class families, does not address this issue. See Susan Kleinberg, *The Shadow of the Mills: Working-Class Families in Pittsburgh, 1870–1907* (Pittsburgh: Pittsburgh University Press, 1989).

18. PAO, F 1350, Box 11, File Mining Association, Letter 12 February 1935 from J.H. Stovel to L.J. Simpson.

19. Interview with her daughter Mary Bilenki, born 1921. See also interviews with Eveline Laplante, born 1911; and Emma Wagner, born 1924.

20. PAO, RG 10, Provincial Board of Health, 30-A-3, Timmins, 1929-43, Report 28 October-8 November 1935.

21. United Steelworkers of America, "A Supplementary Submission Dealing with Health and Living Conditions of the Timmins Gold Miners," 8.

22. PAO, RG 10, 30-A-3, Timmins 1929-43, See, for example, reports 11-15 October, 1932; 10 December 1932; 10 October 1933; 28 October-8 November 1935; 1-9 November 1937.

23. PAO, RG 10, 30-A-3, Timmins 1929-43, Report 10-14 October 1933.

24. PAO, RG 10, 30-A-3, Timmins 1929-43, Report 28 October-8 November 1935. See also PAO, F 1350, Box 11, File, Ontario Mining Association, Letter, 12 February 1935 from J.H. Stovel to L.J. Simpson, Minister of Education.

25. Interviews with Edna Pulmitaka, born 1926; Yvette Blanchard, born 1919.

26. UKM, Workers' Co-operative, Minutes, 1 April 1930.

27. TIM, 985.61, Municipality of Timmins, File Hollinger Disaster 1928.

28. Suzanne Morton, *Ideal Surroundings: Domestic Life in a Working-Class Suburb in the 1920s* (Toronto: University of Toronto Press, 1995), 92-93.

29. For a discussion of the political debate leading up to the Ontario act, see Michael Piva, "The Workmen's Compensation Movement in Ontario," *Ontario History* 67, 1 (March 1975): 39-56. With regard to the difficulties of receiving financial compensation prior to this, see Eric Tucker, *Administering Danger in the Workplace: The Law and Politics of Occupational Health and Safety Regulation in Ontario, 1850–1914* (Toronto: University of Toronto Press, 1990), 50. See also Dennis Guest, *The Emergence of Social Security in Canada* 2nd. rev. ed. (Vancouver: University of British Columbia Press, 1985), 39-40.

30. Ontario, "The Ontario Workmen's Compensation Act, 1914," *Statutes of Ontario*, 1914, Chapter 25, 4 George V.

31. PA, MG 28, III, 81, Vol.23, File 5, Letter 29 June 1933 from Buffalo Ankerite to the Workmen's Compensation Board.

32. *Woman Worker*, February 1928.

33. See Ontario, "An Act to Amend the Workmen's Compensation Act, 1943," *Statutes of Ontario, 1943*, Chapter 37, 7 George VI.

34. "An Act to Amend the Workmen's Compensation Act, 1925," *Statutes of Ontario, 1925*, Chapter 43, 15 George V.

35. *Union News*, May 1938.

36. Ontario, Department of Mines, *Silicosis in Hardrock Miners*, (1958), 20.

37. Ontario, "Workmen's Compensation Act," *Statutes of Ontario, 1914*, Chapter 25, 4 George V.

38. Ontario, *Annual Report of Workmen's Compensation*, 1915, 34.

39. This calculation is derived from 55 percent of the average monthly wages of Ontario goldminers for that year – $105.

40. Ontario, "An Act to Amend Workmen's Compensation, 1920," *Statutes of Ontario, 1920*, Chapter 43, 10-11 George V.

41. See Ontario, *Annual Report of Workmen's Compensation Board*, 1922, 59-60.

42. This estimated figure was tabulated from information in a 1939 Toronto Welfare Council report and from data on the provincial standard of living contained in the *Labour Gazette* for *The Canadian Historical Atlas*, Vol. 3 by Lynne Marks. See, *Canadian Historical Atlas*, Vol. 3, ed. Donald Kerr and Deryck Holdsworth (Toronto: University of Toronto Press, 1990), Plate 32.

43. This tabulation is based on cost-of-living data for Timmins in Canada, *Labour Gazette*, 1939, 234. On the difficulties of living on a widow's pension in the 1930s and 1940s, see interviews with Mary Bilenki, born 1921; and Molly Buzowski, born 1918.

44. Ontario, "An Act to Amend the Workmen's Compensation Act 1943," *Statutes of Ontario, 1943*, Chapter 37, 7 George VI; Ontario, "An Act to Amend the Workmen's Compensation Act, 1948," *Statutes of Ontario, 1948*, Chapter 99, 12 George VI.

45. PAO, F 1350, Box 45, File Workmen's Compensation, Brief on the Ontario Compensation Act Submitted by the Ontario Mining Association, 21 November 1949.

46. While the woman received $74 ($50 + $24) the miner was granted $174 (75 percent of $230 – the average monthly wage of Ontario goldminers that year). Ontario, "An Act to Amend the Workmen's Compensation Act, 1949," *Statutes of Ontario, 1949*, Chapter 114, 13 George VI.

47. For an elaboration of this point, see Mariana Valverde, *The Age of Light, Soap and Water* (Toronto: McClelland and Stewart, 1991), 165.

48. Interview with Theresa Del Guidice, born 1911.

49. The name of this organization was changed to the Catholic Women's League at some point in the early 1930s. For newspaper reports about their charity work see, for example, *Porcu-*

pine Advance, 12 March 1924, 26 August 1925, 7 December 1936; *Timmins Press*, 13 June 1946. See also PAO, RG 10, 30-A-3, Timmins, 1929 –1943, 1940 Urban Health Appraisal, for a summary of local organizations doing social service work.

50. See for example, UCA, Manitou Conference, Timmins, First United Church, Meeting Minutes of the Ladies' Aid, 4 October 1928, 6 February 1929, 4 May 1943.

51. *Porcupine Advance*, 18 February 1928.

52. TMA, Municipal Council Minutes, 15 April 1925. For details of the dispensation of relief, see *Porcupine Advance*, 29 December 1932, 26 January 1933.

53. *Porcupine Advance*, 1 February 1940.

Chapter 17

1. We give special thanks to Barbara Bekooy, District Economist's Office Northern Ontario, who assisted by providing data on government transfers.

2. Quoted in C. Hein, V. Smith-Danyliw, and A.M. Kooiman, "The Effects of Poverty on Children: Perceptions of Social Assistance Recipients," Chapter 6 in *Child and Youth Poverty in Sudbury: A Follow-up Report* (Sudbury: School of Social Work, Laurentian University, 1994): 57-73.

3. Quoted in M. Reitsma-Street, ed., *The Forgotten Cry: Child Poverty in North Bay* (North Bay: The Child Poverty Research Group, Nipissing University, 1989).

4. Quoted in Hein et al., "The Effects of Poverty on Children."

5. Patricia M. Evans, "The Sexual Division of Poverty: The Consequences of Gendered Caring," in *Women's Caring: Feminist Perspective on Social Welfare*, ed. Carol Baines, Patricia Evans, and Sheila Neysmith (Toronto: McClelland and Stewart Inc., 1991), 169-203.

6. See also Noel Beach, "Nickel Capital: Sudbury and the Nickel Industry, 1905-1925," *Laurentian University Review* 6, 3 (1974): 55-74; and Graeme S. Mount, "The 1940s," in *Sudbury: Rail Town to Regional Capital* (Toronto: Dundurn Press, 1993), 168-89.

7. Employment and Immigration Canada, *The Northern Ontario Labour Market* (Sudbury: Northern Ontario Regional Economist's Office, March 1992).

8. Employment and Immigration Canada, *Northern Ontario Outlook* (Sudbury: District Economist's Office, Northern Ontario Economic Services Directorate, Ontario Region, January 1991).

9. Sources used in this chapter include: census data from a variety of sources including census documents from 1971 to 1991; special tabulations produced by the Northern Ontario District Economist's Office on tax file returns; and special tabulations of the 1981, 1986, and 1991 census data for the Sudbury Region obtained by the Child Poverty Network.

10. The one exception is the poverty line for rural areas, which was set at $9,637. It should be noted that this particular cut-off does not apply to individuals living in any of the cities and towns listed in Table 1, since this category would include only those who lived outside cities, towns, and villages in areas with populations under 1,000. See Alan F.J. Artibise and John Sewell, "City," in *The Canadian Encyclopedia* (Edmonton: Hurtig Publishers Ltd., 1988): 428.

11. Canadian Advisory Council on the Status of Women, *Women and Labour Market Poverty*, (Ottawa: The Council, 1990), 12.

12. The contrast with men's average incomes is striking. While the figures are not shown, the average rents in these cities and towns accounted for 16.9 percent (Kapuskasing) to 26.7 percent (Parry Sound) of northern men's average incomes. If Parry Sound is excluded, the gross average rents were less than 25 percent of men's average incomes in all the northern communities listed in Table 1.

13. Northern Ontario Regional Economist's Office, *The Ontario Labour Market: The Labour Force Income Profile, 1992* (Sudbury: Human Resources Development Canada, 1995). On p. 2, the Office explains that the EDR represents "the ratio of federal government transfer payments to every $100 of employment income earned for the area." Northern Ontario's EDR of 32.7 in 1992 means that $32.70 in transfer payment dollars was received for every $100 of income from employment.

14. Timothy M. Smeeding, "Poverty, Affluence, and the Income Costs of Children: Cross-National Evidence from the Luxembourg Income Study," *Journal of Post Keynesian Economics* (1988-89): 222-39.

15. D. Hubka, "Report on Child Poverty: The Efforts of Campaign 2000," *Perception* 16, 4 (Ottawa: Canadian Council on Social Development, 1992): 17-22.

16. See National Council of Welfare, "Fighting Child Poverty," a brief by the National Council of Welfare presented to the Sub-Committee on Poverty of the House of Commons Standing Committee on Health and Welfare, Social Affairs, Seniors and the Status of Women, April 1990. These percentages are based on the low-income cut-offs established by Statistics Canada, which are significantly higher than the $10,000 cut-offs used above.

17. See Carol Hein, "Poverty Rates for Children, Youth and Families in the Sudbury Region," Chapter 2 in *Child and Youth Poverty in Sudbury: A Follow-up Report* (Sudbury: School of Social Work, Laurentian University, 1994): 8-26. In this analysis, poverty rates are identical to low-income cut-offs established by Statistics Canada: those who must spend more than 36.2 percent of their average incomes on food, clothing, and shelter are below the poverty line.

18. J. Oderkirk, "Parents and Children Living with Low Incomes," *Canadian Social Trends* 27 (Statistics Canada, 1992): 11-15.

19. Figures exclude the means-tested income from the GAINS, which could bring income up by another $3,000 per year for either men or women.

20. Statistics Canada, *Profile of Census Divisions and Subdivisions in Ontario, Part B* (Ottawa: Industry, Science and Technology Canada, 1994). 1991 Census of Canada, Catalogue number 95-338.

21. Data supporting these statements is available from the authors.

22. Karen Swift, *Manufacturing Bad Mothers* (Toronto: University of Toronto Press, 1995).

23. Ken Battle, "Income Security for Canada's Children," in *On the Right Side: Canada and the Convention on the Rights of the Child*, Michelle Clark, ed. (Ottawa: Canadian Council on Children and Youth, 1990).

Chapter 18

1. Merci à Marc Charron pour sa collaboration à la rédaction de cet article. Pour un portrait provincial de la pauvreté des Franco-Ontariennes de 45 à 64 ans voir Marie-Luce Garceau et Marc Charron, «La dynamique de la pauvreté: l'exemple des Franco-Ontariennes de 45 à 64 ans,» *Revue du Nouvel Ontario* 19 (1966): 39-58.

2. Adam Smith cité par R.L. Heilbroner, *Le capitalisme: nature et logique.* (Paris: Éd. Economica, 1986).

3. Sur la fonction identificatrice des institutions, voir C.Taylor, «Les institutions dans la vie nationale», *Esprit* 3-4 (1994): 90-102.

4. Envoi de mémoires à plusieurs ministères canadiens et ontariens (logement, pension, santé, etc.), établissement de réseaux d'action, lutte à la violence contre les femmes, etc.

5. Cette définition est largement empruntée à E. Mossé, *Les riches et les pauvres* (Paris: Éditions du Seuil, Points économie, 1985).

6. Dans l'enquête, la spécificité de cette classe d'âge a été étudiée dans les domaines individuel, familial, structurel, culturel et historique. Certains thèmes ont fait l'objet d'une étude approfondie afin de mieux comprendre leurs conditions de vie: comportements linguistiques, travail, éducation, bénévolat, et violence familiale. Voir à ce sujet, M.L.Garceau, «Franco-Ontariennes de 45 à 64 ans: analyse de leurs conditions de vie», Thèse de doctorat (Montréal: Université du Québec à Montréal, Département de Sociologie, 1995).

7. Pour l'année 1992, les mesures de pauvreté les plus utilisées sont celles du Conseil national de bien-être social (1994), de Statistique Canada, et celle du Conseil canadien de développement social – pour ces deux derniers, voir D. Ross, "Current and Proposed Measures of Poverty, 1992," *Perception*, 15-4/16-1 (1992): 60-63. Ces mesures de pauvreté concernant une personne ou une famille varient d'un organisme à l'autre. Par exemple, une personne

sous le seuil de pauvreté pourrait avoir un revenu de 15,452$, 14,070$, ou 13,021$ par an, selon l'un ou l'autre des organismes. Dans l'enquête, nous avons retenu la tranche de revenu se rapprochant le plus de ces indicateurs. Pour une personne seule, la tranche de revenu allant de 0$ à moins de 15,000$ a été retenue. Pour une famille de deux personnes, nous avons retenu la tranche de revenu allant de 0$ à moins de 20,000$. Pour une famille de trois personnes, nous avons utilisé la tranche de revenu allant de 0$ à moins de 29,999$ par année.

8. Conseil national du bien-être social, *Profil de la pauvreté, 1992* (Ottawa: Ministre des Approvisionnements et Services Canada, 1994). L'écart entre notre taux et celui du Conseil national de bien-être social s'explique par le fait que notre enquête repose sur un échantillon strictement francophone, provincial, et dans une tranche d'âge précise.

9. Voir M.-A. Denniger, M. Provost, et Conseil canadien de développement social, *Appauvrissement des jeunes familles québécoises: l'urgence d'agir* (Montréal: Conseil canadien de développement social, 1992); et L. Fortin, D. Fournier, et M. Provost, *La pauvreté change-t-elle nos pratiques? Propos d'intervenantes et d'enseignantes.* (Montréal: Relais-Femmes et Conseil canadien de développement social, 1992).

Chapter 19

1. Ethics procedures for these interviews, including confidentiality and ways to minimize risks to interviewees, were approved by the Ethics Committee for the author's doctoral research at the Ontario Institute for Studies in Education (OISE) in Toronto.

2. L. Chalmers and P. Smith, "Wife Battering: Psychological, Social and Physical Isolation and Counteracting Strategies" in *Women: Isolation and Bonding, The Ecology of Gender*, ed. K. Storie (Toronto: Methuen, 1987), 15-37.

3. Chalmers and Smith, "Wife Battering," 16.

4. J.M. Billson, "Violence Toward Women and Children" in *Gossip: A Spoken History of Women in the North*, ed. Mary Crnkovich (Ottawa: Canadian Arctic Resource Committee, 1990), 156-57.

5. Billson, "Violence," 157.

6. Chalmers and Smith, "Wife Battering," 19.

7. Gretchen Grinnell, "Women, Depression and the Global Folie: A New Framework for Therapists," *Women and Therapy* 6, 1-2 (1987): 41-58.

Chapter 20

1. MOH, *Ontario Health Survey 1990. Highlights* (Toronto: Ontario Ministry of Health, 1992).

2. J.R. Pitblado, R. Pong, and J. Jacono, "Regional Differences in Contacts With Health Care Providers in Ontario, Part 2," in *Redressing the Imbalance: Health Human Resources in Rural and Northern Communities*, ed. Bruce Minore and Connie Hartviksen (Thunder Bay: Northern Health Human Resources Research Unit, Lakehead University, 1996), proceedings of a conference of the same name held at the Valhalla Inn, Thunder Bay, 21-24 October 1993), 403-22.

3. Most of the measures that are reported in this paper are expressed in the form of percentages. As the OHS was not undertaken as a full enumeration, sampling variability exists, and therefore these percentages would normally be annotated according to OHS release guidelines based on categories of a computed statistic known as the coefficient of variation (C.V.). However, all of the estimates that are used here would be categorized by these guidelines as "for general unrestricted release" (C.V. 0.0-16.5 percent). See Part 3 in: MOH, *Ontario Health Survey 1990. User's Guide* Volume 2, Microdata Manual (Toronto: Ontario Ministry of Health, 1992), 1-15.

4. MOH, *Ontario Health Survey 1990. Highlights*, 5.

5. Ross M.G. Norman, *The Nature and Correlates of Health Behaviour* (Ottawa: Health Promotion Studies Series No. 2, Health Promotion Directorate, Health and Welfare Canada, 1986) quoted by: Mike Burke, H. Michael Stevenson, Pat Armstrong, Georgina Feldberg, and Harriet Rosenberg, "Women, Work and Health Inequalities" (Toronto: Working Paper

No. 3, Ontario Health Survey 1990, Ontario Ministry of Health, 1992), 7; Peggy McDonough, Irving Rootman, Paul Corey, and Roberta Ferrence, "Interrelations Among Health Behaviours" (Toronto: Working Paper No. 4, Ontario Health Survey 1990, Ontario Ministry of Health, 1993), 3.

6. MOH, *Ontario Health Survey 1990. Highlights*, 28.

7. Paul Taylor, "Major breast-cancer risk found," *Globe and Mail*, 3 May 1995, 1.

8. MOH, *Ontario Health Survey 1990. Highlights*, 24.

9. See, for example: R.G. Beck, "Economic Class and Access to Physician Services under Public Medical Care Insurance," *International Journal of Health Services* 3 (1973): 341- 55; P.L. Knox, "Medical Deprivation, Area Deprivation and Public Policy," *Social Science and Medicine* 13 (1979): 111-21; J. Eyles and K.J. Woods, *The Social Geography of Medicine and Health* (New York: St. Martins Park, 1983); R.W. Broyles, P. Manga, D.A. Binder, D.E. Angus, and A. Charette, "The Use of Physician Services Under a National Health Insurance Scheme," *Medical Care* 21 (1983): 1037-54; R. Haynes, "Inequalities in Health and Health Service Use: Evidence from the General Household Survey," *Social Science and Medicine* 33 (1991): 361-68; R. Pamplon, "Health Discrepancies in Rural Areas in Quebec," *Social Science and Medicine* 33 (1991): 355-60.

10. MOH, *Ontario Health Survey 1990. Highlights*, 48.

11. MOH, *Ontario Health Survey 1990. Highlights*, 43.

12. MOH, *Ontario Health Survey 1990. Highlights*, 43.

13. Karen A. Blackford, Patricia Hill Bailey, and Ginette M. Coutu-Wakulczyk, "Tobacco Use in Northeastern Ontario Teenagers: Prevalence of Use and Associated Factors," *Canadian Journal of Public Health* 85 (1994): 89-92. See especially pp. 91-92.

14. MOH, *Ontario Health Survey 1990. Highlights*, 24. These statements by the MOH must be examined further as education and income tend to be highly correlated.

15. MOH, *Ontario Health Survey 1990. Highlights*, 48.

16. M. Pirie, "Women and the Illness Role; Rethinking Feminist Theory," *Canadian Review of Sociology and Anthropology* 25 (1988): 628-44; David Coburn and Joan M. Eakin,"The Sociology of Health in Canada: First Impressions," *Health and Canadian Society* 1 (1993): 83-110; Enakshi Dua, Maureen FitzGerald, Linda Gardner, Darien Taylor, and Lisa Wyndels, eds., *On Women Healthsharing* (Toronto: Women's Press,1994).

17. Kelvyn Jones and Graham Moon, *Health, Disease and Society: An Introduction to Medical Geography* (London: Routledge, 1987), 260-61.

18. Ingrid Waldron, "Sex Differences in Illness Incidence, Prognosis and Mortality: Issues and Evidence," *Social Science & Medicine* 17 (1983): 1107-23; Melinda Meade, John Florin, and Wilbert Gesler, *Medical Geography* (New York: The Guilford Press, 1988); Ofra Anson, Esther Paran, Lily Neumann, and Dov Chernichovsky, "Gender Differences in Health Perceptions and Their Predictors," *Social Science & Medicine* 36 (1993): 419-27.

19. Charlotte Muller, "Review of Twenty Years of Research on Medical Care Utilization," *Health Services Research* 21 (1986): 129-44.

20. See Constance A. Nathanson, "Illness and the Feminine Role: A Theoretical Review," *Social Science & Medicine* 9 (1975): 57-62; V. Coupland, "Gender, Class and Space as Accessibility Constraints for Women with Young Children," in "Contemporary Perspectives on Health and Health Care," ed. Health Research Group (London: Occasional Paper 20, Department of Geography, Queen Mary College, University of London, 1982), 51-70; J. Clarke, "Sexism, Feminism and Medicalism: A Decade Review of Literature on Gender and Illness," *Sociology of Health and Illness* 5 (1983): 62-82; and a small number of others.

21. Nathanson, "Illness and the Feminine Role," 57.

22. See Coupland, "Gender, Class and Space"; Clarke, "Sexism, Feminism and Medicalism"; Burke et al., "Women, Work and Health Inequalities"; and a small number of others.

23. David Coburn and Joan M. Eakin,"The Sociology of Health in Canada: First Impressions," *Health and Canadian Society* 1 (1993): 83-110. See especially p. 87.

Chapter 21

1. The author is a feminist activist in the women's health movement.

2. My gratitude goes to committee members Cathy Austin, Raye Desgranges, Bev Dobbins-Blake, Ines Drummond Borges, Heather Easterbrook, Delores Fortier, Kathryn Irwin-Seguin, Donja Jarrett, Vicki MacDonald, Christine McInnes, Janice McKenney, Jackie Moffatt, Margery Wagner, Linda Willet, and especially Mary Stratton. Thanks also to women who were able to provide the committee with occasional assistance: Dyane Adam, Karen Annis, Norma Bisson, Vickie Kaminski, Michelle MacEwen, and Grace St. Jean.

   For the report of the committee, see C.A. Suschnigg, *Women's Health Needs Assessment* (Sudbury: Women's Health Research Steering Committee, Manitoulin-Sudbury District Health Council, 1991).

3. Most needs assessments are carried out using a conventional social science approach. Typically, organizations that require a needs assessment make use of an in-house researcher, or contract out to universities or private companies. Whatever the case, it is the "expert" who is responsible for designing the research, collecting the data, and interpreting the results. In this scenario, "ordinary" people are thought to be incapable of conducting research. Instead, ordinary people are regarded merely as "sources of information, possessing bits of isolated knowledge needed by the researcher.... Interviewees are neither expected nor apparently assumed to be able to analyze a given social reality." See B. Hall, "Breaking the Monopoly of Knowledge: Research Methods, Participation and Development" in *Creating Knowledge: A Monopoly?* ed. B. Hall, A. Gillette and R. Tandon (New Delhi: Society for Participatory Research in Asia, 1982): 13-25, especially p. 17.

4. For a fuller account of feminist participatory research, as well as an assessment of its strengths and weaknesses, see pp. 258-330 in C.A. Suschnigg, "The Community Health Centre: Health Planning for Critical Consciousness?" Ph.D. dissertation (Toronto: York University, 1992).

5. A "random" sample simply means that everyone in the population has an equal chance to be selected as a respondent. In traditional survey research, random sampling is considered essential: without it, the researcher cannot make generalizations about the population. While there are several ways to draw a random sample, social researchers rarely end up with a truly random sample; many people, for example, simply refuse to participate in the research. If such people share certain characteristics, then bias is introduced and generalizations to the population become invalid.

6. In this exercise, respondents are given several slips of paper and asked to write down their most important health issues for women (in our case, we asked women to write down four issues). The group is asked to maintain silence while this activity is going on to ensure that every person forms her own judgement.

   A set of arbitrary symbols is lined up across a wall. Then, women are asked to hand in their slips of paper. One by one, issues are read out and the corresponding slips of paper are placed under the various symbols on the wall. A concern about women's mental health, for example, would be placed under one symbol; a concern about women's reproductive rights would be placed under a second symbol; a concern about breast cancer would be placed under a third symbol; and so on.

   Throughout the exercise, the group is asked to name the heading it assigns to each symbol, and to decide the heading under which an issue should be placed. At the end of the exercise, the group can see clearly the kinds of issues that have been raised, the frequency with which particular issues have been mentioned, and the way in which the issues are ranked.

   If this exercise is done with all focus groups, all the slips of paper can eventually be pooled. Health issues can be categorized and ranked for the entire sample. In this instance, of course, it is the researcher who has control over how an issue is categorized and thus, to some extent, over the way in which issues are ranked.

7. From the perspective of conventional social science, there were obvious technical disadvantages associated with our decision to modify and adapt our original focus group format. Data were not collected in a consistent manner for all respondents; in particular, women with self-administered question packages (English or French) had little opportunity to get clarification

if they did not understand a question. The other major disadvantage was that information from the formal questionnaire was available for only 111 of the 177 women who participated in the survey. Nevertheless, if we had not adapted our original plan for data collection, there is far less chance that francophone women, First Nations women, non-anglo immigrant women, women with low literacy skills, and women with disabilities could have contributed to the project. In the end, the committee felt that a measure of its success was its willingness and ability to be sensitive to the different groups of women in our community; the research design had to be flexible if it were to elicit and register the voices of women from whom we were most anxious to hear.

8. Birth control and sexual assault services exist in our community. Nevertheless, some women reported that they had difficulty gaining access to birth control services. In addition, through our survey of local agencies, we learned that survivors of sexual assault and incest face long waiting lists for counselling.

9. P. Maguire, *Doing Participatory Research: A Feminist Approach* (Amherst, MA: The Centre for International Education, University of Massachusetts, 1987), 197-99.

Chapter 22

1. I wish to thank the Federated Women's Institutes of Ontario and the Social Sciences and Humanities Research Council of Canada for providing financial support for the research for this paper. I am very grateful to the members of the northern WI branches who hosted my research trips and helped me locate local sources in their districts in 1993 and 1994.

2. Ontario, Department of Agriculture, *Annual Report*, Institutes Branch, 1914. Miss S. Campbell, "A Visit to Three Northern Conventions," 52 (hereafter cited as *Annual Report*).

33. Cheryl MacDonald, *Adelaide Hoodless: Domestic Crusader* (Toronto: Dundurn Press, 1986). For background information on the Ontario Women's Institutes, there have been four commemorative volumes to date: Viola Powell, *Forty Years Agrowing: A History of Ontario Women's Institutes* (Port Perry, Ont.: Port Perry Star, 1941); Annie Walker, Edith M. Collins, and M. McIntyre Hood, *Fifty Years of Achievement* (Toronto: Federated Women's Institutes of Ontario, 1948); *Ontario Women's Institute Story: In Commemoration of the 75th Anniversary of the Founding of the Women's Institutes of Ontario* (Toronto: Federated Women's Institutes of Ontario, 1972); and Linda M. Ambrose, *For Home and Country: The Centennial History of the Women's Institutes in Ontario* (Erin, Ont.: Boston Mills Press, 1996).

4. For an academic treatment of the early years up to 1919, see Margaret Kechnie, "Keeping Things Clean for 'Home and Country': The Federated Women's Institute of Ontario," Ph.D. Thesis (Toronto: Ontario Institute for Studies in Education, 1995).

5. Figure 1 was compiled by the author from correspondence with local branches received from 1993 to 1995 as part of the Federated Women's Institutes of Ontario Centennial Book Project.

6. See *Annual Reports*, 1905 and 1906 for the travel itineraries which these women followed.

7. *Annual Reports*, 1905-1922.

8. The female population of Ontario in 1911 was 1,223,984, while women in Northern Ontario numbered 104,412 or 8.5 percent of the provincial female total (see Eileen Goltz, Chapter 1 in this volume). WI membership was 22,042 with 2,131 members from Northern Ontario (*Census of Canada*, 1911, 1, 70).

9. Powell, *Forty Years Agrowing*, 90.

10. Linda M. Ambrose, "What Are the Good of Those Meetings Anyway?: Early Popularity of the Ontario Women's Institutes," *Ontario History* 87,1 (Spring 1995): 1-20. For a Western Canadian perspective, see Catherine C. Cole and Ann Milovic, "Education, Community Service and Social Life: The Alberta Women's Institutes and Rural Families, 1909-1945," in Catherine A. Cavanaugh and Randi R. Warne, *Standing on New Ground: Women in Alberta* (Edmonton: University of Alberta Press, 1993), 19-31. On the educational purposes, see Terry Crowley, "The Origins of Continuing Education for Women: The Ontario Women's Institutes," *Canadian Woman Studies* 7, 3 (Fall 1986): 78-81.

11. Douglas Owen Baldwin, "Imitation vs. Innovation: Cobalt as an Urban Frontier Town," *Laurentian University Review* 11, 2 (February 1979): 23-41. See especially pages 28-29.

12. For a historical description of the organization's official symbols, see *Ontario Women's Institute Story*, 126-29.

13. Much more significant than the grants were the fund-raising events held by the local branches. The Barrie Island Institute in Manitoulin District reported, for example, "We have raised money in many different ways. The following are a few over the years: Bake sales in town, pie socials, garden parties, picnics, fowl suppers, oyster suppers, tickets on quilts, also autographs. Our favourite is a social in the school at which we sell candy, ice cream or hot dogs. We have a program and this seems to be enjoyed by the community. Also we make a nice amount of money usually with not too much expense and very little work." Gore Bay Public Library, Barrie Island Women's Institute Tweedsmuir History, microfilm.

14. *Annual Report, 1916*, 190.

15. *Annual Report, 1918*, 122. The speaker went on to recount, "I remember one woman telling me she went into a shack away out on the prairie, and the woman rushed up to her and put her arms around her neck and cried like a child. She said, 'I have not seen a woman for six months.'"

16. Paipoonge Museum, Thunder Bay District Tweedsmuir History Book, Mrs. J. Hahn. This is an excerpt from a letter written by Mrs. Hahn in 1965 in which she reminisced about her pioneer experience.

17. *Annual Report, 1912*, 35.

18. *Annual Report, 1924*, 29.

19. Richard's Landing Public Library. Kentvale Women's Institute Minute Books, 4 October 1917 and 29 August 1918. Ontario. *Sessional Papers*, v 55 pt 6 leg 15 sess 4, 1923, 43; Fort Frances Museum, Fort Frances Women's Institute Minute Book, 12 January 1922, 16 February 1922, and 2 March 1922; Gore Bay Public Library, Barrie Island Tweedsmuir.

20. Private Branch Collection (Thunder Bay District). O'Connor Women's Institute Tweedsmuir History Book.

21. *Annual Report, 1927*, 31.

22. *Annual Report, 1934*, 60.

23. Premier Drury, cited in: Willing Workers Group of Heaslip, *Memories of the Great Fire* (Cobalt: Highway Book Shop, 1972), 4.

24. *Annual Report, 1929*, 40.

25. Englehart and Area Museum Collection. Marter Women's Institute Minute Book, 5 January 1916.

26. Englehart and Area Museum Collection. Marter Women's Institute Minute Book, 1 July 1915.

27. Englehart and Area Museum Collection. Marter Women's Institute Minute Book, 4 March 1915.

28. Englehart and Area Museum Collection, Dane WI Minute Books, 2 February 1932.

29. *Annual Report, 1916*. Mrs. E. Darlington, "Reports of Women's Institutes: Rainy River District," 137.

30. Ambrose-FWIO Centennial Survey. Moscow Branch, Addington County. Notes sent in from this southern Ontario branch included a reference to the Island Falls branch with the information about membership, and the explanation that Island Falls "was situated at the Abitibi Electric Development Co. Dam. Sometime after 1942 the Company moved to Fraserdale (further north) and the log cabins were dismantled and WI was disbanded on to Fraserdale."

31. *Annual Report, 1914*, 72.

32. *Annual Report, 1914*, 52. This is reminiscent of the style of Nellie McClung's campaign where she satired the Premier of Manitoba with a presentation along those same lines. See Alison Prentice et al. *Canadian Women: A History* (Toronto: Harcourt, Brace, Jovanovich, 1988), 194.

33. *Annual Report, 1914*, 52-53.

34. Private Branch Collection, Monteith WI Minutebooks, 12 October 1916; 9 November 1916; April 1917; 10 May 1917.

35. Richard's Landing Public Library. Kentvale WI Minute Books, 28 September, 2 November, and 7 December 1916.

36. *Annual Report, 1916*, 72.

37. *Annual Report, 1914*, 72.

38. *Annual Report, 1916*, Mrs. E. Darlington, Devlin, ON, "Reports of the Women's Institutes: Rainy River District," 137.

39. *Annual Report, 1917*, Miss Mildred McMillen, Lee Valley Women's Institute, 113.

40. *Annual Report, 1916*, Mrs. Parsons, "An Appreciation of the Northern Conventions, 1915," 190.

41. *Annual Report, 1918*, Mrs. J. Muldrew, "The Women's Institutes of Western Canada," 122-24.

42. *Annual Report, 1915*, 113.

43. *Annual Report, 1919*, 27.

Chapter 23

1. This first paragraph comes from the April 1984 conference brochure for "Through the Looking Glass," the final Northeastern Ontario Women's Conference.

2. Comments from Marguerite Cassin, who was a major resource person for all the conferences, are taken from interviews and written conference commentaries. At the time of the conferences, Gayle Broad was a community activist in Sault Ste. Marie, Joan Kuyek was a community legal worker in Sudbury, and Marguerite Cassin was a doctoral student at the Ontario Institute for Studies in Education (OISE) at the University of Toronto.

3. Joan Newman Kuyek, *Fighting for Hope* (Montreal: Black Rose Books, 1990).

Chapter 24

1. The author wishes to thank all the women of the Sudbury, North Bay, Northern, and Kenora Women's Centres and Phoenix Rising, Sault Ste. Marie and Elliot Lake. In addition, Alistine Andre of Tsiigehtchic, NWT, contributed to editorial content. Special thanks to Leanne Tooley of Thunder Bay who served as research assistant on this project.

2. Kathy Kilburn, *The North Bay Women's Centre Herstory* (unpublished, 1989).

3. Kilburn, *Herstory,* 1.

4. Kilburn, *Herstory*, 4.

5. Kathy Kilburn, *The North Bay Women's Centre Report*, (unpublished, 1982), 2.

6. Kilburn, *Herstory*, 19.

7. Kilburn, *Herstory*, 21.

8. From personal correspondence from Kilburn to the author in June 1995.

9. Karen Dominick, *Fighting for Roses: A Herstory of the Sudbury Women's Centre* (Sudbury: The Women's Centre, 1994), 10.

10. Dominick, *Fighting*, 18.

11. Dominick, *Fighting*, 20-21.

12. Ontario Women's Directorate, *Annual Report* (Toronto: The Directorate, 1993), 43.

13. Ontario Women's Directorate, *Annual Report*, 7.

14. Fiona Karlstedt, *Northwestern Ontario Status of Women Initiatives 1973-1987* (Toronto: Secretary of State Program and Ontario Women's Directorate, 1987), 7.

15. Karlstedt, *Northwestern Initiatives*, 12.

16. Northern Women's Centre, *Annual Report*, Annual General Meeting, 7 June 1994.

17. Karlstedt, *Northwestern Initiatives*, 55.

18. Karlstedt, *Northwestern Initiatives*, 55-56.

19. Ontario Women's Directorate, *Annual Report*, 23.

20. *(Editors' note)* Since this chapter was written, the Conservative government of Premier Mike Harris has cut back funding to Women's Centres in Ontario. With the exception of the North Bay Women's Resource Centre, all of the centres discussed in this chapter are still operating, but with reduced funding. This means that if services to women are to be maintained, fund-raising efforts – an already onerous task for the centres – will have to increase.

Chapter 25

1. Angela C. Mione, *Housing: Not a Gender-Neutral Issue: A Summary Report on Women and Housing* (Sudbury: The Sudbury Women's Housing Network and the Elizabeth Fry Society of Sudbury, October 1994).

2. Gerda R. Wekerle, *Women's Housing Projects in Eight Canadian Cities* (Ottawa: Canada Mortgage and Housing Corporation, Policy Division, Research and Programs Sector, April 1988), 12.

3. John G. Craig, *The Nature of Co-operation* (Montreal: Black Rose Books, 1993), 213.

4. In preparation for this chapter, the authors interviewed four women living in housing co-operatives in northeastern Ontario. For reasons of privacy, their names are not given.

5. Craig, *Nature of Co-operation*, 41.

6. Co-operative Housing Federation of Canada, *What is Co-operative Housing?*

7. Wekerle, *Women's Housing Projects*, 12.

Chapter 26

1. Les collaboratrices (en ordre alphabétique) sont: Denise André, Francine Beaulieu, Denise Bellehumeur, Christine Caveen, Marie-Luce Garceau, Danielle Gervais, Noëlla Lahaie, Sylvie Larocque, Martine Lefebvre, Diane Lemay, Manon Lemonde, Anita Pelletier, Aline Rochon, et Lise Tardif.

2. Statistique Canada/Statistics Canada, *Causes of Death, Vital Statistics IV* (cat. #84-203) (Ottawa: Statistics Canada, Health Division, Vital Statistics and Disease Registries Section, 1986).

3. S. Samuels et P. Cole, *Le Réseau d'entraide des personnes âgées*, (s.l.: s.n., 1988).

4. F. Descarries-Bélanger et S. Roy, *Le mouvement des femmes et ses courants de pensées: essai de typologie (Ottawa: CRIAW\CREF, 1988).*

5. *Relevons le défi! Actes du colloques sur l'intervention féministe dans le Nord-est de l'Ontario* (Collection Actexpress, Ottawa: Presses de l'Université d'Ottawa, 1992), sous la direction de M.-L. Garceau.

6. D.P. Holder and C.M. Anderson, "Women, Work and the Family," in *Women in Families*, ed. M. McGoldrick, C.M. Anderson, and F. Walsh (New York: W.W. Norton, 1989): 57-380.

7. L. Cardinal et C. Coderre, *Les femmes de langue maternelle française vivant à l'extérieur du Québec: des profils provinciaux* (Ottawa: s.n., 1991).

8. R. Mayer et F. Ouellet, *Méthodologie de recherche pour les intervenants sociaux* (Montréal: Gaétan Morin, éditeur, 1991).

9. C. Corbeil, F. Descarries, G. Gill, et C. Séguin, «Des femmes, du travail et des enfants: des vies dédoublées». *Nouvelles pratiques sociales* 3, 2 (1990): 99-128.

10. Corbeil et al., "Des femmes, du travail et des enfants."

11. C. Higgins, L. Duxbury, C. Lee, and S. Mills, "An Examination of Work-Time and Work-Location Flexibility," *OPTIMUM The Journal of Public Sector Management*, 23, 2 (1992): 29-38.

12. Un autre élément important dans les succès du Collectif est le soutien que l'Université Laurentienne a offert au début de nos activités et le support financier que nous avons obtenu des ministères suivants; de la Condition Féminine, des Ressources Humaines, du Secrétariat d'État, du Développement du Nord et des Mines, des Services Sociaux et Communautaires, de l'Office des Affaires Francophones, et de Promotion de la santé.

Chapter 27

1. Linda Ross and Rick Powell, "Women and Distance Education," *Research in Distance Education* 2, 2 (April 1990): 10-13.

2. See: Margaret Grace, "Gender Issues in Distance Education," in *Beyond the Text: Contemporary Writing on Distance Education*, ed. T. Evans and B. King (Geelong, Australia: Deakin University Press, 1991), 152-75; Gill Kirkup and Christine von Prummer, "Support and Connectedness: the Needs of Women Distance Education Students," *Journal of Distance Education* 5, 2 (Fall 1990): 9-31; and B. Spronk and D. Radtke, "Problems and Possibilities: Canadian Native Women in Distance Education" in *Toward New Horizons for Women in Distance Education*, ed. Karlene Faith (International Perspectives. London: Routledge, 1988): 214-28.

3. Ross and Powell, "Women and Distance Education," 10.

4. Susan May, "Women's Experiences as Distance Learners: Access and Technology," *Journal of Distance Education* 9, 1 (1994): 81-98. See p. 94.

5. Spronk and Radtke, "Problems and Possibilities," 224.

6. Interview on 10 April 1995 with Roy Mawhiney, class of 1962.

7. Discussion with the then Director of the Centre of Continuing Education on 15 April 1995 confirmed this.

8. Contact North/Contact Nord is a bilingual teleconference network operating in over 150 communities throughout all of Northern Ontario.

9. We are counting courses here regardless of whether they give three or six credits; the purpose is to determine the gender of the senior course author.

10. Because Laurentian University is a dual-mode university, it was necessary to distinguish between those students studying on-campus and those from off-campus.

11. "Successful completion" is defined as those students who did not withdraw or fail the course.

12. A. Leslie Robb and Byron G. Spencer, "Education: Enrolment and Attaintment" in *Opportunity for Choice: A Goal for Women in Canada*, ed. Gail C. A. Cook (Ottawa: Statistics Canada and the C.D. Howe Research Institute,1976), 53-92. See p. 77.

13. Grace, "Gender Issues," 173.

14. Karlene Faith, "Gender as an Issue in Distance Education," *Journal of Distance Education* 3, 1 (Spring 1988): 75-79. See p. ii.

Chapter 28

1. The authors would like to thank Ashley Thomson, who as Director of INORD asked that that project be carried out, and Barbara Evans and Charlotte Mosher in the CIMMER office at Laurentian University, who typed the chapter, as well as Jane Pitblado of the INORD office for the many retypes of this paper.

2. Stella Thompson (Chair), *Winning with Women in Trades, Technology, Science and Engineering*, (Technology, Science and Engineering Report of the National Advisory Board of Science and Technology Canada), January 1993, 3-4.

3. Sid Gilbert and Alan Pomfret, *Gender Tracking in University Programmes* (Occasional Paper Number 4), Ottawa: Industry Canada, March 1995.

4. Gilbert and Pomfret, *Gender Tracking*, i-iii.

5. M. O'Driscoll and J. Anderson, *Women in Science: Attitudes of University Students Towards a Career in Science: A Pilot Study* (Report Number 4), *PRISM* June 1994.

6. Sheila Tobias, *They're Not Dumb, They're Different: Stalking the Second Tier* (Tuscon, AZ: Research Corporation, 1990).

7. Pat Shipman, "One Woman's Life in Science," *American Scientist* 83 (1995): 300-02.

8. Gilbert and Pomfret, *Gender Tracking*.

9. Joan Jeruchim and Pat Shapiro, *Women, Mentors and Success* (Toronto: Random House, 1992).

10. Frank Feather, *G Forces Reinventing the World* (Toronto: Summerhill Press Ltd., 1990), 73-76.

Chapter 29

1. I thank the tremendous young women who graciously donated their time and shared with me their ideas and insights. Without them, this paper could not have been written. I am also grateful to Heather Sangster and Daniel Wolgelerenter for their constructive editorial suggestions.

2. See, for example, Gloria Steinem, "Why Young Women are More Conservative," *Outrageous Acts and Everyday Rebellions* (New York: Plume, 1983), 211-18; and Nancy Whittier, *Feminist Generations: The Persistence of the Radical Women's Movement* (Philadelphia: Temple University Press, 1995). Danielle Forth provides an excellent analysis of older feminists' criticisms of younger women in "Diving Deep: The Generation Gap Between Older and Younger Feminists," in *Women and Social Location: Our Lives, Our Research*, ed. Marilyn Assheton-Smith and Barbara Spronk (Charlottetown: CRIAW-gynergy, 1993), 69-75.

3. Claudia Wallis, "Onward, Women," *Time* (4 December 1989): 54-61. The exact question asked was, "Do you consider yourself a feminist?" The poll's sampling error was plus or minus 3 percent.

4. Nancy Gibbs, "The War Against Feminism," *Time* (9 March 1992): 38-44. As in the 1989 survey, the phrasing of the question was, "Do you consider yourself a feminist?" The poll's margin of error was plus or minus 4 percent.

5. Sherrye Henry, *The Deep Divide: Why American Women Resist Equality* (New York: Macmillan, 1994), 241.

6. Claire Renzetti, "New Wave or Second Stage? Attitudes of College Women Toward Feminism," *Sex Roles* 16 (1987): 265-277. The statement relating directly to feminist identity was, "I consider myself to be a feminist."

7. Dian Day, *Young Women in Nova Scotia: A Study of Attitudes, Behaviour, and Aspirations* (Halifax: Nova Scotia Advisory Council on the Status of Women, November 1990). The women were asked, "How would you define a feminist?" Responses were then coded into "positive" and "negative" categories.

8. Words spoken by these young women are presented in the indented sections throughout this paper.

9. Alison Prentice et al., *Canadian Women: A History* (Toronto: Harcourt Brace Jovanovich, 1988), 352-56.

10. Arja Lane, "Wives Supporting the Strike," in *Union Sisters: Women in the Labour Movement* (Toronto: Women's Educational Press, 1983), 322-32; Karen Dominick, *Fighting for Roses: A Herstory of The Sudbury Women's Centre* (Sudbury: The Women's Centre, 1994), 14-20; and *A Wives' Tale,* produced by S. Bissonnette, M. Duckworth, and J. Rock (Toronto: Full Frame Film and Video Distribution, 1980).

11. Evelyn Lau, *Runaway: Diary of a Streetkid* (Toronto: Harper and Collins, 1989).

12. Evelyn Lau, *Oedipal Dreams* (Victoria, B.C.: Beach Holme, 1992).

13. See Hélène Jutras, *Le Québec me tue* (Montréal: Éditions des Intouchables, 1995). The description of Jutras' book is from Andrew Phillips, "Quebec's New Voice," *Maclean's* (6 March 1995): 22.

14. Page 3 of every edition of the newspaper features colour photos of sparsely dressed models (who do not receive pay for their work). See Anne Bains, "On the Trail with the Bitch Brigade," *This Magazine* 28, 7 (March/April 1995): 8-9.

15. Naomi Klein, "Salesgirl Solidarity," *This Magazine* 28, 6 (February 1995): 12-19.

16. Laurie Soper, "'Indecent Acts' and Everyday Rebellion: An Interview with Gwen Jacob," *Herizons* (Fall 1992): 16.

17. Soper, "'Indecent Acts,'" 16.

18. Women's Place Kenora, "Womyn Rhythms Conference Summary," 2-3.

19. Women's Place Kenora, "Womyn," 10.

20. Anne Innis Dagg and Patricia J.Thompson, *MisEducation: Women and Canadian Universities* (Toronto: OISE Press, 1988), 82-83.

21. Dagg and Thompson, *MisEducation,* 82.

22. Both Lakehead and Laurentian briefly had women's associations (not full-fledged centres as exist now) in earlier years, but student turnover and opposition from student associations resulted in their demise.

23. Lakehead University Gender Issues Centre, "Gender Issues Centre Director Job Profile," 1994.

24. Laurentian University Women's Centre/Centre des femmes de l'Université Laurentienne, "A Women's Centre at Laurentian: Background and Rationale," 1993.

25. Nancy Adamson, Linda Briskin, and Margaret McPhail, *Feminist Organizing for Change: The Contemporary Women's Movement in Canada* (Toronto: Oxford University Press, 1988), 234.

Contributors

LINDA M. AMBROSE – assistant professor of history at Laurentian University.

MARIAN BEAUREGARD – psychotherapist in Parry Sound and South River, with a doctorate in psychology.

KAREN BLACKFORD – associate professor of nursing at Laurentian University.

HUGUETTE BLANCO – associate professor of commerce at Laurentian University.

GAYLE BROAD – community legal worker at the Algoma Legal Clinic in Sault Ste. Marie.

MARY ANN CORBIERE – lecturer and chair of native studies at the University of Sudbury in Laurentian University.

HELENA DEBEVC-MOROZ – assistant professor in the school of translators and interpreters at Laurentian University.

KAREN DUBINSKY – associate professor of history at Queen's University, Kingston.

DOROTHY L. ELLIS – chair of human services at Cambrian College, Sudbury.

NANCY M. FORESTELL – assistant professor of history at St. Francis Xavier University in Antigonish, Nova Scotia.

MARIE-LUCE GARCEAU – professeure agrégée et coordinatrice des programmes de baccalauréat en français à l'école de service social de l'Université Laurentienne.

DOUGLAS GOLDSACK – professor of chemistry, director of the Centre in Mining and Mineral Exploration Research (CIMMER).

EILEEN GOLTZ – associate librarian at Laurentian University with a doctorate in history.

SHEILA HARDY – assistant professor of the native human services program at Laurentian University.

CINDY IVES-BIGEAU – senior manager for marketing and development in Laurentian University's centre for continuing education.

ROY KARI – director of institutional research at Laurentian University.

CAROL KAUPPI – lecturer in sociology at Laurentian University.

JENNIFER KECK – assistant professor of social work at Laurentian University.

MARGARET KECHNIE – associate professor of women's studies at Laurentian University.

SUSAN KENNEDY – labour activist and program consultant with Human Resources Development Canada in Toronto.

JOAN KUYEK – project co-ordinator of Better Beginnings, Better Futures in Sudbury. In June 1995 she was awarded an honorary doctorate from Laurentian University for her achievements as a community activist.

GINETTE LAFRENIÈRE – assistant professor of commerce at Laurentian University.

ROLLAND LEBRASSEUR – assistant professor of commerce at Laurentian University.

VARPU LINDSTRÖM – associate professor of history and women's studies and master of Atkinson College at York University.

DAWN MADAHBEE – general manager at Waubetek Business Development Corporation on Birch Island, Ontario.

ANNE-MARIE MAWHINEY – director of the Institute of Northern Ontario Research and Development (INORD) at Laurentian University and professor of social work.

BARBARA MILLSAP – executive director of Northern Non-Profit Housing in Sudbury.

KITTY MINOR – mental health specialist for Tsiigehtchic Band, Northwest Territories, and adjunct professor of social work at Lakehead University, Thunder Bay.

K.V. NAGARAJAN – assistant professor of economics and commerce at Laurentian University.

ROSS PAUL – president of Laurentian University.

J. ROGER PITBLADO – professor of geography at Laurentian University.

JOHANNE POMERLEAU – professeure adjointe et directrice de l'école des sciences infirmières à l'Université Laurentienne.

RAYMOND W. PONG – director of the Northern Health Human Resources Research Unit at Laurentian University.

ELAINE PORTER – associate professor and chair of sociology and anthropology at Laurentian University.

MARY POWELL – assistant professor of political science at Laurentian University.

MARGE REITSMA-STREET – associate professor of social work at Laurentian University.

VALERIE SENYK – performance poet and lecturer in theatre arts at Thorneloe College, Laurentian University.

THERESA SOLOMON-GRAVEL – homemaker and a graduate of Native studies and women's studies at Laurentian University.

MERCEDES STEEDMAN – associate professor of sociology at Laurentian University.

CAROL ALEXIS STOS – assistant professor of Spanish language, literature, and culture at Laurentian University.

CAROLE A. SUSCHNIGG – assistant professor of sociology at Laurentian University.

PAT TOBIN – assistant professor of social work at Laurentian University.

SUSAN VANSTONE – graduate student in sociology at the Ontario Institute for Studies in Education (OISE) in Toronto.